THE EMPLOYEE

POLITICS AND CULTURE IN MODERN AMERICA

Series Editors: Margot Canaday, Glenda Gilmore,
Michael Kazin, and Thomas J. Sugrue

Volumes in the series narrate and analyze political and social
change in the broadest dimensions from 1865 to the present,
including ideas about the ways people have sought and wielded
power in the public sphere and the language and institutions of
politics at all levels—local, national, and transnational. The series
is motivated by a desire to reverse the fragmentation of modern
U.S. history and to encourage synthetic perspectives on social
movements and the state, on gender, race, and labor, and on
intellectual history and popular culture.

THE EMPLOYEE

A POLITICAL HISTORY

JEAN-CHRISTIAN VINEL

PENN

UNIVERSITY OF PENNSYLVANIA PRESS

PHILADELPHIA

Published by
University of Pennsylvania Press
Philadelphia, Pennsylvania 19104-4112
www.upenn.edu/pennpress

Printed in the United States of America
on acid-free paper
10 9 8 7 6 5 4 3 2 1

Library of Congress Cataloging-in-Publication Data
Vinel, Jean-Christian.
 The employee : a political history / Jean-Christian Vinel. — 1st ed.
   p. cm. — (Politics and culture in modern America)
 Includes bibliographical references and index.
 ISBN 978-0-8122-4524-0 (hardcover : alk. paper)
 1. Employees—Legal status, laws, etc.—United States—History—
20th century. 2. Industrial relations—United States—History—
20th century. 3. Political culture—United States—History—20th
century. I. Title. II. Series: Politics and culture in modern America.
 HD8072.V56 2013
 331.110973—dc23

                              2013011239

To the memory of Roger Vinel, true leftist

To my parents, with love

CONTENTS

INTRODUCTION
"A Man Can't Serve Two Masters"

ON September 29, 2006, the National Labor Relations Board (NLRB) touched off a rare controversy over labor law when it published its rulings in the "*Kentucky River* cases"—three legal disputes bearing on the definition of workers in American labor law. Holding that nurses acting as "charge nurses" in an acute care hospital in Detroit had no substantive bargaining rights because they were not "employees" but "supervisors" directing other health care staff, the conservative majority of the NLRB elicited a chorus of outraged responses from union leaders and Democratic Party members.[1] Nancy Pelosi, the Democratic Speaker of the House of Representatives, lost no time in condemning the agency. The board's new policy regarding the definition of "employee," she argued, was a "ruthless attack on American workers," one that fitted quite well in the antiunion pattern set by President George W. Bush's labor policies since 2001. "In an economy when wages are down," she lamented, "and the income of middle class families continues to stagnate, the Bush administration continues to undermine hardworking families."[2]

Quite beyond their economic impact, the *Kentucky River* cases also raised important questions about civic belonging for workers seeking to reconcile freedom of association with the ascribed categories of labor law, questions that Cheryl Johnson, the president of United American Nurses, formulated rather well. "I'm a registered nurse. I take care of patients. I'm very good at it. I make decisions every day, and I give a few orders from time to time whether I'm assigned as charge nurse or not. I am a key leader on the health care team. But I'm not a supervisor. Today, we have a Labor Board that makes its bread and butter out of determining who should get the privilege of exercising their democratic rights. When did this become a privilege granted only to a few?"[3]

In 2006, there were no readily available answers to Cheryl Johnson's query. While demonstrators and critics of the NLRB deployed a language of rights that revolved around ideas of justice and democracy, no work of political history offered insight into the origins of the predicament of these aggrieved workers. Responding to ominous reports suggesting that as many as eight million workers would lose their right to organize as a result of the *Kentucky River* cases, the AFL-CIO filed a complaint with the Committee on Freedom of Association of the International Labour Organization, arguing that the United States had failed to respect its membership obligations—indeed, according to international conventions, workers "without distinctions whatsoever" shall have the right to join a union.[4] Yet the legal and political origins of the controversy remained unaddressed. Why the Wagner Act, a law adopted in 1935 to promote economic citizenship and democracy in the workplace, could now be interpreted to exclude millions of American workers from this very right remained an open question.[5]

This book is an attempt to fill this gap in our understanding of the history of American democracy. Behind the *Kentucky River* cases lies a hidden history of power and domination in the workplace. Largely unknown to historians, this history harkens back to the 1947 Taft-Hartley Act, when businessmen pressured Congress into amending the National Labor Relations Act so that foremen in the nation's leading automobile, steel, and mining companies would not be allowed to organize and make common cause with rank-and-file workers. Relying on a concept inherited from the colonial master and servant doctrine (the body of rules and statutes relating to the relationships between masters/employers and workers/servants), corporate America insisted that unless they were production workers, employees owed a duty of fealty and loyalty to their employers, making their participation in unions impossible.[6] "A man can't serve two masters," businessmen repeatedly argued to press their case, suggesting that for supervisors, foremen, and managers, unionism was incompatible with the faithful exercise of duty because it would result in "divided loyalties," that is, these workers would be torn between their allegiance to the union and their responsibilities toward their employer. The loyalty argument was premised on the notion that democracy and individual rights can be accepted only to the extent that they do not disturb existing social and economic structures.[7]

As a result, since the 1940s the protection of the right to organize in the

United States has been structured by a tension between freedom of associ- ation and loyalty with which historians have yet to grapple. Ranging from the courtroom to the workplace and back, this book follows a large cast of characters, including workers, union leaders, labor experts, National Labor Relations Commissioners, members of Congress, judges, managers, and business associations, who were involved in a power struggle *within* what we once thought was the stable "New Deal order." A focus on the history of the legal definition of the worker and the contested meaning and boundaries of workplace democracy thus helps us restore tension to our vision of the politi- cal history of the twentieth century.[8]

This investigation also offers insight into the cultural and political power of American business. Although the result of the struggle over the definition of the worker was never foreordained, in the end it was driven by the ongoing and largely successful exercise in cultural domination that businessmen con- ducted over labor law. In tracing an arc of struggles in which the battle over the legal definition of "workers" was made public and given legal resolution, I hope to shed light on the creation of a discourse making the right to organize incompatible with the faithful performance of duty.

Uncovering this story, one finds that there is more to the history of man- agement than the organizational framework inherited from the work of Alfred Chandler.[9] As this book shows, at different junctures executives were seriously worried about the possible defection of workers they deemed es- sential to their authority over the workplace, including foremen, nurses, pro- curement buyers, and even, in a famous case, university professors. These workers' continued presence in the realm of management as defined by busi- nessmen was secured through the law, not through ideas about strategy or efficiency or middle-class, individualist values. Hence the traditional idea that white-collar employees are not interested in unions can be qualified in important ways. While the workers featured in this book never knew "mo- ments of madness" during which they collectively transformed their fate and let politics burst into their lives, they did believe that they stood to gain much from collective bargaining and little from the individualism and the corpo- rate ethic that businessmen sought to impose as their social role.[10]

In thinking about this history, I largely benefitted from the work of the legal scholar James Atleson, who demonstrated some thirty years ago that after the New Deal, the Supreme Court vitiated the democratizing potential of the right to organize created by the Wagner Act by upholding an implicit set of nineteenth-century "values and assumptions" about business prerogatives,

including "loyalty" and "management rights."[11] In a way, this book is a political historian's follow-up on Atleson's analysis of business hegemony, which
was more narrowly focused on the law. However, I depart from Atleson's rich
exposition on one important count. Atleson believed that in the post–New
Deal era, legal conservatism had thwarted the very real possibility of workers'
control in the United States. I do not share this view. There is scant evidence
that a majority of workers really wanted and sought this kind of control—
rather, most wanted to gain a freedom from arbitrary treatment, and a voice
in the company choices and decisions that affected both their working and
living conditions.[12] As I argue in this book, the alternative that existed to the
conservative definition of the worker was the progressive language of social
harmony that undergirded the labor expertise of NLRB members for several decades, one that implied not a working-class takeover of the plants, but
rather a robust individual right to organize accruing to all workers regardless
of their role in the hierarchy and organization of a company.

"We're All Workers Here"

To justify their restricting the labor perimeter under the Wagner Act, from
the 1940s onward businessmen insisted continuously on the essential difference between "labor" and "management" and stressed the adversarial character of their relations. This is surprising, and can seem even paradoxical, for
the unity of workers and employers has long been a staple of social discourse
in the United States. Indeed, in 1949, a mere twelve months after businessmen had convinced members of Congress to prevent the unionization of
foremen by adopting a law forcing their participation in managerial culture,
Philip Murray, the head of the Congress of Industrial Organizations, proved
his American mettle by insisting, "We have no classes in this country. That's
why the Marxist theory of the class struggle has gained so few adherents.
We're all workers here. And in the final analysis, the interests of farmers, factory hands, business and professional people and white collar workers prove
to be the same."[13]

While Murray's statement should be placed in proper context—it was no
doubt a response to the conservative turn in American politics in the late
1940s—it echoed many other declarations by nineteenth-century liberal pundits such as William Graham Sumner. Rooted in the nation's egalitarianism,
and reinforced by the lack of a class-based political system, the axiom of social harmony has often stymied rhetorical and political appeals to class. "You

can't talk about social classes in America," the New Dealer Herman Oliphant remarked in a private letter to French finance minister Vincent Auriol in 1936. Even with Popular Front politics at high tide, the Roosevelt administration refused to publicly couch its support for a devaluation of the franc in terms suggesting that this would enhance the standard of living of "all social classes."[14]

It is tempting to dismiss this talk about social harmony as empty rhetoric. Indeed, three generations of labor historians have taught us to lay both American exceptionalism and the midcentury notion of political consensus to rest. While linguistic, ethnic, and religious fault lines prevented the formation of a coherent working class projecting a distinct political identity in America, there is no doubt that a majority of workers never accepted the unity between "employer and employee" that supposedly characterized labor relations in America from the Gilded Age onward. Rather, from the 1877 railroad strike to the Lordstown Strike in 1972, strikes and conflict were the drumbeat of American social history.[15]

This mythologizing notwithstanding, it remains possible and useful to historicize social harmony as an ideology and, in fact, a contested ideal.[16] This book argues that during the Progressive Era, labor reformers—mostly middle-class men and women—minted their own version of the nineteenth-century conservative discourse of social harmony and used it to create and defend a via media between the traditional liberal state and socialism. The dominant figure in this effort was John R. Commons, whose sociology of labor relations offered a new vision of social harmony based on an extension of the democratic principle into the workplace. Speaking the language of the emerging social sciences, Commons argued that harmony was a social product; that is, by fostering collective bargaining, it was possible to instill faith in cooperation in the minds of workers and so deflect class antagonism. Commons and his students did not simply play an active role in the shaping of the New Deal; they also bequeathed later generations of labor economists a language on which they could draw to protect the right to organize beyond the blue-collar world to which businessmen continuously tried to limit it. After the New Deal, this language of harmony was the main alternative to the doctrine of loyalty in the contested struggle over the legal definition of the worker.

In showing this Progressivism at work over the course of the twentieth century, this book challenges the traditional vision of labor expertise. According to historians such as Nelson Lichtenstein and Christopher Tomlins, John R.

Commons and the scholars who later worked in the theoretical framework he had established in Wisconsin—industrial pluralism—mostly conceived of collective bargaining as a way to defeat labor strife and defuse workers' militancy.[17] While I do not disagree with this analysis, in this book I seek to shed light on what I call "the other side of industrial pluralism." Indeed, the industrial pluralists who staffed the National Labor Relations Board from the 1930s to the 1970s always sought to expand the definition of "worker" under the Wagner Act, even if it meant cutting against the grain of the business vision of the workplace and the social groups of which the Fordist system of production was composed. Indeed, I argue that it was precisely their moderate language of social harmony—one that hearkened back to the beginnings of Commons's sociology in the early twentieth century—that allowed them to countenance the idea that foremen or white-collar professionals with managerial duties should be classified as "employees" and allowed to bargain collectively.

By contrast, businessmen rejected this language of social harmony after the 1940s, when their cultural domination seemed at risk, insisting instead that the concept of worker loyalty should prevail over the right to organize. This book thus presents a different picture of the ideal of social harmony and classlessness in America. In the nineteenth century, liberal pundits and businessmen were united in their defense of the traditional harmony of the workplace, but in the twentieth century, it was middle-class progressives who defended this ideal, while businessmen and top managers now insisted that labor relations were inherently adversarial and that the relations between the two groups should be kept in proper balance.

Moreover, I emphasize that these labor experts who defended harmony through an expansive workplace democracy wore an empty suit: their authority was acknowledged only to the extent that a large number of political actors subscribed to their views. In fact, this was never the case, and from the late 1930s to the late 1990s, the National Labor Relations Board's efforts to expand the sociological realm of collective bargaining were recurrently stymied by an odd alliance of conservative and liberal voices. Businessmen prevailed in the struggle over the definition of employee because liberals, progressives, and unionists themselves were unable to agree on who should count as a worker under the Wagner Act. A product of the progressive search for order, their vision of workplace democracy was incomplete. Lacking a clear class-based or rights-based discourse when it came to unionism, liberals never united on a response that could be offered to the business claim to a "right to manage."

In highlighting these labor experts' unsuccessful efforts, I shed light on a lost cause of the past, one that, in the words of critic Paul Goodman, "haunts us in the present as unfinished business."[18]

The reader might note that race and gender do not figure prominently in this book. This is not for lack of interest. As I argue, during the 1930s African Americans were among the first contestants of the meaning of "worker" in the implementation of the National Labor Relations Act. That said, the thrust of this book is that in the United States the freedom to join unions and bargain collectively—an essential attribute of democracy—will never be secure as long as it is not enjoyed by all workers across the "collar" lines. To the important point that there can be no sustainable democracy at work if race and gender remain fault lines separating employees, I wish to add a complementary one: as long as the right to organize and bargain collectively is *conceded* to only specific groups of workers as an *exception* to the American grain of individualism and corporate values, associational freedom will be in danger. To return to the *Kentucky River* cases, many of the nurses who lost their bargaining rights as a result of those decisions were women or African Americans, but they lost these democratic rights because embedded in today's labor law is a prejudice against collective action and unionism that has resulted in a collective bargaining right that is granted to some workers while others are required to be "loyal" to their company. As this book argues, there is nothing natural or inevitable to the idea that the right to organize is incompatible with the faithful performance of duty when the job of a worker involves more than mindless routine. Rather, this idea is the product of business anxiety in the face of the democratization of the workplace. This book tells the history of this conservative response, and by showing the paths not taken, it suggests possibilities for a different future.

What follows is a narrative that traces the impact of the ideologies of harmony and loyalty on the definition of the worker and workplace democracy in chronological order. The first part of the book, "The Struggle for Harmony," offers a political genealogy of the Wagner Act. It shows how opposition to class antagonism shaped elite conceptions of labor relations in the late nineteenth and early twentieth centuries and informed the democratization of the workplace. I begin by reviewing the nineteenth-century origins of the ideal of social harmony by looking at the emergence of the term "employee" in American usage. By the end of the nineteenth century, the term was used commonly by Americans, and yet its social and legal meaning remained uncertain, particularly for judges who struggled with its definition

in the interpretation of lien laws and needed to differentiate more clearly between those who stood "inside" and "outside" modern corporations. Indeed,
it was the rise of economic liberalism and the eclipse of republican fears of
wage slavery and hirelings that had driven the adoption of "employé" in the
American language, for this term was well suited to express faith in the unity
between "employer and employee."

By the late nineteenth century, this classic, liberal vision was increasingly
frayed. But faith in social harmony endured. The Progressive struggle against
class antagonism shaped the transformation of the legal definition of the
worker in a way that allowed reformers to carve exceptions to the liberal and
common-law notion of the employer and employee as juridical equals. Labor
progressives shaped the Wagner Act as a law that made it possible to protect
the freedom of association of some workers while denying it to others, and
by the 1930s, labor reformers had come to believe that collective bargaining
would pave the way to social peace and cooperation between employers and
workers. Importantly, these reformers conceived of labor relations as involving two social entities, namely, "management" and "employees," thus reinforcing the notion that not all workers should be allowed to join unions.

The second half of the book, "The Battle for Loyalty," shows how the
Progressive search for social harmony through collective bargaining was stymied by businessmen who successfully invoked the need for loyalty to secure
the exclusion of an ever greater number of workers from the purview of the
law. By chronicling the history of foremen's unionism in the late 1930s and
1940s, we see that foremen did not necessarily want to make common cause
with rank-and-file unions. In fact, as the movement developed, it increasingly
defined itself as a third group between "labor" and "management." Sill, foremen argued that they were "employees," and they demanded the same kind
of economic citizenship and protection that the law now afforded unionized
production workers.

Businessmen, however, perceived this movement as a threat hanging over
both their authority in the workplace and their cultural domination. Industrial
pluralists, including labor experts, judges, and policy makers, reinterpreted
the main tenets of the science of labor relations pioneered by Commons to
support the claim that foremen were indeed "employees." Combined with
the pressure of foremen on the factory floor, the NLRB's decisions opened
the door to a broad sociological transmutation of labor relations, one that
would have wrested the legal definition of the worker away from its manual
roots. While this transmutation took place in a country like France, in the

United States it did not come to pass. Instead, the pressure exerted by corporate America and the lack of support that rank-and-file unions—particularly the United Auto Workers (UAW)—afforded the foremen's struggle closed the door on this possibility, allowing businessmen to secure the recognition of the need for managerial loyalty in the Taft-Hartley Act.

By the 1960s, white-collar workers loomed large on the horizon of American unions, whose leaders were worried at the declining numbers of blue-collar factory jobs in the United States. Yet when unions such as the UAW became committed to expanding their reach across the collar line, they found that the legal definition of the worker to which they had lent their unfortunate support in the context of the foremen's movement was a serious obstacle to their organizing plans. In the 1960s and early 1970s, the "new frontier NLRB" tried once again to expand the legal definition of the worker, this time challenging head-on the notion that managers should not be allowed to organize. Even with the support of CIO unions, however, once again the democratic efforts of the NLRB came to nothing. *In Bell Aerospace v. NLRB*, a case involving procurement buyers employed by the Bell Aerospace company, a coalition of liberal and conservative judges chastised the board for its new definition of the worker, suggesting that, far from being a liberty essential to citizenship, the protection of freedom of association was only part of a progressive search for order that might well leave many workers with no freedom to associate.

By the 1980s, it was becoming clear that the large numbers of knowledge workers on whom the American economy increasingly relied would find themselves at the center of the conservative struggle against unions and the Wagner Act. It was in the health care industry—the theater of one of the few union successes in the last two decades of the twentieth century—that the conservative battle for loyalty was taken to a new level, leading to the current controversy over the *Kentucky River* decisions. The rise of nurse unions precipitated a fresh battle over the legal definition of worker because such unions cut against the grain of the cost-cutting politics of managed care. Nurses, it would seem, are a far cry from the midcentury foreman and have few if any of the indicia of industrial managers and supervisors. Yet hospital managements were able to secure the help of conservative judges, who used the interpretive methodology of "textualism" to argue that many nurses fall in the managerial category. By 2006, as progressives lamented the *Kentucky River* decisions, the legal definition of the worker had lost much of its social relevance—it was a morbid symptom of a dying order.

PART I

The Struggle for Harmony

CHAPTER 1

The "Employé"

I N an article bearing on the "legal duties of employer and employed" published in 1893 in the *American Law Register*, jurist Richard McMurtrie railed against the growing use of the terms "employed" and "employee" to refer to American workers. According to McMurtrie, these terms were too broad and too vague. "A passenger on a ship is the employer of the master, but there is not the faintest resemblance to that of the relationship between master and servant between them," he explained. Instead, McMurtrie suggested that Americans should retain the words "master" and "servant," whose meaning was very clear: a servant, he said, was someone whose work was directed by another, which implied legal liabilities for the master. Their relationship arose by contract, and its duration was "at will." By using terms such as "employee," McMurtrie contended, Americans risked losing sight of the rights and duties of employers and workers in common law. Lamenting that there should be "something derogatory to recognize the relation of Master or the position of Servant," McMurtrie denied that there was any "servility imported from the word servant."[1]

In fact, McMurtrie had it wrong. A sense of servility *was* attached to the term "servant" at the end of the nineteenth century. Yet McMurtrie's lament reflected a confusion that was quite real. Although they had used the term "employee" since the middle of the nineteenth century, Americans—particularly judges—were confounded by its meaning. As the case of James E. Vane, an electrician who filed a lien notice against the Bankers' and Merchants' Telegraph Company (BMTC) of New York in October 1884, reveals, the term "employé," a French import, posed significant interpretive problems to judges. Vane contended that the struggling corporation owed him $16,000 for the work he had done. Yet the receivers of the corporation denied the validity of his claim to a lien on the grounds that Vane was not an "employé," but a general contractor. Surprisingly, the conundrum posed by the meaning of the term "employé" in law was such that Vane's legal matter was solved only by a Supreme Court decision five years later, in 1889.[2]

In the mid-1880s, a skilled worker like James Vane was hardly representative of the American workforce. Tellingly, the amount of the lien he claimed represented a sum of money many American workers would have taken many years to earn. An old-stock citizen in the Midwest, Vane represented that segment of the labor force comprising men who earned a high return for their skill and enjoyed a large amount of autonomy in performing the work they had agreed to do. In many ways, his experience of paid work was comparable to that of the men rolling iron or blowing glass; midway between a craft worker and a small entrepreneur, Vane could claim to be a part of what today would be called the middle class.[3]

Vane's decision to turn to the judicial system to vindicate his rights was equally suggestive of his social position. In the waning years of the nineteenth century, few American workers eagerly called on the courts to intervene in their relationship with their employers. Experience had taught them that usually courts did so only at the behest of capitalists and on behalf of capitalism and production. While in Vane's case no injunction was published against a labor union and no army was sent to crush a worker rebellion, the result was no more satisfactory and every bit as final because the Supreme Court refused to grant him the lien he claimed on the corporation because he was not an "employé."

Vane's suit against the BMTC of New York has long been forgotten, but it offers a revealing insight into the history of labor relations at the end of the nineteenth century. Indeed, the debate surrounding the legal meaning of "employé" in turn highlighted the extent to which its social meaning was also uncertain. Peering into obscure cases like James Vane's, we glimpse the dominant discourse of social harmony that pervaded not only the law but also American thinking about the relation of worker and employer. The confusion over the social meaning of "employé"—which has largely escaped the attention of historians—stemmed from the political values that had facilitated the word's adoption in American English. More than any other word in the developing lexicon of nineteenth century labor-capital relations, "employé" reflected a refusal to recognize class antagonism in America, where powerful actors—including judges—were determined to affirm the purposive unity of capital and labor.

"A Meaning Not At All Uncertain"

The BMTC was a company for which Vane had installed wires and telegraph poles on an existing line and constructed two others. For this work, Vane had hired several workers and assisted them in person. The company, however, failed to fulfill its part of the contract. It did not furnish the materials, leaving the men Vane had hired without work for some time, but nevertheless requested that the men be kept together during the delay. To be able to proceed with the work, Vane provided the materials himself, and arranged and paid for their freight, although the contract he had signed with the BMTC made no provisions for such expenditures. By September 1884, Vane notified the managers of the company that he intended to seek a lien on the company's earnings "for the labor performed after the 15th day of June 1884." Vane filed his complaint in October, and at this time the work was practically done, although he had not finished the connections. In November, he came to an agreement with the two receivers of the company whereby he would finish the connections, allowing the company to use the wires—an agreement that was not meant to contradict his claim to a lien. Overall, Vane claimed that the company owed him $16,000.[4]

In trying to convince the courts to enforce his lien against the company that had contracted with him, James Vane reflected the political tensions at work in America at the time. While mechanics' liens already had a long history in the United States, they were an important part of the populist revolt against corporations in the Midwest and in the South and thus provided one of the first attempts to regulate the work relationship in a mature, industrial economy.[5] Like the millions of workers, immigrant or not, who supplied the labor sustaining the country's economic progress, Vane underwent the destabilizing effects of industrial capitalism and its impact on the experience of work.

James Vane's claim to a lien was premised on an 1877 Indiana law providing that "[t]he employés of any corporation doing business in this State, whether organized under the laws of this State or otherwise, shall be, and they are hereby entitled to, have and to hold a first and prior lien upon the corporate property of such corporation, and the earnings thereof, for all work and labor done and performed by such employés for such corporation, from the date of their employment by such corporation."[6]

Whether Vane shared a social and economic position with the workers and farmers who were part of the populist impulse, however, the courts could not say precisely. Because the receivers of the corporation claimed that Vane's relationship with the company was not that of an "employé," but a general contractor, the claim was referred to a master, who decided that Vane was indeed an "employé," and awarded him a lien of $13,771. The circuit court, however, took exception to the report, ruling that Vane's claim to a lien was groundless, for Vane was a contractor. Vane, the court explained, "was only bound to produce, or cause to be produced, a certain result—a result of labor to be sure—but he was free to dispose of his own time and personal efforts according to his pleasure, without responsibility to the other party." The court argued that Vane was no "employé" because there was no bond of subordination between him and the corporation. "The employé must have been a servant," the court went on, "bound in some degree at least to the duties of a servant." Because Vane organized his work without direct supervision of the person who had hired him, he was not a "servant" at law, hence not an "employé."[7]

Other courts disagreed with this interpretation of "employé." Earlier, in *Water Co. v. Ware*, the Supreme Court had required that a company be held responsible for damages produced by the workers of a subcontractor. Such workers, the Court had ruled, were indeed "employés" of the company even if they were not servants of it.[8] A similar decision suggesting that "employee" was broader than "servant" had been made in 1874 by a New York state court in *Gurney v. Atlantic*, a case Vane's attorney cited in his brief. In that decision, the court interpreted an order to "pay arrearages owing to laborers and employés of the company for labor and services actually done in connection with the company" and found the order broad enough to include a lawyer who had done work for the railroad company. In this expansive definition, compensation for professional services, although they were not closely supervised, fell within the ambit of "employé."[9]

Sometimes judges simply—and carefully—avoided defining "employé." The decision of the Supreme Court of Indiana in an 1887 case involving a law punishing embezzlement by an "officer, agent, attorney, clerk, or employe of any person or persons" is illustrative. In this case, the defendant asked the court to invalidate his indictment on the grounds that the lower court had ruled that he was an "employe," without defining the term. The court, however, dismissed the appeal, contending that "the word employe, although of French derivation, was long since transplanted and adopted as an English, or at least, American, word. In this country it is of such common use that its meaning is not at all uncertain." Nonetheless it too failed to provide a definition. Six years later, the same court found it much easier to focus on the words "servant, clerk, and agent"—suggesting that the world "employé" covered all three—to determine whether the defendant was guilty under the statute. In the end, the court was content with reaffirming a most equivocal and circular definition of "employee": "one who is employed."[10]

As Richard McMurtrie's 1894 lament on "employee" reveals, this confusion extended to law treatises and debates in the legal profession.[11] In 1895, a leading legal scholar like James Schouler, for example, associated "employees" with "servants." "Servants," he explained, were "persons commonly known in popular speech as workmen or employees. . . . In this case are included day laborers, factory operatives, miners, colliers, and numerous others, of whom nothing more definite can be said than that they are hired to perform services of a somewhat unambitious character." By way of contrast, another jurist, I. Browne, defined a "servant" as being less inclusive than "employee," "as including all such employees as are in the exclusive service of the employer and constructively under his supervision, as clerks in stores, operatives in mills, persons employed on public conveyances and the like."[12]

In Vane's case, the Supreme Court did not solve this confusion, offering instead a narrow decision. In his majority opinion, Justice Blatchford noted that the lien covered neither the materials furnished nor the advances of money. It was limited, as he explained, "to the work and labor done by the employés of the corporation." Comparing the Indiana lien law used by Vane to other lien laws, Blatchford argued that other lien statutes were broader in their coverage. For example, the Indiana law covering miners explicitly covered "the miners and all persons employed in and about the mines," while the law protecting mechanics covered "mechanics and all persons performing labor." According to the Court, the language of the Indiana lien statute on which Vane based his claim covered only "the employés of a corporation" and was thus more limited—it did not cover contractors such as Vane.[13] Tellingly, a precise definition of neither "servant" nor "employé" was suggested by the Court, which was content with writing contractors out of a statute covering "employés."[14]

What, then, was an "employé"? It took the Supreme Court another two years to provide a more specific definition. Once again, the case arose out of a claim to a lien, and once more it bore upon the complex organization of the corporations that came to dominate the American landscape at the end of the Gilded Age—*Louisville, Evansville and St. Louis Railroad Co. v. Wilson.*[15]

The Louisville, Evansville and St. Louis Railroad Company was a struggling concern in the highly competitive context of the 1870s and 1880s, when railroad companies were the biggest corporations in the country and tried to consolidate to reinforce and secure their position. To help this company, which could no longer pay for its operating expenses, some of the managers of the railroad decided to advance some money and thus prevent a legal foreclosure proceeding, to no avail. The concern was put in the trust of a receiver, who sold it to a new corporation, namely, the Louisville, Evansville and St. Louis Railroad Company. In the meantime, a judge ordered the receiver to pay "all just claims and accounts for labor material, supplies, salaries of officers and wages of employés that may have been earned or furnished within six months prior to the [time when the concern was put in the hands of the receiver]." Bluford Wilson, an attorney, requested to join the suit against the company on the grounds that he had provided services, helping the company lease engines to another railroad company, and thus came within the ambit of the court order, which covered "employés." The lower court had agreed, requesting the new company to pay him $7,650 for his services.[16]

This decision was congruent with the 1874 New York case mentioned below, according to which anyone performing paid services for another was an "employé." Comparing the two cases, we see the inconsistent use of "employé" by judges and receivers. In the New York case, the receiver was told to pay arrearages to "laborers and employés," suggesting that "employé" referred to people on the white-collar side of the class line. On the contrary in *Louisville*, the order referred to "salaries of officers and wages of employés," suggesting this time that employés were the blue-collar railroad workers.

No sociological consideration, however, led the Court to outline more precisely the contours of the category of "employés." Rather, Justice Brewer, who would later pen the ruling in the infamous *In Re Debs* decision, chose to emphasize the need to protect investment and capital: "We would not be understood as asserting, even by implication, that the terms of an order of appointment of a receiver vest in all claimants an absolute right against the security holders." The first definition of "employé" given by the Court, then, was one that arose from the movement that had grown stronger in the legal world since the creation of the American Bar Association in 1878—the determination to reassert the role of the judiciary in the American system of government and use its powers to protect property and the "use of capital," as Brewer himself explained in a speech delivered in 1893. As a result, in 1891 the Court defined "employés" as "those in regular and continual service. Within the ordinary acceptation of the terms, one who is engaged to render service in a particular transaction is neither an officer nor an employé."[17]

This was a small, but important step. In determining paths of dependency and autonomy in the modern industrial world, the Supreme Court had given "employé" its first concrete technical definition, ending the general confusion over its meaning. The following year, in a similar case, a New York tribunal ruled that a lawyer who had served as the counsel of a railroad and was hired at a salary of $200 per month to provide his services was an "employé" of the railroad company and could claim a lien on the company.[18] By 1910, *Black's Law Dictionary* defined the relationship in the same terms, although some hesitancy still transpired: "As generally used with us, though perhaps not confined to any official employment, it is understood to mean some permanent employment or position. The word is more extensive than 'clerk' or 'officer.' It signifies anyone having charge or using a function, as well as one in office."[19]

Yet this confusion remains puzzling. Why did judges take so long to define "employé," when the legal meaning of terms such as "servant," "clerk," or "agent" was so well established? And how can we explain that "employé" seemed to be purposefully devoid of social connotations, referring to white-collar and blue-collar workers alike, at a time when class formation was clearly under way in the United States?

Operatives and Professionals

Although it is commonplace today, the term "employee" was not part of the everyday language of American society in the antebellum era. While "employ" and "employment" appeared frequently, there were other words more commonly used to refer to those who furnished the country's manual but necessary labor. "Mechanic," "workingman," "journeyman," and "laborer" adequately conveyed the social position of workers in the young republic, one that did not derive from tensions inherent in the wage relationship.

At the turn of the century, journeymen and artisans inhabited a world based on household production, a preindustrial setting in which master craftsmen, journeymen, and apprentices often worked and lived together. While this organization of production did not prevent tensions (journeymen created unions as early as the 1790s), it was based on a cooperative culture that revolved around the acquisition of skills. Learning a trade opened the door to advancement and independence, and both the apprentice and the journeyman could work toward and look forward to becoming independent artisans themselves through what was a predictable, community-based life cycle. Indeed, in the young republic, the artisan, like the farmer, was a social figure embodying a freedom that combined a strong sense of individual proprietorship and a sense of interdependence coming from a local, moral economy.[20]

"Employé," which entered *Webster's Dictionary* first in 1849, did not convey these social assumptions, and its emergence in the American language no doubt owed to its lack of artisanal connotations—an important element in a country transformed by the industrial revolution. In 1849, "employé" was simply defined as "someone who is employed," a cryptic explanation that the reader might elucidate by looking up "to employ": "1. To occupy the time, attention and labor of, to keep busy, or at work, to use. 2. To use as an instrument or means. 3. To use as materials in forming anything. 4. To engage in one's service. To use as an agent or substitute in transacting business. 5. To occupy, to use. To apply or to devote to an object; to pass in business; as to *employ* one's time—to *employ* one's self, is to apply or devote one's time and attention, to busy one's self."[21]

"Employé" ("employee," according to the dictionary, was not accepted yet) thus did not speak to any social condition or any economic relationship—rather, it denoted an individual situation, the fact that someone was "used." One might employ someone else's help just like someone might employ a tool or a method, or simply one's self. In English as in French, the roots of the word "employé" in the Latin *implicare* ran deep. Employment was first and foremost "usage."

But this "usage" was not restricted to manual work, and implied no lack of dignity. In 1890, the report of the eleventh census provided a clear picture of the growing number of Americans who did not work independently: the "Employés and Wages" section offered a table titled "Total Employés and Number and Percentage of Males, Females and Children." Their number had risen from 957,059 in 1850 to 2,053,996 in 1870 and to 4,470,884 in 1890. From 1880 to 1890, the increase was staggering, over 65 percent. Importantly, the report further divided the category "employés" into five "classes": (1) operatives, engineers, and skilled workers, including superintendents; (2) firm officers; (3) clerks; (4) laborers and unskilled workers; and (5) piece workers. Farmworkers and domestic workers were not included—an exclusion that would prove long-lasting.[22]

"Employe" thus cast a broad sociological net over the American workforce. In fact, it is striking that the term was adopted in American English during a period—roughly the end of the Civil War to the early twentieth century—that witnessed two profound evolutions. The first was the growth of large-scale enterprises and the concomitant need for white-collar workers to assume the bureaucratic tasks that made it possible to coordinate production. While this meant a development of a stable work relationship in the office, many skilled and unskilled workers, by contrast, experienced the irregular, seasonal aspects of labor and were forced to go from town to town to find the means to provide for themselves; as a number of historians have noted, that period was also the golden age of "tramping."[23] At the turn of the century "employé" might have been used to refer to all these social worlds and experiences of work, although, as a number of scholars have argued, class distinctions between manual and nonmanual workers were increasingly drawn even in the antebellum period.[24] By the end of the century, American dictionaries gave it a very broad definition—"one who works for an employer; a person working for salary and wages."[25]

This classless dimension was most visible in language: as the *Centennial Dictionary* explained in 1890, a sense of respectability attached to "employ" that did not exist in "hire": "*Hire* and *Employ* are words of different meaning. To *Hire* is to engage in service for wages. The word does not imply dignity. It is not customary to speak of *hiring* a teacher or pastor. We *hire* a man for wages; we *employ* him for wages or salary. To employ is thus a word of wider signification. A man *hired* to labor is *employed*, but a man may be *employed* in a work who is not *hired*." The concomitant displacement of *hireling* by *employee* was thus no mere linguistic refinement—in calling manual workers "employees," the American language bestowed on them a respectability that bridged social classes.[26]

At this point, we can understand much better why James Vane believed that he could stake a claim to be an "employee." This generic term simply referred to the fact that someone provided labor or services and might be a professional or a skilled mechanic working without direct supervision as much as a manual worker. As Vane's attorney noted in his brief, "The word [employé] has recently come to us from a foreign tongue, but receives a broader meaning here than it has in its natural home. Its brevity has led to its adoption in our tongue as it comprehends many classes of people which otherwise we must name respectively." Vane could indeed claim to be an "employé."[27]

The sense of dignity that attached to "employ," however, requires additional investigation. Looking at the history of "employé" in France, Great Britain, and the United States provides a brief but important glimpse at the political assumptions that underwrote the all-inclusive social character of "employé" in the United States. This expansive definition, which included all Americans at work, was also a political construction rooted in opposition to class antagonism.

From France to Great Britain and the United States: The Many Worlds of "Employé"

In France, "employé" originally referred to workers employed by the state, particularly those whose work was routine and did not imply the use of judgment, as opposed to the "commis." It did not apply to manual workers, who in the nineteenth century were still expected to carry a *livret*, even though bound labor had been abolished at the time of the Revolution. In the mid-nineteenth century, however, "employé" was given a much wider—albeit abstract—definition in the work of liberal political economists known as the "laissez-faire ultras" who sought to promote free trade in the Third Republic and emphatically denied the main claim of radical movements of the time—that the wage relationship was inequitable. "Les fonctions du maître et de l'employé sont réglées par un contrat, c'est à dire un acte de la volonté libre de l'un et de l'autre [the rights and duties of the master and the employee are fixed by contract, that is, a voluntary act on both sides]," Courcelle Seneuil explained in 1867 in his *Manuel des affaires*, while his fellow ultra-liberal Frédéric Bastiat sang the virtues of the division of labor in a book aptly titled *Harmonies économiques* (Economic Harmonies). It was at that time that "employé" was paired in French with "employeur," a term liberals deemed more adequate than the traditional "patron," for it conveyed more clearly the idea of freedom and the lack reciprocal obligations between the "patron" and the "ouvrier."[28]

"Employ" migrated across the English Channel very early on, and as in France, the term strongly connoted the idea of freedom in the work relationship. In *Customs in Common*, E. P. Thompson recounts an encounter, early in the eighteenth century, between a justice and a local journeyman weaver who was accused of neglect of duty:

> Justice: Come in, Edmund, I have talk'd with your Master.
> Edmund: Not my Master, and't please your Worship, I hope I am
>   my own Master.

> Justice: Well, your employer, Mr. E_____ the clothier; will the
>   word employer do?
> Edmund: Yes, yes, and't please your worship, anything but
>   master.[29]

Both the judge and the journeyman interpreted *employer* and *master* to convey opposite meanings when it came to the freedom of the worker. For Thompson, this was the sign of changing social relations, a symbol of the decline of hierarchical relations and the rise of free labor as the basis of a new social order. To use another example, prosecutors in a late eighteenth-century North Carolina case explained that "the mechanic to whom we send our job is not our servant. . . . There is not authority on one side, and subjugation on the other. His time is his own, not ours. He may postpone work to make room for another's." Such a worker, the legal historian Christopher Tomlins tells us, was said to be "employed."[30]

Yet if we follow the thread of language, we see that the path to freedom for British workers was actually as tortuous as for French ones. "Employé" was used in Great Britain in the nineteenth century, but interestingly that term was not used to refer to manual workers before the beginning of the twentieth century. As in France, "employé" referred only to white-collar workers, clerks, managerial workers, and professionals, excluding from its purview all the workers who were still subject to the strictures of Master and Servant Law, under which breach of service was a felony. Indeed, the rising demand for freedom identified by Thompson was actually largely contained over the eighteenth century as the British Parliament enacted laws that returned the work relationship to the previous model of authority. The Master and Servant Law was not abolished until 1875, and its legal influence obtained long afterward through the disciplinary powers given to employers and the duty of obedience bestowed on workers. What characterized the "employés" in Great Britain, then, was the capacity to sign a contract of employment, a freedom that set them apart from manual workers, many of whom did not have the right to vote before the 1867 and 1884 reforms and were seen as an unprovided class. Tellingly, it took the rise of the welfare state and Beveridge's vision of a new social order in the twentieth century to fully bring the British industrial worker safely under the purview of "employee."[31]

The British case is quite illuminating because in the United States, unfree labor was abolished (with the obvious exception of slavery) very early on, in the 1820s, as the Supreme Court moved against the system of indentured servitude.[32] In 1849, the liberal *Philadelphia Ledger*, the first penny paper of the nation, captured the liberal individualism that was developing in America, paving the way for the adoption of "employed" and then "employé(s)" as generic terms: "A compromise between employer and employed. In other words, a contract between two free contracting parties. This is precisely where the law must leave it under a free government. Compulsion upon either is a violation of natural right. Competition among employers will raise wages, and competition between employed will depress them. Yet competition must be free to both, for it cannot be restrained without violation of natural right."[33]

Such a contractual reading of the wage relationship was at odds with the republican persuasion that still dominated the nation thirty years earlier. Whether it came through a Jeffersonian rejection of the wage system or through a defense of workingmen's rights to combine, as in the streak of cases that led to *Commonwealth v. Hunt* (1842), American Republicanism had woven tropes such as public interest, virtue, and independence into its definition of free labor, none of which was present in "employé," which symbolized the ascendency of a free-market-based definition of the rights of the worker and implied that the wage relationship had become respectable. Consider, for example, this famous comment made by a Massachusetts congressman ten years later during the state's constitutional convention: "In a free country like ours employment is simply a contract between parties having equal rights. The operative agrees to perform a certain amount of work in consideration of receiving a certain amount of money. The work to be performed is, by the contract, an equivalent for the money paid. The relationship, when properly entered into, is therefore one of *mutual benefit*. The employed is under no greater obligation to the employer than the employer is to the employed. . . . In the eye of the law, they are both freemen, citizens having equal rights and brethren sharing a common destiny."[34] Over forty years later, the *New York Times* illustrated the social and cultural change that had attended the linguistic evolution from "employed" to "employé" and "employee," emphasizing the logic of contract that undergirded it: "Why should the French word employé be so much used when we have at hand the English form of the same word? Employee is surely the correlative of employer. When we want the correlative of examiner we say at once examinee, and so in analogous cases, licensee, assignee, addressee, consignee, mortgagee."[35]

Such paeans to the powers of individualism were a fitting expression of Marx's lament that "Liberty, Equality, Property and Bentham" reigned over the industrial labor market.[36] Indeed, one may argue that the term "employee"

and the pair "employer and employee" were particularly suited to express the idea of harmony between capital and labor that attended the rise of economic liberalism in the United States. While Marx saw the wage relationship as inherently exploitative because workers did not receive the full product of their labor, the idea expressed by advocates of the free market through the idea of "employee" was that the market was a harmonious space where capital and labor naturally associated to produce goods. Tellingly, one of the best-known exponents of the theory of social harmony was Henry Charles Carey, an economist who butted heads with Karl Marx in the pages of Horace Greeley's *New York Tribune* and whom Karl Marx bitterly criticized in *Capital*. Carey, who was active in Whig and then Republican politics and was mentioned in 1860 as a possible candidate for the presidential nomination, developed a home-grown analysis that contradicted much of the classical theory expounded by the British School, particularly the opposing interests of capital and labor. In his *Principles of Social Science* (1858) and his aptly titled *Harmony of Interests* (1857), Carey explained that wages did not need to fall to the "subsistence level" because in America capital increased faster than the population—as society developed and as the national income increased, the workers were bound to see their standard of living increasing, as had been the case so far. "The interests of the capitalist and the laborer are thus in perfect harmony with each other, as each derives advantage from every measure that tends to facilitate the growth of capital, and to render labor productive, while every measure that tends to produce the opposite effect is injurious to both." It is no surprise, then, to find that Carey also talked about the "harmony between the employer and the employed."[37]

In similar fashion, from the early nineteenth century onward, a number of pundits emphatically denied that American society was composed of classes. Ranging from Daniel Webster in the antebellum era to E. L. Godkin and William Sumner in the 1870s and 1880s, these "literary champions of capitalism," as the Socialist Labor Party called them in 1880, deployed in the pages of the *Nation* and the *North American Review* a dominant discourse depicting class antagonism as a European phenomenon that could not take root in America. Reading into the nineteenth-century economy the workings of the market as described by eighteenth-century observers, they insisted that every laborer was an incipient capitalist, and that the market produced a harmony of interests. "There are no classes of men born, none formed, none recognized in any way, who have the right to do any conceivable thing to which other men have no right," the linguist Richard Grant White explained in 1883.

To White, as to others before him, social differences in America were rooted in education, talent, and virtue; to be sure, such qualities were not distributed equally, but the American republican form of government did not upset or trump any individual's chances in the market or in society. As William Dolby, a man of letters, had suggested in the 1840s, "classes" existed in America, but only in the form of a "classification of *employments*" rather than a "classification of interests."[38]

This defense of an American social order premised on a harmony of interests was reinforced by the end of slavery, for abolitionism had lent a positive sanction to wage work and the right to contract and removed the republican critique of wage slavery from the debate on free labor.[39] As the lawyer James Schouler explained in his 1870 law treatise, "In these days we dislike to call any man master. The recent abolition of slavery has well nigh removed all traces of an institution known to the ancient Roman empire. . . . Master and Servant is a rather repulsive title, and is fast losing favor in this republican country."[40] Schouler suggested that lawyers and legal pundits should use "principal" and "agent" instead of "master and servant," a proposal that found little echo. Seven years later, instead, one of the most influential treatises of the day, Horace Wood's *Treatise on the Law of Master and Servant*, reflected the evolution of American legal English with the subtitle *Covering the Relation, Duties and Liabilities of Employers and Employees.*[41]

Wood's treatise was significant because it offered the first definition of the employment relationship as being "at will," meaning that both the employer and worker were free to end it as they pleased. For workers, this was a development with mixed blessings. Until the 1880s, under the "entire contract" rule, it was understood that payment for work done came at the end of the duration of the contract—if workers quit their jobs before the end of the contract, they forfeited any wages that had not been paid them for the work already done. So in this respect, the "at will" rule did represent progress for workers. Still, even as they conceived of the employment relationship as one based on consent, nineteenth-century judges expected workers to submit voluntarily to forms of obligation derived from the status-based master and servant model, according to which servants were to accept any work given to them, follow instructions, and not break their ties to the master. As a number of scholars have argued, remnants of feudalism were thus visible in post–Civil War labor law.[42]

One such doctrine was employers' right to control the work of those they employed: according to the famous treatise author Horace Wood, workers

had a duty to obey their master's "reasonable commands," which was a remnant of the old servant's duty of allegiance. This meant that factory rules often prescribed not only working hours and quota outputs, but also obedience to usages and customs imposed by the employer. Beyond the essential right to control work, remnants of the master and servant idea of loyalty were visible in the fact that trying to entice a worker to leave an employer was illegal and in the fact that money earned by workers during the time they were employed by someone else was their employer's, not theirs. The continuing importance of loyalty was further manifest in the legal sanction given to yellow-dog contracts, whereby workers pledged not to join a union. Additional protection against outside interference by unions in the relations between employers and workers was provided by judges who used the doctrine of conspiracy to defend American workplaces against attempts at collective control.[43]

Writing in 1885 as the receiver of a railroad company, Justice Brewer offered a sharp defense of the idea of worker loyalty and its incompatibility with unionism: "I do not know of any large organization of business, or any aggregation of labor, where there is more imperative demand for almost military law and discipline. You must have a corps of employés who are loyal to the road, who are looking after its interests ungrudgingly, without divided allegiance." Thomas Cooley, another nineteenth-century conservative luminary, similarly insisted that "confidence" was essential to "friendly intercourse" in employment relations, and although he blamed employers for their workers' turn to unions, he still believed that unions did not belong in the workplace and that workers should be made to feel that they had a reciprocity of interests with their employers.[44]

Yet these limits on the freedom of workers were deemphasized by the ideal of social harmony conveyed by the "employer and employee" coordinates, thus giving rise to confusion as to the sociological makeup of the group of "employees." This ideal rested on three assumptions. The first was an important *tradition of equal rights*, a feature of Jeffersonian and Jacksonian America that was still present in legal discourses on workers at the end of the century. As the Supreme Court of Tennessee argued in 1884, "Men must be left to buy and sell where they please, and to discharge or retain employees at will for good cause and no cause, or even for bad cause. . . . It is a right which an employee may exercise in the same way, to the same extent, for the same cause or want of cause as the employer."[45]

The second one was the idea that the relationship between "employer and employee" was *mutually beneficial* and was tied to the success of a company.

When strikes broke out, conservatives were quick to point out that collective action was detrimental to both sides of the conflict because it resulted in a waste of the capital that made economic activity possible: "The day of the inauguration of the trades union and labor organizations in this country was a day of the blackest and fullest menace to the popular prosperity and peace that ever dawned on this nation. They have been an unmitigated curse on employer and employees alike," said the *Scribner's Monthly* in 1877, as the railroad strikes jolted the nation. By contrast, the *Scranton Times* contended, "Labor is the great moving power of this world. If the railroads have the right to reduce the rate of workmen, the workmen have the right to dissolve the partnership [note the term] and take their labor out of the firm."[46]

Third was *social mobility.* The idea that the worker of today was the master of tomorrow remained influential late in the nineteenth century and even prevailed in modern form at the beginning of the twentieth century. Opposing an arbitration bill supported by President Grover Cleveland in 1887, the Colorado Congressman Henry M. Teller contended that "no laboring man should for a moment surrender the right to free contract either to the state, to his fellow workmen, or to capital. His labor is valuable to him only as it is at his uncontrolled disposal. . . . The difference between a slave and a free man consists mainly in the fact that the freeman may freely dispose of his labor. Today an employee, tomorrow an employer."[47] In 1907, a Texas judge concurred: "In this country the employee of today may be the employer next year, and laws treating employés as subjects for protective legislation belittle their intelligence, and reflect on their standing as free citizens."[48] These were words Abraham Lincoln might have used in the early 1860s, when no permanent class of wage earners was visible as yet, but in the late nineteenth century, when a majority of Americans worked in the industrial sector, it reflected a strong, willful denial of social stratification.

Employees and Producers

For years, liberal pundits such as E. L. Godkin had resisted restrictive definitions of terms of identity such as "laboring classes," "workingmen," and "producers" on the grounds that such definitions implied an unnatural social division. Instead, they tried to impress on Americans an expansive vision of laborers or producers that included every person involved in stimulating industry and production in one way or another. Thus, the astronomer Simon Newcomb argued in the *North American Review* that the "laboring classes" included all who worked "with head or hand," including "intellectual labor-ers," those in professions, and those involved in "planning, directing and managing."[49]

Similarly, in *What Social Classes Owe Each Other* (1883), the Yale scholar William Graham Sumner—one of the foremost champions of liberalism and social Darwinism—took exception to the meaning of the terms "labor" and "capital" in the producerist culture of American labor. Sumner defined *labor* as "toil, irksome exertion" and *capital* as "any product of labor used to assist production" and lamented that the discussion over the wage rela-tionship was made difficult by other uses of these two terms—particularly the idea that *labor* might refer to all those contributing production except merchants, bankers, and professionals, and that *capital* might be reserved for large-scale employers. Breaking with this political definition of labor and la-borers, Sumner fell back on the more neutral pair "employer and employed." Comparing the "employer" and "employé" to " buyers and sellers, borrowers and lenders," Sumner argued that their relationship was governed by the "uni-versal law of supply and demand" and was on the whole advantageous to the worker. The employer, he explained, "takes all the risks, assumes the direc-tion of business," while the employé "is free from all responsibilities, risk and speculation." Including all workers in the category "employes," he argued that wage earners were in the same advantageous situation as salaried men. Like them, "physicians, lawyers, and workers paid by fees are workers by the piece. To the capital in existence all must come for their subsistence and tools."[50]

Yet at the end of the nineteenth century, these exercises in cultural hege-mony increasingly fell short of their aims. In 1887, as the country awoke to the reality of deep-seated social antagonism, the Knights of Labor leader George McNeill delivered in *The Labor Movement: The Problem of Today* a classic indictment of industrial capitalism, warning that workers would not be lulled by rhetorical appeals to partnership:

> The old cry of partnership between labor and capital has finally
> awakened in the minds of the silent partners in the concern a
> demand for an examination of the accounts, as well as a more
> equitable division of the profits. Heretofore, the laborer, having
> no right of free contract, sold his labor at such terms and for such
> times as the proprietor or employer should fix; and if, at any time,
> the laborer asked for higher remuneration, he was informed that
> the interests of the enterprise would not permit an advance, and

that, as one of the partners in the labor and capital combination,
he must waive any right to increased payment lest he should
hazard the existence of such enterprise.[51]

To McNeill, there was no doubt that a "crisis of mighty import" would take place unless workers forced the nation to restructure its politics and economic organization and create a "Republic of Labor."[52]

For labor radicals, the individual right to pursue a calling in industry as either employer or worker did not suffice to satisfy the needs of a republican society based on equal rights. Insisting that the workers' social position mattered just as much as their individual rights, they defended, through the term "producer," a vision of free labor that stressed the importance of community concerns for the welfare of all and reaffirmed the principle of individuals' voice in shaping their political and social environment. In their view, no social harmony characterized American society in the Gilded Age, for the republic was being corrupted by an elite of financiers and industrialists who had gotten hold of the transportation system, public land, and the financial system, but also of the polity and the courts in particular. Such a system, they said, fomented social antagonism because it was incompatible with the principles of democracy and equal rights. Increasingly, American workers and farmers were deprived of the just reward for their labor and of their social independence.[53] Henry George's widely read *Progress and Poverty* made this point eloquently when he denounced both the increased poverty and lack of education of workers in the United States and England.[54]

Yet neither George nor other labor radicals spoke the language of Marxism or claimed that there were antagonistic interests between employers and workers. "The principles of the Knights of Labor make no war on the Vanderbilts, but upon the system that makes the Vanderbilts possible," McNeill explained.[55] In fact, the producerist critique of capitalism was not aimed at the idea of social harmony. "The capitalist, seeking profit or gain, and the worker, seeking better and easier condition, may work as partners, with common interests, or wage unrelenting war for the mastery," McNeill commented. Nor did this critique challenge the theory of freedom of contract as such. Rather, the Knights and their followers lamented that these ideals were no longer possible in the present economic system, which favored individualistic capital accumulation. McNeill thus noted in his pamphlet that during the 1886 congressional hearings on relations between capital and labor, an employer had emphatically asserted that he did not wish to "run his business on the town meeting plan," a statement that in his view illustrated the fact that freedom of contract did not exist.[56]

For all the clamor arising from workers and farmers, attempts to restructure American politics and its economic organization around the interests of "producers" were short-lived. The Knights of Labor foundered on the shoals of political repression after Haymarket, and the Populist movement did not survive the fusion with the Democratic Party during the 1896 campaign.[57] As for the American Federation of Labor, the only federation of unions in the country, although it was founded on the need to represent "the working classes" of the country, it soon limited itself to the craft workers for whom the struggle for independence and dignity remained possible. Law and deep-seated prejudices against immigrants thus combined to create a segmented market in which many "employés" enjoyed no citizenship at work.

Still, the emergence of the labor question as the dominant question of the day proved that nineteenth-century economic liberalism was increasingly untenable. In due time, the idea that negotiation between employers and workers should be based on a true negotiation and reflect democratic principles such as the "town meeting plan" would be essential to the shaping of labor relations. Before this could happen, however, two developments were necessary. First, it would be necessary to lay the legal framework necessary to wrest American workers from the tendrils of the free labor ideology. Second, a fresh rationale for the democratization of the workplace—one that would not simply look back to preindustrial America, but would also speak to the needs of a nation with a majority of people working in an emerging Fordist, mass-production economy—would be needed.

The ideal of social harmony, however, like the term "employee" whose introduction to American discourse it had facilitated, did not disappear with traditional liberalism. Rather, it was reconstructed by a generation of progressives who accepted the reality of the class struggle but nonetheless believed that class interests—defined now as the "correlative interests" of employer and employee—could be reconciled and industrial conflict contained.

CHAPTER 2

Struggling Against Class

THEY exploit the employés to the utmost to compensate themselves
for the exactions of the manufacturers and the competition among
themselves. . . . It is the judgment of the employes in the trade, and most
emphatically my judgment, that any measure which does not prohibit the
manufacture of clothing in any dwelling by any woman or child will wholly
fail of its object." Social reformer Florence Kelley's sharp denunciation of the
sweatshop system in the tenements of Chicago perfectly illustrated the social meaning of "employé" at the end of the nineteenth century. No worker,
indeed, could have been further removed from the modern organization of
wage work taking shape in the rising corporations than those whose toil she
brought to light in her report to the Illinois legislature—an "employé" was
still simply someone who was "used."[1]

Kelley was a tireless advocate of the regulation of the economy through
the intervention of the state, and her report, which was soon to be translated
into a law regulating the work of women and prohibiting the employment
of children, illustrated the dynamics behind the rise of the labor question in
America. Earlier in the nineteenth century, many middle-class Americans,
like their European counterparts, saw in vagrants and paupers dangerous un-
incorporated social figures. By the end of the century, the rapid industrialization of American society and the centrifugal forces it generated had changed
the terms of the debate on the social body. Workers, although they were
not idle, had come to embody the problem of social disaffiliation, and wage
work was the object of renewed attention. The labor question—a mixture
of class antagonism, worker poverty, and social strife—encapsulated both a

middle-class feeling of alienation from society and definite programmatic responses moving beyond the orthodoxy of acquisitive liberalism.[2]

An upheaval in social values and norms was at hand in many Western countries, one that came largely, as in Kelley's report, from the emergence of realism and its ultimate product—the notion of social fact. From Mary Van Horst's experience as a factory girl and E. C. Moore's studies of working-class saloons to Robert Hunter's analysis of the dynamics of poverty in the United States, a large number of reform-minded scholars now tried to use sociological and statistical techniques to move beyond Victorian moral strictures and abstract free-market principles. Probing the ways in which American society and its economy produced social inequality and economic coercion, they laid the groundwork for a reappraisal of the meaning of wage work.

The input of the social sciences thus simultaneously revived and transformed the old ideal of social harmony. Indeed, these reformers did not wish to enter the class struggle on the same terms as the Industrial Workers of the World or European socialist parties. They saw class antagonism as a pathology that could be remedied and dealt with. With the help of Progressive political leaders convinced that the pursuit of private interests could no longer be expected to produce a social good, they worked to redefine employment and wage work as a source of obligations for employers and of social rights for workers. This was a long and sustained effort that consumed the energies of advocates of social reform well beyond the chronological limits through which the "Progressive Era" is usually understood. Only in the late 1930s, when the Federal Labor Standards Act was adopted, did this movement lose its impetus. By then, "employee," the legal definition of the worker, had become the mainstay of a new and capacious vision of economic citizenship.[3]

The Wagner Act, which was adopted in 1935, was no doubt the keystone of the legislative edifice that Progressives and New Dealers built to remedy the patterns of coercion and subordination that they identified at the root of the labor question. By democratizing the workplace and allowing an upward shift in working-class purchasing power, the law came to symbolize the politics of economic security that characterized the reconstruction of the wage relationship. Coming as it did after decades of legal injunctions and battles with employers, the Wagner Act seemed to many workers to be nothing short of a revolution. It was, in William Green's words, "Labor's Magna Charta."

This, however, was a somewhat restrictive vision of "labor," for the adoption of the Wagner Act also gave rise to a debate over the contours of the legal definition of the worker. While many workers enjoyed the benefits of unionism, others were now engaged in a struggle for inclusion and for recognition as "employees." Indeed, the benefits of the law were not universal, and opposition to the democratization of the workplace now developed along a participatory axis, with employers seeking to define workers out of the group of "employees." Tracing the political and constitutional genealogy of the Wagner Act back to its Progressive roots, this chapter explains why at the end of the New Deal, the legal definition of workers had become a contested battleground on which employers and unions now waged their struggle over the limits democracy at work.

From Working-Class Empowerment to Employment Regulation

"The question that forces itself upon us, and imperatively demands an immediate answer, is this: in the great strife of classes, in the life and death struggle that is rending society and its foundations, where do I belong?" Florence Kelley asked in 1887.[4] Progressives emphatically responded that they stood on the side of those who were victims of the industrial capitalism, and yet most of them did not deal in the rhetoric of class, preferring to emphasize the pursuit of the public interest, which they identified with the regulation of the employment relationship rather than its abolition.[5] As Jane Addams explained in an article published in the *American Journal of Sociology* in 1899, social reform should not be effected on behalf of one particular social class, but rather with a view toward fostering social cohesion. "The habitual use of 'the people' as a phrase practically equivalent to the 'working classes,'" she explained, "is a constant admission of the fact that the proletariat is not, properly speaking, a 'class' at all, but the body of society itself."[6]

Indeed, Addams argued that the labor question and the social strife that attended it were really a failure of the American social body, which had grown so distended as to allow for structural inequality and for the existence of economic social classes. Like organized labor and socialist politicians, Progressives like Addams understood that social change was possible on a relatively short term. Yet the task of resolving this question was not to be left to labor unions alone. Social amelioration should not be primarily a working-class movement, for in promoting their interests, unions, like corporate America, might be oblivious to the common good. For Progressives, an objective and positive observation of social facts, not class consciousness, should form the basis of social policies. As Addams explained, "The trades-union movement secures its lower objects best where there is a well-defined class feeling among the proletarians of its country, but it accomplishes its highest objects in proportion as it is able to break into all classes and seize upon legislative enactment."[7]

Those Progressives who took interest in the labor question can be seen as pioneers of a "new liberalism" that also existed in England and thrived in a common ground of shared interests with the left. Progressives did assist workers in their struggles, whether it was Florence Kelley in Lawrence in 1912 or Lincoln Steffens and Walter Lippmann joining Bill Haywood at the Paterson pageant organized by John Reed in 1912 at Madison Square Garden, but this support can be misleading. They were legatees of a liberal world whose values they found jarring and hollow. Yet while they often interacted and rubbed shoulders with socialists and unionists, Progressive reformers were not members of the Socialist Party and did not want to live under working-class rule. They saw the empowerment of the working class and the promotion of its welfare as a means toward social cohesion, a stepping stone to a different social order. The interests of the working class and those of the "public" were so enmeshed as to be sometimes undistinguishable in practice, but in theory there was a great difference—Progressives championed the interests of the working class, but they opposed class politics all the same. This led them to deemphasize the socialist ambition to empower the working class and to seek instead the regulation of employment and the protection of "employees" by weighing on the incidents of the workers' relationship with employers.[8]

Notably, many reformers in the Progressive Era were steeped in the language of pragmatism. According to men like John Dewey and William James, truth was essentially contingent; it was the product of social inquiry and experience. In this perspective, there was no such thing as an abstract, coherent working class; rather, there were a diversity of workers and a multiplicity of interests. True to this pragmatic approach, in their efforts at social amelioration, reformers did not tackle the labor question in a broad, structural way, but rather aimed at one specific social ill they could attempt to remedy, usually by marshaling the vocabulary of science and efficiency. This often involved building local coalitions of lawyers, journalists, and working-class advocates to accommodate the demands of party machines. However, it also led reformers to focus their reformist efforts on specific groups of workers rather than on classwide reform.

The adoption of the New York Bakeshop Act in 1895—the law that generated the *Lochner v. New York* case—is illustrative of this early type of "issue
politics," to use historian Daniel Rodgers's apt phrase.[9] This law resulted
from the investigations of the muckraker journalist Edward Marshall into
the squalid bakeries housed in New York tenements. With the help of Henry
Weisman, the secretary of the local Journeymen Bakers Union as well as several "social gospel" groups, Edward Marshall was able to rouse public attention by shedding light on the disastrous consequences of long hours (it was
not uncommon for bakers to work more than one hundred hours a week)
spent in an unsanitary environment where dampness, gas fumes, and flour
dust generated lung diseases. Tellingly, the Bakeshop Act mostly targeted
master bakers or "boss bakers," whose small establishments employed fewer
than five workers—very often French, Italian, or Jewish—and did not bring
large profits. Larger, more modern bakeries supported the law, hoping that
their English, Irish, and German workforces would no longer suffer from the
competition of the tenement bakeries.[10]

With an editorial published in the *New York Press,* Marshall was able to
launch a local campaign, enlist a large number of urban reformers, and secure
the support of the local union of bakers, who had grown frustrated with their
unsuccessful attempts to win the ten-hour day through collective bargaining.
In a state dominated by the Republican machine of boss Thomas Platt, this
campaign ended with a unanimous vote for the following law:

> No employee shall be required or permitted to work in a biscuit,
> bread, or cake bakery or confectionary establishment for more
> than sixty hours in any one week, or more than ten hours in any
> one day, unless for the purpose of making a shorter work day on
> the last day of the week; nor more hours in any one week than
> will make an average of ten hours per day for the number of days
> during such week in which such employee shall work.[11]

The New York Bakeshop Act thus helps us lay bare a number of important elements in the way Progressive quest for harmony reshaped the social meaning of wage work and displaced the idea of a political working class. First,
through this law, the New York legislature obviously recognized that there
were elements of compulsion in the wage relationship, thus changing the social and cultural meaning of "employee." Although the law was based on a report highlighting the unhealthy sanitary conditions prevailing in the baking

industry, it covered only those who were deemed to lack the freedom to protect themselves from the effects of these conditions. "Our aim is primarily
to protect the employee," explained Henry Weissman after the bill had been
amended to exclude the employers, who thus remained free to work as much
as they wanted in spite of the health hazards.[12]

Still, the recognition of the lack of freedom of the wage worker came with
a drawback insomuch as it did not entail a full recognition of the asymmetry
and inequity of the wage bargain that radicals denounced. First, this recognition was limited to specific groups of workers who could be linked to a social
problem—whether it was bakers in the New York law or women in the famous case of *Muller v. Oregon* in 1908 (where the Supreme Court sanctioned
a law mandating shorter hours for women), the group of "employees" covered
by the Progressive laws was not universal, but rather determined through a
specific social purpose, whether it was the regulation of a specific industry
(railroads, bakeries, restaurants) or the protection of women and children
workers because of preconceived ideas as to their role and place in society.
This fragmentation of workers into specific groups of employees was reinforced by the character of the American polity, which made it difficult to contemplate national social laws at first, but also by the Progressive movement
itself—a local impulse that only gradually developed a national dimension.[13]

Second, in protecting some workers from the overweening power of their
employers, such laws also, *sub silentio*, legitimized and objectivized the workers' lack of discretion on the job and their submission to managerial rule.
As the social insurance expert Charles Richmond Henderson explained, the
worker "has special claims upon collective consideration because he no longer has any ownership in the materials and instruments of production, nor
any voice in management of the process nor control of the conditions under
which his mind and body may suffer." As the legal scholar Jonathan Witt has
suggested, some Progressive laws such as workmen's compensation even
strengthened managerial rule by leading employers to increase safety procedures and reinforce their control of the workplace to avoid civil penalties. The
protection of the "employee" was thus thoroughly congruent with Taylorism.
In fact, Progressive laws strengthened the inequity of the wage bargain by
making it the source of a number of social rights that were trade-offs for the
worker's social and technical submission to the new industrial order. In this
respect, the path trod by American Progressives was quite similar to the one
taken by reformers in European countries such as France, which provides a
useful point of comparison.[14]

In France, it was the *solidaristes* led by Léon Bourgeois who left their imprint on the legal definition of the worker during the third Republic. *Solidarisme* was in many ways the political translation of the sociological analysis pioneered at the turn of the century by Emile Durkheim, who argued in *De la division du travail social* that social interdependence was both inevitable and necessary, and needed to be founded on social justice. As a result, returning modern societies to harmony meant fostering the social bonds that had weakened with industrialization. Law was most important in this respect, because it could engineer social solidarity and integration. Seeking to act upon this idea, solidaristes conceived of society as built on social debts and credits. In *La solidarité*, Bourgeois explained that every individual is indebted to society in that he or she benefits from the achievements and decisions made by former generations.[15] But society was equally indebted to individuals, for its role was to make sure that their expectations for social justice were met. The ideal of *solidarité* packed a new social contract that justified the adoption of social laws to promote the security of the working class without accepting socialist collectivism.[16]

Indeed, although they sought to address the same social issues and sometimes collaborated, socialists and solidaristes had different approaches to class politics. Opposing the logic of class, solidaristes marshaled the concept of "society" to push for social laws that would "restore" equality between employers and employees. In their view, the state should now act as an agent of "reparative justice," for it had become impossible to maintain that employer and employee were always two free and equal individuals.[17] Accordingly, solidaristes pushed for a number of legislative reforms such as progressive taxation, but the crux of the rearticulation of social relations that their political and social outlook engineered was a new legal definition of wage work and of "employé" that incorporated the concept of subordination, namely, the *contrat de travail* or *contrat salarial*. First used in a 1901 law, the concept of contrat de travail (employment contract) stemmed from the implementation of an 1898 law that enacted the liability of businessmen in all work-related accidents of workers. As in the case of lien laws in the United States, the implementation of this legislation raised questions about the sociological limits of the group of potential beneficiaries—what, indeed, constituted an *ouvrier* or an *employé*? As defined in the contrat de travail, an employé or—to use the term that would be more commonly used—a *salarié* (wage worker) was someone who submitted to the employer, who ceded the employer the right to direct the work that was to be done.

Importantly, this idea of subordination included in the law went beyond affirming the authority of the manager over the worker. This was no doubt one of the goals sought by the proponents of this legal reform, who sought to adapt labor law to the needs of the growing corporations. Yet the contrat de travail was also premised on the idea that there were elements of social and economic compulsion in the wage relationship that needed to be acknowledged. Therefore this contract also enacted the dissymmetry inherent in the wage relationship—the employer and the employee were not equal at the moment when they concluded the contract, and the contract involved more than labor power—it constructed the worker as a person *dependent* on the employer.[18]

Language bore the mark of the defeat of the ideal of working-class emancipation. A term singled out by Proudhon for its negative social implications and rejected by workers throughout nineteenth century, *salariat* (wage work) gradually lost its meaning as wage slavery. Rather, it was now a legal category spelling a number of social rights stemming from the legal definition of subordination included in the contrat de travail. Having renounced his freedom to subject himself to a master or a manager, the worker (*salarié*) was to regain his or her social identity through social laws providing a specific and well-defined social status. Indeed, it was the recognition of economic subordination that made it possible to adopt laws to progressively *emancipate* workers: the ten-hour day was adopted in 1904, in 1906 work was prohibited on Sundays, in 1919 the working day was shortened to eight hours, and the first law on collective bargaining was passed the same year. Significantly, by 1910 labor law—which covered all those who were seen as "socially dependent"—had been separated from civil law.

The evolution of labor law in France and the United States thus proceeded from a similar ideological impulse against social fragmentation and class identification. There was, however, a marked difference. In France, no doubt reflecting the centralization of the country, the new legal definition of the worker was a universal one. By contrast, in the United States the structure of the polity—particularly federalism and separation of powers—made the general recognition of the socially subordinated character of labor extremely difficult to achieve. Indeed, it was in the course of a dialogue between labor reformers and the courts that the American "employee" assumed a distinctive, limited character—it was built on the foundations of free labor, and it resulted in labor laws protecting some workers while leaving others out of its safety net.[19]

An Industrial *Plessy v. Ferguson*

In 1895, the Supreme Court handed down its decision in *Ritchie v. People*, the case bearing on the constitutionality of the eight-hour law that Florence Kelley, Jane Addams, and the Chicago Federation of Labor had successfully pushed through in 1893. The decision came as big disappointment to the "eight-hour club" that now met weekly at Hull House to discuss labor legislation. Taking its cues from the brief written by the Illinois Manufacturing Association, the Court struck down the eight-hour section on the grounds that it violated the right to make lawful contracts, a substantive property right protected by the Fourteenth Amendment.[20] Underlying this decision was the reigning public/private legal distinction—the idea that through their police powers, states could legislate private behavior and activity only when such legislation was clothed within a public interest. The Court found none of it in the regulation of women's employment.[21]

The idea that signing contracts was a substantive property right was of recent coinage, *but it* was not long in finding a national translation, particularly in *Lochner v. New York*, a case that—in the Progressive milieu—came to symbolize the judiciary's determination to reify an abstract, universal legal norm in the face of pressing social needs.[22] In 1902, Joseph Lochner, a German immigrant from Bavaria and a master baker in Utica, was found guilty of violating the first provision of the New York Bakeshop Act and was fined $50. Notably, Lochner stood in adamant opposition to the union and had already been convicted for violating the statute a few years earlier. Upon his second conviction, Lochner decided to ask the State Association of Master Bakers to help him challenge the law in court. The request came at a propitious time, for during its 1902 convention the association had decided to find a test case to challenge the law, as it believed that it was used as a bludgeon by unions to attack nonunion bakeries. Defending their legal action in the *Bakers' Review*, the association reaffirmed the voluntary, free labor roots of the employer-employee relationship: "[The masters] cannot see why the matters of settling hours of work should not be left to employers and employees in the baking trade as it has been settled in any other trade."[23]

The Court was receptive to this argument. In the opinion it handed down on April 17, 1905, the majority vindicated Joseph Lochner's claim and put forward an abstract defense of "individuals, both employer and employee, to make contracts regarding labor in such terms as they think best, or which they may agree upon with the other parties to such contracts." Tellingly, the Court argued that the New York legislature had actually impaired sui juris individuals in their ability to make decisions "with regard to their means of livelihood." In its brief, the state of New York had made the argument that the law was necessary because the baking industry mostly comprised immigrants who needed this kind of regulation, but the majority opinion denied the social and economic dynamics structuring the employment relation, and instead reaffirmed the principle that the employer and the employee were strictly on equal footing: each individual was to make his or her own decisions free from interference from the state.[24]

This principle was sharply criticized by the proponents of legal realism, particularly Roscoe Pound and Oliver W. Holmes, for whom this liberty of contract was nothing more than a social and legal construct. Holmes famously took the majority to task for attempting to read Spencer's *Social Statics* into the pithy wording of the Fourteenth Amendment. The public/private distinction, Holmes suggested, was nothing less than a formal legal reasoning cloaking a political one. As he had explained in an earlier opinion, the Constitution embodied only "relatively fundamental rules of right, as understood generally by all English speaking communities."[25] Beyond their duty to protect this kernel of Anglo-Saxon liberties, the courts were to defer to the legislative process and the definition of the public good that it produced.

Following Holmes, many reformers doubted whether a substantive freedom of contract really constituted a natural right, and were quick to point out that the courts had seized on this concept precisely at the moment when there was an increase in available evidence showing that the freedom of workers was restricted in many ways. In an article lamenting the Court's "mechanical" reasoning, legal scholar Roscoe Pound argued that the holding was not adequate to modern industrial conditions. "Why is the legal conception of the relation between employer and employee so at variance with the common knowledge of mankind?" he asked, citing the sociological work of Richard T. Ely and Carroll D. Wright.[26]

Yet the Court took its defense of an abstract, universal employment relationship one step further in 1908 in *Adair v. United States*, when it invalidated the Erdman Act, a federal law prohibiting yellow dog contracts—contracts whereby workers pledged not to join a union—in the railroad industry. Citing the work of the Jurist Thomas Cooley, who had penned influential defenses of liberty of contract denying that the interests of employers and workers might ever be at variance, Justice Harlan—himself the author of a famous dissent in *Plessy v. Ferguson*—reaffirmed the sanctity of the principle of employment at will:

> The right of the employee to quit the service of the employer,
> for whatever reason, is the same as the right of the employer
> for whatever reason to dispense with the services of the
> employee. . . . In all such particulars, the employer and the
> employee have equality of right, and any legislation that disturbs
> that equality is an arbitrary interference with the liberty of
> contract that no government can justify in a free land.[27]

Interpreting this determined defense of laissez-faire and liberty of contract has been no easy task. Progressive historians have long argued that in the Gilded Age judges indulged in their personal faith in laissez-faire rather than legal interpretation. Moreover, progressive historiography insists that decisions such as *Lochner* exemplify judicial activism, one that stemmed from the judge's misgivings about the democratic process. Rufus Peckham, the author of the majority opinion in *Lochner*, was a conservative Democrat and a former corporate attorney who believed, as he noted in his opinion, that many health statutes were passed for "other political motives" rather than the workers' health. Similarly, justices such as David Brewer spoke for a large number of property-minded conservatives when he declared in 1893 that the role of the judiciary was to protect the individuals and their rights from the majoritarian process, "the danger is from the multitudes—the majority with whom is the power." From the 1895 *Pollock* case—in which the Court had ruled the federal income tax unconstitutional—to the 1897 *Debs* decision, the Court had evinced a decided interest in negating the very nature of social interactions and conflicts that now ran through American society, refusing to conceive of social relations in any other terms than individualist ones. In point of fact, in *Pollock*, Justice Field had expressly stated the Court's determination to not to let the political process drift into an all-out struggle between the rich and the poor.[28]

More recently, scholars have argued that such judges did not simply read their own political views into the Constitution. Their decisions also made sense within the framework of Jacksonian and Republican principles, which implied a tradition of equal rights and an opposition to monopolies that led judges to oppose "class legislation." Historians have also pointed out that the Court actually supported more pieces of protective legislation than it actually struck down. In this perspective, the Court's preindustrial faith in the purposive equality and unity of the "employer" and the "employee" did not prevent it from sanctioning legislation that seemed to serve a legitimate social purpose.[29]

We will dwell with such laws and cases in just a moment, but before we do so, we need to note that by the early twentieth century, whether it stemmed from an antidemocratic impulse or from a nostalgia for a bygone, preindustrial era, liberty of contract was indeed legal fiction for most workers, particularly those whom protective legislation targeted. The effect of the jurisprudence on freedom of contract was to disconnect the purchase and selling of labor from the worker's social position. What the Court actually secured is a status quo keeping the employee in a state of subjugation, a reality it halfheartedly acknowledged in 1915 in its *Coppage* decision as it struck down yet another law prohibiting yellow-dog contracts: "It is *from the nature of things* impossible to uphold freedom of contract and the right to property without at the same time recognizing those inequalities of fortune that are the necessary result of the exercise of those rights," the Court tersely concluded.[30] The phrase must have rung a bell to reformers, for it was used in the *Civil Rights Cases*, in which the Court held that the 1875 Civil Rights Act was incompatible with the public/private dichotomy. Like the phrase "separate but equal," the definition of the employment relationship as one involving two equal parties thoroughly concealed one essential feature of modern societies, in which an individual's liberty was exercised within a tangled web of relations of power. In this respect, the triad *Lochner*, *Adair*, and *Coppage* can be seen as an industrial *Plessy v. Ferguson*.

Most important, although these rulings were subsequently overruled—and although substantive due process was abandoned as a standard for reviewing the constitutionality of economic regulation—there was no general statutory reform of the employment relationship. Indeed, the drift and logic of Progressive reform was to carve exceptions to the at-will common-law rule and its underlying principle of equality rather than fully discard it and give all workers the same economic rights.[31]

To understand the full significance of *Adair* and *Lochner* for the history of the definition of the worker in labor relations, it is the dissenting opinion penned by John Marshall Harlan for himself and two other justices that should command most of our attention. For while he stood by the precept that the "employer" and the "employee" were social equals, Harlan believed that laws protecting "employees" might nevertheless pass constitutional muster. In contradistinction to Holmes, Harlan agreed with the majority that the Bakeshop Act may have stemmed from the ill-conceived notion that "the employer and the employee do not stand on equal footing in such establishments"—an agreement largely congruent with his opinion in *Adair*.

Harlan departed from the majority opinion, however, when he contended that the Court had passed too quickly on the possibility that the hours law might constitute a valid exercise of police power in the public interest. Using the public-private distinction, he suggested, required the Court to probe all the available economic and sociological evidence to determine the re-lationship of a law to the public interest. In a kind of proto-Brandeis brief, the "Great Dissenter" culled evidence from a number of studies produced in the United States and in Europe since the early eighteenth-century plague to demonstrate that the Bakeshop Act was no oddity in the larger international movement to protect the health of workers and of those dependent on them. As such, it constituted the legitimate expression of the belief held in New York that sixty hours a week was the limit of reasonable exertion in bakeries, which may not be the case in other industries.[32]

Harlan's dissent bears rereading because of its implications. What he sug-gested was that it was really possible to adopt social legislation and still retain the nineteenth-century notion that the employer and the employee were ju-ridical and social equals. Under Harlan, the common-law definition of em-ployers and employees as free contractors would remain the default one, with legislatures intervening in this equal relation only to serve the public interest, but without fundamentally affecting the theoretical and legal definition of the worker as a free seller of labor. Far from becoming a new anthropological norm, the recognition of the subordination of the worker would be condi-tional and would be linked to the pursuit of a specific social and economic end. The definition of employee would be not political but thoroughly instru-mental, and it has remained so to this day.

Indeed, it is possible to discern a jurisprudential undertow that, through the public-private distinction, allowed American states to remedy what they saw as the worst evils arising out of the industrial revolution. Thus, in the 1898 *Holden v. Hardy* case, the Court had sustained a law limiting to eight hours a day the work of miners in Utah. Admitting that "law is, to a certain extent, a progressive science," the Court drew an important distinction between the fact that the miners were "full of age, and competent to contract," and the "state's power to interfere, where the parties do not stand upon an equality, or where public health demands that one party to the contract shall be protected against himself." In view of the dangerous working conditions of miners, the Court held, the state of Utah could legitimately intervene and regulate the miners' work. Moreover, the Court noted that the claim that workers should enjoy an unfettered freedom of contract was made not by miners, but rather by mine owners whose interest was in long hours. "The argument would come with better grace and greater cogency if it came from the other class," the Court concluded.[33]

This does not mean that the Court admitted that liberty of contract was mere legal fiction. Rather, *Holden v. Hardy* was important because it implied that the courts were willing, in specific cases, to admit exceptions to the theory that freedom of contract was a model of social interaction that would go of itself. "Freedom of contract is a qualified, not an absolute right," the Court proceeded to explain in 1911 as it passed upon the validity of an Iowa law that made companies liable for their workers' injuries even when the latter had signed contracts that said otherwise. At issue in this case was a railroad company relief department which awarded benefits to injured workers provided that they had signed contracts in which they waived the right to sue the company for damages incurred. "There is no absolute freedom to contract as one chooses. Liberty implies the absence of arbitrary restraint, not immunity from reasonable regulations," the judges concluded.[34] In the meantime, the Court had handed down the *Muller v. Oregon* case, in which the famous Brandeis brief opened the door to regulation of hours and working conditions of women. Notably, the court followed this jurisprudential vein in 1917, when it once more sustained the state of Oregon, this time sanctioning a law that limited the working hours of "employees"—not just women—in mills, factories, and other manufacturing establishments, and required that overtime be paid to those requested to work over the limit.[35]

Who's an "Employee"?

Still, the limitations inherent in this reconstruction of the wage relationship could be quite significant, for the question of who counted as an "employee" was essential to the making of Progressive laws. Paradoxically, it seems that it was employers who first challenged the restrictive sociological purview of Progressive laws on equal protection grounds. In 1915, in the case *Miller v. Wilson*, it was the owner of a Riverside hotel arrested for asking a chambermaid to work nine hours a day who asked the Supreme Court to invalidate the Women's Eight Hour Law adopted in California in 1911. According to the plaintiff, the law was not simply an unconstitutional violation of freedom of contract; it also needed to be struck down because it violated the Fourteenth Amendment equal protection clause. Indeed, the law omitted from its protective ambit large numbers of women, excluding from its definition of

"employee" (1) women employed in "harvesting, curing, canning, or dry-
ing of any variety of perishable fruit or vegetable," (2) women employed in
"boarding houses, lodging houses, etc.," and (3) "stenographers, clerks, and
assistants employed by the professional classes, and domestic servants."[36]
Earlier on, a similar argument had been made by a businessman opposed
to a law regulating the working time of women in Ohio. Yet in both cases,
the Court rejected the argument, holding that laws protecting only certain
groups of workers were perfectly legitimate.[37]

A quick look into the personal journey of Charles Evans Hughes, who
drafted the opinion of the court in the *Miller* case, offers interesting insights
both into the logic of the Court's response and into its implications. In 1915,
Hughes was reaching the end of what legal historian James Henretta has
termed the "19th century transition from Mugwump to Progressivism."[38]
Raised according to strict Calvinist principles, Hughes was a hard worker
who shared the American bourgeoisie's concern over democracy and universal suffrage. A Wall Street lawyer, he became a local popular hero in 1905
when he contributed to a high-profile investigation of the corrupt business
of the public utilities industry in New York, before turning his attention to
the rule of law to conduct an equally devastating investigation of the life insurance business. In the 1906 gubernatorial race, he ran a Progressive campaign against the radical platform of Hearst, condemning "legislation for
classes . . . working classes or any other classes"—words reminiscent of the
political outlook of the likes of Jane Addams and many other middle-class
reformers. As governor, Hughes proceeded with his struggle against corrup-
tion, but he also supported the National Consumers League's efforts to impose
minimum wages on department stores and regulate child labor. Meanwhile,
he developed ties with the American Association for Labor Legislation and,
using the current distinction between ordinary and hazardous labor, supported barring the employment of young men in some occupations. As James
Henretta notes, by the end of his mandate Hughes had moved so close to the
principles of the new liberalism as to acknowledge, like Roscoe Pound and
sociologists like Arthur Ross and Richard Ely, that society was an organic
whole. As a result, once on the Court Hughes was prepared to assert the protective power of states and uphold regulation in the public interest. "The opportunities for Labor (should be) protected and enlarged by state action," he
explained.[39]

Yet there was a significant difference between this quest for social cohesion and the recognition of the subordinated social and economic position of

wage workers. Hughes was willing to admit that in some cases workers and employers did not stand on equal footing (he did so in the case of an Iowa law that nullified contracts limiting workers' rights), but he really believed that the recognition of this inequality was necessarily contingent on specific industries and well-defined groups of workers. It was a matter of legislative power, not class. As a result, he explained in *Miller v. Wilson*, legislatures were not expected to couch their laws in "all embracing terms," "extending the regulation to all cases where it might potentially reach." Rather, he said, they were "free to recognize degrees of harm," and may confine regulation to "those cases where the need is the clearest."[40]

Such were the origins of the contemporary debate over the meaning of "employee." Erected on the legal basis of the public-private distinction, the definition of the worker in Progressive laws was a far cry from the Marxian collective worker, a political figure bound by economic pressure to attempt to emancipate himself. Used as it was by reformers and Progressive judges to break down the labor question into a large number of specific socioeconomic problems arising within the framework of the capitalist system, this definition conveyed a vision of the working class that bore two characteristics: it was sociologically fragmented and sought to combine the individualism inherent in freedom of contract with the need to expand the police power of the states. In many ways, the restrictive, contingent character of the legal definition of the worker illustrated the Progressive search for order, a limitation that would prove hard to transcend.[41]

Indeed, one may argue that by the end of the Progressive Era, most reformers had grown accustomed to thinking about social reform in those restrictive terms, even if talk about "industrial democracy" carried considerable universal appeal.[42] To be sure, in the coming two decades the Great Depression would give labor reformers the opportunity to think about American workers on a much broader scale, pushing for an ideal of "economic security" covering all American workers. In his famous Commonwealth Speech in San Francisco in 1932, Roosevelt called for a "new constitutional order," one that would protect a number of economic rights as well as political ones. No doubt, as a number of scholars have noted, the Wagner Act was a pillar of the attempt to protect a citizenship writ large.[43] Yet as they built the right to organize, reformers and labor progressives continued to work within the conceptual regulatory framework that they had established during the Progressive Era, building the state's visible hand on labor relations by adopting a law that protected some workers while it excluded others.[44]

Toward a New Deal in
the "Employer-Employee" Relationship

Historians of the New Deal often give pride of place to the strikes and movements that swept the country from the mining districts of Pennsylvania to
the Port of San Francisco. Such movements are significant because they reveal the role played by workers in the process that led to the adoption of
the law recognizing their right to organize. As in France, where working-
class mobilization forced obdurate employers to bargain with the leaders of
the sit-down strikes in 1936, American society gained in 1933–1934 what the
historian Melvyn Dubofsky has called a "practical education in industrial
warfare." Without this mobilization, it is quite unlikely that laws such as the
Wagner Act would ever have been adopted.[45]

Tracing the legal and constitutional logic of the law, however, requires
that we take a different approach, one that can tell us what reformers had in
mind when they responded to social pressure. When the Great Depression
set in, the 1925 Railway Labor Act—the first federal law protecting the right to
organize—figured prominently in the minds of labor liberals because of a two-
year struggle between the Brotherhood of Railways and Steamship Clerks and
the Texas & New Orleans Company.[46] In May 1927, the union officials requested
a wage increase that the company, although it had traditionally been open to
negotiations, firmly refused. When the union petitioned the U.S. Mediation
Board, the tripartite agency created by the Railway Labor Act to solve such matters, the company hastily set up a company union with the intent of bypassing
the American Railroad Union. Determined to enjoy the benefits of its statutory
rights, the union decided to sue the company and, in an irony of history, secured an injunction against it for violation of the Railway Labor Act; the federal
court ordered the company to disband the company union.[47]

By 1930, the stakes were high indeed as the Supreme Court prepared to pass
on the constitutionality of the law. Before the Court, the company argued that
the Railway Labor Act was unconstitutional on two grounds. First, the law
protected an "abstract right" (i.e., the right to organize) with no real legal
foundations. Second, because the law prohibited employer interference in
the selection of the railroad workers' delegates, it violated the property rights
and the freedom of speech protected by the First and Fifth Amendments.
The company therefore contended that the *Adair* decision should remain
controlling—employers and employees being equal in the railroad industry
as in others, no departure from free contractual relations was constitutionally
permissible.[48]

The Supreme Court firmly rejected the company's argument, and once again Charles Evans Hughes was the author of the majority opinion. Relying on a 1921 case in which the Court had ruled that picketing was legal—*American Steel Foundries*—Hughes rejected the idea that the right to organize was an "abstract right." In *American Steel Foundries*, the Court had ruled that while it was limited by other rights and freedoms such as freedom of contract, the right to associate and bargain for better working conditions did exist. To be sure, in and of itself this was no breakthrough. The *American Steel Foundries* decision was so limited in its endorsement of the right to organize that it had hardly made a dent in the free labor legal apparatus that had construed the employee's economic citizenship as the right to contract freely.[49]

However, what Hughes was intent on establishing in this case was different—reaffirming the *American Steel Foundries* decision was only a logical segue to the main part of its holding, which was that the federal government could legitimately intervene in the employer-employee relationship if it did so to protect the public good. In his dissent in *Coppage v. Kansas* in 1917, Hughes had contended that "the right to join a union is undisputed . . . and may be the legitimate subject of the protection of the police authority of the States," which to him included the power to prohibit yellow-dog contracts. He followed this idea in the present case, ruling that the Railway Labor Act did not infringe on freedom of contract because it did not provide the U.S. Board of Mediation with the power to force an employer to hire or fire a railroad worker. Rather, the law simply protected the railroad worker's right to organize with the intent of doing away with labor strife in railroads:

> We entertain no doubt of the constitutional authority of Congress
> to enact the prohibition. The power to regulate commerce is the
> power to enact "all appropriate legislation" for its "protection or
> advancement"; to adopt measures "to promote its growth and
> insure its safety." . . . The legality of collective action on the part
> of employees in order to safeguard their proper interests is not
> to be disputed. . . . Congress was not required to ignore this right
> of the employees but could safeguard it and seek to make their
> appropriate collective action an instrument of peace rather than of
> strife.[50]

Following a legal logic that hearkened back to—but went beyond—Harlan's seminal dissent in *Lochner v. New York*, Hughes had thus adumbrated the possibility of a new deal in the employer-employee relationship. This new deal was a far cry from the legal recognition of the existence of an American working class with rights stemming from the workers' social and economic subordination, for the *Texas* decision left the generic, common-law definition of the employer and employee as equal, free contractors intact. Now, however, the Court allowed the federal government to superimpose on that definition a specific category of "employees" made up of railroad workers only, a category whose existence rested on a more expansive reading of the regulatory rights of the government under the Commerce Clause, not on a novel reading of workers' rights. As a result, while it was in theory nothing more than a limited right to associate, the right to organize and bargain collectively of *a specific group of workers* could be strengthened and actively protected by the federal government if such was the object of a public policy designed in the *public interest*.

What the Court recognized in *Texas*, then, was the government's visible hand on labor relations. And much of the subsequent debate on the legal definition of the worker would stem from the fact that because the New Deal collective bargaining regime was premised on a novel, expansive reading of the government's regulatory power rather than on the individual rights of workers, it did not have to include all American workers in the category of "employees" it protected.

The *Texas & New Orleans* case was not widely noted at the time. However, its significance was not lost on labor reformers and jurists determined to challenge the formalist notion that law and politics were fundamentally distinct. Thus, the *Harvard Law Review* explained that the case marked "a definite departure from the strict policy of laissez-faire" and insisted on the need to shift the emphasis of law from abstract principles to social engineering.[51] Legal realists were not alone, however, in hoping that labor reformers stood on the cusp of a new era. Edward Berman, a liberal labor economist with the University of Illinois, explained approvingly that in the *Texas & New Orleans* case, the Court had produced a "very considerable extension of constitutional boundaries within which social legislation had been confined."[52] The American Federation of Labor was equally interested in the case, which figured in its brief defending the legality of the Norris La Guardia Act, a 1932 law forbidding the use of injunctions against unions.

Yet only in 1934, when labor progressives were faced with the difficulties associated with the implementation of Section 7a of the National Industrial Recovery Act (NIRA), did the *Texas & New Orleans* case become directly relevant to the goal of reforming the workplace. Beginning in 1933, New York's Senator Robert Wagner—by then the foremost labor reformer in Congress—and other liberals had sought to include American labor in the Roosevelt's administration attempt to rationalize the economy. This effort stemmed from the numerous proposals for economic planning that were publicized and debated at the time, many of which did not include unions in the reorganization of the economy.[53] To Wagner—whom Roosevelt had asked to synthesize the various proposals that circulated for an economic recovery bill—protecting the right to unionize was first and foremost a matter of political principle. Like Roosevelt, he had risen politically by advocating a transition from the sway of political machines to state welfare programs, but unions occupied a much more important place in his variant of urban liberalism. A former judge, he had collaborated very early on with Progressive jurists seeking to challenge the legality of the yellow-dog contract, and in the 1930s, he stood at the core of a network of labor-oriented reformers running the gamut from Taylor Society engineers like Morris Cooke to labor economists trained by John R. Commons and legal realists. Wagner was also close to important union leaders who advocated the rationalization of the economy. Relying on the experiences conducted in the 1920s in the mining and textile industry, where unions collaborated with management to stabilize labor relations, establish production goals, and uphold efficiency schemes, Wagner argued that collaboration and mutual respect between workers and employers were necessary for the NIRA codes to succeed.[54] As we will see in the next chapter, in the 1920s and 1930s labor reformers did not abandon, but rather refurbished, the old ideal of industrial harmony.

This said, in spite of the spectacular rise in organizing that followed the adoption of the NIRA, the democratization of industry that Wagner envisioned when he secured the adoption of Section 7a in the NIRA did not take place.[55] In many mass-production industries, businessmen countered this organizing tide by setting up company unions or, as in Ford factories, by creating a surveillance system. Far from agreeing to negotiate working rules with workers, some employers took advantage of the large pool of available workers to "speed up" the line and introduce labor-saving technology that reinforced unemployment, a strategy denounced in an NIRA Research Planning Division report in which economists Isador Lubin and Leon Henderson concluded that the automobile industry was "socially inadequate to meet its responsibilities."[56] As for the Roosevelt administration, it saw the workers' increasing militancy as an obstacle to economic reform and remained doubtful that independent labor organizations were preferable to company unions, to which the president actually lent his support in a number of industries.[57] Indeed, FDR's only concession to the right to organize came in 1933, with the creation of the National Labor Board, which was charged with the responsibility to mediate labor conflicts but had no power to enforce its decisions. A year later, responding to the upheaval that swept through America in the spring of 1934, when 1.4 million workers staged over eighteen hundred strikes, Roosevelt also agreed to the creation of a stronger NLRB, but the defeat of the textile strike in the fall of 1934, with twelve Democratic governors moving against the strikers, revealed how shaky the administration's labor policy really was. Disenchanted, NLRB Chair Francis Biddle lamented that the right to organize and bargain collectively was merely "a paper right."[58]

Faced with employers determined to retain their authority over the workplace, labor reformers sought to reassert the constitutional language of rights and democracy that had animated talk of industrial democracy since the early days of the twentieth century. As they testified in favor of the Labor Disputes Act in 1934 (the first bill introduced by Senator Wagner) and its successor bill in 1935, the National Labor Relations Act in 1935 (also known as the Wagner Act), both of which were aimed at spelling the contours of the freedom to organize by protecting workers against a list of specified "unfair labor practices," labor reformers couched their defense of the right to organize in terms that came close to making it an individual civil right. Commenting on the meaning of Section 7a a few days after the reintroduction of the Wagner Bill in 1935, Pennsylvania representative and majority whip Patrick J. Boland explained that "the ideas underlying this section are very simple. The worker is treated as a free man. He is accorded the right to associate with fellow workers, to join or refrain from joining any labor organization. He is protected from acts of aggression by his employer. His helplessness as an individual in bargaining with his employer is recognized." The labor lawyer Francis Haas, then on the board of the NIRA's National Labor Board, framed his defense of the bill in equally ambitious language: "Section 7(a) of the NIRA declares that workers may exercise rights that nature gives them, the same as our Federal and State constitutions declare that they may exercise rights which nature gives them to elect their representatives in Government, whether local or national."[59]

Moreover, labor reformers deployed a Whiggish reading of history to depict the workers' right to join a union as an essential step in the ongoing struggle for individual freedom against tyranny. "It is the next step in the logical unfolding on man's eternal quest for freedom," Wagner explained in defense of his bill in 1935. Echoing Roosevelt's own allusions to the economic checks hanging on individual freedom in modern industrial society, Wagner continued, "Only 150 years ago did this country cast off the shackles of political despotism. And today, with economic problems occupying center stage, we strive to liberate the common man from destitution, from insecurity and from human exploitation."[60]

Indeed, New Dealers argued that in the modern economy the asymmetry of power between the employer and the worker was so great as to foreclose the possibility that the worker might exercise his citizenship through individual bargaining.[61] As the labor economist Harry Millis explained, "Of course, if there were perfect mobility of labor and keen competition for labor, and no concerted control of wages and hours by employers the case for collective bargaining would be less conclusive in the modern industry." "The actualities of present-day life impel us to recognize economic duress," Wagner concurred. "We are forced to recognize the futility of pretending that there is equality of freedom when a single workman, with only his job between his family and ruin, sits down to draw a contract of employment with a representative of a tremendous organization having thousands of workers at its call."[62] Wagner suggested that in the tense international context of the 1930s, denying this fact meant putting democracy in jeopardy, for disillusioned workers would turn to either fascism or communism to remedy their lack of freedom.

Yet as they built and defended the Wagner Act, labor reformers did not seek to constitutionalize associational freedom.[63] Nor did they seek to revert the shift from working-class empowerment to employment regulation that Progressive reform had effected. Rather, following the drift of employment regulation since the late nineteenth century, they insisted on the positive social and economic effects of unionism, not the philosophical rationale that undergirded it. In a sense, this was a consequence of the *Texas* decision, in which the Court had affirmed the existence of the right to organize, leaving it to reformers to make a case for a public law providing it with additional protection. During the hearings, Senator Wagner and the jurists Robert Hale, Milton Handler, and Francis Biddle all insisted on the importance of the *Texas* decision and its main consequence—namely that the *Adair* and *Coppage* decisions had been overruled *sub silentio* and were no longer controlling. Consequently, Congress could enact a collective bargaining law without running into a Fifth Amendment due process wall. Wagner even pointed to Hughes's dissent in the *Coppage* case, in which Hughes had noted that "the right to join unions . . . may be the legitimate subject of the protection of the police authority of the States." The question that remained at this stage was whether the Court would sanction an interpretation of interstate commerce that would include federal regulation of the manufacturing sector.[64]

But equally important in the case for labor reform was the Progressive and new liberal idea that the regulation of the employment relationship produced *positive* freedoms, that is, freedoms that did not inhere in the citizen but rather in the public interest for a well-ordered society. Here, the ideology of harmony and the constitutional and legal drift of Progressive reform intersected. As the lawyer Francis Haas explained, the time had come to part with the idea that the "the wage contract concerns only an employer and an employee. . . . It concerns everybody else," Haas contended."[65] The right to organize and to bargain collectively, in other words, was to make a contribution to the common good.

Accordingly, in making their case for a policy protecting collective bargaining, labor reformers insisted on the detrimental character of work stoppages for the flow of commerce. During the 1934 debates, the National Labor Board's Milton Handler provided statistics showing the steady growth in the number of cases handled by his agency. By March 1934, the agency had intervened in over two thousand cases and passed the one million workers mark. The reports judiciously stressed the increasing number of strikes that had been settled, but also the number of strikes averted in places where both workers and employers had chosen the arbitration of the NLRB. Similarly, in the spring of 1935, reformers pointed to the declining militancy of the workforce—by then the 1934 strike wave had ebbed—as a sign of the success of the NIRA procedures, and labor leaders such as William Green testified about their recent efforts to prevent strikes in the automobile and rubber sectors. If the Wagner Act did not pass, Green explained, the menace to "industrial peace could not be exaggerated." Indeed, the threat of worker militancy remained constant during the debates, giving the labor reformers a definite edge as they pressed the argument that strikes actually derived from the lack of workers' rights.[66] Harmony would come first in the guise of social peace.

Whether this argument would suffice was unclear. According to Leon Keyserling, the main drafter of the bill, the most important point to be made in the preamble was a broader one—that unionism was necessary to protect purchasing power and that a higher level of purchasing power was necessary to absorb the output of the American economy. The argument had been made since the debates over the adoption of the NIRA, but now the third draft of the bill made this point clearly: "[T]he failure of the total wage payments to advance as fast as production and corporate surpluses has resulted in inadequate purchasing power, which has accentuated periodic depressions and disrupted the flow of commerce," the preamble now declared. Keyserling and Wagner believed that the interstate commerce argument would be stronger than the argument for industrial peace.[67]

The notion that mass production required mass consumption, of course, was at the heart of the Fordist production system and had led to the famous $5 day as early as 1914. Yet the appeal of the purchasing power rationale among reformers in the 1930s can be explained only by looking at the broader movement of businessmen, economists, and policy makers who had laid the theoretical groundwork for policies protecting purchasing power in the previous two decades. Businessmen such as Lincoln Filene, Eugene Grace, and Waddell Catchings had long argued that it was necessary for business to expand its pool of consumers, while economists such as Paul Douglas had provided statistics showing that productivity was rising faster than wages, thus creating an imbalance that might lead to an economic crisis. In the meantime, a consumer culture had enveloped both middle-class and working-class households, leading to social movements for lower prices, to which policy makers had responded by creating statist structures such as the Consumer Advisory Board.[68]

But the purchasing power argument mattered to the reconstruction of the wage relationship precisely because it fit squarely in the general pattern of labor reform, and labor reformers used it to win over the members of Congress and legitimize the intervention of the government in the employment relationship. To do so, they could point to *America's Capacity to Consume*, a report in which Brookings Institution scholars Maurice Leven, Harold Moulton, and Clark Warburton likewise rejected the notion that the crisis originated in what a banker called the "glorious" overcapacity of the economy, which produced more than what American society actually needed. Their study revealed that 70 percent of American families lived under the threshold of $2,500 a year, which the authors of the study believed represented the poverty line in 1935.[69] Whether the American economy actually had the capacity to produce enough to bring those families the earnings that they needed, the authors actually doubted very much.

The crisis thus reinforced the reformers' tendency to focus on the ultimate economic aims of the regulation they sought rather than working-class empowerment. Indeed, the severity of the Depression and the causes New

Dealers ascribed to it—insufficient consumption by the masses of workers—suggested that the labor question could not be solved by simply looking at the place of the worker in the production system. Rather, it was precisely through the worker's social role as a consumer that the worker's social inferiority would be solved. In his statement to Congress, Sidney Hillman, the president of the Amalgamated Clothing Workers of America, noted that the average worker did not have the ability to buy one set of clothes per year.[70] In making this case, New Dealers thus suggested that the right to organize would buttress economic harmony and prevent future depressions.

By 1935, then, labor reformers had fully charted the path of a via media between socialism and unregulated capitalism. Although they sincerely believed that they were democratizing American industries, they addressed the question of subordinated labor only indirectly. In the Wagner Act, unionism was as much an economic means as a philosophical end. Throughout the hearings, reformers had built the strongest case possible for a *public policy* fostering unionism. Notably, industrial peace and the purchasing power argument dovetailed because they abutted on the same institutional venue—collective bargaining. Indeed, the law did not simply protect workers' right to join a union; it also imposed on employers the duty to bargain with the workers' representatives and sustained collective bargaining through the adoption of majority rule and the decision to give the new NLRB the ability to decide what bargaining units would be most adequate to the goal of bargaining.

On April 12, 1937, in *NLRB v. Jones and Laughlin*, the Supreme Court lent its support to this reasoning. Following the argument laid out in his own opinion in *Texas & New Orleans*, Charles E. Hughes, once again the author of the majority opinion in *Jones and Laughlin*, reaffirmed the idea that the right to organize was a "fundamental right," one that that the Court had long recognized.[71] The main part of the holding, however, bore upon the right of Congress to enact a law fostering the practice of collective bargaining. On this question too, Hughes followed his previous opinion, arguing that the power of Congress to regulate commerce was the power to enact "all appropriate legislation for its protection and advancement." This power, Hughes concluded, was "plenary."[72] Moreover, the Court said that it refused to "shut its eyes to the plainest facts of industrial life," and deal with the definition of interstate commerce "in an intellectual vacuum." Given the size and organization of companies on a national scale, the Court insisted, it had become impossible to continue to hold that their labor relations were in essence a local matter.[73] Even if a company's relation to interstate commerce was only indirect, Congress could legitimately decide to steer it toward labor peace rather than strife.

In *Jones and Laughlin,* the Supreme Court thus completed the slow juris-prudential evolution it had started in the Progressive Era. In validating the Wagner Act, it sanctioned a serious exception to the at-will rule that had come to dominate employment contracts in the second half of the nineteenth century. The Wagner Act, however, did not erase the at-will rule from the nation's common law. Nor did it construe *all* workers as subordinated labor. Rather, it built the government's right to foster collective bargaining in the nation's factories and offices and left to the government the possibility to de-cide *which* workers would be covered by this policy. In doing so, the act, like other New Deal laws, built a definite gap between the worker and the worker's legal definition—the "employee"—which was now the main legal fulcrum upon which labor relations turned.[74]

Protecting "the Working Class Generally"?

Like its Progressive forebears, the Wagner Act made only a passing reference to "workers" and focused on "employees," whom it defined thus:

> The term "employee" shall include any employee, and shall not be limited to the employees of a particular employer, unless the Act explicitly states otherwise, and shall include any individual whose work has ceased as a consequence of, or in connection with, any current labor dispute or because of any unfair labor practice, and who has not obtained any other regular and substantially equivalent employment, but shall not include any individual employed as an agricultural laborer, or in the domestic service of any family or person at his home, or any individual employed by his parent or spouse.

In a sense, this was an expansive definition of the worker meant to include all workers involved in a dispute rather than only the workers employed by a given company. Indeed, because Wagner and his advisers remembered how the Clayton Act had been eviscerated by the courts through a narrow definition of "employee," in the National Labor Relations Act (NLRA) they purposely defined "employee" as including not simply workers who stood in a proximate employer-employee relationship with an employer, but also all the workers who had an indirect stake in an ongoing labor conflict ("and shall not be limited to the employees of a particular employer"). Overcoming resistance from members of Congress who argued that the law would allow outside agitators to come and fan the flames of labor strife, Wagner and other reformers suggested that the right to bargain collectively would not be made effective if sympathetic strikes were illegal and more generally if industry-wide bargaining was not established.[75] In this respect, the definition of "employee" reflected his view that collective bargaining would be ineffective unless the masses of workers cohered in large enough movements.

Interestingly, the Supreme Court sanctioned this recognition of working-class power precisely because it saw the definition of "employee" as being subservient to the a public policy: the aim of Congress was not to "adjudicate private rights," it explained in 1941, but rather to give effect to a broad economic policy. Citing the decision a few years later, the NLRB commissioners applauded this expansive definition of "employee," saying that it was "broad enough to include members of the working class generally."[76]

Yet one can say that the Wagner Act protected the "working class" through its definition of "employee" only if one recognizes the thoroughly contingent, contested character of the concept of class and its evolution over time. As the main legal vehicle through which this policy was delivered, the definition of "employee" certainly eased the transition from ethnic to class consciousness that Lizabeth Cohen has described.[77] Not only did it bestow a common legal identity on workers that facilitated this transition, but it also fostered class consciousness by allowing them to forge social links beyond individual locales. This explains why to the millions of workers who joined the CIO after 1935, there was no significant difference between the terms "worker" and "employee." With the Wagner Act, labor progressives had instilled a class dimension in "employee," one that allowed workers to use either term to refer to the newfound sense of economic security that unionism had nurtured among them.

To others, however, it made all the difference. In 1934 and 1935, civil rights organizations watched helplessly as members of Congress winnowed the definition of "employee" to exclude agricultural workers. In 1933, during the legislative debates over the NIRA, southern politicians such as Huey Long had lamented that Section 7a applied to "all laboring men," and although the text was not amended, it was implemented in a restrictive fashion, leaving most agricultural workers outside of the law. The question was raised again, however, in March 1934, when the Labor Disputes Act was introduced, for at first it contained no provision excluding agricultural workers and was understood to apply to all workers. When the bill was referred to the Committee of Education and Labor, Alabama Senator Hugo Black—later Roosevelt's first appointment to the Supreme Court—and Senator Trammell from Florida worked with three senators, from Iowa, Montana, and Utah, and wrote an agricultural exemption in the bill that reflected the ability of what a historian has called the "marriage of corn and cotton" in applying brakes on labor liberalism and containing the reform to the modern factory. Wagner knew fully well that given the number of votes that these men represented in Congress, there was no avoiding the agricultural exception, but "employee" was malleable enough to be interpreted as covering industrial workers while excluding others. Its definition thus registered the conservatism of a large group of states that would launch the right to work movement a few years later.[78]

For black organizations, this defeat mattered enormously because in spite of the deep-seated racism of many labor organizations, their relationship to unionism was then in a state of flux. The National Urban League had shed its erstwhile opposition to unionism, and, along with the National Negro Congress, it now stressed the economic character of social inequality in America. This "proletarian turn," as historian Thomas Sugrue has called it, was precisely facilitated by the upsurge in union organizing in transportation, where a clause equivalent to the NIRA's Section 7a, existed but also among sharecroppers and farm tenants in Arkansas, where the possibility of an interracial unionism could now be glimpsed.[79]

Indeed, African American organizations were certainly among the first to gauge the importance and the nature of the change that the Wagner Act had wrought in the working-class struggle, which was no longer limited to the defense of labor solidarity on the shop floor or in the farm. To travel the via media charted by the New Dealers, workers now had to be officially recognized as "employees." Black workers learned this lesson very early because they chafed under the discriminatory practices established by most unions in northern cities. Although black Americans composed 8 percent of the nonagricultural workforce, they accounted for only 1 percent of unionized workers, with half of this membership in the Brotherhood of Sleeping Car Porters. In general, blacks were either kept out of unions altogether or, when they were accepted, remained relegated to the lowliest jobs and were forced into segregated locals. As a result, as the National Urban League's Arnold T. Hill explained in a letter to Robert Wagner, "It's been through going in to break strikes that many [black workers] have found employment in coal mines, steel plants, and other important industries." Indeed, in the 1920s black workers helped defeat strikes in a number of industries such as coal and steel, but also in automobile textile manufacturing and slaughterhouses.[80]

Yet the first drafts of the Labor Disputes Act in 1934 explicitly excluded "strikebreakers" from the definition of "employee." This was an attempt to correct earlier National Labor Board decisions, according to which an employer was free to engage replacement workers during a strike and retain them when the strike was over as long as the strike was an "economic" one, and did not stem from a violation of the Section 7a disposition in the NIRA. In excluding strikebreakers from the statutory definition of "employee," the drafters of the act hoped to strengthen the recall rights of strikers and vindicate their claims to reinstatement.[81]

When combined with the provision for majority rule that drafters had included to forestall company unionism and facilitate collective bargaining, the bill, although aimed at protecting workers, thus threatened to reinforce the discriminatory pattern from which black workers already suffered. Notably, the Harvard sociologist Kelly Miller indicated that if it were left unamended, the bill would have detrimental consequences in the very few places where black workers had gained an industrial foothold—Ford factories especially.[82] The National Negro Congress and the National Urban League already denounced discrimination in New Deal programs, and they pointedly pleaded with Roosevelt to address the question of discrimination in labor unions.[83] When the Wagner Act was first introduced in 1934, they promptly reacted, sending numerous requests for an amendment protecting black workers, who were kept outside of the world of labor: "The term 'employee' shall not include an individual who has replaced a striking employee, *except when the labor organization either by direct constitutional or ritualistic regulation and/ or by practices traceable to discriminatory policies bars an individual from joining such labor organization or restricts rights, privileges, and practices usually accorded members of such labor organizations*" (my emphasis).[84]

Overall demands for amendments to protect African Americans from Jim Crow were usually of no avail because of the concerted opposition of AFL and southern lawmakers, but in this precise case the demands arising from the African American organizations drew support from other sources—not only did corporate America express its opposition to a clause that would severely hamstring its control of the workplace, but even liberal lawmakers balked at the idea that replacement workers would not be able to shed their "nonemployee" status if they retained their new job. Indeed, Professor John

Fitch of the New York School of Social Work convinced Senator Wagner that the purposes of the bill would be better served by allowing all replacement workers to bargain with their new employer, a position that can be explained by the fact that the employers' right to hire replacement workers was not in doubt and that excluding strikebreakers would not directly contribute to developing collective bargaining.[85] Accordingly, when the bill was reintroduced and later adopted in 1935, the reference to strikebreakers had disappeared from the definition of "employee."

"No Word of Art"

The limits inherent in the definition of the worker for labor relations were made obvious a few years later in a case that directly harkened back to the Progressive struggle to root out injustice in the workplace—child labor. In *NLRB v. Hearst Pub. Inc.*, the Court passed on the case of newsboys, whose bargaining rights were denied by their employers on the grounds that they were not "employees" but "independent contractors." Upholding the NLRB's decision that the boys were "employees," the Supreme Court once again reaffirmed the specific character of "employee" under the Wagner Act. Indeed, the high tribunal denied that Congress had imported in the Wagner Act either the common-law definition of "employee" or a social definition of worker whereby anyone hired—that is, all workers—would be protected by the law.[86] "Congress did not treat employee as a word of art having a definite meaning," the Court explained. Rather, "it ["employee"] takes its color from its surroundings, in the statute where it appears, and derives meaning from the context of that statute which must be read in the light to the mischief to be corrected and the end to be attained."[87]

No opinion better expressed the promise and limitations inherent in the Wagner Act. While the intervention of the government in the employment relationship liberated millions of workers from the arbitrary rule of management, the Wagner Act raised, but did not solve, the question of which workers would be defined as "employees." Indeed, what Progressives intent on deflecting class antagonism had really built was the government's visible hand on labor relations. But the Wagner Act protected no substantive civil right. As the Supreme Court explained in 1944, a pattern of inclusion and exclusion was at the heart of the logic of the reshaping of labor relations.

As a result, included as "employees" were the workers who toiled by the thousands in the mass-production industries on which the Fordist economy relied. For them, the right to organize went hand in hand with the evolution of personnel policies, which sought to foster their long-term attachment and fidelity by offering promotion patterns and social benefits. The growth of unionism and the security it brought, then, paralleled its evolution in management policies. For many others, the Wagner Act laid the groundwork for a struggle for inclusion. To paraphrase E. P. Thompson, the "employee" was to be made and remade, not "given." But to make themselves "employees," workers would have to fight more than a cultural struggle—theirs would be a legal and political struggle in the arenas of the NLRB and the courts as much as a social one.

In the 1930s these limitations did not worry labor reformers, who believed that they had fundamentally reshaped labor relations according to the needs of a mass-production economy. Notably, this faith stemmed from the fact that labor reformers such as Robert Wagner and Leon Keyserling had built strong ideological ties with the labor economists trained by John R. Commons in Wisconsin. What undergirded their faith in the Wagner Act was the sociology of labor relations developed by Commons, according to whom collective bargaining could deliver this most wanted social product—harmony and partnership between "employer and employee."

CHAPTER 3

The Sociology of Harmony

ACCORDING to his autobiography, it was around 1885 that John R. Commons started the intellectual journey that later brought him to the forefront of the Progressive impulse. He was working in a printing office in Leesburg, Florida, when he stumbled on a book in which Herbert Spencer contended that according to the science of physics, it was impossible to pitch a curve ball. To the young Commons, this was an egregious mistake. "He knew not the seams on the ball and forgot the friction of the air," Commons noted. "His was evidently a single-track mind. Ever after, I looked for the omitted factors, or the ones taken for granted and therefore omitted, by the great leaders in the science of economics. That was how I became an economic skeptic."[1]

Quite beyond Spencer's gross error, John R. Commons was well situated to contemplate heterodox ideas and join the Progressive banner. Born in 1862 to a Quaker father and a Presbyterian mother who had been active in abolitionist feminist advocacy, he was steeped in a tradition of reform that caused him, like a generation of middle-class Americans, to look uneasily at the growing social dislocation of the country. At Oberlin, where he spent seven years between 1881 and 1888, he was a mediocre student who spent a lot of time earning money as a typesetter—and trying to pitch curve balls, which he achieved at least once. But in Cleveland, Commons was also immersed in the daily toils of printers who tried to exercise control over their working conditions by associating, and he received his first bit of education by heeding a fellow printer's advice—reading Henry George's *Progress and Poverty*, by that time a well-known denunciation of growing social inequalities. George was no advocate of labor unions or class consciousness, preferring to agitate for a single tax, but his argument that unions could not really improve the rate of wages failed to sway Commons, who had a decided knack to put a premium on empiricism over theory: "In my own case, I knew [trade unions] resulted in conditions of employment preferable to those existing in the open shop across the way."[2]

It was upon moving to Johns Hopkins in 1888 that Commons gained the intellectual ability to put a theoretical spin on his skepticism. In completing his education with Richard Ely—one of the main advocates of the ideal of industrial democracy—Commons was plunged in the transnational academic élan that engulfed the energies of Progressive scholars who believed the market and the economy should be seen as social constructions. Seeking to analyze these constructions, Sidney and Beatrice Webb in Great Britain, Emile Durkheim and his followers in France, Thorstein Veblen in the United States, and Gustav von Schmoller and Max Weber in Germany all sought to develop a kind of economic sociology that aimed at determining what subjective and contingent forces acted as social determinations of human choices.[3]

After graduating from Johns Hopkins, Commons eventually decided to embrace an academic career, which proved to be a rocky path. In spite of Ely's prominence, at the time the field of labor relations was only emerging, its scientific contours unclear and its legitimacy in doubt. Hired in 1890 at Wesleyan, Commons taught political science for two years before losing his job. At Oberlin and Syracuse, he taught sociology but was dismissed in 1898 for his "radical" ideas. His academic exile ended only in 1904, when Commons landed a permanent appointment—this time in economics—at the University of Wisconsin. By then, the Progressive legislative impulse was gaining strength, and Commons subsequently made the most of his position, translating his expertise into political action with his contribution to the Wisconsin idea.

"Class conflict may be growing," Commons contended, "but it's not inevitable." From his post in Madison, Commons conducted the research that provided the intellectual underpinnings of the Progressive transformation and revival of the ideology of social harmony. He trained a significant amount of students in the new discipline of "institutional economics," which conceived of class conflict as a pathological social fact that could be remedied. Alongside the process of natural selection described by Spencer, Commons argued, there was an equally important process of social selection whereby society chose the institutions most adequate to further its goals. Through institutions, society could "subordinate" the individual by "institutionalizing" his or her mind.[4] Indeed, it was his grounding in the emerging social sciences that led Commons to discard Marxist materialism and focus instead of individual behavior as a social product built through institutions and mental habits, and therefore susceptible to constructive change. Unions and trade agreements, Commons taught, should be seen as engines of cooperation in the workplace.[5]

When the Wagner Act was passed in 1935, Commons had passed from the scene, but under his academic influence the ideal of the harmony of interests between capital and labor had been refashioned into an academic discipline that paved a Progressive, scientific way out of the labor question. Indeed, Commons's vision of industrial democracy and collective bargaining would remain influential for decades to come, guiding the efforts of two generations of labor experts eager to proceed with the search for order he had pioneered, one that included an orderly process of negotiation between "employers and employees."

The Long Conceptual Road to Industrial Democracy

"The masses of this country want not less democracy but more. They want . . . industrial democracy added to political democracy. Their problem is not how to limit the suffrage but to protect the liberties of the people."[6] The entry "democracy" in the 1897 edition of the *Encyclopedia of Social Reform* reminds us that the term "industrial democracy" came in use well before Commons and the Wisconsin school left their mark on labor relations. At the time its meaning was ambiguous, and the degrees of "democratization" that advocates of industrial democracy envisioned were quite different, ranging from collective ownership of the means of production to cooperative partnerships, trade agreements, and even profit-sharing plans offered by enlightened businessmen who wanted both to cultivate their workers' loyalty and foster a definition of industrial democracy that would not threaten managerial prerogatives.[7]

Still, an important element in the rise of the ideal of industrial democracy was the American egalitarian tradition. Many of its first advocates hoped to secure the recognition of the *individual* rights of workers. Like Knights of Labor leader George McNeill, who suggested that a company should be run on the "town meeting plan," labor advocates who agitated for the extension of the principles of democracy to the workplace sought to make a claim on the country's political culture. The influence of this egalitarian tradition remained very strong well after the decline of the Knights of Labor, and even during the Great War, workers demanded forcefully that the American struggle for democracy in Europe be replicated by a democratization of the factories in which the weaponry used to wage the war was produced. Frank Walsh, the head of the National Labor War Relations Board, created in April 1918 to arbitrate labor conflicts, then became one of the main proponents of industrial democracy: "political democracy, he explained, is an illusion unless builded upon and guaranteed by a free and virile industrial democracy."[8]

Like Walsh, Commons agreed that a profound sociological imbalance now characterized the American polity. The recognition that all classes have rights, he explained in *Labor and Administration*, was essential if civil war was to be avoided in America. In fact, Commons's early work was precisely aimed at securing the political representation of the working class in Congress by shifting the dynamics of representation from a geographical to a social basis. The reorganization of political power he called for would send representatives of business and workers to Capitol Hill along with economists standing on either side of the labor question. "As long as an economist does not recognize the existence of classes, he will fail to see the need for this readjustment of electoral machinery, which shall represent all classes," he explained at a meeting of the American Economic Association in 1899, trying—to no avail—to defend his plan.[9]

Had this focus on individual rights and equality been enough to justify industrial democracy, Commons's role would have been quite modest. Yet, like other Progressives, Commons spoke a language emphasizing social bonds as much as individual rights, and it was precisely because he helped develop a sociology that constructed collective bargaining as a vehicle of social harmony, and not simply as agencies of worker empowerment, that his vision of democracy at work became dominant and was translated into an academic discipline. Therefore we need to try to reconstruct his intellectual journey, keeping in mind that the democratic ideal did not, in and of itself, solve the labor question.

One difficulty in approaching Commons's work is that his writings span a long period—roughly from the late 1890s to the 1934 publication of *Institutional Economics*. This is clearly a long enough period for any active scholar to evolve, particularly if, like Commons, one was involved in the building of a whole scientific paradigm. Yet Commons's research was conceived from the outset as a study of the dynamics of coercion in society, not historical materialism. In "A Sociological View of Sovereignty" (1899), he argued that there is no such thing as individual freedom, for "coercion is the decisive social relation." The struggle for the control of material goods governed human actions and preceded all institutions (the family, political parties, corporations). Because self-interest and scarcity of material resources and services led to sharp conflicts between individuals over the acquisition and control of property, men designed institutions whose natural evolution drove them to become monopolistic and centralized, thus turning coercion into the dominant social relation. In the course of history, a number of social organizations, ranging from English barons and chartered companies to the church, political parties, and the patriarchal family, had evolved and developed, gaining political privileges that allowed them to mediate the allocation of property in disproportionate fashion toward the few.[10]

However, this in turn led to collective responses by the subordinated to force their superiors to redirect the use of monopoly in a way that serves the interests of the community as a whole.[11] In "A Sociological View of Sovereignty," Commons contended that throughout its history, the state had grown by "abstracting" the coercive power of an institution (its capacity to use violence), leaving it with only "persuasive" powers, thus giving a specific social group a new right that served as the basis for a new order based on negotiation.

According to Commons, because the "institutionalized" power of corporations was so great, they were able to exercise a disproportionate amount of economic coercion on workers. American companies had acquired a political privilege that was the source of conflict. For this conflict to disappear, workers had to "enter the constitution" too, that is, judges had to provide general rules of conduct setting limits on the corporations' ability to exercise economic coercion, even if Commons was wise enough to admit that economic coercion would never disappear altogether. Still, Commons argued that by setting limits on the coercive power of companies, the reform of the common law would put employers and workers in a situation of cooperative dependency—such was the very logic of his vision of industrial democracy.

Commons's analysis therefore discarded very early on the possibility that labor conflict might stem from the inherent inequalities or imbalances in the capitalist system, which explains that he was more attracted to the language of social harmony than to the Marxian language of class. Indeed, Commons's approach of society through "institutions" that were gradually divested of their coercive powers allowed him to sketch a positive evolution from "conflict to order and interdependence." As he noted in 1901, the main result of collective bargaining and trade agreements was the "new feeling of equality and mutual respect that *springs up* in both employer and employee."[12]

Yet the common law, which represented the evolutionary body of working rules of society, was only the first level of this "institutionalization" of minds. It remained for Commons to show that in the very field of labor relations, institutions could indeed produce norms that would, as he claimed in "A Sociological View of Sovereignty," regulate the economy and deflect class polarization. Such was the task he took on in 1909 by launching a historical investigation titled "American Shoemakers: A Sketch of Industrial Evolution," in which he retraced Sidney Webb's footsteps in opting for a kind of ethical positivism that put customs and legal norms at the center of experience and meaning of wage work.[13]

Cast in the mold of the German historicist tradition, "American Shoemakers" was aimed at showing how industrial evolution had deprived a "homogeneous craftsman"—combining the functions of merchant, master, and journeyman—of "property rights," that is, control of over earnings. The dynamic driving this process, Commons explained, was the gradual expansion of markets, which had gradually created gaps within the three functions that were united in the journeyman. In the late nineteenth century, some masters had become retail merchants, thus separating the merchant function from the master-journeyman ones. Then, in the early nineteenth century, better modes of transportation and access to credit had turned merchants into wholesale dealers looking for outside markets, thus widening the gap between them and the master-journeymen on the other side. In the 1830s, larger credit flows from the North had resulted in the rise of the merchant capitalist, who no longer obtained his goods from a master, but from a contractor who himself employed several journeymen—the functions of master and journeymen were now distinct, and Commons saw in this stage of industrial evolution the emergence of the "worker" in the modern sense, an emergence symbolized in the word "boss." Finally, in the middle and late nineteenth century, it was the tools of production—heretofore unaltered—that evolved to allow the merchant capitalist to redefine the market and expand it once again, leading to a fresh attempt at regulation on the part of the union to impose "working rules."[14]

Written against the "abstractions of Marx," this historicist analysis led Commons to reject the existence of a proletariat, or any other unitary division of society. Indeed, Commons argued, the centrality of the expansion of markets in American industrial history suggested that the driving force precipitating these successive "realignments of interests" among journeymen, masters, and merchants was actually the tension between the producer and the consumer. Harmony between master and journeyman and a commonality of interests had obtained through the first stages in the expansion of markets until the emergence of the merchant capitalist made it impossible to pass the cost of the worker's standard of living onto consumers because the employer and the retailer were no longer the same. Throughout his career, his sociology was aimed at restoring this harmony, which he described in "American Shoemakers" as the "primitive harmony of capital and labor."[15]

Commons argued that tensions arising in the wage relationship could be solved through the negotiations of norms and the creation of institutions. Following the model established in "A Sociological View of Sovereignty," Commons suggested in "American Shoemakers" that at all stages, unions of workers made coercion impossible and led to negotiations based on persuasion—"institutionalized" workers had recovered their property rights, thus reverting to a harmonious relationship with employers. This historical analysis echoed the history of labor written by Commons's students at Wisconsin in the early 1900s and foreshadowed the work of Selig Perlman on the working class. Not only was the American working class "job conscious" and conservative, but from the standpoint of the Wisconsin school of evolutionary sociology, the disappearance of social harmony could be interpreted as a temporary historical process, and reformers could hope to restore harmony through institutions.

The ambition to restore industrial harmony was pursued through the Wisconsin version of the ideal of industrial democracy, which in many ways was a quest for a return to preindustrial norms of social order and interdependence, an ideal expressed once again through the anticlass implications of the pair "employer and employee." As Commons's student Jett Lauck explained in 1926 in his aptly titled—and influential—*Political and Industrial Democracy*, industrial democracy meant returning to peaceful relations that obtained before the industrial revolution: "The effects of this development [the industrial revolution] upon social and political life were serious," Lauck noted, "the breakdown of personal relations between employer and employee was complete. . . . Cooperation between employer and employees rapidly disappeared. It was supplanted by industrial strife and industrial dislocations."[16]

In Commons's later work, particularly *The Legal Foundations of Capitalism* and *Institutional Economics*, this interest into organized forms of collective action led him to develop a new concept to express the centrality of harmony in any capitalist enterprise, namely, the *going concern,* which he defined as "a living body . . . animated by a common purpose, governed by common rules of its own making." A "going concern" was first and foremost a voluntary association, since employers did not enjoy the power to force workers to stay on the job and workers had no property rights in their jobs—the going concern was based on the voluntary cooperation of both employers and workers. This cooperation Commons explained through the idea of *futurity*—what shaped the employment relationship was not the atemporal law of supply and demand for labor, but the expectation on both sides of future benefits deriving from the cooperation. What made this futurity possible was the fact that both employers and workers had internalized a number of customs and rules that allowed them to project themselves in the future: what Commons and his students often defended as industrial democracy was simply the notion that the employment relationship was not the meeting of two individuals, or a group of individuals, but a "collective act" resting on established social relations that made this joint expectation possible.[17]

Quite clearly, Commons's goal was social harmony, not social strife, and by his own admission his sociology of labor relations was designed to place restraints on individuals. Tellingly, his definition of institutional economics was "collective action in control of individual action."[18] Equally important to understand his sociology, however, was his weariness at the "new immigrants" who were transforming the social makeup of the American working class. Like many of his contemporaries, Commons doubted that these immigrants had the same democratic inclinations as the English middle class, whose struggles he had depicted in "A Sociological View of Sovereignty," and from whom American workers were descended. Yet his sociology and the discipline of industrial relations he was trying to build precisely allowed him to think that immigrants could be led to share in cooperation and compromise—as long as experts were there to guide their negotiations with managers—rather than turning to radical political activities. Quite beyond his conservative weariness of immigrants, unionism was to Commons a true American freedom because it was an engine for assimilation.[19]

However, there were other limitations to Commons's Progressive vision of labor relations. In fact, what he had painstakingly conceptualized was the process whereby employers and employees could develop a relationship based on cooperation and compromise, not the constitutional rights of American citizens.

"Employee" not "Citizen":
The Limits of the Constitutional Metaphor
in the Rise of Industrial Democracy

True to the realist spirit of the age, Commons found an empirical base for this new reading of the employment relationship in his involvement with the National Civic Foundation, an organization created by the AFL with open-shop leaders hoping to thwart the rise of radical unionism. In 1900, he witnessed the proceedings of the annual Interstate Joint Conference, which brought together the companies of the Central Competitive Field and the United Mine Workers to decide matters pertaining to wages, working conditions, and output goals. To Commons, the most striking feature of this negotiation process was that it was premised on the equality of the parties and was patterned like the British Parliament—the unelected members of management met with the elected representatives of the workers. Commons thought that in place of strife, he had discovered a parliamentary process based on ordered liberty, a total redefinition of democracy and representation that promised to solve the labor question.[20]

Such political metaphors, however, must not be misunderstood, and should be seen in the broader context of Commons's sociological research. Tellingly, the tables of contents of his main works of economic sociology do not feature the term "industrial democracy." By contrast, in the public sphere it was through the metaphor of the democratic political process that the new "institutionalization" of the employment relationship was promoted, with recurring attempts to invoke the memory of British parliamentary struggles. Indeed, the analogy between the collective bargaining process and the British parliamentary system became the crux of the defense of American workers' right to organize. Commons called it "constitutional government" in industry, and his protégés, particularly William Leiserson, Jett Lauck, and Edwin Witte, followed suit. In his *Political and Industrial Democracy*, Lauck squarely planted the struggle for industrial democracy in a Whiggish historical account that started with the American and the French Revolutions and followed a predictable republican thread weaving the basic principle of the consent of the governed with the importance of checks and balances and respect for individual rights—a process that pointed naturally to the need to extend democracy in industry.[21] Tackling the issue from the angle of his struggle against trusts, the jurist Louis Brandeis sounded the same theme in his testimony at the Industrial Commission in 1915. Industrial unrest, he explained, flowed from the absolutism of business executives, with the result that "we lose the necessary contact between employers and employees, which the American aspirations for democracy demand." "We Americans are committed not only to social justice, like unjust distribution of wealth, but we are committed to democracy. The social justice for which we are striving is an incident of our democracy, not the main end. It is rather the result of democracy—perhaps its finest expression—but it rests upon democracy, which implies the rule by the people."[22]

Yet industrial democracy can be a slippery doctrine, particularly because it was used more to promote than to conceptualize the reform of labor relations that Commons and his students were advocating. Indeed, neither legal realists nor institutional economists ever tried to give a concrete, legal dimension to the right to organize. As Brandeis himself explained in 1921, the right to organize would serve a useful purpose, but it was not a fundamental one: "Because I have come to the conclusion that both the common law of a state and a statute of the United States declare the rights of industrial combatants to push their struggle to the limits of justification of their self-interest, I do not wish to be understood as attaching any moral or constitutional sanction to that right. All rights are derived from the purposes of the society in which they exist."[23]

The Progressives' defense of unions was no doubt replete with constitutional references, and Commons even emphasized that contrary to classical economics, institutional scholars did not view workers as "commodities" but as "citizens." Yet those AFL leaders who preached for a constitutional right to unionize premised on the Thirteenth Amendment found little support in the Commons school, and one may say that they couldn't have.[24] Cast in the mold of the debate over institutions in the economy, the regulation of the employment relationship was impervious to the rhetoric of individual rights, and focused on the need to promote collective bargaining. To the extent that institutional economics conceived of the worker as a citizen, it was not through natural rights, but as a citizen of a given, *institutionalized* social group with a number of duties and rights conceived during a negotiation—an "economic status," spelling security through conformity.[25] In Commons's work, the language of democracy occupied the same function as Calvinism in Max Weber's *Protestant Ethic and the Spirit of Capitalism*—it was an ethos, a mental habit. But Commons had reversed the focus of European economic sociology, for he proposed to foster the mental habit so as to obtain the social result.

The main idea stemming from this sociological perspective was the notion that there was not one class struggle, but myriads of legal disputes between employers and groups of employees that could be easily remedied by adopting institutions that produced peaceful labor relations. Some years on, reflecting on the contribution of institutionalism to the reconceptualization of the employment relationship, William Leiserson, one of Commons's most prominent heirs, took pride in the success of this endeavor, noting the conceptual gap between capital and labor and employer and employee and the consequent disappearance of the "labor question":

> Employee and Employer are no longer the economists'
> abstractions, Capital and Labor, but personalities bound together
> in contractual agreements not unlike the relations set up by a
> marriage contract. The search for a theoretical labor problem
> therefore appears as futile as a search for a solution of an abstract
> marriage or family problem. Instead, we seek methods of securing
> mutual accommodations and adjustment. . . . The change from
> the Labor Problem to Labor relations was no mere academic
> refinement.[26]

Leiserson believed that "employee" and "employer" had acquired an important, concrete social meaning in the lives of workers and employer, one that had displaced the class struggle by instituting new social norms of industrial relationships. Indeed, one may contend that what institutionalists believed they had achieved was in fact similar to the social regulation that Durkheim called for by producing a new social fact, that is, "a system of representation and mental states" in different industrial settings.[27] Institutionalists believed they had given American society the conceptual and technical toolbox for the resolution of the labor question, and it was no coincidence that they were able to develop a whole academic field—industrial relations—to that effect. No longer the natural consequence of the harmony of the market, the harmony between "employer and employee" would return as a social product.

The economic sociology of institutionalism had profoundly reignited the traditional hope that class polarization could be prevented, opening a reformist venue that guided efforts through the New Deal. By then, the trade agreement—the central institution according to institutional economics—stood at the heart of the reformers who drafted and promoted the nation's first attempt to afford unionism the protection Commons had long called for.

The Wagner Act's unambiguous affirmation of American workers' right to organize only partly satisfied the industrial pluralists because the law made no provision for the actual mediation of labor disputes by arbitrators such as Leiserson. Nevertheless, they joined in the effort to defend Wagner's bill because they realized that it was necessary both to sustain the level of wages and to affirm the political legitimacy of unionism. In fact, the Wagner Act represented the first stage that Commons had identified in the transition from economic coercion to order and interdependence. As Leiserson explained to labor journalist John Fitch in 1936, "the New Deal has accomplished this much: it has convinced people that men have a right to organize." To Leiserson it remained for labor progressives to build a structure that would help managers and employees develop the working rules needed to resolve their conflicts peacefully. Collective bargaining would not magically work by itself—rather, it would require the guiding hand of labor expertise.[28]

Whether such as structure was necessary in the eyes of New Dealers such as Robert Wagner and Leon Keyserling was doubtful. Yet this was not because they defined their task as simply empowering workers in their struggle for better working and living conditions. On the contrary, the main tenets of industrial democracy as defined by the pluralists had been so extensively discussed since the Great War that by the 1930s the idea that collective bargaining was a vehicle of social peace was endorsed by many labor progressives who had been in contact with the pluralists. "The cooperation between employer and employee is boldly written in the law," Wagner joyfully explained about the inclusion of Section 7a in the National Industrial Recovery Act.[29] Indeed, Robert Wagner always couched his defense of associational rights in a language that reflected the staying power of the ideals of social harmony and comity between "employer and employee." Although Section 7a in the NIRA put the weight of the federal government for the first time behind the process of collective bargaining, it was not meant to simply empower the working class in the class struggle, as socialists would have demanded. Rather, cooperation was to *end* social strife, which was a fixture of the "old order." Lamenting the existence of "cross currents of distrust and antagonism between labor and industry that have no substantial basis in fact," Wagner contended that "cooperation based on trust and understanding must be the keynote henceforward."[30]

The main problem behind the depression, the ill apportionment of income, would thus be solved by a partnership for economic reconstruction. As Wagner himself noted in a congressional debate in 1932, workers should not feel alienated from management; rather, they should feel like "partners, shouldering the responsibilities of management."[31] Workers were not simply expected to regain a freedom of which modern industrial society had deprived them (the preindustrial ability to bargain with the employer), but they were expected to use this freedom in an ethical fashion, to pursue a common goal. In a prominent interview with the *New York Times*, Wagner referred to the NIRA experiment as a "moral" one, in which various social groups should try to reach beyond their immediate interest and fulfill a common goal. "Partnership," "harmony" equally pointed to the hope that both employers and employees would go beyond the enjoyment of individual, positive rights and attempt to cooperate for the common benefit of what Dewey called "socialized intelligence." Sounding a sociological theme that harkened back to the beginning of institutional economics, Wagner and others saw the NIRA as the best protection against "social disintegration."[32] Cooperation, he argued, was an ethos that should develop in the "hearts and minds" of all Americans. The macro-management of the economy was to be based on a cultural and psychological change. The cartoonist Clifford Barryman aptly captured the essence of this new language of harmony with a cartoon titled "The Spirit of the New Deal," which depicted Uncle Sam standing between a happy "employer" dressed in a suit and a merry "employe" wearing overalls, Sam's arms outstretched around their shoulders as a sign of unity.[33]

One of the problems with the language of harmony, of course, was that it could easily be captured by conservatives opposing the development of unionism, particularly those who had defeated the radical impulse for industrial democracy after the Great War.[34] Thus, Paul Litchfield, talking to Goodyear employees in March 1934, undercut much of the argumentation for Section 7a by sounding the very Progressive themes of social cohesion and efficiency that labor reformers had marshaled earlier in their defense of the NIRA: "I view the service Goodyear renders the public as being the product of a partnership effort in which men, money and management are pooling their strength and intelligence. Each branch of the partnership contributes an indispensable part to the whole, and each branch must depend of the other branches for the balanced support which is the value measure of the final product."[35]

After the NIRA was adopted, labor organizations did march in strides in the mining, textile, and construction industries, as militancy reached levels unseen since 1921. And in 1933 alone, the AFL added five hundred thousand members to its existing ranks.[36] But in many mass-production industries, businessmen countered this organizing tide by setting up company unions. In September 1933, a National Industrial Conference Board study revealed that the proportion American workers covered by an Employee Representation Plan—45 percent—had increased by 169 percent since 1932. Notably, this trend was even stronger in companies with a workforce of more than five hundred workers, which means that the biggest engines of the Fordist economy were unwilling to follow Wagner's calls for a "partnership" with labor.[37]

Indeed, it was those companies that had always frowned upon company unions that now set them up: General Motors, Chrysler, and RCA, for example. In the steel industry, ever the antiunion citadel, some 85 percent of the workers were covered by an Employee Representation Plan.[38] In the spring of 1934, as Congress debated a bill to create the NLRB to arbitrate disputes, U.S. Steel, which had created an ERP in June 1933, still felt confident enough to hand out to workers a leaflet arguing that the Wagner Bill would "legalize the closed shop and force all employers to operate under it" and "force all employees into labor unions." Ironically, the leaflet listed all the advantages workers might derive from the law, but portrayed them as so many threats hanging over "Friendly Relations between Employers and Employees."[39]

Corporate America was not about to let labor reformers capture the language of industrial harmony. ERPs, after all, were businessmen's most recent victory on industrial unionism. In the aftermath of the Great War, "employee representation" had been management's most effective device against the growth of a working-class conscious of its political power. Designed to foster "factory solidarity" at the expense of "class solidarity," ERP plans usually followed the model established in 1913 by John Rockefeller in Colorado—which granted workers an "Employee's Bill of Rights"—in creating a communication link between managers and workers. Coming as they did with other programs composing welfare capitalism, ERPs promised to solve the atomization of individuals in modern society by conceptualizing the worker as a social figure dependent on social bonds forged and maintained at the local and community level by business benevolence. Whether they relied on constitutional metaphors as in the Colorado plan or portrayed the company as a " family," they reflected the growing purchase of personnel management and constituted a recent but determined attempt to build a social edifice on the nineteenth-century legal notion that the "employer-employee" relation was a naturally peaceful and beneficial one for both parties.[40]

Why then, did not Wagner and other labor progressives part with the language of harmony? Although he often emphasized the idea that the right to organize was a fundamental one, Wagner was sometimes at pains to reaffirm the difference between his vision of industrial harmony and that of corporate

America: "A tranquil relationship between employer and employe, while emi-
nently desirable is not a sole desideratum," he argued in 1934 as the nation
debated the virtues of company unionism. "It all depends on the basis of that
tranquility. The slave system of the Old South was as tranquil as a Summer's
day, but there is no reason to perpetuate in modern industry any of the aspects of master-servant relationship."[41] The reason why Wagner did not part
with this ambiguous ideal is that he shared with Commons the basic belief
that it was the legal context that structured economic exchanges. Once a social group "entered the constitution," Commons explained in *A Sociological
View of Sovereignty*, duress could no longer be applied in relations with its
members, and negotiation became inevitable. Wagner made very much the
same point regarding workers when he argued that labor conflicts stemmed
from the workers' lack of industrial rights.

Furthermore, this faith in harmony derived additional impetus from the
Taylor Society, which was created in 1910 as the Society to Promote Scientific
Management, and was renamed after Taylor in 1915.[42] Prominent among its
members were the engineer Morris L. Cooke and the jurist Louis Brandeis,
who had been trying to refurbish the theory of scientific management
by remedying its main lacuna, its inability to obtain the workers' consent.
Calling on businessmen to accept the authority of claims for industrial democracy, Cooke argued that class consciousness in the United States was
weak and limited enough for a spirit "partnership" and "cooperation" to develop in American workshops, one in which union leaders would accept de-
ferring to the demands of science in the organization of production.[43] Overall
the Taylorites had few followers, but the application of their principles in the
needle trades did reveal that technocratic management, planning, and unionism were compatible. In the prolabor group assembled by Wagner, Sidney
Hillman, the leader of the Amalgamated Clothing Workers of America, spoke
for a "new unionism"—a theory of mass-production premised on unionism
as a means to stabilize an industry by homogenizing costs and production
methods, but also as a means to provide workers with the purchasing power
they needed as consumers to make mass production viable.[44]

Hence even as he pushed a proto-Keynesian argument to defend his bill
and as he stressed the nugatory economic effects of company unions, Robert
Wagner held fast to the idea of harmony between managers and workers,
explaining that the NLRB he wanted to create was "an agency designed for
harmony and mutual concessions . . . where employers and employees could
appear as equals, where they could look with frank and friendly eyes into

each other's problems, where they could banish suspicion and hatred, and where they could sign contracts of enduring peace rather than mere articles of uncertain truce."[45] No doubt, Wagner's ambition was to make the worker a "free and dignified workman," but this emancipation would not simply come through a Marxist recognition of the structural inequity of the wage bargain. Rather, the process of collective bargaining and the enhanced consuming capacities were the New Deal's version of the old leftist utopia that worker and capital could be reconciled.

Naturally, there were dissenting voices. One came from the social reformer Mary Van Kleeck—a sharp critic of the New Deal—who registered her opposition to the Wagner Bill in a letter sent to Wagner in March 1934. Van Kleeck, who had spent almost two decades studying women's work and labor relations, harbored less sanguine views about collective bargaining than the labor reformers working with Wagner. It is "impossible to equalize the bargaining power of employers and employes," she noted, "since the decision to produce at all and in what quantities and by what processes . . . rest with the employer." Consequently, she argued in private correspondence with Wagner, the list of unfair labor cases included in the bill offered no real protection to workers—rather, it would discourage strikes by triggering the intervention of the government in disputes, thus favoring the "status quo."[46] "I need not say to you that a strike in itself often generates strength for the workers and has indeed been an important method of organization."[47] One year later, Roger Baldwin, the director of the ACLU, sent Wagner a letter in which he sounded the same notes. Contrary to union sentiment, Baldwin argued, the bill would not help strengthen the position of workers in their struggles with employers because it did not sufficiently protect the right to strike, but also because the very preamble of the law suggested that strikes were to be condemned rather than supported.[48]

Much later, the work of Christopher Tomlins and other critical scholars would vindicate the concerns expressed by Van Kleeck and Baldwin, but Wagner himself disagreed. Section 7a, he argued, had not "lulled labor into a sense of security," as Baldwin suggested, but had rather been a "galvanizing force."[49] While the senator politely acknowledged the two letters, he held fast to the idea that it was possible to equalize the bargaining power of employers and employees to such a degree that cooperation and mutual gains would be possible. In this respect, the spirit that underwrote the Wagner Act was aptly captured by the labor economist Harry M. Millis in his testimony before the Senate Committee on Education and Labor in 1934: "If and when collective bargaining is freed from undue militancy, as it can be when wise management and good labor leadership are brought into cooperation, special problems connected with collective bargaining clear up and there are opportunities to gain to all parties," Commons's student declared.[50]

However, this harmony depended on a clear definition of the two entities that were expected to cooperate and bargain with one another, namely "labor" and "management." There again, the influence of Commons's work was significant. Indeed, Commons's work premised social harmony on a restrictive sociological view of the worker. Although he was quite close to the AFL and the skilled trades—they had served as a model for the job conscious working class that he and Selig Perlman had analyzed—in his later work he provided a sociological definition of "employees" that actually reflected the organization of work in the modern, Fordist companies. Indeed, it was restricted to manual workers who followed the foremen's orders, but it excluded those higher up in the hierarchy. In Commons's prescription for a new industrial order based on the harmony of the collective bargaining process, we thus find some of the origins of the contemporary problems associated with the legal definition of workers.

Defining Workers: The Sociology of Harmony and the Labor of Superintendence

Whether those who conduct and lead the work of others are workers themselves was never an easy question. In *Capital*, Marx emphasized the "double nature" of the labor of superintendence. On the one hand, he compared the work of foremen and managers to that of the conductor of an orchestra and firmly situated their role in the realm of productive work. Indeed, he noted, any cooperative work required "commanding will to coordinate and unify the process," and socialist cooperatives amply revealed this need, as they too were organized to make this coordination possible. As Marx further explained in the unpublished chapter 6 of volume 1 of *Capital*, foremen and managers were part of an abstract, collective worker, a "socially combined labour capacity," including engineers and manual workers.[51]

On the other hand, Marx contended that in the capitalistic system, the labor of superintendence sprang from the sheer antagonism between workers and capitalists—it was necessary to the submission of the former to the latter. Moreover, it was used to justify the inequalities between the social classes, as economists argued that workers should not simply be expected to produce the maximum surplus value, but also the wages of those overseers and su-perintendents who helped to turn them into useful social beings. As a result, for Marx overseers and superintendents had a "divided allegiance" typical of the petty bourgeoisie—they were wage laborers, sprang from the same social classes as the workers, and took part in the productive endeavor, yet their role in the exercise of social control aligned them with capital.[52]

Commons's economic sociology, however, identified no such divided al-legiance, for he perceived no structural antagonism between workers and capitalists. Commons agreed with Marx that labor combined "mental and managerial faculties" as well as "manual" ones, but he did not conclude that all workers using such faculties made up an abstract, collective entity.[53] In fact, very early on Commons repudiated the theory of labor's right to the en-tire product as passé: ever true to the perspective of evolution, he saw this theory as the mere product of a moment in the history of political economy when it was a "science of the production of wealth"—an allusion to the fact that Marxist theory, like all classical economics since Adam Smith, was fo-cused on the liberty to produce and, following Locke, posited the right of people to their own labor. As Commons, noted, the Marxist definition of the worker derived from this approach.[54]

Commons meant to operate a break with the Marxian association of labor with the physical product. As we have seen, he conceived of the labor pro-cess as a process implying interdependence between employers and work-ers, whose joint expectation of a future profit entailed mutual interests and order—this collective act he called "going concern." Moreover, he approached this going concern from the standpoint of *consumption*. The "gross income" that both workers and employers expected ultimately derived from the ex-change value of the commodities they produced on the market. To produce this commodity, employers and workers engaged in three successive trans-actions that, for Commons, were the core of economic activity. If we look further into this part of his sociology, we can understand why he ended up offering a restrictive definition of the worker in labor relations, or "employee."

First, workers and employers engaged in a *bargaining transaction* in which they were equals, that is, both sides enjoyed an intangible property, sanctioned by the Supreme Court in 1897 in the *Allgeyer* case—the right to a future expected earning.[55] This property right, Commons explained, in-cluded the right to withhold services one may need but did not own. Workers needed the job, and employers needed the workforce of workers. So there was no alienation in the employment relationship—what the workers really sold, he argued, was neither their body nor the use of their body, which were inalienable. Rather, workers, like employers, sold their *goodwill*, the workers their acceptance to follow the commands of the employer and the latter their acceptance to furnish the means of production. The key to this bargaining transaction between equals was that the worker became a creditor, owning an "encumbrance" on the future benefits of the company, while the employer was to become the owner of the product of the work. A bargaining transaction necessarily grew out of a relation among five parties—the employer, the worker, the two (at a minimum) alternatives to which each could theoretically look, and the state that institutionalizes this transaction, setting limits on the ability to coerce in the public interest.[56]

The second transaction, the *managerial transaction*, creates wealth, and thus derives from a technological imperative—to organize the work according to efficiency principles. To Commons, this meant that this transaction was necessarily between a legal superior—management, foremen—and a legal inferior, namely, the worker. Command and obedience govern the managerial transaction, which means that through the bargaining transaction, the workers commit to renounce their liberty and place themselves under the authority of the manager. To Commons, this renunciation of liberty was inevitable and did not constitute a problem because the managerial transaction was nonetheless to be governed by working rules and custom, and more generally the need to find lasting expedients to solve disputes. Moreover, it squarely fitted with the idea that what brought workers and employers together in an ongoing concern was an expectation of earnings, and this renunciation reflected Commons's long-standing belief that unions should not concern themselves with the management of production and should rather focus on the distribution of incomes.[57]

The third transaction was the *rationing transaction*, whereby the distribution of the wealth produced was conducted. Collective bargaining and trade agreements were examples of this type of transaction just like legislatures dealing with economic questions of courts of justice solving disputes. In all these cases, the institution in charge of the rationing was the legal superior, and the participants the legal inferiors. The boards of mediation and arbitration that Commons advocated throughout his career and helped create in Wisconsin were prime examples of this type of transaction. More than the two others, it was the rationing transaction that exemplified the potential for social harmony that Commons sought to demonstrate. In this respect, there was no better example than the policy set by Herbert Hoover during the Great

War to set the price of wheat. Indeed, Commons applauded Hoover's decision to ask associations of farmers and the AFL to negotiate and agree to a compromise on the price under the aegis of the government. It was, Commons wrote, "representative democracy in industry . . . a procedure of appealing to the harmony of interest of both classes for the public good."[58]

Not only did this theory of economic transactions offer a rebuttal to the inevitability of class polarization, but it also led Commons to suggest that in labor relations, foremen did not belong with "employees." According to him, foremen and managers, who had to accept or reject the laborers' output, were not "employees," for they stood on the opposite side of workers in the managerial transaction.[59] This was an important difference between scientific management advocates and Commons. The former believed that both engineers and workers should cooperate to maximize the output of the company. But, very early on, Commons disagreed with this notion on the grounds that in "modern industry it is the employer upon whom the responsibility of production is placed." Indeed, Commons believed that this was an employer prerogative and that unions had no right to bargain over production or investment. Moreover, Commons insisted that cooperating with employers on the question of production or investment would compromise the ability of the union to bargain over its share of the final product. The creation of wealth was the sole responsibility of the employer, and the union bargained only over wages.[60]

Commons's sociology thus legitimized relations of power within the modern factory because he believed that ultimately, the harmony that prevailed in a "going concern" rested on the common expectation of a gross income. However, Commons did not hold that all participants contributed equally to that goal, nor even that workers were the most important element in this endeavor. Rather, he argued that in modern enterprises the pursuit of this expected joint income was conducted through a vertical, hierarchical organization of people whose individual influence on the total product differed greatly—it was great at the top but insignificant at the bottom. Speaking the Progressive language of efficiency, Commons suggested that it was necessary to differentiate between two types of actions in the workplace—there were "discretional" and "ministerial" "acts of will," with the latter term conveying the nearly total absence of discretion. To Commons, manual workers naturally stood at the bottom of this hierarchy because they mainly acted "in subjection to the will of others," while foremen, superintendents, and managers had greater discretional influence.[61]

Moreover, Commons connected the notion of "employee" with "ministerial" acts rather than "discretional acts." In modern factories, this implied a link between "employee" and physical exertion, arduous labor, as opposed to the use of mental faculties—a link that limited the idea of the worker to the blue-collar world. "The agent deals with people, and therefore must rely on persuasion and coercion, whereas the employee deals with physical and animal forces," he explained in *The Legal Foundations of Capitalism*.[62] In this respect, Commons seems to have followed a tradition going back to English political economists, according to whom productive work was the transformation of nature into objects.[63] Most important, as we will see in the next chapter, his definition of "employee" was also in tune with the new organization of work in the Fordist system—the industrial sector organized around the methods and objectives of mass production—where the new foremanship closely allied foremen and many supervisors with management and separated them from "employees," that is, line workers. A Progressive endeavor, Commons's sociology of the factory world nonetheless justified—and to some extent reinforced—the social organization of the Fordist factory, for the main element characterizing the "employee" was precisely his or her inability to use discretion on the job, whereas discretion was an attribute of "agents" who were really agents of efficiency because they used their knowledge to influence the objectives and prospects of production. By contrast, "employees" were only the means of this efficiency, as they provided the brawn.

This traditional vision of the worker, however, was only one part of the definition of "employee," which to Commons really revolved around the lack of discretionary powers. In fact, to Commons, "employees" were not necessarily manual workers. As he noted, the American government had long called some of its workers "employees," although they were white-collar workers. But what mattered to him is that these governmental clerks were indeed "employees" because their duties were largely instrumental, or "ministerial" in his vocabulary: "The State itself is but one of many going concerns, whose sovereign working rules are but a larger collective will, and the behavior of whose officials is collective behavior. It too has its ministerial agents with such slight discretionary powers that they are held in law to be only 'employees.'"[64]

This definition of "employee" had significant consequences for Commons's theory of collective bargaining, for it was the basis for the definition of the two social entities involved in the bargaining process. As William Leiserson explained to the members of Congress in 1939, it was important for these two entities to remain stable over time:

> Quite frequently, individual members of a board of directors and
> individual managers, superintendents, or foremen, differ with the
> majority of the directors or managers regarding wages, hours, and
> conditions of employment. But they are not permitted to bargain
> as individuals . . . there must be collective, unified bargaining on
> behalf of the management of the corporation. Similarly . . . there
> must be unified bargaining by the whole of the employees who
> constitute an appropriate bargaining unit.[65]

Leiserson's description of the two social groups involved in collective bargaining left the labor of superintendence squarely planted in the realm of
management. Indeed, the labor sociology developed in Wisconsin implied a
link between unionism and tedious, routine work. It moved the idea of collective bargaining away from the egalitarian tradition that had first underwritten the claims to industrial democracy—the idea that the right to organize
and bargain collectively might be a political right accruing from citizenship.
Commons simply never envisioned that "agents" might demand the right to
organize too, and he did not do so because he did not believe that unionism
should challenge managerial prerogatives. Moreover, he understood collective bargaining as a vehicle for harmony because it was first and foremost a
process of negotiation between well-established social entities.

As we have seen, Wagner, Keyserling, and other labor reformers believed
that the legal definition of the worker they had adopted—although lacking in
some respects—was broad enough to cover the industrial working class and
thus solve the labor question. Similarly, Leiserson believed that the representation of the social world of the workplace as one made up of two distinct
social groups, "management" and "labor" or, as they were now increasingly
called, "employers" and "employees," was essential to the Progressive axiom
of reconcilable social interests. In either case, there were limits to the recognition of workers' individual rights to organize, and this recognition stemmed
precisely from contemporary perceptions of who a worker was.

The Common Interest of Employer and Employee

In November 1945, Governor Thomas Dewey of New York celebrated the
creation of the New York State School of Industrial Relations at Cornell
University with a nationally broadcast radio address that Commons, who
had recently passed away, would certainly have applauded:

It is a school which denies the alien theory that there are classes in
our society that must wage war against each other. This is a school
dedicated to the common interest of employer and employee
and the whole of the American people. It is dedicated to the
concept that when men understand each other and work together
harmoniously, then and only then do they succeed. The State of
New York will here provide the equipment to abate the fevers
which rise from claims and counter-claims which are now the
language of industrial relations.[66]

Later known as "industrial pluralism," this science of social peace dominated
the theory and practice of labor relations well into the 1970s, providing a
source of inspiration and beliefs for three generations of labor economists
interpreting the Wagner Act.

Even as Thomas Dewey gave his radio address, however, the sociological
assumptions that guided such encomiums to the "common interest of employer and employee" were coming under severe strain because of the unionization wave that had swept through the ranks of foremanship during the war,
and it was not clear any more what groups of workers should be included in
the category "employee." More than any other, it was the case of Packard foremen that exemplified the first challenge that the heirs of John R. Commons
would have to confront—reconciling the tenets of their science of social harmony with the egalitarian claims stemming from the democratic principle.

PART II

The Battle for Loyalty

CHAPTER 4

Is a Foreman a Worker?

L ATE in 1938, Clarence Bolds, a foreman with Kelsey Hayes Company in Detroit, convinced some of his fellow supervisors to follow in the footsteps of the company's workers and create a small group to defend their interests. This was a brash move on the part of first-line supervisors, who had often been instrumental in the managerial struggle against unions, but Bolds was no stranger to the labor movement. The brother of an officer of the International Typographical Union—which organized foremen—he had long held positive views of unions. Although he had earned his position as a supervisor shortly after he was hired in 1929, Bolds had lent a helping hand to the AFL as it sought to organize automobile workers during the yeasty years of the New Deal.[1]

A few months later, on the other side of town, Thomas Dwyer, a foreman with Packard Motor Company, decided to join the movement launched by Clarence Bolds, which was morphing into a fully fledged union. It is unlikely that the two men knew each other, and Dwyer's political background differed from that of Bolds, as unionism had never played an important part in his life or that of his family. Dwyer's career at Packard rather exemplified the profile of the modern foreman. Trained as an electrician, Dwyer was hired in 1905 and was offered a position as assistant foreman six years later. He supervised the electrical assembly operations, directing the work of some five hundred men. Six years on, he was promoted to the grade of foreman and oversaw several departments where workers were involved in electrical setup.[2]

In spite of the sharp contrast between these two supervisors' backgrounds, by 1939 they were both part of a rising wave of unionization that that seemed to cut against the grain of the CIO's growing difficulties. "New Allies in Guise of Foremen Keep Rallying to CIO Banner," the *Kelsey Hayes Picket* proudly announced. To be sure, the United Foremen and Supervisors–CIO (UFS-CIO) was a very modest organization—it counted a mere twelve hundred members. But the American labor movement as a whole was still a foundling at that time, its hold on workers precarious. In the uncertain aftermath of the victories at General Motors and U.S. Steel, local labor organizers at the militant Kelsey Hayes factory saw in the victory of a handful of foremen over the determination of Chrysler management yet another sign heralding the promising future of American labor. Two years on, World War II opened a window of opportunity that helped foremen fulfill the hopes expressed in 1939. The UFS-CIO had disappeared by then, but two larger unions had come to replace it: the Foreman's Association of America (FAA) and the United Clerical Technical and Supervisory Employees (UCTSE). Together, they combined for a membership of over 120,000, and by 1945 polls revealed that over 70 percent of foremen believed that unionism was an interesting and legitimate venue to defend their interests.

The frontier of managerial control thus became, during World War II, the crucible where the dynamics of labor relations were being reassessed and redefined. At issue in the foremen's movement was whether one of the rights spelling economic citizenship—the right to organize and bargain collectively—should remain merely for manual work. Foremen's unionism suggested that far from being a kind of "Fordist compromise" providing a social compensation for mindless, manual work in mass-production industries, the right to organize and bargain collectively should benefit anyone engaged in a working activity for wages or a salary, regardless of his or her duties. The social and political meaning of foremanship would thus be construed in light of the objectives of the policies underwriting the nascent American welfare state. As with all social laws since the Progressive Era, the legal definition of the worker—employee—would depend on the public policy pursued by Congress.

"Is a Foreman a worker?" *Fortune* pointedly asked in 1945. The question was paramount to representatives of corporate America, who adamantly refused to bargain with foremen's unions and argued that foremen were managers who should not and could not be allowed to organize. Underlying this reading of the social world was the organizational logic of Fordism, in which foremen played a pivotal role. Foremen were the voice of top managers on the shop floor, and corporate executives forcefully maintained that they belonged with management and should not forsake managerial values such as individualism and competitiveness. Explaining that collective bargaining required two well-identified social entities, labor and management, top managers contended that foremen could not "sit on both sides" of the bargaining table. Their participation in unions, they insisted, would foster a divided loyalty—to the employer and to the union—that was incompatible with their role in the production process. "A man can't serve two masters," they often repeated, suggesting that the master and servant rule of fealty and loyalty to the employer had not been totally superseded by the Wagner Act and even justified excluding some workers from its purview.

This chapter traces the social dynamics of this renewed debate over worker loyalty. From the creation of the first foremen's union in 1947 to the exclusion of first-line supervisors from the definition of "employee" in the Taft-Hartley Act, a window of reformist opportunity opened as a large number of political and social actors debated the norms and values that were to underwrite work in postwar America. The debate assumed national proportions, involving miners in Pennsylvania, chemists in Louisiana, labor leaders in Detroit, conservative senators from the South, Supreme Court judges, and many others. Yet the legal logic that underwrote the debate soon focused the eyes of the nation on one outstanding NLRB and later Supreme Court case, *Matter of Packard Motor Company v. NLRB*.[3]

The Social and Organizational
Construction of Foremanship

In a well-known article on the UFS published in 1940, Ira B. Cross, a scholar with the Graduate School of Business Administration at Harvard, emphasized that foremen's unionism seemed an absurdity to many people. The UFS was the first foremen's union, and shortly after it had obtained a charter from the CIO in 1938, Cross explained, it opened an office in Detroit with the name "UFS" displayed on its front windows, eliciting many surprised responses from passers-by who wondered why on earth foremen and supervisors would need a union. "Truly," Cross concluded, "it was a little difficult to understand." Cross believed that the UFS was a temporary aberration to which sound management would quickly put an end, which is not surprising from a man trained under John R. Commons's supervision in Wisconsin. Like Sumner Slichter, his colleague at the Harvard Business School, and most industrial pluralists, Cross had always taken foremen to be an integral part of management, and his surprise at the emergence of foremen's unions was illustrative of the social identity of foremen in the 1930s.[4]

In point of fact, foremen's unions were not a new development in the United States. After the Civil War, many skilled workers unions had developed the practice of organizing supervisory workers along with the rank and file, and by 1900 this had become the norm in the printing, building, and metal trades as well as in the railroad and the maritime industries. Notably, this practice had been endorsed in the formulation of the policy of the Railway Labor Act, which was adopted in 1925 to regulate and pacify labor relations.[5] By contrast, in the industries that were part of what Daniel Nelson has called the "new factory system" that emerged in the 1880s, foremen's unions did not exist. In such industries, first-line supervisors had a more limited but essential role: they were expected to "get out production," that is, they were to be the managers' voices and arms on the factory floor. As a result, in such industries foremanship was a cultural and organizational construction that had come to maturity in the 1920s with the rise of personnel management, a construction that put foremanship squarely within the contours of management and thus constructed foremen and employees as two different social groups.[6]

In *Shop Management* in 1911, Frederick Taylor criticized the system of management in use in many American factories, lamenting the extensive powers and latitude granted to foremen. To Taylor, the managerial performance of foremen was poor at best, as it lacked method, rigor, and objectives. Indeed, while from the 1880s most American companies had acquired the facilities necessary to aim at new productive levels, managerial techniques had not yet adapted to the potential offered by the new scale and scope of enterprises. Many of these were still highly decentralized and largely depended on the authority of foremen whose autonomy turned the shop floor into a virtual local empire.[7]

The case of James R. Wilkins, who was hired at Packard in September 1909, is illustrative of the foreman's empire denounced by the most famous advocate of rationalization. Wilkins was first taken on as a major parts assembler and was promoted to foreman five months later. His duties included going out on the street to hire the people he would supervise, training them, deciding on their wages (from 28 cents to 40 cents at the time depending on the performance of the laborer), and assigning them a job to do. Wilkins also determined both the methods of production and the general pace of the work. He used an expense account to pay his workers' wages and for the tools and scrap material needed by them. Tellingly, a part of his own wages depended on his ability to save money on this fund.[8]

At the beginning of the century, this combination of skill and power made the foreman the linchpin of the production system, surpassed in autonomy only by the contractor who was more typical of New England mills. Foremen were also intent on retaining these prerogatives, as Packard's campaign to "Americanize" its workers during the Great War revealed. Like those at many other American companies in the mid-1910s, Packard managers tried to enlist the twelve hundred foreign workers working on East Grand Boulevard in public evening schools. But they soon realized that the foremen were unwilling to sign up the workers they supervised for fear of losing authority over them. In the end two-thirds of the "foreigners" did not sign up for the classes, a figure revealing the determination of the company's foremen to oppose outside interventions on the shop floor.[9]

Yet even as Taylor commented on the inefficiency of foremen, the movement toward rationalization and planning that he had helped to create—which involved deskilling many elements of craft work and creating multitudes of semiskilled machine operatives to do the work once done by highly experienced all-around machinists—had also started eroding the foreman's authority. To be sure, Taylor's own answer to this problem, "functional management," never really took hold, but by the 1920s, a "new foremanship" had emerged in place of the old imperial one all the same. The rise of personnel management after World War I certainly had the greatest impact on foremanship. Indeed, to reach levels of mass production, companies needed a much more stable workforce, one that would accept, not escape, the rigid constraints of the assembly line. While few companies at first followed Ford's lead in offering workers the compromise known as the $5 day, many realized the need to put an end to labor turnover and to rationalize and standardize employment procedures. As early as 1914, Ford, Packard, and Dodge divested foremen of the absolute right to hire and discharge and created personnel departments to assume these responsibilities, thus leaving foremen only the possibility to recommend such actions. Concurrently, as historian Alfred Chandler has shown, companies developed new hierarchical structures in which middle managers played a horizontal and vertical role at once, thus coordinating the departments of companies together. As a result, the tasks of planning and organizing production were devolved to engineers while the ever-more-important tasks of accounting and organizing the flow of materials were assumed by other middle managers. The organizational logic of throughput had taken many of the emperor's clothes away.[10]

This was most visible at Packard in the 1930s, where several lines of foremanship existed (straw boss, assistant foreman, foreman, general foreman), but where foremen did not really influence the organization of work.[11] At the start of a program, the Process Department sent time engineers on the line to estimate the time necessary to perform each task (at Packard by the 1940s, each task was tried out three times) and assess the overall cost of the program for the Planning Department. Decisions to hire, promote, or discharge the men on the line rested with the Employment Department. At the beginning of every shift, foremen were presented with a "route sheet" that told them how much their line should produce during their shift. They were expected to decide how many men they needed to accomplish this objective, but they were not allowed to change the pace of work or the disposition of machines on the shop floor. Along with the responsibility to maintain productivity rates, they were supposed to maintain safety standards and watch the quality of the pieces they produced. In case of a deficiency, however, a special assignment man was sent by the Process Department to see what changes needed to be made.[12]

To be sure, one should not exaggerate the extent of this organizational revolution, as foremen retained their empire in many industries. The "new foremanship" was really a product of the mass-production system, and it developed in large companies that had achieved significant rationalization. In the aftermath of World War I, which had witnessed a flurry of union activity, the defeat of labor activism often meant a return to the nepotism and arbitrariness of foremen, both of which were clearly visible in the labor struggles that followed the adoption of the NIRA in 1933, particularly in the steel industry.[13]

In mass-production industries, however, the foremen's fairly brutal methods could not really obtain. Foremen did retain a vital importance in the Fordist environment—while the techniques of work rationalization and control developed by Taylor and Ford engineers had curbed their prerogatives, foremen were also, paradoxically, expected to be the very *agents* of the process of rationalization on the shop floor, that is, they were to "get out production." Yet there was strong resistance to these new managerial practices in the serried ranks of semiskilled operators who now labored in factories. As a result, top managers in large corporations such as Ford Motor Company and efficiency-minded economists such as Paul H. Douglas came very early on to see discipline and the handling of labor as the fulcrum of the new industrial system (tellingly, Ford even extended supervision to leisure time).[14]

This problem led Ford to create the $5 day—which gave workers a higher than market wage—and management consultants to suggest schemes of employee involvement, but it also led top managers to put a premium on the reconstruction of the foreman as a loyal manager. Indeed, if the Fordist system largely rested on the agreement of workers to the new mode of production, then foremen were to be firmly associated with management, that is, they were to be able to take the side of management and defend its policies when workers challenged them. This was particularly important because in the modern manufacturing system, the ratio of foremen to workers had largely increased. In 1938, at Packard there were 313 first-line supervisors for 8,200 workers, a ratio of one to twenty-six. At Ford, the ratio had gone from one to fifty-three to one to fifteen.[15]

The concern for efficiency thus led engineers and top managers to reckon with the despotic methods of foremen, and in the postwar era foremanship was reconstructed as a managerial activity, namely, supervision, that could be learned and practiced—notably, foremen were to be instructed in more democratic and scientific methods of management.[16] The movement started with the creation of foremen's clubs, which held management workshops, but it soon evolved into a more structured form. Foremen's training programs and then foremen's schools flourished in American companies in the 1920s and 1930s. The idea underwriting these programs was that while foremen's prerogatives had been diminished, to be effective leaders foremen should be conversant with the methodologies employed by middle managers to establish production schedules, calculate costs, and compensate workers. They were also increasingly expected to understand safety procedures. Finally, foremen were expected to be personnel managers of their own—to "get out production" in the most efficient way, they were supposed to be able to understand and motivate workers, which implied a basic training in the psychological techniques developed in the wake of Elton Mayo's research. Finally, with the arrival of the shop steward in his department, the foreman had to develop a keen understanding of the logic of labor law and more precisely of the impact of the labor contract on this work as supervisor.[17]

This evolution was obvious in the classes taught at the Foremen's School that Packard had set up in the early 1930s. The school was run by a manager who organized a series of conferences, choosing the topics with the industrial relations manager of the company. The conferences were held during working hours and were attended by groups of twenty-five foremen. The following list of conferences organized in 1939–1940 is illustrative of what had come to differentiate foremen from the workers they supervised, namely, educational credentials.

Interestingly, this list of classes reveals that at the same time, the organizational evolution of American companies had associated foremen much more closely to management. While in the former industrial system the main division had been between craftsmen and the laborers they directed, in the emerging mass-production system the division that structured social groups on the workplace was the one separating planning and supervising from doing.

What is most striking in this list of classes is that they were not simply designed at providing technical training through classes that had a professional-like flavor. Equally important was the exposition of the social meaning of foremanship. Conferences such as "Fundamentals in Business," "Management in Business," and "Men and Money in Business" ring like an in-house version of the efforts led at the time by corporate America to reestablish the legitimacy of capitalism in American society, while others dealt with values sustaining it, such as self-advancement, "Personal Improvement," and the work ethic "Getting a Full Day's Work" (taught in 1941). Finally, conferences such

Table 4.1. Conferences Taught at Packard in 1939–1940

• Distribution and Reading Aloud of the New Contract	• Organization—General
• Discussion of the Contract	• Principle—General Policies
• Fundamentals in Business	• Amendments to the Social Security Act
• Getting Along Better with People	• The Learning Process
• Safety Accident and Accident Prevention	• Deputizing
• Raw Materials in the Automotive Industry	• Speech Habits
• Taxation—Income and Public Welfare	• Foreman-Employee Relationships
• Men and Money in Business	• Understanding Problem Employees
• Management in Business	• Discipline
• Waste—General	• Developing Company Understanding
• Waste—Present and Future	• U.S. Constitution—Our Constitutional Rights
• Personal Improvement	• Morale
	• What It Takes to Be a Foreman
	• Increasing the Personal Efficiency of Executives and Foremen

Source: "Brief for Packard Motor Company," *Packard v. NLRB* Supreme Court case file, 1947 (330 U.S. 485), 10–12.

as "U.S. Constitution—Our Constitutional Rights" remind us of the contested debate over the meaning of Americanism and the American experiment that had developed in the 1930s. Obviously, Packard understood the need to have technically proficient foremen who would also be loyal purveyors of the values sustaining the conservative capitalist order top managers and executives had defended throughout the New Deal—foremen were to be capitalism's noncommissioned officers.[18]

This construction of the foreman as a conservative man loyal and faithful to the organization employing him went along with the activities of the National Association of Foremen (NAF). Modeled after professional societies, the NAF was created in 1918 with the support of the National Association of Manufacturers to give foremen a patina of social respectability.[19] As foremen were usually recruited from the ranks of skilled workers, NAF actions emphasized self-advancement and highlighted the social mobility that foremanship afforded any worker who was willing to learn and use his qualities. It published a monthly journal, *Foremen's Magazine*, where articles on success, character, faith, and individual ambition abounded.[20] To promote the idea that foremen were the proud depositories of a specific know-how, the NAF also organized classes and lecture tours to reinforce the links between foremen and managers and foster a sense of identity among foremen. Key to its efforts was the propagation of the idea that foremen were an integral part of management, and that foremanship was incompatible with the logic of unionism. The main purpose of the foreman, the president of the NAF thus explained in 1927, is to "enable the securing of profit in industry"—a point of view echoed in *Foremen's Magazine* that same year: "The Foreman's job is economic, he must make a profit," a general manager in a machine company explained.[21] The NAF was largely dominated by conservative company executives, but even enlightened corporate managers such as Cyrus Ching and labor economists such as Don Lescohier believed that the foreman's legitimate place in the labor relations system was with management. With adequate training, Ching and others argued, the foreman could contribute to the emergence of peaceful "employer-employee" relations.[22]

At Packard, this construction of the foreman as a manager found echoes in several symbolical markers that emphasized the difference between foremen and the rank and file with whom they interacted and worked all day long. Unlike workers, first-line supervisors did not have to change clothes when they arrived at the factory and were allowed to wear street clothes. Except for those who bore the title of "assistant foreman," they were placed on salary

rolls, which brought them together with office employees and top management. A directory listing their names and positions was on display on the
walls in every part of the huge Packard complex, a sign of individual existence and achievement in an environment that literally produced the working
class by bringing hundreds of workers together every day. They usually had
an office on the factory floor and could count on a secretary to type out the
requests that they made to their superintendents when they wanted to make
changes in the work process, require additional help, or discipline a worker.

Finally, foremen were not subjected to the same factory discipline as blue-
collar workers—they could report to work late by as much as half an hour or
obtain a short leave of absence and still be compensated. They were entitled
to a one-week vacation after six months of work, whereas the workers had to
wait for one year. Last, they were given "separation pay" if they were let go.
Most important, these markers also pointed to important differences between
the workers and foremen: their employment was generally more regular and
stable. At Packard during slack periods, for example, when there was a model
change, the foremen were kept on the job or their vacations were scheduled
for that time and, most important, they took home a better paycheck.[23]

"Foremen are born, not made," explained a general superintendent of
General Electric at the end of the 1930s in *Foremen's Magazine*. The statement
was rhetorical, but in calling on foremen to discover in themselves the potential for leadership, James A. Smith sought to appeal to one of foremen's most
distinctive social traits, their Protestant religion. Indeed, to fully understand
the social meaning of the various class markers we have just pointed out, one
needs to remember that while foremen were overwhelmingly native born or
of older immigrant stock, they supervised a workforce that composed a mot-
ley social quilt. Indeed, it is no coincidence that the names of the leaders of
the UFS and the FAA all had an Anglo-Saxon or Northern European ring
(Bolds, Keys, Traen, Dwyer, etc.). Since the beginning of the century, the ethnic and religious gap that separated these Protestants from the Catholic immigrant workforce had been so wide that foremen kept themselves removed
from workers, culturally and socially.[24]

This combination of organizational and cultural forces resulted in a limited
definition of "employee" on the factory floor, one that, as we have seen, John
R. Commons accepted in his sociological and legal investigation of American
capitalism. For while the term "employee" was still used in conjunction with
all the hierarchical levels of a corporation (including white-collar employees, and managerial employees), when used alone, in the mass-production

environment, the very term "employees" bore the organizational imprint of Fordism and referred to blue-collar workers. Most important, such was its social and legal meaning in labor relations. For if we may return to the foremen's classes for a short moment, we can easily see that in the managerial logic of the company foremen were not part of employees in the mass-production environment. The conferences dealing with their relations to blue-collar workers are edifying in this respect: "Relations with Employees" (1943), "Understanding Problem Employees," "Foreman-Employee Relationships." That foremen were included in management was obvious in conferences such as "Developing Company Understanding" and "Increasing the Personal Efficiency of Executives and Foremen."

Notably, the codification of labor relations through the contracts that had been signed between unions and companies in the wake of the adoption of the Wagner Act in 1935 on the factory floor had further reified the foreman/ employee distinction. Thus, in the contract that the UAW signed in 1937 with Packard, the union acknowledged the limits of its sociological terrain: "(d) The Union will not accept for membership direct representatives of the Management such as superintendents, foremen or supervisors in any class of labor, time study men, plant protection employees, confidential clerks and salaried employees."[25] In union parlance, this practice soon became known as "stipulating out," for in many contracts such as the one it signed with Packard, the UAW agreed to leave the white-collar world unorganized.[26]

The very logic of this division of the social world in American factories was authority—it was intimately linked to the managers' need for control, in that the superiority of managers over workers was essential in the mass-production system. Yet by the 1940s, these categories had been so entrenched that they actually provided the conceptual bounds of the debate over the social organization of capitalism. Thus Fritz Roethlisberger, a sociologist who had assisted Mayo at Hawthorne Works during his famous experiment, excoriated the scientific pretenses of Taylorism in his analysis of foremen's unionism, but like Commons, he did not question the very categories to which this logic had given rise:

> At the bottom of the organization are people who are called
> *employees*, who are in general merely supposed to conform to
> changes which they do not originate. . . . Directing them there is
> a group of *supervisors* who are again merely supposed to uphold
> the standards of performance and policies decided by other

groups . . . a group of *technical specialists* who are supposed to originate better ways and better standards through which the economic purpose can be secured and more effectively controlled by a group of *top management* men who in their *evaluation* of the workers' behavior assume that the major inducement they can offer to cooperate is financial.[27]

True to the ideas of pioneered by his mentor, Roethlisberger argued that managers erroneously believed that authority was to be wielded from the top down, through a hierarchical process that actually left no place for the sentiments and psychological needs of workers that the Hawthorne experiments had revealed.[28] This necessarily placed foremen in an impossible position— they might either seek to meet the expectations of top managers and expose themselves to an aggressive response on the shop floor, or try to secure the workers' cooperation and risk failing to meet these objectives. As a result, Roethlisberger argued, the foreman's loyalty tended to shift with the pressures that were brought on him, which could be explained by the fact that foremen were marginal to managerial circles and that many felt removed from them. Indeed, although they represented managers on the shop floor, they were totally excluded from the planning and decision making that characterized managerial work in modern factories, something that foremen would complain about throughout the 1940s.[29] In spite of the training they had received, foremen often entered into informal agreements with the workers and thus escaped the psychological difficulties of their marginal position.[30]

Yet the foremen's quest was not merely the stigma of a managerial pathology; theirs was a defection also endowed with logic, one that ultimately led to a reckoning with the social meaning of the category employee and pointedly showed that foremanship was indeed made, and could be remade.

Packard Foremen and Unionism

In point of fact, Packard Motor Company was an unlikely candidate to become the legal epicenter of a large-scale labor struggle. Created in 1900 in Ohio by James Ward and William Doud, Packard had none of the features that made companies such as General Motors, Ford, and Republic Steel the tuning forks of labor relations in America. At the beginning, the company represented barely 4 percent of a competitive market in which forty to fifty manufacturers produced some four thousand cars a year, and very early on investors pushed the company's top managers to move the company to Detroit, where expansion would be easier. There, Packard quickly came into its own as a high-end car manufacturer whose stylish cars were prized by Tsar Nicholas II, the shah of Iran, and many other people of means. Between 1906 and 1912, the Packard 30, priced at $4,000, sold more than nine thousand vehicles. Later on, when the hard times ushered in by the 1929 crash restricted the automobile market, the company decided it should expand its purchase on American consumers—capitalizing on its image, in 1935 it introduced the Junior Line, with cars that cost less than $1,000, a very successful move. Indeed, production moved from six thousand cars a year to fifty-two thousand. By the end of the 1930s, Packard employed over eight thousand workers in its factories on East Grand Boulevard.[31]

This rather secure economic standing explains why the foremen's collective movement did not arise at Packard. The spark was provided by an automobile parts maker, Kelsey Hayes Wheel Company, a seedbed of rank-and-file militancy where Eastern European production workers had displayed particular energy in claiming the economic citizenship now protected by the Wagner Act. In this pursuit they had benefited from the radical, socialist culture of a local union cadre composed of prounion foremen such as Clarence Bolds. Having witnessed the birth of West Side Local 174, Walter Reuther's original turf, some of these foremen endeavored to join the new UAW-CIO as early as February 1938, but the union rebuffed them. However, in November, when the company cut back on the compensation of its first-line supervisors and moved them from a salary to an hourly rate, Bolds and others decided they could not accept this 10 to 15 percent pay cut and needed to organize all the same. Kelsey Hayes was mostly trying to adapt to the economic downturn that affected the industry of that year, but its decision to target only supervisors stemmed from the commitments it had made to rank-and-file workers in the contract signed with the UAW, which forced the company to look higher in the hierarchy of its employees to find the flexibility it needed. Caught between the anvil and the hammer, the foremen decided to create a bargaining unit of their own in November, and in spite of CIO infighting over the foremen's status in labor relations, they found enough support from Adolph Germer and Homer Martin to obtain a CIO local international union (LIU) charter in December, namely, United Foremen and Supervisors LIU 918.[32]

The CIO charter had a notable impact on the fledgling local—very soon, all 150 supervisors at Kelsey Hayes were organized, and the local proceeded to expand in the Detroit area. By June 1939, it had close to one thousand members and had signed its first collective bargaining contract with Universal Cooler in Detroit. Bolds and his comrades were tirelessly canvassing the city and giving speeches to groups of foremen, and soon they had a foothold in some of the bigger companies of the city such as Ford, Chrysler, and Murray-Ecorse. Most important, the movement was starting to spread along the geographic ramifications of the automobile industry. In August 1939 the CIO agreed to grant a new charter, LIU 984, to a group of foremen at Electric Auto Lite in La Crosse, Wisconsin, who also staged the first foremen's strike—one that was indicative of some of the political, legal, and social dynamics of the foremen's movement even as it was a its incipient stage. The company refused to bargain with the foremen, but the rank-and-file workers—UAW members—decided not to cross the foremen's picket line. As a result, the company obliged the foremen with an informal agreement and a wage increase.[33] This social pressure was necessary because the Wagner Act made no mention of foremen—Section 7a applied to "employees"—and the NLRB, following the tenets of industrial democracy as developed in Wisconsin by Commons and his students, had always believed them to be associated with management. Doing so, it was able to find that employers committed an unfair labor practice if foremen impeded organization drives.

No such solidarity between workers and foremen occurred at Packard, however. The group of foremen who began stirring toward unionism in 1939 was rather small—about 15 men out of the 340 first-line supervisors employed by the company—which shows that to many foremen, it remained at least unclear whether joining a union was the best way to improve their working conditions. But the company took a firm stand all the same and either demoted them to production work or encouraged them to leave. The cases of Thomas Dwyer and James Beyerley, two veteran supervisors, are illustrative: one month after he joined the UFS, Dwyer was called into the office of his superintendent and told he would have to take a pay cut from $260 a week to $200. Dwyer refused and tried to get a job through the Employment Department of the company but had to struggle for forty-five days before he was given one. Beyerley, a former arc welder, was given a job as an hourly production worker.[34]

Packard was not alone in adamantly opposing the UFS. In November 1939, as the UAW was working to translate the benefits of a long and bitter strike at Chrysler into a collective bargaining contract, Dodge Company fired several dozen foremen who had joined the UFS. The foremen petitioned the NLRB, arguing that the company had committed an unfair labor practice. When the board officially accepted to hear their case, the foremen's movement made the headlines, with Chrysler accusing the UAW of violating the principles of collective bargaining by trying to "sit on both sides of the table." Soon, it appeared to CIO leaders that the foremen's local was a liability to the UAW, and in August 1940 the decision was taken to disband it.[35] The AFL's comparative hospitality to the foremen's culture had not been passed on to the new confederation that its most militant cadre had helped to build. In fact, with a few exceptions, foremen and CIO workers would never make common cause.

The lack of CIO support notwithstanding, two years later, in October 1942, a group of Packard foremen created the fifth chapter of a new union, the Foremen's Association of America (FAA). The development of the FAA was largely reminiscent of the tentative rise of the UFS—unlike CIO unions, both were built from the bottom up with little funding and very limited organizational capacity. The FAA originated in the creation of a "fellowship club" in August 1941 at the Ford River Rouge Plant, where many foremen were wary of the impact that the company's recognition of the UAW breakthrough would have on their own position in the company. Although it was at first limited to the foremen of the Aircraft Building, the success of the club was such that it was easily transformed into a bona fide union in November 1941, with over twelve hundred members.[36]

The FAA's road to viability was equally rocky at first—Ford managers had no intention to bargain with the FAA and dismissed 170 foremen in May 1942 to thwart the growing union. By that time, however, the FAA represented 3,700 out of the company's 18,000 first-line supervisors and threatened to stage a strike if the men were not promptly reinstated. In November, the company gave in, granting its supervisors a 15 percent increase and creating a Foremen's Personnel Office to handle the grievances arising from what it still adamantly considered to be the lower rungs of its managerial hierarchy. By then, the FAA was developing at a very fast clip and had gained a foothold in many of Detroit's bigger companies such as Briggs and Chrysler. The case of Packard foremen was illustrative of this impressive rise—while the UFS had only made a very limited inroad at Packard, the FAA could count on the support of most first-line supervisors when the chapter was created, so much so that it was confident enough to ask the company to agree to an official NLRB election. Held in February 1943, the election was a ringing victory, with only 2 foremen voting against the FAA and 486 casting their vote in favor of it.[37] Two months later, the FAA was poised to present twenty similar petitions to the NLRB, a sign of the quickening pace of its development.[38]

Packard's decision to agree to an election, even one that had to be held outside the premises of the company in city voting booths, reflected the changing social and political context in which foremen made their claims to collective independence. Like many Detroit concerns, Packard had shifted to war production in 1939, when it started producing the marine engines that were mounted on American PT (patrol) boats. In addition, in 1940, Packard workers began work on Rolls-Royce engines, which were used on a number of American, British, and Canadian war planes. The first marine engine was built early in 1940, but the company could produce them serially only in 1942. Indeed, aircraft engines required small-batch production and skilled workers, which meant that untrained semiskilled workers could be employed in this process only if provided with machine tools, dies, and jigs that took a long time to produce. Catering to the military's cost-plus orders was difficult enough for the company to decide that it needed to stabilize its relationships with first-line supervisors. Indeed such was the logic that led Ford to negotiate, if not to officially bargain, with the FAA.[39]

In addition, the institutional ground had shifted in June 1942 when the NLRB handed down its decision in the *Union Collieries* case, which involved the bargaining rights of foremen in the mining industry, the other seedbed of foremen's unionism. Taking stock of the growing unrest among supervisors, the NLRB ruled that foremen were "employees" with full bargaining rights protected by the Wagner Act.[40] The case had a strong impact on the unionization of mining foremen, which had been somewhat hesitant, leading the United Mine Workers to affiliate the heretofore independent Mine Officials Union of America (MOUA). In point of fact, this NLRB policy was to be short-lived—in May 1943, the nomination of a new member at the board led to a reversal in the *Maryland Drydock* case. This latter ruling helped C. E. Wilson, GM's chief executive, to avoid an election involving over four hundred foremen, but it did not thwart the development of the FAA, for the 1942 ruling in *Union Collieries* was influential enough to encourage foremen throughout the country to begin stirring toward organization. Indeed, as 1944 dawned, foremen's unionism was no longer limited to the automobile industry—the FAA was making quiet but important inroads in the rubber, steel, aircraft, oil, and aluminum industries.[41]

Yet there was something paradoxical in the FAA's rise, as its ability to recruit an ever larger number of members was rarely translated into collective bargaining contracts. Except for the official agreements reached with United Stove and Ford in 1944, the FAA was unable to obtain recognition from corporate managers. Packard embodied corporate America's opposition to the FAA. Following the consent election won by the FAA, the company refused to bargain with the FAA because it sought to represent general foremen, who headed departments. After the NLRB's decision in May 1943 in *Maryland Drydock*—which took foremen out of the purview of the Wagner Act—the company had no incentive to acknowledge the legitimacy of the FAA, and Packard managers were content with suggesting that should the Packard chapter disaffiliate from the FAA, bargaining would become possible. When irate foremen struck for three consecutive Sundays in October, the company went as far as setting up a representation scheme whereby one foreman was designated to present any foreman grievance to members of management, who also pledged to communicate with the foremen through this representative. But no bona fide collective bargaining was in order.[42]

By the end of 1943, the FAA thus found itself in a difficult position—its raison d'être was the quest for a measure of collective independence, but such independence could accrue only from collective bargaining agreements. The lack of contracts did not mean that the union was powerless; indeed, its strength lay partly in the indirect influence it exercised over foremen's working conditions. Thus the FAA prided itself on having pushed Packard managers to grant foremen some wage increases, overtime pay, and better vacation pay. At many other concerns such as Hudson and U.S. Rubber, the union obtained similar results. Considering the cultural forces weighing against foremen's unionism in the mass-production industries, however, such results were meager and might have placed the organization on the road to oblivion as much as on the road to social respectability.[43]

Underlying the FAA's predicament was the fact that since the New Deal labor relations had been fully institutionalized, turning the notion of "employee" into a legal category carrying enormous weight in the ability of men and women to fight successful collective struggles at work. Faced with adamant and bitter opposition from corporate managers, the FAA could not expect to enhance its strength in factories as long as the federal agencies dealing with labor relations refused to admit the legitimacy of foremen's labor struggles. This meant that foremen needed to persuade the NLRB that they should be classified as "employees" or, alternatively, to push the National War Labor Board (NWLB) into categorizing foremen's strikes as "labor disputes" within the meaning of the War Labor Act of 1942. Since neither recognition was forthcoming, the only way for the FAA to challenge these sociolegal norms was to resort to strikes, even though there was less legitimacy in those collective actions during the war than at any moment in peacetime. But the FAA, after all, had never been asked to sign a no-strike pledge—ironically, such a pledge was a measure of success for CIO unions. Historians have largely documented the negative effects of this pledge on militancy, but by 1944 the FAA precisely needed the official, legal legitimacy that New Deal policies had bestowed on CIO unions. Lacking this official sanction, the FAA had to be content with publishing "We Don't Want to Strike" notices in newspapers.[44]

The FAA thus entered the political and institutional arena by challenging the social consensus that underwrote the war effort. Starting in July 1943, when six hundred foremen walked away from their jobs at Murray Ecorse in Detroit, tensions simmered and production was often hampered even if workers did not refuse to cross the foremen's picket lines or to work without supervision (which was often the case). In May 1944, the FAA shifted gears by organizing a twenty-day walk out at six different concerns with thirty-three hundred foremen participating. At Packard, more than nine hundred foremen were on strike, but the company still refused to bargain with the FAA. The cost of these "showdown strikes" was immense, with almost seven hundred thousand man-days lost. Moreover, Packard became the first indirect victim of the strike, as Military Procurement Officials announced on May 13, 1944, that they would not accept products manufactured without supervision, leaving the workers of the company idle for several days.

The strikes generated a large-scale controversy, and a bevy of proposals ranging from "work or fight" orders to legislation prohibiting foremen's unionism, but the FAA had made its point. By the end of May, as the *New York Times* explained, it had forced the foremen's issue in the political scene. At the end of 1944, the NLRB accepted a petition from the FAA in the matter of Packard, and the NWLB was conducting extensive hearings on the foremen's issue. Meanwhile, the union kept growing, and counted over thirty-two thousand members in 1945 as the war's end drew near. The NLRB and the Supreme Court yet had to pass final judgment on the meaning of the term "employee," but foremen's unionism seemed to be established.[45]

By the mid-1940s, it was obvious to many observers that notwithstanding the efforts led by the NAF and other associations promoting supervision as a managerial activity, many of its practitioners did not feel as if they fully belonged to the managerial world. "The Foreman Abdicates," *Fortune* explained in 1945, while the *New Republic* explained that the "Foreman Goes Union." By that time, the notion of defection dominated explanations of the growing foremen's movement. In an account of the movement ending with a bit of corrosive wit, *Factory Management and Maintenance* argued that unless management took drastic steps to keep its foremen, "some of them will be singing 'Solidarity Forever.'"[46] Yet such fears spoke less to the political meaning of the foremen's movement than to the essential role they played in mass-production industries: more than anything else, the FAA introduced a disjunction between the technology of managerial practices and the culture sustaining them.

The Logic of Exit

The efforts made by corporate managers to construct first-line supervisors as managers in the 1920s and the 1930s were certainly not exerted to no avail, but their effects were blunted by the reformist impulse of the New Deal and the logic of social citizenship that laws such as the Wagner Act purveyed. Insecurity and instability came to characterize the social position of foremen, who increasingly saw themselves as the "forgotten men of industry," and the particular context of the war provided them with a choice and an alternative to the identity that corporate leaders had been seeking to bestow upon them.

In a booklet providing practical guidelines to the growing number of shop stewards, the UAW explained in 1940 that they should stand firm with the front line of management, for "with the coming of the Union, the foreman finds his whole world turned upside down. His small dictatorship has been overthrown, and he must be adjusted to a democratic shop government."[47] Indeed, in many ways foremen had been the very target of the project to democratize American factories since the Progressive Era, when reformers such as William Leiserson had traced the outlines of an "industrial jurisprudence" whereby factories would be run. Many of the rules that were thus adopted further eroded the authority of the foreman, but even when they did not do so, he found that he could execute them only by interacting with the shop steward.

Richard Bone, a foreman with Packard, acknowledged the extent to which the arrival of the shop steward had ground down his authority: "There is never a move I make in the department that the steward doesn't know it. We talk things over, seniority, raises, movement of men. If the night shift is short of a man, he even allows me to put an extra man in there, running, say, three men on two machines."[48] Indeed, in a context in which every job was listed in a classification and given a specific price, there was little the foreman could do to redistribute his men around the shop without the steward's approval. Very often, however, this interaction was difficult. Foremen had to contend with the workers' recurrent complaints that the line was too fast or that they were underhanded to carry the job. In response, however, a foreman could only show the steward the "route sheet" he had been provided, and which he was merely trying to follow. Adding to this friction was the constant absenteeism of many workers, which foremen deemed to be their biggest problem. The contract that the company had signed with the UAW allowed workers to take up to three days off without warning their foreman. Workers were also allowed by contract to request a pass to go home early if the steward agreed, and the foremen's authority in such cases was so limited that they routinely issued up to twelve passes every day. Hence conflicts between foremen and time-study engineers recurred, with the former accusing the latter of being oblivious to their manpower difficulties.[49]

In reducing or opposing the authority of foremen on the shop floor, shop stewards inevitably challenged their fragile social identity as managers. Top managers, moreover, compounded their difficulties by issuing troublemaking orders to test the militancy of the workers. When the orders were resisted, managers were not reluctant to fire a foreman or two to emphasize that the mistake was theirs. This no doubt cut against the grain of managerial unity, and first-line supervisors felt even more stranded from the true managerial circles in their dealing of grievances. Not only were they excluded from the negotiations of collective bargaining agreements, but unless they were able to solve a grievance informally with the steward, each complaint triggered a grievance procedure involving the Labor Relations Department, one that did not involve the foremen and often ended with rulings that were the opposite of the position they had defended.[50]

We would be mistaken, however, to see the foremen's response to this "industrial jurisprudence" only through the lens of their decreasing authority and prestige on the shop floor. Most important, foremen witnessed every day the benefits that workers derived from the communal logic of unionism and the importance seniority had acquired in their lives. For now the process whereby workers were demoted, discharged, and promoted to better-paying jobs followed closely the requirements of seniority, giving workers a sense of entitlement that foremen sorely lacked. Thus Prosper Traen tried several times to promote a worker endowed with skills he deemed superior, to no avail. Even the utility man, who was expected to be an all-around worker able to help with minor technical problems, was chosen on a seniority basis.[51]

By contrast, theirs was a more fragile situation. As Robert Turnbull explained, "My idea of a union is to see that a fair standard of wages is provided." Indeed Packard foremen grievously lamented over their compensation system, which ensured no status. While many foremen, like white-collar employees, were on salary, their compensation ranged from $250 per month for assistant foremen to $300 for foremen, although there was no tangible difference in the work they performed. Compounding this lack of uniformity, some assistant foremen were on an hourly rate, which barely put their earnings above of those of the workers they supervised, who received overtime pay. In some companies, workers refused to take orders from supervisors who did not make more money than they did.[52] Finally foremen protested against their rates of pay, which were not commensurate with the hours they spent on the shop floor on weekends.

At Packard, foremen further complained that there was no rule governing promotions or demotions, which were decided by top managers alone. Unlike rank-and-file workers, foremen could not expect to be notified by managers about the reasons of their change in status. This was particularly irksome to them because it was common for managers to decide to put foremen on an hourly rate when production slackened, which made it easy to temporarily let them go. By 1944, as the war's end drew nearer, fear of such demotions prevailed among them.

The spread of unionism throughout American factories thus indirectly highlighted the infirmity of foremen's position in industry and their limited cultural authority.[53] Ernest Gordon summed up the problem rather well: "When I ask for a raise all I can get is another alibi every time. The best one was when there was talk going around the shop about the Foremen's Association. I was told that nothing could be done now, but that there would be a 'utopia' for foremen soon." Packard foremen typically complained that managers did not take their grievances seriously and refused to consider them, and by the late 1940s, Packard foremen had come to the conclusion that they needed a place where, as they put it, "redress," could be obtained.[54] In may 1944, a few days before they went on strike, they sent a letter to the industrial relations manager, a letter that reveals the extent to which they had accepted and integrated the idea that employment should provide a status governed by contract: "All the other employees of Packard Motor Company belong to organizations affiliated with the CIO and enjoy the privilege of collective bargaining, and the opportunity to protest against discrimination. They also have the opportunity to protest against unfair labor practices and the enforcement of unjust and unfair practices. All these things are denied to the petitioners in their present state of disorganization, and they are desirous of obtaining the same privileges."[55]

Notably, foremen interpreted this industrial jurisprudence through the political language that had animated much of the 1930s, namely, security.[56] To be sure, foremen had not participated in the social struggles that had shaped the political meaning of reconstruction of the country after the crisis, but the logic of security, although it had stirred the masses of workers into political action behind the banner of the Democratic Party, did not have a purely working-class cast making it appealing only to manual workers. Speaking on the radio to expose the objectives of the FAA, Robert H. Keys thus explained that the Wagner Act had been adopted to help the workingman "get an adequate wage, raise his standard of living, and gain for himself and his family a reasonable degree of security."[57] Indeed, the ideology of security was exposed by Franklin Roosevelt as an American project designed to retrieve the original design of the founders—the promotion of general welfare—and its very malleability had allowed companies to endorse it and try to harness its political potential. Thus, in 1936, Alvin McCauley, the president of Packard Company, had published an article in *Factory Management and Maintenance* claiming that the company could provide security through its paternalistic policies: "We work toward worker security," McCauley claimed.[58]

The ubiquitous nature of the language of security and the fact that it had been adopted by corporate America suggest why it was possible, in the 1930s and the 1940s, for first-line supervisors to resort to the very collective actions that they had been trained to fight for a long time. The association that the New Deal had created between security and unionization offered a framework within which the foremen could make sense of their situation. Tellingly, by the mid-1940s foremen defined unionism in those very terms. James Beyerley, who had joined the UFS union in 1938, explained that he had done so because "it looked like a pretty good organization so I joined it. I needed protection the same as anybody else," while Thomas Dwyer explained, "My meaning of unionism is security, is job protection and you cannot get away from it in my case."[59]

While the New Deal had produced an alternative to the individualistic ethos promoted by corporate America, it was actually the experience of mobilization that tipped the scales and allowed the rapid development of foremen's unions in the automobile industry. In this respect, one event largely symbolized their lack of representation to foremen: the company's decision to produce a company magazine, *Work to Win*, in order to shore up its workers' motivation to reach production goals. The magazine was created after managers met with representatives of the CIO, while foremen, although they were expected to reach those production goals on the lines they supervised, were totally left out of the process.[60]

The impact of the war on foremanship was particularly significant because of the intersection of two elements: the statist policies adopted to contain labor conflicts and the swelling ranks of first-line supervisors. In the wake of Pearl Harbor, as the United States started gearing up toward full-scale war, President Roosevelt issued Executive Order 9017 to create the National War Labor Board (NWLB), a tripartite body with members representing corporate America, labor, and the public interest. An obvious heir to the National War Labor Board created in 1918, the NWLB was charged with the mission to facilitate the war effort by preventing labor struggles while the NLRB continued to implement the Wagner Act. To that end, the NWLB conducted hearings and had the ability to dictate the contents of collective bargaining contracts.

The statist structure set up to mediate labor relations thus mirrored the traditional construction of the groups out of which American society was composed—workers, businessmen, and the general public. In this respect the absence of representatives of foremen's unions revealed the difficulties that lay ahead as they sought recognition. By contrast, the CIO and AFL derived important benefits from their contribution to labor peace. After Pearl Harbor, unions had agreed to a no-strike pledge, but had traded militancy for a policy of union security that allowed them to recruit a large amount of new members.[61] The unions' leverage on working conditions, however, was not totally neutralized by this trade-off—in July the NWLB announced an increase of 15 percent to make up for the inflation that had eroded workers' purchasing power since January 1, and in October Roosevelt issued EO 9240, which forced businesses with war contracts to pay workers overtime (i.e., time and a half pay) for all the hours worked during federal holidays and to grant them double pay for the work done on any seventh consecutive day.[62]

Thus, while workers were forced to put their militancy in abeyance during the war, the quest for security—even with unsatisfactory results—could be pursued through an interaction with the federal government. Except for foremen paid on an hourly rate, however, first-line supervisors did not gain the same benefits because they lacked representation in the NWLB. Indeed, foremen actually fell within the orbit of the Treasury Department's Stabilization

Unit, which did try to grant them a salary increase but apportioned it to their earnings. Foremen whose yearly income was below $2,400 received a 15 percent increase, 10 percent if they earned less than $4,000, and 5 percent if they earned less than $7,500.[63] The difference in the two schemes thus worked to create important discrepancies: in spite of the wage freeze, workers could increase their earnings thanks to the large amount of overtime work that mobilization required. By contrast, foremen's earnings were, indeed, frozen. At Packard, even hourly rated foremen were galled by the tiny difference separating their earnings from those of the men they supervised—an hourly rated foreman would receive between $1.30 and $1.50 an hour, while a job setter might receive $1.40 to $1.45.[64]

Most important, EO 9240, which created a temporary exemption to the Fair Labor Standards Act by giving workers overtime pay for the seventh consecutive work day, did not apply to salaried foremen, whom it defined as "managers." As a result, the discrepancy between the status accruing from a wage job and the one based on salary was obvious—hourly rated foremen received time and a half for work above forty hours a week, but the salaried foremen received overtime up to ten hours each week. In the same fashion, the Treasury's Salary Stabilization Unit rejected Packard's bid to pay its foremen a 5 percent increase for night work (equivalent to what the workers had received), agreeing only to a bonus of 5 cents. Clearly, mobilization had made the ability to claim the "employee" status even more crucial to first-line supervisors.[65]

Meanwhile, the war effort transformed the social landscape of American factories. Historians have largely documented the cultural and social consequences of the war on the American workforce. The war opened the gates of American factories to millions of African Americans and women who had until then been kept at bay from industrial jobs, paving the way for a new assessment of racial and gender roles in American society.[66] Notably, the same forces provided a large number of workers with an opportunity to move into the ranks of foremanship, workers who in many cases were beholden to the social culture of the new unionism. The history of foreman's unionism at Packard reveals the importance of this element in the rise of the FAA, as thirty-six of the forty-seven foremen who signed the request of certification by the FAA in October 1942 had been foremen only since 1941. One of them, E. Gordon, begged congressional investigators to "remember the foreman was once a soldier of labor. Let's give him a fair break."[67] In 1943, at General Motors, 42 percent of the nineteen thousand foremen had worked in that capacity for less than one year. The cultural meaning of foremanship was already in flux before the war, but the quickening rhythm of mobilization, by transferring thousands of workers across management lines, had replaced the slow pace of cultural change.[68]

Counteracting as it did the logic of industrial democracy and collective bargaining that had animated reformist circles since the early days of Progressivism, foremen's unionism was bound to raise interest in the social and organizational position of foremen. Chief among these commentators was C. Wright Mills, who a few years later took stock of the set of transmutations that had affected white-collar classes in America since the turn of the century and did not fail to remark on the changing status of the foreman, whom he referred to as the "managerial demiurge." Mills did not share the faith of human relations scholars such as Fritz Roethlisberger in the managerial system—even with a psychological spin on it—but rather lamented that the white-collar workers to whom he was devoting his attention exhibited none of the political awareness and political organization necessary for their maturation into a political movement. The politics of white-collar workers, Mills regretted, were those of the rearguard, as they were bound to follow either business or labor.[69]

The Meaning of a Voice

But Packard foremen, like tens of thousands of their fellow travelers, were no rearguard. Rather, they were at the front lines of a transnational movement that promised to shake the social classes on which Fordism rested. In France, for example, in the aftermath of the adoption of the Accord Matignon—the French Wagner Act—in 1936 the logic of unionism spread to the ranks of foremen and engineers, thus questioning the long-held idea that salaried workers who did not sell their manual labor could not claim the status of "employee." The Accord Matignon, it was thought, had been adopted for the *travailleurs*, that is, the working class.[70] French foremen and engineers were not necessarily intent on joining the ranks of the communist-led Confédération Générale des Travailleurs, but they were determined to be officially recognized as "salariés" (employees) nonetheless.[71]

The trajectory of Robert H. Keys, the president of the FAA, is largely illustrative of the common travails of American and French foremen. Keys was removed from the radical militancy of the men who had presided over the incubation of the UFS at Kelsey Hayes a few years earlier. A member of the

NAF, Keys was educated at Detroit's High School of Commerce and at the Ford Trade School. Trained in Ford's nonunion culture, he was hired at Ford as a machine operator in 1935 and was promoted to foremanship six months later, at a time when foremen were overwhelmingly agents of managers in the struggle against the insurgent UAW. When Ford signed a collective bargaining contract with the UAW in June 1941, it also granted a modest wage increase (65 cents) to foremen—obviously with the intent of lessening the impact of the arrival of the CIO in the citadel of antiunionism. Yet even to moderate men such as Keys, the lesson was unmistakable—the foremen had indirectly benefited from the CIO, gaining an increase they would not have gained by themselves. The logic of organization beckoned, and from then on the youthful Keys, who was twenty-nine years old, applied his skills and energy with brio, presiding over every minute aspect of the development of the organization while he juggled congressional testimonies, the publication of the *Supervisor*, and the promotion of the FAA in weekly radio broadcasts.[72]

But the man who stood at the origins of what top managers would soon call "industry's most pressing problem" preached a kind of neo-business unionism, and the most salient aspect of the foremen's movement and the way it was promoted is that on the whole foremen did not try to pass as workers joining the labor movement. Keys did offer a scathing criticism of the rugged individualism that still underwrote American businessmen's attitudes toward unions and welfare. But this critique did not stem from a growing proletarian consciousness. While foremen tried to act collectively on their subordination, their quest for collective independence first rested on the belief that any improvement in their employment would come with the ability to speak as a group. In what was a nascent industrial pluralism, Keys argued that the individualism that was still purveyed by managerial thought was a mere anachronism. In modern society, when individuals had lost all ability to influence their environment, collective action was inescapable, but foremen argued that their organization and motives were no different from those of bankers, dentists, or lawyers. "This is an age of collective pressure which in turn has resulted in the modern, acceptable methods of collective bargaining used in industry," Keys argued in one of his weekly radio broadcasts, echoing the declarations of members of the Packard chapter to members of Congress or the NLRB.[73]

Indeed, Packard foremen, along with the members of the FAA in general, strove to be identified as an objective, intermediate social category between management and labor, which they referred to as *supervision*. Emphasizing its independence was certainly a wise policy for an association accused by businessmen of being a CIO stooge, but the phrase also included an organizational and social endeavor, the importance of which has gone unheeded, and which was encapsulated in the association's motto, "leadership, fidelity." First, organized foremen strove to demonstrate that leadership was not a quality inherent in successful businessmen, but a specific *know-how* that combined a working knowledge of mechanical engineering and an understanding of the human dimension of work on the assembly line. Criticizing Taylorism and its defenders for their inadequate understanding of worker's motives, Keys called for the creation of tripartite factory boards including labor, management, and supervision and repeatedly explained that only the recognition of supervision as a technical activity would make it possible to reach the production levels required to win the war. Squaring the movement that he led with the Americanism inherent in the participation in the war effort, Keys argued that foremen were essential to the arsenal of democracy precisely because they had no stakes in the labor-management struggle—their raison d'être was the increase in production, not the battle over profits and conditions of labor.[74]

In that sense, the organized foremen's movement was clearly a legacy of the new foremanship that had emerged in the 1920s. Tellingly, key members of the FAA such as Clarence Bolds, who had originated the movement at Kelsey Hayes, had previously belonged to the NAF. Neither Keys nor Packard foremen, however, could have spoken on behalf of supervision if the phrase had been only a rhetorical construction—it also reflected a shared experience in the factories in which foremen had organized. As Theodore Bonaventura explained, the FAA generated an important sense of belonging. Foremen called themselves "Brother"; they read a journal—*The Supervisor*—that was full of pictures and anecdotes that fostered their sense of identity; and the various chapter leaders organized picnics, talks, and other events that bestowed a broader social dimension on the foremen's struggle for status. Furthermore, the FAA nurtured a social bond that had put an end to the foremen's individualism—an evolution reflected in the motto "fidelity." While rivalries between foremen had been very common in mass-production industries, now a spirit of cooperation suffused relationships among foremen, which meant that dealing with technical or manpower problems was much easier.[75]

Most important, then, foremen could simultaneously embrace collective bargaining and reject the larger political principles of unionism, that is, the idea that the working class should come together to push for social and political change. Prosper Traen, the leader of the Packard chapter, exemplified this avowed political moderation. Indeed, Traen had not been part of the small cohort that had joined the UFS in 1939. A native of Belgium, Traen immigrated to the United States in 1913 and worked in Illinois coal mines before hiring on at Packard as an assembler in 1926. Promoted to foreman in 1932, Traen supervised chassis assembly when the UFS was created, but declined to join. Like James R. Wilkins and other veteran foremen, his was a concern for security that could be expressed only through a union that remained independent from the rank and file, a concern that had grown more acute with the war effort in the production needs it generated. Pointedly, Traen referred to the FAA as "a labor movement, just like any other labor movement."[76] Like the engineers who, in the words of the American Association of Engineers, wanted to enjoy the protection of the Wagner Act but were intent on avoiding "the amalgamation of the professions in a 'labor front,'" Packard foremen and their fellow FAA members claimed that theirs were by no means radical motives. Indeed, they pithily claimed the right to organize for the purposes of collective bargaining not because this right was theirs as members of the working class, but because it accrued to *employees*. The nineteenth-century origins of the term thus had a strong echo—because "employee" was devoid of radical political connotations, it enabled the FAA to claim a white-collar right to organize and formally question the link between unionism and class. "Who is an employee anyhow?" Keys asked. "Isn't he a man who works for wages or salary in the service of an employer, just as the dictionary defines the word?" Notably, mine supervisors, in the first legal cases stemming from their movement, offered a similar justification, saying that the Wagner Act applied to "employees," not "workers," and was therefore more inclusive.[77]

The FAA defined management as the process of formulating policies: since their duty was only to carry out the managers' orders, supervisors were indeed "employees." While this legal reasoning was plausible, it nevertheless cut against the grain of the history of the progressive quest for industrial harmony and the tenets of the sociology developed in Wisconsin. As we have seen in the previous chapter, in the minds of reformers the right to organize was first and foremost linked to the subordination of blue-collar workers providing their brawn. Not only did the FAA come to contradict this logic with the idea that the recognition of the existence of *supervision* was essential to the success of industrial democracy, but to justify the union rights of supervisors they had started shifting the terms of the debate. In the end, the FAA argued, foremen should not be deprived of the right to organize because they enjoyed it as citizens. Ultimately, their quest was one for the full enjoyment of the privileges and liberties protected by the Constitution—free speech and free assembly foremost among them.[78]

This claim is not surprising if one remembers that many workers interpreted the Wagner Act in the very same terms. It also reflected the growing appeal of the language of rights in a political context dominated by conservative attempts to grind down labor unions' influence in the American political economy. Tellingly, the bills explicitly depriving foremen of bargaining rights that were debated in Congress as of 1943 were only part of a larger assault that was most active in southern states, where labor laws were being whittled down one by one. Yet in seeking a constitutional justification for their definition of employee, foremen tacitly admitted that the weight of values and assumptions that underwrote the definition of the worker in labor relations was a formidable obstacle.

The Fight for Loyalty

The contract that the FAA signed with Ford Motor Company in 1944 came as an early crowning glory substantiating the theory that the foremen's movement was a viable one. However, Ford's decision to come to terms with his foremen's new collective persuasion was by no means indicative of the way corporate America intended to deal with the FAA and other supervisory unions. Whether they were directly affected by the growing unionization drive or not, on the whole executives and top managers in large companies responded to it with utmost anxiety and a forceful determination to preserve both the power and the identity of management as a social and cultural group. Indeed, the movement was spearheaded by C. E. Wilson, although the FAA had had far less success at GM than at other places. Moreover, the briefs filed by companies like Packard or Chrysler, the testimonies brought in Congress, and the pamphlets published to blunt the growing appeal of foremen's unions reveal a significant degree of cooperation: the evidence cited in exhibits, such as local union journal articles and specific events during local strikes, was often the same. Ironically, it was through an obvious association and group logic that the automobile industries and the mining industries were defending individualism in Washington. The irony notwithstanding, it was at their behest that Congress began considering the Smith Bill in 1943, which purported to explicitly limit the sociology of the category "employee" to blue-collar workers.[79]

Packard's brief in the NLRB case that grew out of the company's refusal to bargain with the FAA exemplified this strong resistance and the arguments on which it rested. First, the brief denied that the term "employee" in Section 2(2) of the Wagner Act might be construed as covering foremen, and reaffirmed the idea that only two social groups existed in the factory system: "Historically there has always been management and workers," the brief stated. "The persons in the Management group are the 'employers' and the persons in the worker group are the 'employees.'" Pointedly, the company's lawyers argued that the words "worker" and "employee" were both used in the language of the law, particularly in the statement of policy, and that the social and political history of collective bargaining left no doubt as to the objective pursued by reformers. Wagner himself had defined his design as "the ideal of employers and workers meeting together with friendly and open minds." Nor did the rationale for the Wagner Act seem to offer any justification for an extensive definition of employee: how could a law adopted to improve the purchasing power of workers be construed as covering those who did not need it?[80] Packard managers were certainly not so naive as to think that this call for original intent would be enough to sway the NLRB. The board had decided once in favor of foremen in the *Union Collieries* case in 1942, then had reversed itself, and might change its position again. Rather, managers cried foul because they hoped that Congress would support their restrictive interpretation of the term "employee."

Indeed, the foremen's strikes, along with the wildcat strikes in which manual workers engaged, nursed a conservative backlash that was to lead to the Taft-Hartley Act. As early as 1943, the more conservative membership in Congress and the increasing difficulties of the NLRB seemed to have reshaped the political landscape in a way that made it plausible to successfully oppose the redefinition of employee that the FAA and other supervisory associations were advocating. To that effect, during the congressional hearings held that year, CEOs and conservative lawyers such as Walter Gordon Merritt painted a bleak picture of constant turmoil should foremen be allowed to organize: they would either remain independent and feud with a rival organization or collaborate with them, and discipline would be lax and degenerate into a kind of "mob production." In either case confusion would dominate the industrial scene, and instead of winning the war, the United States would know a fate similar to "once free France."[81]

The argument that the fall of France in 1940 stemmed from the debilitating social reforms of the Front Populaire is indicative of the reactionary political outlook of the men who were most active in the struggle over the meaning of employee. Unlike the CEOs and top managers who contributed to the war tripartite boards—mostly members of the Business Council and the Council for Economic Development—men such as C. E. Wilson estimated that restoring managerial authority was most urgent, and they did so precisely because they were as yet unreconciled to the idea that unions were legitimate organizations within the walls of American enterprise. Thus, in 1943 the *Detroit Free Press* estimated that if the foremen were allowed to organize, then the "debate over the closed shop would be settled for good," a consequence to be avoided by all means. In the same fashion, the brief submitted by Packard reveals the animus that corporate America still directed at labor unions: "The first objective of union leaders is to engender and foster in the employees a feeling of unavoidable hostility against an employer. This is accomplished by unsupported accusations of unfair treatment, improper charges and is apparently based on the philosophy that an untruth or a series of untruths repeated often enough will finally be accepted as the truth."[82]

Such candor in a brief officially filed with a federal agency is indicative of the bitterness that then dominated managerial circles. In the case of Packard, as in most cases, this bitterness stemmed from the changes that mobilization had wrought on the shop floor. Not only had unions gained a secure foothold in American factories thanks to the Roosevelt administration and the NWLB, but they had managed to challenge managerial authority in many ways. What with the shortage of manpower and the ambitious U.S. production goals, companies such as Packard had found that they could not oppose workers' attempts to unilaterally improve and redefine their working conditions. Thus, although the collective bargaining contract provided that seniority would be the controlling factor for promotion or demotion only whenever two workers displayed similar merit and ability, the company had been forced to agree to make all promotions and demotions based on seniority. The UAW local insisted on participating in the setting up of production schedules, and workers in the naval section, where PT boats were made, refused to let time-study engineers perform their studies. In the plane section, where there was a surplus of workers, the steward had concluded an agreement with the foreman whereby when the daily production goal was reached, workers could play cards or simply rest. Summarizing corporate America's dismay, one manager estimated that "if any manager in this industry tells you that he has control of his plant he is a damn liar."[83] Notably, in 1944 Packard executives, like those of General Motors, had started an offensive against the UAW by trying to remove the most militant shop delegates and by demoting some workers to lower their wages. Top managers had been intent on using foremen in their struggle against unions before the war, hoping that they would peddle the manager's point of view and values on the shop floor, and they saw no reason to concede defeat on that front.[84]

Corporate managers thus believed that their leadership and authority on the shop floor would seriously be at risk if foremen were unionized—a fear that was compounded by John Lewis's decision to call a bitter strike in the spring of 1943 to obtain a wage increase and the inclusion of foremen in the United Mine Workers' contracts.[85] Considering the critical importance of foremen in the mass-production hierarchical scheme, their fears are hardly surprising. To be sure, the UAW could shut down a plant without the help of the FAA, but the prospect of cooperation between foremen and workers was alarming because it would enable workers to fully regain the independence they had lost to Taylorism, a point made by C. E. Wilson in April 1945, when the foremen's movement was at its apex:

> From our experience both before and during the war, we
> are certain that the accepted American method of spreading
> managerial authority and responsibility among foremen—so
> that management is in close, direct contact with comparatively
> small groups of workmen—is the best and only sound method
> of handling day to day relations with the thousands of employes
> engaged in modern mass production. Anything which would
> require a change in this set-up would interfere with employer-
> employe relations and with production.[86]

"Take away the foremen from us and we are lost," a businessman later explained.[87] In fact, although corporate America knew they had lost their battle for the ideological loyalty of the workers, they still expected deference to managerial prerogatives. In framing the issue of supervisory unionism in terms of discipline and control, what businessmen really suggested was that the Wagner Act had not superseded common-law principles such as the right to control the work, which harkened back to the colonial master and servant doctrine and remained at the heart of the legal definition of the employment relationship. As the legal scholar James Atleson has argued, from the late 1930s onward, businessmen pressed judges to hold that the status of Americans workers still remained subservient to imperatives of production and efficiency.[88] As early as 1943, the Smith Bill sought to inscribe these ideas in Selective Training Act:

> In the discharge of his obligations to the Government every contractor shall be responsible for achieving and maintaining maximum efficiency and continuity of operations. . . . He shall be responsible for acts of his executive, administrative, professional, or supervisory employees within the scope of their employment, and such employees shall not be eligible to membership in any labor organization engaging in collective bargaining the contractor, not shall such contractor be required to engage in collective bargaining with any labor organization including any of such employees in its membership.[89]

Moreover, in the case of foremen's unions, what this meant was that business-men had to reframe the link between the old doctrine of worker loyalty and the right to organize. Now they argued that loyalty and unionism were not in-compatible in the case of manual workers because these workers sold only their capacity to work and perform tasks that did not require the exercise of judg-ment. By contrast, foremen should not be allowed to join unions because of their role in the production process—maintaining discipline. Quoting the Bible, businessmen repeatedly argued that they could not dispense with the foremen's full loyalty because "a man can't serve two masters": "A foreman, a supervisory employee should keep faith with his employer and not be on both sides of the fence. . . . There should be no twilight zone in this thing. A man cannot serve two masters. Let us provide that he shall be true to his trust, work for the people who hire him and to a specific job."[90] Such statements echoed the prescriptions of nineteenth century judges such as David Brewer who stood firm against the intrusion of unions in relations between employers and workers. The foremen's struggles revealed the tenacity of such ideas in the post–New Deal era.

The stakes inherent in the definition of the notion of employee thus become fully apparent—the cultural status of corporate America had seriously suffered as a result of the Great Depression. It was not lost on these men that organized foremen might be more receptive to ideas of planning, economic security, and other collective nostrums. In point of fact, Keys himself advocated economic planning in his weekly radio broadcasts in 1943. Indeed, debates over ques-tions of political economy in the 1930s and 1940s largely reflected a move away from the idea that businessmen and top managers could be trusted to oversee

the capitalistic system by themselves. Tellingly, such fears were given full air-
ing in the Packard brief, which argued that "the public will realize, late enough
perhaps, that the unionization of supervisors for collective bargaining purposes has given alarming impetus to the collectivization of industry now going
on." In Congress, C. E. Wilson, the head of General Motors, sounded the same
note when he asked the members of the House Military Affairs Committee,
"Where are you going to stop it? Are you going to have the whole country go
into a union and then have a Socialist State?"[91]

Over the same period, under the aegis of the budding modern presidency,
the federal government had largely extended its reach over the economy
through agencies such as the National Labor Relations Board and the National
Planning Resources Board, and this institutional development had proceeded
apace since Pearl Harbor as the government became involved in regulating
wages and prices. In that respect, the influence of Walter Reuther's proposals
for a corporate organization of the economy—even if they did not come to
fruition—and Franklin Delano Roosevelt's 1944 call for an "Economic Bill of
Rights" were indicative of the forces bearing against unmitigated freedom of
enterprise. Notably, corporate managers chafed at Roosevelt's Four Freedoms,
which left out Freedom of Enterprise, or, as General Motor's director of labor relations, Harry Coen, speaking at the annual meeting of the American Society of
Mechanical Engineers in November 1943 put it, "The Freedom of Opportunity
or perhaps it should be called the freedom of Individual Initiative."[92]

Anticipating Friedrich von Hayek's own definition of freedom as "freedom
from coercion," Coen exhorted his audience to see the foreman question as
one that involved the status of freedom in the United States:

> If the foreman is willing to trade his faith in his ability to get
> ahead on the basis of his own individual initiative for the lulling
> influence or the creeping paralysis of mass security on a lower
> standard of living, he does not have the stuff that it takes. It any
> part of management has softened up to the point of a willingness
> to trade mass action for the freedom of opportunity which is
> inherent in a free economy, it is high time that we face the issue
> and purge management of all such parasitical influences that
> would tend to weaken and destroy that kind of economy.[93]

Tellingly, the brief for Packard Motor Company in the NLRB Packard case
sounded the same cultural themes:

When the worker leaves the rank and file and becomes a
foreman he voluntarily casts his lot with management. He leaves
the collective bargaining group and as an individual joins and
becomes part of the management group. . . . If he wishes to trade
this opportunity to advance as an individual for the questionable
security of collective bargaining, he can do so by remaining with
the rank and file. . . . Those who have the desire to succeed, who
are willing to study and better themselves should not be held
down by those who do not have the desire or ability or the same
courage or energy.[94]

The struggle against foremen was thus a struggle for cultural hegemony.
What ultimately lay at the heart of the battle over foremen was top managers' drive to defend the symbolic values that had underwritten their own
rise to predominance—and power—since the end of the nineteenth century
and shaped the transition from a proprietary to a managerial capitalism. The
time was ripe for such an endeavor, as industry's contribution to the war effort had at least partly restored its image and now enabled it to reaffirm the
"American" principles of industrial management, that is, a line of authority
linking top executives to workers.[95] Most important, then, these managers
connected middle-class Protestant values such as hard work, moral courage,
and individualism with management in a business faith in a way that made it
impossible to conceive of *supervision* as a specific group whose own professional ethos would reconcile industrial leadership and the principle of collective bargaining. The American free enterprise system, they contended, rested
on the merit and individual achievement of managers seeking to climb the
ladder of self-advancement. Accordingly, they sincerely believed that competition among foremen was necessary to the free-enterprise system. Work
should define foremen according to their performances in comparison to
others. As for collective bargaining, it was fit only for those who had foregone
the freedom that the United States afforded them.[96]

What Industrial Harmony?

In a famous ruling handed down in 1953, the Supreme Court reminded
American workers that the goal of the national labor law, as expressed in
the Taft-Hartley Act, was to "strengthen cooperation, continuity of service
and cordial contractual relations between employer and employee that is

born of loyalty to their employer."[97] Indeed, Taft-Hartley was a clear victory for conservatives and businessmen, for the industrial harmony it pursued included a larger protection for management and the pursuit of economic imperatives. Most important, to that effect the Taft-Hartley Act also offered a statutory definition of "employees" that excluded foremen and supervisors from the Wagner Act and ensured their full loyalty to the employer. As had been the case since the beginning of the Progressive Era, the legal definition of the worker remained sociologically limited and subservient to a broader economic policy. Yet the exclusion of foremen from the Wagner Act was not a foregone conclusion. On the contrary, the supervisory exclusion was opposed by industrial pluralists sitting on the NLRB, who reinterpreted the main tenets of the social science pioneered by John R. Commons and defended a vision of societal harmony predicated on a broad right to organize accruing from employment in general. It is to their unsuccessful efforts that we now turn.

CHAPTER 5

The Other Side of Industrial Pluralism

SHALL I get down on my knees, or shall I bludgeon you to go over to the NLRB?" Franklin D. Roosevelt's blunt ultimatum to William Leiserson in October 1939 revealed his determination to send the seasoned labor arbitrator to the agency created by the Wagner Act four years earlier. Leiserson himself had no inclination to leave his post at the National Mediation Board, the agency in charge of the implementation of the 1925 Railway Labor Act. Trained under the supervision of John R. Commons in Wisconsin, he believed that his expertise lay in helping managers and workers reach compromises and live by the strict rules that collective bargaining contracts contained. "I give the decision to one side, but I give the language to the other side," he said of his work in the contested labor relations of the needle industry. Arbitrating disputes was not something he would be able to do at the NLRB, whose mission was only to promote the right to organize by developing a law of unfair labor practices. As Leiserson knew, the NLRB was the province of progressive jurists, many of whom had no background in industrial relations, and he would not be happy there.[1]

At fifty-six years old, Leiserson was older than many of the young, enthusiastic lawyers that the New Deal had channeled toward the nation's capital. He belonged to an earlier generation of Jewish immigrants who had carved a place for themselves in American society by pushing it to live up to its democratic ideals and its promise of upward mobility. The time when he earned a living by cooking flapjacks at a one-minute coffee shop on the campus of the University of Wisconsin was long gone, but Leiserson's faith in the progressive opposition to class antagonism had not weakened since his student days.

While he shared the liberals' faith that a large upward shift in workers' purchasing power could be effected by protecting unions—in fact he had often
agitated for it—he did not believe that societal harmony could be attained
simply by protecting the right to organize against recalcitrant employers.
Independent unions were indeed essential to comity, but comity required the
visible hand of an outside party, a hand Leiserson had exerted for the NIRA
and the petroleum field before moving on the National Labor Mediation
Board. Leiserson's reputation as a fair arbitrator was formidable, and it was
precisely his ability to make decisions while placating unhappy companies
that Roosevelt found appealing—as *Time* noted, the president wanted him to
go over the NLRB to "sweeten" its interpretation of the law.[2]

In 1939, the NLRB was going through an institutional crisis that threatened
to weaken the New Deal. A large part of public opinion, including liberal observers such as Walter Lippmann, believed the board was biased toward the
radicalism of the CIO and fostered class warfare instead of harmony. In fact,
the agency's difficulties mostly stemmed from its almost paradoxical mission:
created in the Progressive mold of administrative agencies, it was designed
to act in the public interest by promoting the right to organize. As it did so,
however, it came under increasing pressure from businessmen who, having
lost their constitutional struggle in 1937, now argued that the agency did not
promote the workers' freedom of choice, but worked in favor of unions. With
the general political climate becoming more conservative after the 1938 elections, fulfilling the NLRB's mission became a self-defeating approach. Faced
with conservative political pressure and a possible refusal of Congress to vote
the appropriations of the NLRB, FDR decided to appoint experienced but
moderate labor experts who would carry out the board's mission at a lower
key, a decision that hardly concealed his misgivings toward an agency it had
never wanted, let alone trusted—Roosevelt had never really accepted the
premise of the act, that sustaining the right to organize would help to deflect
class antagonism.[3]

Historians have seen in Leiserson's arrival at the board—and in the subsequent appointments of Harry Millis and Paul Herzog, two labor experts
equally steeped in the Wisconsin tradition—an important turning point in
the history of labor relations in the United States. According to the standard account, this "reshaping" of the NLRB ended the democratic impulse
of the New Deal as the board shed its bold defense of unionism. Millis and
Leiserson engineered a new jurisprudential course, restricting workers' rights
both at union elections and during the duration of the contracts. The quest

for social harmony came at the price of militancy, and as a result the sap was slowly drawn out of the labor movement, which later on found itself unable to fend off the conservative assault that depleted labor's ranks after the 1970s.[4]

While there is indeed much archival and legal evidence to buttress this argument, the way Leiserson, Millis, and later on Paul Herzog dealt with foremen's unions could help us to revise partly the standard account on industrial pluralism. Indeed, as they dealt with the definition of "employee" under the Wagner Act, the industrial pluralists who sat on the board cut directly against the grain of corporate America, its shrill defense of the "right to manage" and insistent demands on foremen's loyalty. To the pluralists, indeed, there was no fundamental contradiction between the labor of superintendence and union membership. Reassessing the main tenets of the economic sociology they had inherited from John R. Commons, they offered a capacious definition of "employee" that opened the door to the full democratization of American work across class lines, one that turned the Wagner Act right to organize into a civil right that every person employed should enjoy even as it served to promote social harmony through bargaining.

Combined with the social pressure exerted on the shop floor by Robert H. Keys of the FAA, the board's new definition of the worker under the Wagner Act thus offered a rare instance of an alliance between experts and civil society working together to redefine social norms.[5] However, the window of opportunity that was thus opened closed rapidly. In 1947 the foremen's struggle for a new social and legal identity ended when Taft-Hartley Act specifically excluded foremen and supervisors from the definition of "employee" and returned them to the ranks of management. For industrial pluralists, the victory of managerial loyalty over their vision of industrial harmony was a serious defeat, one that signaled their relative impotence in shaping new labor relations.

The Institutional Context

"When these cases reached the Board, we were not sure of what the right course of action was," William Leiserson recalled of the first foremen's cases after he had left the NLRB. "We had to feel our way." Indeed, it is fair to say that when the foremen of the Auto-Lite Company in Wisconsin, having secured their affiliation with the UFS-CIO, sent their first petition request in 1939, the board was largely caught by surprise.[6] Since the late nineteenth century, the ideal of industrial democracy and collective bargaining had revolved around the worker's dream of ending the foreman's petty dictatorship on the shop floor.[7] To effect the protection of the freedom to unionize contemplated by the act, the board had used very early on the legal doctrine of *respondeat superior*, which established the employer's liability for his employee's conduct. Because the board consistently ruled that when foremen committed an unfair labor practice by hindering unionization of workers, they did so as "agents" of the employer, businessmen were prevented from fighting a vicarious struggle against independent unions.[8]

This was made possible by the very definition of "employer" in the law, as Section 2(2) stipulated that "the term 'employer' includes a person acting in the interest of an employer, directly or indirectly." The legal definition of foremen as part of the social entity "employers" rather than workers (employees) was thus key to the development of industrial democracy, particularly in the automobile and the steel industry, where managers had long relied on foremen to oppose the democratization of the factory. As late as 1940, foremen at Ford were found pressuring workers to obtain letters in which they pledged that they were satisfied with their working conditions and earnings, and did not need a union.[9]

Yet at first corporate executives denied that foremen qualified as agents of "employers" in labor law. Indeed, it is a measure of corporate America's determination to exert its hegemony on American law that the first political debate on the status of foremen under the Wagner Act stemmed from their attempt to convince the members of Congress that the board erred in associating foremen and supervisors with "employers" and management. Against the board's rulings that any person in charge of maintaining discipline or production goals was not an "employee" when he or she expressed an opinion about labor relations, company executives argued that foremen did not have the power to hire and fire, and thus should not be assimilated with the managers included in the category "employer." In 1939 corporate America enlisted conservative members of Congress such as Fred Hartley to amend the law so as to shield themselves from the legal penalties accruing from foremen's antiunion activities—an odd historical irony since a few years later Hartley would spearhead the legislative drive to classify foremen as managers.[10] Along with their restrictive definition of "management," those amendments specified that foremen had the right to unionize, although they should not take part in the selection of shop stewards. No longer union busters, the foremen would now pass as workers debating the virtues of unionism. As the board noted in its report to the Senate, "These proposals are in direct conflict with the basic principles of the Act, they would ... result in nullification of the right of employees to freedom in self-organization and would lead to an increase in industrial warfare."[11] Congress followed the NLRB on this question, and the amendments to the NLRA were not adopted.

Having secured the legal classification of foremen and supervisors as "employers," the board thus found itself in a precarious position to respond to the request of the UFS and grant foremen the legal status of "employees." Indeed, the foremen's movement raised three thorny doctrinal questions. First, was whether recognizing the right of foremen to bargain collectively would give them a freedom of speech about unionism that might constitute a violation of the workers' right to choose without interference from the employer and the employer's agents. By wearing union buttons, for example, foremen might be seen as offering an influential opinion. Second, the board had to decide whether foremen should be allowed to join rank-and-file unions or rather should be allowed to join a union of their own. Finally, given the centrality of the foremen in the modern production system, the members of the board feared that if they sustained the right of foremen to bargain collectively, they would be accused of allowing rank-and-file unions to sit on both sides of the negotiating table, which seemed to contradict the basic principles of collective bargaining.[12]

Such questions were compounded by the thoroughly legalistic turn that labor relations had taken after the Wagner Act. As Christopher Tomlins has noted, the board had adopted court-like procedures from the beginning, and a legal discourse suffused its approach to all the cases with which it dealt. As its use of the concept of *respondeat superior* in unfair labor practice cases indicated, the board lawyers developed labor law as a set of coherent doctrines that made rights and duties predictable on both sides. As for labor disputes, they were *adjudicated* rather than mediated or studied. Each party was represented by a lawyer, who was free to summon witnesses and cross-examine the other party's witnesses to convince the commissioners.

This legal discourse was not necessarily well adapted to the rethinking of the parameters of industrial relations that foremen's unionism required. It forced the board to apprehend the foremen's question from an abstract standpoint instead of a case-by-case basis—which the pluralists would certainly have preferred. Furthermore, it gave any of its decisions on the definition of "employee" a jurisprudential, national dimension that exacerbated the political stakes involved in each matter involving foremen. However, the board was deprived of the means to buttress its decisions with material explaining how they related to its overall mission, which was to promote industrial peace and collective bargaining.[13] In fact, the board did have one structure designed to investigate and research the social and economic origins of labor disputes—the Economic Research Division, which was headed by Commons's student David Saposs—but it was eliminated by Congress in 1940 in response to the investigation of the board led by the Smith Committee during that year. A response to both business and AFL criticism of the board, the commission was created at the behest of a group of assertive southern Democrats and northern Republicans eager to amend the act and whittle away the protections it afforded. Putting a spotlight on potential links among the board, the CIO, and the Communist Party, the investigation easily made the headlines, and in the House of Representatives, its criticism of the board's decisions even resulted into a lopsided vote in favor of the amendments favored by the business community and the AFL, which wanted to check the growth of the CIO and did not benefit from the Wagner Act as much. Labor progressives held the line in the Senate, but the investigation was just a harbinger of the reactionary crusade to come.[14]

As a result, one may say that in the years 1939–1947, the time when the board consumed a significant part of its time dealing with the issue of foremen unions, this legal discourse was probably the board's strongest claim to political legitimacy. At the time, the agencies created during the New Deal were coming under intense legal scrutiny and political criticism because of their allegedly obscure and unfair procedures. In the increasingly tense international context of the late 1930s and early 1940s, with totalitarianism looming in the background, the idea that nonelected experts should be trusted with important policy-making responsibilities was increasingly challenged. Given the alleged presence of members of the Communist Party at the board, it received special criticism for "administrative absolutism."[15]

Still, events at Chrysler in the fall of 1939 revealed just how difficult handling the foremen's issue would be. The UAW was then in the midst of a struggle against Chrysler, which had taken advantage of the bitter factionalism opposing the UAW-AFL and the UAW-CIO to cancel its collective bargaining contracts with the union. Instead of negotiating, the company organized a speedup and laid off "slow workers." After the landslide victory of the UAW-CIO in September 1939, the union leadership called on the company to end the speedup, but the company countered that the union was using unauthorized committeemen to organize slowdowns. At Dodge Main, the company contended, these new shop stewards outnumbered foremen and directed the workers themselves. In October, when Chrysler fired some 105 Dodge Main shop stewards, the workers responded with "job skipping"— letting every second car go by unfinished—until the company simply closed the factory. After a forty-seven-day lockout, Chrysler gave in because it could not recruit enough strikebreakers to operate the plant. The shop stewards were reinstated, and the company agreed to negotiate production standards with the union.[16]

It was at that precise point, as the process of bargaining was about to start, that the UFS filed a fresh petition with the NLRB, this time to protest the decision by Dodge managers to lay off a number of foremen because of their membership in the union.[17] The company immediately argued for their "right to manage," and negotiations broke down over the foremen's issue. To Chrysler executives, this time alert to the possibility of a union of foremen, foremen's unionism would only reinforce the UAW's "dual power," which it considered as nothing short of an ongoing attempt to turn the factory into a soviet. The fear may have been exaggerated, but the company managed to force the issue into the main newspapers of the nation, accusing the union of violating the main tenets of collective bargaining. "Chrysler Asks CIO to End Bid to Foremen," the *New York Times* explained in 1939.[18]

Determined to hasten slowly on the question of the UFS-CIO, the board convened CIO leaders to discuss their views on the integration of foremen's unions in the collective bargaining landscape. But like the members of the board, they had no clear suggestions to offer, and in fact they were divided over the issue. Adolph Germer and Homer Martin—the first president of the UAW-CIO—had assisted the UFS in its quest for recognition by the CIO, but R. J. Thomas, the new president, opposed it, contending that foremen represented first and foremost a liability in negotiations, and a rather unfortunate one at the very moment when the CIO unions needed to sign important contracts.[19] As a result, the short-term goal of signing a contract with Chrysler prevailed. Seeking a way out of the impasse in which the foremen's issue had put it, the CIO and the UAW made the decision to disband the Local 918 of UFS. As John Brophy—John L. Lewis's CIO man—explained in a letter, "under the present circumstances, nothing more can be done about [this] group." The UAW went on to renew its contract with Chrysler, but the CIO had given a first glimpse of what its position on foremen's unions would be—while it did not oppose the labor rights of any group of workers, groups seeking to be included in the category "employee" for collective bargaining purposes would have to fight this battle on their own. For now, it was content with a legal definition of the worker that was rooted in manual factory work and did not directly challenge the authority of management. This was a policy it would be at great pains to reverse.[20]

As for the NLRB, it was in no position to adopt a policy that the CIO did not fully support and was not willing to defend. No doubt sensing that it was unwise to spend what political legitimacy it had left on such a controversial issue, it decided to decline to respond the petitions of the UFS.[21] As William Leiserson explained, "We decided that we would wait and see whether the foremen really wanted to organize, or whether the movement was only a mere flash in the pan." With no more than a thousand members, the UFS certainly was not worth an uphill political battle.[22]

Toward an Employment Democracy

The foremen's movement might have been deprived of the protection of the state, but it did not lie dormant for long. By 1941, it reemerged through the creation of two new unions: the Mine Officials Union of America (MOUA) and the Foremen's Association of America (FAA) in the automobile industry. By 1942, strikes had erupted in the mining industry, idling thousands of miners. Meanwhile, the growth of the FAA in the Detroit area was impressive— it had over ten thousand members by December 1942. Seeking to translate this new power into official recognition, in the spring of 1942 it submitted to Frank Bowen, the regional director in Detroit, a list of five thousand foremen at Ford who wanted to form a collective bargaining unit. As Henry Ford was willing to negotiate with the FAA, Bowen proceeded to suggest to the board that the time had come to start revising the NLRB's policy regarding foremen. At the same time, the NLRB was receiving petitions from unaffiliated foremen working in other industries, especially steel and aeronautics. Thus, by 1942, with economic mobilization in full swing, the social and political environment in which the NLRB determined the sociological boundaries of the legal definition of the worker in labor relations had been fundamentally transformed. Now there was no denying that foremen's unionism was developing and that a clarification of the foremen's status was in order—social strife made it possible to envision collective bargaining by foremen as being necessary to industrial harmony.[23]

The NLRB, however, did not follow Bowen's suggestion that Ford Motor Company might prove a good testing ground for a fresh definition of "employee," opting instead for the mining sector. Like the FAA, the MOUA grew out of the gap that New Deal legislation had created between rank-and-file workers and first-line supervision. The mine bosses were systematically excluded from the collective bargaining contracts signed by the United Mine Workers (UMW) after 1933, and they had felt the brunt of the depression of 1937–1938. At Ford Collieries, the bosses were shifted to the hourly wage in 1937, and they worked only an average of three days a week when the union was created, in December 1940. By 1941, however, demand for coal rose again because of the military support offered by the United States to its allies. Once again Ford Collieries changed the status of foremen, putting them back on a monthly salary and extending paid vacation and health benefits to them. Still, it refused to bargain with the union, which petitioned the board for an election in December 1941.[24]

By then, William Leiserson and Harry Millis had decided that the time had come to change course. In the *Union Collieries* decision in 1942, the board ruled that all assistant foremen, checkweighmen, and night bosses were "employees," with full bargaining rights, and that they should constitute a separate bargaining unit. Only general foremen (whom, importantly, the MOUA did not wish to include in the bargaining unit) were still classified as "employers." The reports filed by the field examiner and the regional director, who suggested this new definition, shed light on the rationale of the board's decision, which was deeply rooted in the workers' experience of the mine and the organization of work. None of the assistant foremen could hire or fire miners, and they did not take part in the grievance procedure protecting rank-and-file miners (this was the role of the general foreman). None of them had the responsibility to "get out production"—the assistant foremen enforced the general managers' assignment of a job to each worker; the fire boss was in charge of security, and the weigh boss assessed the amount of coal extracted. The coal inspector was in charge of quality. In fact, like the miners, these bosses were paid by the hour, and could be let go when demand slowed.

Moreover, the reports also revealed that the mine pit generated a spirit of camaraderie among miners and foremen, which separated this group from the general manager who never went down the mines. This camaraderie was based on shared experience—all the bosses had started out as miners—and was reinforced by the impervious need for security that all men felt. But the field examination also revealed that the mine was a social milieu in which men interacted in other ways, exchanging jokes and political opinions when they changed shifts. Finding against the company's attorney, who struggled to make his case that a sharp managerial line separated the workers from the bosses, the board adopted a definition of "employee" that ran deep roots in the social character of mine work.[25]

Other contextual elements sustained the board's decision to redraw the social contours of "employee." The company, although it refused to formally bargain with the union, had already met with union representatives and agreed to improve their status—hence there was some bargaining *before* the NLRB acted. The board's decision to intervene in this dispute could find further legitimacy in the fact that a strike by the union would idle some thirty thousand miners, for in Pennsylvania, as in all mining states, the law prohibited miners from going down the pit without supervision. The board could thus claim to be fulfilling its mission—promoting industrial peace.

Following a jurisprudential logic, four months later, the board sustained the bargaining rights of foremen in a case involving the Godchaux Sugar Company. Once again, it sidestepped in the automobile industry, but what mattered is that this time it went one step further in the protection extended to foremen. The board reasserted the idea that all foremen who did not have the power to hire and fire were "employees" and could form an independent bargaining unit, even though this time the foremen were members of the same union as the rank-and-file workers, namely, the United Sugar Workers–CIO.[26]

Unlike corporate America, Millis and Leiserson did not see foremen's unionism as being the key to the transformation of labor relations. As we have seen, one of the main tenets of the labor sociology they had inherited from Commons was the notion that there was not one class struggle, but myriad legal disputes between employers and workers that could be easily remedied by adopting institutions that produced peaceful labor relations. Still, by sanctioning a new definition of the term "employee," these industrial pluralists did break the link between "employee" and subordinated, manual labor that the theory of industrial democracy—particularly in the work of Commons—had established, and doing so, they laid the groundwork for a fundamental evolution of labor relations. Such a course of action requires some elaboration. If, as has been argued, by 1941 Millis and Leiserson had altered the course of the NLRB and redirected it in a more conservative direction, emphasizing not the rights of employees but industrial peace—one of the original goals of the Wagner Act—and "orderly" labor relations, how might we account for their decision to protect foremen's unionism?

First, Leiserson and Millis believed that labor relations must always be sui generis, that is, they did not conceive of collective bargaining as a process involving fixed social entities. Rather, they saw it as a means to resolve disputes between opposing groups, be they workers, foremen, or white-collar workers. As Leiserson explained, "Whether these foremen or any other group organize, or should organize, will not be determined by any theory that you or anyone else works out. It will be determined solely by the way the men in these groups feel." By the early 1940s, the board had received enough petitions from foremen in various industries to understand that the social and economic position of foremen had suffered since the recognition of CIO unions. Since the purpose of collective bargaining was to achieve social peace, it would have been illogical not to extend it to foremen: "Therefore the direction in which we must go is toward more collective bargaining . . . and that is true regardless of which group may be involved, whether manual workers, clerical or professional employees, straw bosses or foremen." "Insofar as recognition is withheld, foremen must 'grin and bear it,' or resort to the use of their economic power, an alternative which the Act was meant to discourage," Harry Millis explained.[27]

One critical element in these men's thinking was, of course, the extent to which it was their depoliticized vision of the labor relations in the workplace that allowed them to envision a further development of the industrial democracy that they and their mentor, John R. Commons, had been advocating since the early days of the twentieth century. Notably, their defense of foremen's unionism was cast in the same mold as the early Progressive calls for industrial democracy. This defense relied on a vision of employees as men and women divested of their class interests. As we have seen, industrial pluralists such as Leiserson had long argued that labor relations were actually "problems of human relationships" akin to those occurring in family relations and requiring perpetual adjustments. Because the theory of industrial democracy had long been rooted in the denial of the existence of a working class as an agent of political and social change, it was easy to argue that foremen and white-collar workers were no different from manual workers and could be trusted to carry legitimate union activities, as Leiserson explained: "And why should we be afraid? Because these people are employees, though a notch or two above wage workers. They do not become different people merely because they are in a union or not. They are the same human beings."[28]

Indeed, Millis and Leiserson were unswayed by businessmen's argument that the "right to manage" was at stake in the debate over foremen's rights, largely because they had never seen collective bargaining as a purely adversarial process. "We perceive no necessary conflict between self organization for collective bargaining and the faithful performance of duty," they explained, thereby denying that the right to organize should depend on the employee's function.[29] On the contrary, they believed collective bargaining fostered cooperation, and thus brought gains to both parties—a point that they had made during the congressional hearings for the Wagner Act. Key in the business unionist view of Leiserson, for example, was the idea that businessmen had to give workers a voice in the determination of their working conditions if they were to ensure their full participation. Hence, there again, it seemed illogical to these men to deny the right to organize to foremen, as Millis explained: "Whatever may happen, any attempt to frustrate the legitimate desire for self-organization and collective bargaining by such groups can only be harmful to the cause of good industrial relations and efficient production."[30] Clearly, the idea that collective bargaining actually sustained the production process, which had been a staple of the new unionism advocated by Sidney Hillman, did not prevent industrial pluralists from contemplating the unionization of the lower rungs of management. On the contrary, it actually made it possible—what was defection to business executives was democratization to the pluralists.

However, it would be a mistake to conclude that the commitment of these former students of John R. Commons to the principle of collective bargaining and to its extension to other social groups was merely a manifestation of their Progressive quest for social order. Indeed, they took the right to organize very seriously for two reasons. First, like other industrial pluralists such as Jett Lauck, Millis and Leiserson had long seen collective bargaining as the natural expression of humankind's democratic impulse, an impulse that could not be denied. To be sure, the view that the labor question originated in autocratic labor relations was not simply theirs—Frank Walsh had largely publicized it from his pulpit as president of the U.S. Commission on Industrial Relations in 1917, millions of American workers had defended it during the war effort, and Senator Wagner had in turn defended it in the 1930s. Industrial pluralists nevertheless subscribed to it, first because they believed that the process of democratization was a natural, historical process, but also because, having been arbitrators in various industries, they knew exactly how the right to organize could be used to foster industrial peace. Following the logic of the evolutionary sociology first exposed by Commons in "A Sociological View of Sovereignty," they contended that the extension of democratic principles to foremen so as to avoid strife was only the latest stage in the rise of democracy and in the substitution of negotiation for duress. Harry Millis gave this

Whiggish persuasion a clear formulation in his *Maryland Drydock* dissent: "I don't see why History should stop now," he explained.[31]

Indeed, both Leiserson and Millis believed that the Wagner Act had fundamentally transformed the substance of labor relations by shifting the onus of the law to the protection of the right to join unions and bargain. In this respect, they spoke in tune with a generation of reformers and the public as a whole. As Eric Foner has shown, although the New Deal was technically about governmental power, it was widely interpreted as having promoted a new definition of freedom. Hence Leiserson and Millis were not loath, in the *Godchaux* decision, to remind opponents of foremen's unions that in 1937, in the *Jones and Laughlin* case, the Court had elevated the right to organize into a "fundamental right."[32]

Consequently, to Millis and Leiserson the question of whether foremen really had the right to organize was moot. "[Foremen] cannot, in a free country, be prevented from organizing," Leiserson explained. By 1945, writing to Senator Wagner about bills aiming to strip foremen of the protection of the act, Leiserson clearly expressed his support for foremen's rights under the law: "And just why are supervisory employees not entitled to equal treatment with employers and workers? Why should they be pushed around?" he asked.[33] To be sure, Millis and Leiserson were no socialists, and their political thought was undoubtedly moderate in that they sought to reform capitalism, not abolish it. Nor did they conceive of labor relations through the lens of class. Theirs was a democratic idiom that was congruent with the American grain. True to the sociological perspective established by Commons in Wisconsin, they argued that collective bargaining would re-create the harmony necessary to ensure the consent of workers to capitalism.

Still, in their minds this consent should come at a price that few employers, if any, were willing to pay—the recognition of a right that Leiserson defined as "the right of human association, the same freedom to associate with their fellows for common benefit that their employers enjoy in their manufacturers associations, chambers of commerce or trade associations." Seen from this angle, it is hardly surprising that Leiserson and Millis should have been unwilling to ascribe sociological or organizational limits to this right. In many ways, they were transcending the limits and objectives of the Progressive language of industrial harmony, which was anchored in what seemed to be fixed social entities. Leiserson and Millis's vision of harmony constituted a total break with class—it was an employment democracy in which anyone working for wages or a salary would have an individual right to organize and bargain collectively.

By contrast, the third member of the board, Gerard Reilly, stood in dissidence precisely because he didn't see why, based on the reasoning of Millis and Leiserson, all the managers and executives could not organize—in his eyes an absurd idea revealing Millis and Leiserson's perverse interpretation of the Wagner Act. A former labor reformer who had been involved in the drafting of the Railroad Labor Act—which allowed foremen to organize in that industry—Reilly was by then moving to the right on labor matters. Interestingly, he fell back on the idea that Commons himself had defended in the 1920s, to wit, that foremen were "agents" of the employer, not "employees."[34]

A Broad Sociological Transmutation?

To fully gauge the significance of the stance that Millis and Leiserson had taken on the question of foremen, one needs to revert to the hearings organized by the NLRB late in 1941 in the *Union Collieries* case. For then union officials and businessmen had provided distinct definitions of the term "employee," with sharply differing implications. In the briefs they filed with the board, the foremen's union never made the argument that mine bosses were "workers" falling within the ambit of Section 7a like rank-and-file workers. As they knew, in most of the contracts signed by unions in the post-1935 era, including the contract signed by the UMW in the present case, the definition of "mine worker" or "employee" excluded supervisory, clerical, and professional employees. In lieu of a class argument, they contended that in the Wagner Act the term "employee" was not synonymous with "worker," and that it was broader: "According to the Act the term 'employee' ... is more inclusive than the term 'worker.' The definition is at least co-extensive with the definition of *one who is hired.* The word 'employee' may include professional, salaried or highly skilled employees. ... There is nothing in the act to prevent professional or 'executive' employees from organizing themselves for mutual benefit and thereby becoming entitled to the guarantees of the Act as any other class of employees."[35]

In other words, the brief argued that the Wagner Act allowed for a profound sociological transmutation of unionism. To justify its assertion, the brief submitted by the union's attorney pointed to the many decisions in which the agency had included white-collar employees of all kinds in industrial units or even in separate units.[36] Hence what the MOUA and its attorneys argued was that the Wagner Act should actually be read not as a statute primarily favoring collective bargaining by rank-and-file laborers, but as a law protecting an individual legal right to organize, a right that was not subservient, but prior to, the negotiation of trade agreements and the search for industrial peace. The logic of this argument was that the Fordist production system would be enveloped by a form of social regulation giving anyone employed by a company the right to bargain collectively for wages and benefits. Erected on the basis of the right to organize, the social status of all employees across the hierarchical ladder would be a social product. Significantly, testifying at congressional hearings in 1943, Alice Balmer, the head of the United Office and Professional Workers of America (UOPWA) in Washington, argued that "if the rights and procedures of collective bargaining through organizations of their own choosing can secure . . . results among industrial workers, then they certainly can secure the same results from administrative, executive, professional and supervisory workers."[37]

The communist-led UOPWA soon fell prey to McCarthyism, but the notion that the realm of collective bargaining should expand well beyond the blue-collar world retained its significance. What underwrote this sociological evolution was the growth of white-collar employment. As C. Wright Mills noted in *White Collar* in 1951, a new class of managers, salaried professionals, salespeople, and clerks now constituted 25 percent of the workforce, while the old middle class of small businessmen and independent professionals was quickly declining. As the foremen's movement suggested, these white-collar workers were attracted to unionism and collective bargaining because it was a source of social rights and allowed a secure integration in the middle class. Tellingly, in the 1950s, as public employment grew, pressure for an extension of the collective bargaining principles into the governmental administrative offices was growing too. In 1958, Wisconsin was the first state to formally recognize the bargaining rights of its employees.[38]

Corporate America was alive to this possible evolution. Companies like Chrysler and General Motors had been involved in cases growing out of the CIO's forays into white-collar ranks. Since 1936, in a number of cases the board sustained the organizing rights of office workers, plant guards, design engineers, and shift engineers. These cases were too few to really constitute even a fledging movement, but they were indicative of the fissures that the Great Depression and Popular Front politics had opened in social groups that were once considered as solidly antiunion. Most important, these cases explain why in the 1940s their executives immediately identified the issue of foremen's unions as key to retaining their cultural hold on the factory, but also the disciplinary power that accrued from it.[39]

Yet this issue is best seen in transnational perspective. Again, France offers an important point of comparison: there, the notion of salariat (wage work) had always been rooted in the blue-collar world and did not refer to executive or white-collar workers before the 1940s, largely because the test used to identify the "salariés" was an economic dependency test that highlighted the social condition (*condition ouvrière*) of the workers. By the late 1930s and early 1940s, however, the legal ground was shifting as public workers, engineers, foremen, and clerical workers argued that they too were salariés, and claimed the protection of the law. At the same time, judges shifted to a new test to identify the salariés, a test similar to the American common-law test whereby any worker placed under the authority of a manager or executive was a salarié. Interpreted broadly, this allowed judges to extend labor law protections to a large number of white-collar and managerial employees and to rule that they too were indeed endowed with the right to organize.[40] Notably, the result of this development was the gradual recognition of a third social group in French factories and companies, *les cadres*, who like the FAA, claimed a separate technical and social identity from the workers and top managers and resorted to organizing to assert it.[41]

As in the United States, this was a development that *displaced* and *superseded* the class struggle rather than reinforcing it. The movement of foremen, engineers, and managers toward a collective organization was owed, as in the United States, to the changing social character of white-collar employment, and it started in the late 1930s in response to the collective bargaining contracts of the Front Populaire. After World War II, it derived additional impetus from its members' strong opposition to the communist unions. The consequences on the social meaning of unionism were significant; with large numbers of white-collar workers unionizing, the link that had previously existed between unionism and the working-class condition—the idea of social subordination—gradually disappeared. Furthermore, many of the managers who increasingly claimed the social identity of cadre were influenced by Mayoite human engineering and also, quite interestingly, by the American idea that it was possible to reconcile class interests and promote labor peace in the name of productivity—an idea that the United States promoted in France through the Marshall Plan. Cadres saw themselves as buffers and negotiators between businessmen and blue-collar workers, which also meant that the theory of the class struggle based on the ownership of production no longer held.[42]

By contrast, corporate America held fast to the idea that there were only two social groups on the shop floor—managers and employees—and opposed the idea defended by the FAA, to wit, the recognition of "supervision" as a group that could be inserted between them as a third element. This was because they had nothing to gain from an independent "supervision" with collective bargaining rights. In the United States, collective bargaining had been conceived from the start as a form of cooperation, and businessmen really feared that the legal recognition of "supervision" would foster a kind of producerist ethic among workers and foremen making common cause. "Solidarity of labor is not an empty phrase, but a strong and active force," a counsel to Ford Motor Company explained. Although they were never able to prove that supervisory unionism was detrimental to production, executives warned members of Congress that American capitalism could not survive without a social order premised on the prerogatives of management.[43]

Hence from the *Union Collieries* onward, businessmen insisted that classifying foremen as "employees" was a profound misreading of the Wagner Act, which properly applied to "workers" only, although they did not make it immediately. In the *Union Collieries* case, the company executives contended that the definition of the term "employee" should be decided in light of the purposes of the Wagner Act, which were to promote collective bargaining between management and "workers." Hence it would defeat the purpose of the act to classify as "employees" anyone who did not work at the production level. A unified management, they argued, was necessary for collective bargaining to work well.[44] The company lost this argument, and two months after the *Union Collieries* decision had been handed down, with the *Godchaux* case still undecided, several business associations petitioned the board for a rehearing in the *Union Collieries* case. This time, company officials, led by Senator Burke, dropped the reference to collective bargaining. Shifting the onus to Section 7a of the law and its preamble, they claimed that a proper interpretation of the Wagner Act would necessarily limit its protection to "workers," for it was the freedom of association and the right to select representatives of "workers," not of "employees," that the law purported to protect in its statement of policy.[45]

Seen from this perspective, the social character of Fordism took on a much different aspect—the right to organize was not a universal social right of the wage or salary worker, but rather a kind of compensation for factory workers who accepted the strict work regime of the mass-production system. Ultimately, Congress would adopt this view, with the House report on Taft-Hartley mentioning that the production needs of the country required restoring the authority of managers over American companies.[46]

The Limits of Expertise

In spite of their depoliticized vision of the workplace, Leiserson and Millis were never able to convince reluctant liberals and conservatives that collective bargaining and managerial loyalty were not mutually incompatible in a capitalistic system of production.[47] As we saw in the previous chapter, the debate over foremen's unions gave business executives the opportunity to reaffirm the cultural values—individualism, risk taking, initiative—that had undergirded the managers' own rise to social dominance since late nineteenth century and that the Depression had briefly seemed to consign to oblivion. Opposing the pluralists' defense of industrial harmony through reasoned bargaining, conservatives insisted at length on the debilitating effects of the collective logic of unionism.

It matters now to note that the weakness of the NLRB's institutional position in this debate was patent. It failed to fence off this assault, mostly because it was deprived of the means to do so. Indeed, for lack of social science studies, neither Leiserson nor Millis could really challenge businessmen's assertions that foremen's unions made for diminished production and lower levels of safety on the factory floor. Nor could they escape sharp criticism for holding that in mass-production industries, foremen could be at the same time representatives of "employers" and "employees" with rights of their own. Legally, as we have seen, this made sense, but how could this dual status be worked out on the factory floor? According to the jurisprudence they had established, foremen were allowed to organize, but they could in no way take part in the union activities of rank-and-file employees, nor even comment upon them—because doing so would constitute an unfair labor practice. Moreover, the decisions of the board seemed all the fuzzier because it had held that nothing in the act prevented foremen from joining rank-and-file unions, and the fact that foremen in all cases were to form collective bargaining units of their own was not enough to assuage the fears to which businessmen had given rise. In point of fact, both Millis and Leiserson privately expressed the opinion that it would be preferable for rank-and-file workers and foremen to belong to distinct labor organizations—the foremen's ability to maintain discipline and the worker's freedom of choice would be easier to secure—but the legal toolbox with which they were required to operate was ill fitted to deploy a general vision of industrial relations and production. Had they been able to mediate disputes, they might have offered independent unions as solutions, but from the NLRB's vantage point, they could work only within the parameters of the law as it stood.[48]

Finally, the agency's decisions were weakened by its court-like procedures, especially dissenting opinions. Such a practice dated back to the early days of the NLRB, when the many lawyers staffing the board had adopted legal procedures that seemed to best represent the impartiality and neutrality of the administrative process. Yet in such a contentious issue as foremen's unionism, this practice was at cross-purposes with the idea that the agency worked for the public good in a disinterested fashion. Rather, the dissenting opinions written by Gerard Reilly—the third member of the board—further diminished the board's public standing by legitimizing businessmen's criticism.

A mere few months after the *Godchaux* decision, the board's extensive definition of "employee" fell prey to political pressure, although in fact, Congress did not have to act. In March 1943, William Leiserson left the board to go back to the National Mediation Board, where he could escape the institutional constraints of the NLRB and revert to the work he liked most—mediation. To replace him, FDR named a businessman with no labor background, John Houston, a Democratic representative from Kansas operating an open-shop lumber company. In many ways, this appointment, which had been made in spite of the opposition of union leaders, reflected FDR's preoccupation with both congressional pressure and the conservative evolution of public opinion. As *Business Week* noted, "It was Franklin D. Roosevelt, the politician, not the leader of the New Deal, who appointed John Houston to the NLRB. . . . He took account of the strongly anti-labor sentiment, bowing to it by refusing to appoint a man with a labor background."[49] Indeed, the nomination was decided in the midst of a huge wildcat strike launched by John Lewis to obtain a $2 per day increase and recognition of the rights of foremen represented by the MOUA, which he had integrated into the UMW in November 1942. Meanwhile, antilabor sentiment was rising, as evidenced by the bevy of antilabor laws that were adopted by the states, especially in the South and Midwest, in 1943.

The result of that "board packing" was not long in coming—on May 11, 1943, eight days after the arrival of John Houston on the board, the *Maryland* decision overturned the *Union Collieries* and *Godchaux* decisions, putting foremen outside the province of the Wagner Act. In the majority opinion, Gerald Reilly gave corporate demands of foremen loyalty a strong boost by relying on an opinion penned by a famous New Deal liberal, namely, Benjamin Cardozo. In a famous case bearing on the traditional duty of loyalty imposed by the common law on people having fiduciary duties, Cardozo explained, "Many forms of conduct permissible in a workaday world for those acting at arm's length are forbidden to those bound by fiduciary ties. A trustee is held to something stricter than the morals of the market place. Not honesty alone, but the punctilio of an honor the most sensitive, then, is the standard of behavior."[50] Reilly thus suggested that because managers did not directly supervise foremen, but rather trusted them to carry out their plans, there was between them the kind of fiduciary duty that Cardozo had eloquently described.

The main paradox of the *Maryland Drydock* decision is that it was released precisely at the moment when the organizing drive of foremen was gaining momentum, and at the time when the war production effort was in full swing, giving foremen significant leverage. As a result, while industrial pluralists at the NLRB were unable to preserve this enlarged definition of the realm of collective bargaining, foremen forced a reckoning with their movement and their rights through social pressure. Detroit bore the brunt of this militancy. The first strike occurred at the Murray Cy in July 1943 (with 600 foremen walking away), and tensions simmered until spring 1944, when industrial production was crippled by a strike involving 3,300 foremen working for six manufacturers. These strikes, which often enjoyed the support, and sometimes the participation, of rank-and-file workers, had such an impact—about 669,156 man-days lost between July 1943 and November 1944—that by January 1944, the three members of the board asked the legal division to research the possibilities that the law afforded if one wanted to protect foremen as "employees" without questioning the *Maryland* decision.[51]

Drafted by two jurists, Mervin Bachman and Guy Farmer, the reports offered a commentary on the legal framework of the Wagner Act suggesting that it was indeed possible to craft a middle ground legal status for foremen. To deny that foremen were "employees," the *Maryland Drydock* majority had relied on Section 9b of the law, according to which it is up to the NLRB to decide what bargaining units can appropriately further the objectives of the act. But this did not exhaust the possibilities offered by Section 7a, the scope of which, the two jurists insisted, was greater than collective bargaining, since it protected the right "to self organization, to form join, or assist labor organizations to bargain collectively through representatives of their own choosing, and to engage in other concerted activities, for the purpose of collective bargaining or other mutual aid or protection." Even if the protection of collective bargaining was not extended to foremen, it was still possible to read the act as protecting the right to organize—one that it did not create, since even foremen enjoyed it at common law—in other ways, for example by prohibiting any layoffs for union activities.

In a sense these two jurists were odd bedfellows. While Mervin Bachman, a graduate of Harvard Law School, was the typical New Deal liberal lawyer, Farmer was a Republican who would later be appointed by Eisenhower to the board. Yet Farmer was a moderate who believed that the government intervened too much in labor relations and should limit itself to helping unions when they were too weak or, alternatively, when their excesses had to be restrained.[52] Together, however, they stirred the board toward a recognition that even if foremen were not fully "employees," they were still "workers and part of labor in the generic sense." Undergirding this approach was the idea that the right to organize was a "fundamental right," the protection of which should be extended, in one way or another, to all people working.[53] On May 8, 1944, the board handed down two decisions laying out the new contours of the legal status of foremen by finding against two companies whose managers had fired members of the FAA. The two decisions contended that "from the premise that supervisory employees, under the Board policy, may not constitute appropriate units and thus utilize the processes and sanctions of the Act to compel bargaining, it does not follow that an employer many therefore disregard the rights to self organization and to engage in concerted activities for mutual aid or protection."[54]

This did not quell foremen's militancy, and by then, the NLRB's legalistic approach was in competition with the investigatory powers of the NWLB, which the president had created on January 12, 1940, to forestall labor strife by way of mediation while the NLRB kept enforcing the Wagner Act prohibition of unfair labor practices. The NWLB was under pressure from the military to find a solution to the conflicts involving foremen—a task for which it seemed better equipped than the NLRB, as its tripartite structure included representatives from labor and management and experts representing the public, and it was headed by William H. Davis, a well-known labor mediator with a background firmly anchored in labor progressivism. Davis was a former member of the 20th Century Fund, one of the main institutional sounding boards for industrial pluralism, the philosophy of labor relations pioneered in Wisconsin. In June 1944, having extended its jurisdiction to all foremen's cases, the board created an investigatory commission headed by another important figure of Wisconsin labor progressivism—Harvard's Sumner Slichter.[55]

Released in January 1945, the report of the Slichter Commission was no full-scale endorsement of the foremen's cause. The report noted that some of the foremen's contentions—regarding the narrowing gap between their earnings and those of rank-and-file workers and regarding management's failure to support them in their dealing with shop stewards—were unjustified at the time of the investigation (the commission noted they may have been easier to buttress earlier on). However, the Slichter Commission pointed out the deficiencies of the policy of the "open door," which high managers and executives touted as the best managerial policy with foremen and supervisors: "The insistence by management that its representatives deal with each foreman only individually and then only about his own grievances impedes, if it does not preclude, the initiation of grievance cases affecting groups of foremen. But even on his own behalf a single foreman may be at a disadvantage in presenting his case. Being one among many, the foreman is individually dispensable and replaceable."[56]

This portrayal of the foreman as a helpless individual in the modern corporation cut directly against the grain of managerial talk. Most important, it was coupled with a sharp analysis of the changing nature of foremanship in modern industry. The report analyzed the gradual reduction of the foreman's role in modern industry to one limited to merely giving orders. Anticipating the work of Alfred Chandler and Daniel Nelson, the members of the Slichter Commission explained that this declining status was a product of the emergence of middle management—and with it modern management practices. Countering corporate managers' assertions that foremen embodied the enduring spirit of American individualism, the report noted, "Despite the exacting nature of the foreman's responsibilities, a large proportion of foremen sincerely do not regard themselves as part of management. This is a natural result of the growth of central management and the development of foremen into executors of policies and recommenders of decisions rather than makers of decisions."[57]

What the NWLB had done was thus to provide the social science expertise that the NLRB—being confined to a legal approach—had missed from the beginning. In point of fact, the Slichter report was released during the hearings conducted by the NLRB in the *Packard* case, which the board had selected in late 1944 to review the *Maryland* decision. By then, much to the chagrin of Gerard D. Reilly, the other conservative member sitting on the NLRB, John Houston, had become a strong advocate of union rights, and he was ready to change his position on the definition of "employee."[58] At the same time, there was internal pressure from men such as Frank Bloom, the head of trial examiners in the Detroit office, to move beyond a purely "legalistic approach" on this question. This was the time when the board finally made a decision in the case that encapsulated all the stakes inherent in the foremen's movement—*Packard Motor Company.*[59]

Taking stock of the numerous strikes that had taken place since the *Maryland Drydock* decision, in *Packard*—which was handed down in March 1945—Houston and Millis reaffirmed the progressive logic of the Wagner Act, which was to promote industrial peace. Quoting extensively from the Slichter report, the decision argued that the foreman was not a manager making important decisions but only a "traffic cop" whose social trajectory was similar to that of rank-and-file employees in the 1920s and 1930s. According to the decision, both the logic of the act and the realities of power in the modern corporation led to the conclusion that foremen were "employees" with collective bargaining rights of their own.[60]

Moreover, the board used the Slichter report to offer a new representation of the social world of the factory that implicitly rejected the idea of a large militant working class, and instead endorsed the business unionism propounded by the head of the FAA, Robert Keys. Foremen, it said, should constitute a bargaining unit of their own because their interests were different from those of workers—they did not do manual work, but had no decision-making responsibilities. At Packard, what characterized them was the work of supervision, their ability to make recommendations, and the fact that they had been trained in the foremen's school. Thus, the NLRB now offered to grant the FAA what it had demanded all along—the acknowledgment of the existence of a third social group in American factories, namely, supervision. "They consider themselves a middle group between the rank and file on the one hand and the management on the other, and the facts of modern mass production industry, which we have discussed earlier support this view," the board said.[61]

This important step toward a possible shift from industrial democracy to an employment democracy based on a multifaceted collective bargaining process was confirmed when Truman, in a widely publicized appointment, named another industrial pluralist to preside over the board—Paul Herzog. No choice could have been more meaningful, for, as a member of the New York State Labor Board, Herzog had supported foremen's collective bargaining claims. In a subsequent decision condemning Packard for refusing to bargain with the FAA, Herzog reaffirmed the pluralist ideal of peaceful and consensual labor relations: collective bargaining was the *solution* to, not the *cause* of, the problems existing between management and foremen: "Fear, perhaps more than self-interest, is a ready cause of industrial strife. In the long run, collective bargaining will tend to reduce both the cause and effect. Bargaining can only succeed, however, if responsible unions representing supervisory employees, once their legal rights are established, recognize the validity of some of management's special fears, and seek to dispel them by the terms of the ultimate bargain."[62]

By the mid-1940s, industrial pluralists working in the reformist vein established by John R. Commons offered the only solution available to restore the traditional American ideal of social harmony because they owned a virtual monopoly on the scientific and academic discourse on labor relations. To the conservative *Detroit Free Press*, however, the *Packard* decision was only "peace at any price." The ruling would be short-lived, the paper predicted, and would obtain only until the end of the war. Indeed, it was clear that with the inevitable termination of government contracts, the NLRB would not have the power to secure this holding by itself. In spite of the prevalence of Wisconsin labor economics and the prominence its practitioners had achieved in the political sphere since the New Deal, what really sustained the expansive definition of "employee" and the faith in social harmony that underwrote it was pressure from the bottom up, not the ability of labor experts to orchestrate labor relations. Once the war was over, the foremen's ability to exert this pressure would decline.[63]

Packard Motor Company lost its battle against the NLRB for good in 1947, when the Supreme Court ruled that the NLRB's definition of "employee" was in tune with the general objectives of the act. Speaking for the majority, Judge Jackson refuted the idea that there was an inevitable contradiction between the foremen's role in the production process and their desire to organize, and thus supported the industrial pluralists' analysis: "Though the foreman is the faithful representative of the employer in maintaining a production schedule, his interest properly may be adverse to that of the employer when it comes to fixing his own wages, hours, seniority rights and working conditions," the opinion read. According to Jackson, the company's objection was rooted in what he denounced as a "misconception," that is, the view that because it was entitled to the loyalty of its employees, the company should not let them organize. If that notion had been repudiated for production employees, surely the same could be done for foremen.[64]

Coming from a judge who was at the forefront of the criticism of the New Deal administrative state, this was valuable support. But the Court's decision also revealed that the debate over the rights of foremen was not simply one pitting liberals against corporate conservatives. Equally significant was the debate within liberal ranks. Indeed, dissenting from the majority's opinion in *NLRB v. Packard* were none other than Justices Douglas and Frankfurter—two notable labor progressives. In a blistering opinion, Douglas couched his dissent in words that conservatives had used throughout the 1940s in their criticism of foremen's unions. According to Douglas, the act was really meant to apply only to "workers," "wage earners," and "laborers"; otherwise the danger of the employers' "arms and legs" being sympathetic to manual workers instead of directing them would be too strong. The main obstacle faced by the industrial pluralists, then, was that their vision of harmonious labor relations was rebutted by more than a few liberals who were receptive to business claims to managerial loyalty because they remained thoroughly wedded to the free enterprise system.

Indeed, on the foremen's issue, American liberalism and conservatism easily overlapped. Douglas did not deny that the objective of the Wagner Act was to deflect social antagonism and bring managers and workers closer together. However, this was to be done *in the interest of capitalistic production*. The Court's decision, he contended, transformed social relations instead of pacifying them, for it would allow labor and management to form "a solid phalanx," with "the struggle for control or power between management and labor becoming secondary to a growing unity in their common demands on ownership." In a sense, Douglas's dissent exemplified the "end of reform" that characterized American liberalism in the 1940s, for his defense of management stood squarely against the more reformist vision laid out by Adolph Berle and Gardiner Means in their 1932 opus, *The Modern Corporation and Private Property*, in which they exposed the unaccountability of managerial circles to society as a whole.[65] As we will see in the next chapter, in time Douglas's own vision of industrial harmony though unionism was much less ambitious than that of the rights-based approach of the pluralists, for it applied only to factory workers. In fact, his moderate views would offer significant ammunition to conservatives in their struggle against the NLRB's efforts to expand the definition of "employee" beyond the blue-collar world.

The legal status of foremen, however, remained fragile for other political reasons. Once the country had been returned to peace, management circles launched a legislative and media campaign designed to amend the Wagner Act, which left no doubt about their commitment to the exclusion of foremen and managers from the purview of the act.[66] The failure of the National Labor Management Conference, held in the winter of 1945–1946, enabled the unions to gauge the determination of businessmen to prevent any further development of unionism and sharply limit the scope of collective bargaining as well. As it put a premium on industrial peace, the Truman administration refused to invite the two main foremen's unions—the FAA and UCTSE, which was affiliated with UMW. The question of foremen's unionism did figure on the conference agenda, but it was added only *after* the conference had actually started.

Most important, the conference laid bare the positions of the respective parties on this question. The business representatives of the conference made it clear in their report that the defense of the "right to manage" made the definition of foremen as "employees" simply unacceptable. By contrast, the CIO refused to take a stand on the issue, simply saying that it should be solved by the NLRB and the courts. In fact, in March 1945, the CIO had signed a charter with the Chamber of Commerce in which each party pledged to respect the rights of the other side, which meant that the CIO accepted the "right to manage." Overall, in the years that followed the war, the CIO was too concerned by the antilabor bills submitted in Congress to defend foremen's unions. Internal reports on such bills did not even mention the foremen's question— the memory of the post–World War I debacle was such that the young confederation was focused solely on securing the collective bargaining edifice.[67]

Meanwhile two dynamics largely reinforced the businessmen's position. First, public opinion largely turned against labor unions—a movement that was already at work during the war and was largely accelerated by the 1946 strike wave. The congressional elections held in 1946, in which Republicans regained control of Congress, paved the way for labor reform. By then, the argument made in the 1930s in favor of the Wagner Act—that it would foster social harmony because strikes stemmed form the lack of democracy at work—seemed a bit worn and made it difficult to justify protecting foremen's unions on the same terms.

Second, this growing insistence on industrial peace was compounded by the demands of foreign policy. As early as 1945, Truman insisted on the need to develop commercial exchanges with Europe to avoid a new depression, which meant garnering the support of isolationists in Congress and preparing for the Marshall Plan, which had been in the works, in some form or other, since 1944. Much to the dismay of union leaders, many liberal policy makers consequently shed their unswerving commitment to an unamended Wagner Act. In June 1946, before the congressional elections that returned the Republican Party to majority status, Congress voted on the Case Bill, which contained all of the elements of the Taft-Hartley Bill, adopted a year later, including the exclusion of foremen from the category "employee." As

Lee Pressman, the CIO counsel, noted, "It is the liberals who are capitulat-ing . . . congressional liberals are not as firm against anti-labor legislation as are reactionaries against the FEPC."[68]

In this context, the voices of labor experts such as William Leiserson and Paul Herzog, who testified against conservative bills stripping foremen of their rights, could play only a minor role, for too few liberals were willing to defend the idea that the right to organize was a "fundamental one." The Truman administration's response to the Case Bill is illustrative. In his testi-mony in Congress, labor secretary Lewis Schwellenbach opposed the provi-sion of the law exempting foremen, but did so mostly on the grounds that it would jeopardize industrial peace at a time when the United States could ill afford it. In his draft of Truman's veto speech, Clark Clifford sounded a simi-lar theme, noting that the exemption of foremen from the Wagner Act was not in tune with the administration's economic policy, which was centered on increased production.[69]

Yet administration officials were unable to offer a clear defense of the foremen's right to organize. As Schwellenbach explained in an internal memorandum,

> the question of supervisory employees is a complicated
> one. . . . During the Labor-Management conference we had many
> arguments upon the subject. Clearly the right of supervisors to
> have the protection afforded to them by the right of organization
> cannot lightly be thrown aside. The fact is that the supervisors
> won't permit it to be thrown aside. On the other hand
> management is entitled to its protection. Somewhere in the area
> of disagreement between the parties the line can be thrown with
> reasonable accuracy.[70]

Where and why this line should be drawn, however, the Truman administra-tion never said. On June 11, Truman's veto of the Case Bill did mention that the "full right of supervisory employees to collective bargaining is one that cannot be lightly thrown aside," but it reiterated the notion that "somewhere in the area of disagreement," the line could be thrown with "reasonable accu-racy." Going any further would have meant responding to business represen-tatives' contention that the act should apply to manual workers only and that for philosophical, technical, and social reasons, one should not allow fore-men's loyalty to management to be compromised. This was not a conceptual effort that the Truman administration was willing to undertake. American liberals as a whole had never been able to decide to what extent the right to organize should be seen as a civil right. By contrast, Republican members of Congress doggedly pressed the business case for loyalty. Denouncing the "folly" of allowing supervisors to unionize, the House report on the Taft-Hartley Bill contended, "The evidence before the committee shows clearly that unionizing supervisors under the Wagner Act is inconsistent with . . . our policy to protect the right of employers. They, as well as workers, are entitled to loyal representatives in the plants. There must be in management and loyal to it persons not subject to the influence or control of unions."[71] The Senate report sounded a similar theme, noting that "it is natural to expect that unless Congress takes action, management will be deprived of the undivided loyalty of its foremen. There is an inherent tendency to subordinate their interests whenever they conflict with those of the rank and file."[72] As a result, in June 1947 Congress adopted the Taft-Hartley Act over Truman's veto, excluding foremen from the Wagner Act. According to Section 2(11),

> The term "supervisor" means any individual having authority,
> in the interest of the employer, to hire, transfer, suspend, lay
> off, recall, promote, discharge, assign, reward, or discipline
> other employees, or responsibly to direct them, or to adjust
> their grievances, or effectively to recommend such action if in
> connection with the foregoing the exercise of such authority is
> not of a merely routine or clerical nature, but requires the use of
> independent judgment.[73]

A profound mistrust of unionism thus continued to characterize American labor law, which accepted it only to the extent that it could be embedded in the logic and structures of capitalistic production. This mistrust, however, was not simply the product of a dominant discourse. It was also vindicated from the bottom up by the very unions that company executives feared might forge alliances with foremen.

The UAW and the Redefinition of "Employee" on the Factory Floor

Legal concepts are not inherently legitimate; rather, they find some of their legitimacy if they can acquire social meaning and thus be the embodiment of a social contract. Thus, the fate of the foremen's organization drive, and the future of the labor relations regime, was determined as much on the factory floor as in the halls of Congress. Indeed, the Taft-Hartley Act was passed a few days after the FAA had launched a strike at the Ford factories in Detroit. While the company had been one of the first manufacturers to sign a contract with the FAA, it had decided, under the pressure of General Motors and other manufacturers, to put an end to collective bargaining with foremen. The strike began on May 21, 1947, with a sanguine Robert H. Keys (the president of the FAA) predicting that, with over thirty-five hundred foremen out, production would shortly be stopped. A few days later, however, it became apparent that the strike could not be won without the support of the UAW, which was itself involved in the negotiation of a new contract. Once the Taft-Hartley Act had been passed on June 23, Keys had no choice but to ask for the UAW's help.[74] Yet, in spite of the repeated demands of the FAA, the UAW refused to ask its workers to respect the foremen's picket line and simply tried to mediate the conflict, to no avail—the strike was called off forty-seven days after it had begun, on July 7, 1947.

This negative response might seem surprising in light of the UAW leadership's own recurring official statements in favor of the foremen's right to join a union and bargain collectively.[75] To several UAW leaders, however, there was a line between supportive declarations and actual assistance that should not be crossed. Throughout the war the UAW had followed the policy of the CIO, which was to ask production workers to walk through the picket lines of foremen but refuse to take up their jobs. In the context of the war, this policy had not hampered the FAA, whose leverage on companies was significant because of the needs of production. Unlike the United Steelworkers of America (USWA), as yet, the UAW had not decided to take advantage of the *Packard* decision to take in foremen. Indeed, not only had it turned down affiliation demands made by foremen who did not want to join the FAA, but it had even carried a motion urging the CIO not to set up any LIUs for foremen.[76] In September 1945, when, in the midst of a foremen strike, the UAW local at Hudson officially voiced its desire to respect the foremen's picket line, the leadership opposed them, arguing that the foremen's cause should remain foreign to them.[77]

In a way this policy was also the legacy of the negotiations for a contract at Chrysler in 1939, when the UAW had come to the conclusion that representing foremen was not possible given the adamant opposition of businessmen. It also reflected the obvious, long-standing hard feelings against foremen, whose arbitrary power had long justified the calls for a democratization of the workplace. Men such as Richard Addes, R. J. Thomas, and Richard Frankensteen were either skeptical about the prospects of an alliance with the FAA or downright hostile to it.[78] As for the *United Auto Worker*—the main publication of the UAW—it had remained conspicuously silent on the foremen's issue since the creation of the FAA in 1942.

More generally, however, one may say that the CIO unions and their members did not share in the industrial pluralists' faith in harmony because they had never articulated this discourse. Opposition to social antagonism had always been a thoroughly middle-class endeavor, even if it had engulfed the energy of numerous labor reformers. The unions' experience of collective bargaining remained anchored in a strong sense of class, and in mass-production industries—as opposed to the skilled trades—this class consciousness had rarely included cooperation with foremen. CIO unions could not ignore the existence of foremen's unions and their potential consequences on labor relations, but, on the other hand, the fact remained that no common social or political struggle as yet united the two social groups that history had divided for so long.[79]

Interestingly, this isolation had also made the FAA a union whose institutional culture was geared toward independence. While the first foremen's union in the automobile industry had developed under the aegis of CIO leader Adolph Germer, the FAA had been created on the assumption that it would be easier for a foremen's union to become established if it were independent.[80] Significantly, in 1946, its leaders had refused an offer of the FAA to become an affiliate of the CIO, which seemed to have anticipated the move for some time.[81] Hence, nothing, in the short existence of the FAA, had prepared the two unions for what the FAA now requested—a common fight against one of the major automakers.

Be that as it may, the UAW could not afford to ignore some of the issues attendant on the foremen's struggle. Walther Reuther, for one, understood the stakes inherent in the foremen's struggle. With over a thousand workers laid off temporarily because production had become lax at Ford, it seemed obvious to Reuther that the UAW could hardly cohabit with a union whose actions it did not control. Yet more was at stake in the Ford strike than the coherent organization of labor unions in the automobile industry. Indeed, the sanctity of the picket line that American labor unions had taken years to build now seemed in jeopardy, and Reuther did not fail to understand how eerie it was for the UAW to adopt such a tepid policy at a difficult time for

American unionism: "As stated before, the foremen's strike is now in its third week and it is a very serious situation to see our people crossing picket lines as though it were nothing. In the face of some of the anti-labor legislation facing the labor movement it is important that there be established in the minds of our people some respect for authorized picket lines regardless of what union they are."[82]

According to Reuther, Ford could not afford two strikes at once. All the UAW had to do was to indicate to the Ford management that no contract would be signed until the foremen's situation was settled.[83] The UAW could not, he argued, take the responsibility for breaking the foremen's movement, but it would also be in a better position to bargain if the two contracts were negotiated at once. Reuther was not alone in defending this idea. Significantly, the day before the UAW International Executive Board convened to discuss the foremen's matter, the executive board of the Ford local (Local 600) had sent a cable urging it to announce to the management at Ford that unless top managers bargained with the FAA, the UAW workers would start respecting their picket line.[84] But R. J. Thomas and Richard Leonard, who were also Reuther's political opponents in the UAW, would not budge. While no contract had been signed yet, they had by then an agreement with Ford that the pending contract would include a pension plan, and they were extremely reluctant to jeopardize this provision for the sake of the foremen. Accordingly, they argued that the FAA had not consulted with them prior to starting the strike and that the UAW had no business stepping into it. Coldly, Thomas argued that the FAA should have cast its lot with the CIO in 1946 when the offer was made.[85]

The UAW thus willfully accepted a very restrictive definition of the term "employee" and provided this legal concept with social meaning on the factory floor.[86] Indeed, the defeat of the foremen's strike at Ford dealt a deadly blow to foremen's unionism. Shortly after the strike was called off, the FAA lost its fight to get contracts at two other Detroit companies—Midland and Garwood. Many companies then adopted and implemented the policies and ideas hatched at GM or Ford during the war to make foremen feel that they were part of management. The pay differential with production workers was widened. Foremen often received special lunch rooms, parking lots, and badges and were enlisted in extensive training programs. As a manager explained, all these changes aimed to transform foremen's self-perception, so that "the mere suggestion of organization would outrage his sense of loyalty and obligation."[87]

Opportunities Found and Lost

In a noted article, the historians Robert Korstad and Nelson Lichtenstein have argued that the 1940s witnessed a historic missed opportunity—the possibility of a civil rights movement firmly anchored in the energy and ideals of organized labor.[88] The foremen's movement was yet another opportunity "found and lost" to buttress the political legitimacy of American unions. What was lost in the 1940s was not necessarily the opportunity to build a broad, radical labor movement. Whether at the end of the war the social gap between workers and foremen and beyond them white-collar workers had been narrowed remains open to question. But this is beside the point, for the success of foremen's unions would have durably altered the *common sense* of the social meaning of unionism by turning the right to organize and bargain collectively into a right that all citizens enjoyed in the American democracy.[89] To be sure, the Taft-Hartley Act expressly protected the rights of professionals to organize. Nevertheless, the supervisory exemption and the doctrine of loyalty now hung over this right, as industrial unions learned when, in the 1960s and 1970s, they made a sustained effort to beyond the blue-collar world.

CHAPTER 6

Loyalty Ascendant

O N July 30, 1970, the UAW filed a representation petition with the NLRB, seeking to be certified as the representative of the twenty-four buyers working in the purchasing and procuring department of Bell Aerospace in Wheatfield, New York, near Buffalo. A division of Textron, Bell Aerospace was a midsize company employing 4,637 workers whose skills allowed them to sit at the heart of the military-industrial complex. The company produced engines for helicopters and rockets, a cutting-edge technological process that had earned it lucrative contracts related to the Minute Man Missile Program, which was then the pillar of the U.S. Air Force's defensive nuclear capabilities.[1]

Many of the companies taking part in the country's military apparatus were located in the Sunbelt, well beyond the sphere of influence to which American unions had been relegated since the end of World War II. There, the federal government had massively invested its resources, and conservative ideas thrived along with economic expansion. Yet Bell Aerospace was largely removed from the cultural environment in which advocates of antistatism and individualism labored to remake American society. Sitting across the country from the right-to-work states where Barry Goldwater, Ronald Reagan, and George Wallace had made their first political marks, the factories of Bell Aerospace were a non-Fordist complex in a thoroughly Fordist political and social environment. The UAW was no newcomer there—it had represented production workers since the end of the 1940s and had even secured a solid foothold among office employees and supervisors. Now the company's engineers and technicians—Local 1286—were the ones trying to expand the ranks of their unions by including procurement buyers.[2]

Yet even though it had accepted unions, Bell Aerospace's response to the UAW's election was adamantly negative. The company was encountering financial difficulties, and it bitterly opposed the new organizing drive, arguing that the buyers were not "employees" but "managers" with no bargaining rights.[3] All the same, one year later the NLRB proceeded with the election, which the union won by fifteen votes to nine, but the company immediately challenged the legitimacy of the election in court. As for the UAW, it could not have been surprised at the company's position. Since it had decided to devote the means necessary to make inroads in the white-collar world in the mid-1960s, creating the Technical Office and Professional Workers Division (TOP) to that effect, the union had come to grips with the problem arising from the exclusion of managers and supervisors from the purview of collective bargaining law—an exclusion to which it had lent its unfortunate support in the 1930s and 1940s.[4]

What made the case of the twenty-four Bell Aerospace procurement buyers so significant, however, was that they were not managers in the traditional meaning of the word. Far from the Chandlerian managers who had engineered the transition of American companies to their modern divisional structure, the buyers represented a new breed of workers, semiprofessionals whose knowledge was essential to productive production, but whose semiautonomy found no relevance in the categories that heretofore had been used to construct the social meaning of work—employee and manager.

"The position, function and fulfillment of the knowledge worker is the social question of the 20th century," Peter Drucker argued in 1966. To the Austrian-born theorist of the modern corporation, the knowledge worker—a term he coined in the 1950s—was a new development challenging the dominance of managers over work just as skilled workers had challenged the domination of business owners before the advent of Taylorism, and he dedicated himself to contrive managerial practices to ensure these new workers' loyalty. Further to the left, however, the emergence of this new industrial class excited the hopes of theorists such as Daniel Bell, who coined the term "postindustrial society" to express the idea that these workers might be the sociological mainstay of a new sociopolitical equilibrium.[5]

What the legal case *Bell Aerospace* suggested, then, was that the making of the postindustrial society would not simply rest with the tasks and self-perceptions of the men and women toiling within its womb—it would also be conducted by the labor experts who still guided the federal government's visible hand on labor relations. For these men, who saw themselves as heirs to the Progressive tradition established by Commons in Wisconsin more than a half century earlier, the 1960s and 1970s offered as many possibilities and opportunities as the 1930s and 1940s. Indeed, during this period the "new frontier NLRB" feistily laid the groundwork for an expansion of unionism among white-collar workers. Renewing their predecessors' quest for an "employment democracy," they also challenged head-on the meaning and breadth of the managerial exemption in American labor law, suggesting that the right to organize and the faithful performance of duty were, in many cases, not incompatible.

In 1970, as the board tackled the *Bell* case, the stakes were indeed high. As the country moved toward a new economic environment, one in which manual factory workers would be a declining social force while workers working with and developing information and knowledge would compose an ever greater part of the workforce, the future of American unionism depended on the capacity of American liberalism to effectuate the transformation that had failed in the 1940s. By 1974, however, any hope that the legal definition of "employee" would be wrested from its Fordist roots had died, as the Supreme Court ruled in *NLRB v. Bell Aerospace* that all managers were excluded from the protection of the main legislation protecting the right to organize.[6] This defeat was not simply handed to liberals by conservative Justices—the project of social harmony through associational freedom no longer defined the ambition of the liberal community as a whole. In the 1960s and early 1970s, liberalism was not simply beset by a conservative assault launched from the unreformed South and West; it was also weakened by the incapacity of some of its agents to transcend its limitations.

Knowledge Workers and the New Struggle for Loyalty on the Workplace

The buyers who elected to join the UAW at Bell Aerospace were a far cry from the automobile workers who had animated the labor movement in the 1930s and forced recalcitrant companies to accept the tenets of industrial democracy. Yet their organizing drive rekindled the battle over managerial loyalty because like skilled workers in the late nineteenth century and foremen in the mid-1940s, they occupied a key role in the production process. As in the 1940s, the company demanded their full loyalty because it exerted over them none of the control that it enjoyed on production workers through scientific management.

The fifteen procurement buyers were in charge of purchasing the materials and devices used by the company in the production of the engines. Every day they received purchase requisitions that they processed according to specific technical and financial imperatives laid out in a procurement manual.[7] The requisitions were sent to one of the eight supervisors of the Procurement Department, who then passed them on to the buyer with the highest expertise in the technical area of the requisition, for each buyer had a specialty. These requisitions came in three different types. First, they could be a simple request for a part or a tool produced by one company in the United States only, a General Motors engine for example. In this case, all the buyer had to do was to order it and make sure the device was delivered on time. Second, there were "off the shelf" requisitions—orders for basic items available at standard prices such as oil, tools, or technologically advanced pieces such as radars and black boxes that were produced by several companies. To place an order for such items, buyers were expected to use their knowledge of the specifics of the market of each item and favor products meeting high quality standards. However, if the order specified "brand name or equivalent," the buyers would then assess the alternatives and try to select a cheaper but adequate product.[8]

These two types of orders represented the bulk of the buyers' work—some nineteen thousand to twenty thousand orders per year. Requisitions for expensive, technologically cutting-edge devices, however, triggered a much longer process. In this case, the buyers advised the company as to whether the item should be bought or made on the premises. If the decision was made to select a supplier that would make the item according to the company's specifications, the buyers prepared a file presenting the information necessary to launch a bid—technical requirements, quality standards, price, production schedule. To prepare this file, they would assemble an ad hoc team of technicians, engineers, and jurists who all weighed in at different stages in the process, as each part of the contract, from the production methodology to the overall cost, was minutely scrutinized. In some cases, to gain a better understanding of the particulars of the contract that was being negotiated, the buyers would even go with a technician from Bell Aerospace and visit the facilities of the company bidding for the contract.[9] Most important, the buyers were allowed to pledge the company's credit up to $5,000. Committing the company to bigger contracts required the approval of a procurement department supervisor. Even then, the buyers retained an important role, as they oversaw the production of the piece by establishing "milestone events"—specific junctures in the production schedule where they would meet with representatives of the company and check on its performance. If a problem emerged, the buyers tried to solve it, renegotiated the contract if it was necessary, and might even prepare for a full-scale cancellation.[10]

Still, Bell Aerospace buyers were not certified professionals in the same way as lawyers or physicians; indeed, only one of them was a college graduate. Rather, their trajectory was that of skilled workers who had decided, in the 1950s, to "change collars" and use their skills in a different way. Their know-how rested on the unique synthesis of a specific technical expertise, of knowledge of the legal and commercial dynamics underwriting the market of each product, and of knowledge of the rules published by the Defense Department for the production of military equipment. Bell Aerospace buyers thus epitomized the growing importance of technology and information in the American economy. But this "new industrial middle class," as management expert Drucker first labeled it, was a variegated lot. In a sense the concept of "knowledge worker" was ill-defined and included a large array of technicians, nurses, engineers, administrators, teachers, and others still who identified neither with management nor with manual workers. Yet there was something common to all of them—unlike lawyers or physicians, their identity at work did not stem from their belonging to a professional association speaking on their behalf and defining their social, technical, and cultural position. Rather, their identity was a function of the unique configuration composing their working conditions.[11]

Most important, these workers did not fit neatly into an industrial hierarchy premised on the difference between planning (managers) and doing (employees), as they were neither managers who strategized the organization of work nor manual workers whose productive capacity depended on a mental vacuousness inherited from the earliest Taylorist schemes.[12] From this ambiguous social and technical position stemmed an inherent challenge to managerial authority, for the modern enterprise rested on the superiority of management over workers performing extremely segmented work. No close supervision, however, could ensure these workers' commitment to organizational goals. As Drucker explained, only if knowledge workers internalized corporate objectives and accepted an "implicit contract" to exercise autonomy in the interest of the company would managerial rule be secure—unionism had earned corporate managers the participation of workers in the pursuit of corporate productive goals, but for knowledge workers it was unacceptable. Their values and norms must of necessity be managerial ones.[13]

The conflict at Bell Aerospace largely illustrated this tension between unionism and the managerial quest for loyalty. In its challenge to the NLRB decision to organize an election, the company argued that the procurement buyers were "managers," not "employees." Prominent in its argumentation was the fact that the company practiced management by objectives, a managerial technique pioneered by Peter Drucker in the 1950s and 1960s to help managers promote the legitimacy of their business goals among knowledge workers and secure the latter's acceptance of their authority. Indeed, the buyers set spending objectives at the beginning of each year and devoted much time to finding products that would enable them to meet these objectives.[14] During the investigation organized by the NLRB, Frank Seitz, the director of the procurement department, emphasized that the buyers exercised a large amount of discretion in their spending, for contracts worth less than $5,000, which amounted to a total of $7 million in 1969. Furthermore, when they prepared bigger contracts, the buyers headed a team composed of managers from several services, a prestigious role according to the company's top managers, who stressed that they were the voice of this team in the negotiations with the vendors. Finally, to defend the idea that the buyers were managers, the company pointed to the fact that nine of them were members of the National Association of Procurement Management, an association created in 1915 after the model of professional associations to cultivate the buyers' middle-class status.[15]

As in the case of organized foremen in the 1940s, cultural assumptions went hand in hand with concrete questions of power on the shop floor. Bell Aerospace top managers feared that if they were allowed to unionize, the buyers would more often than not base their decisions on the logic of collective solidarity instead of favoring the economic interests of the company. "If union considerations were to influence, as they well might, the decisions as to selection of vendors and price, the employer's business would be in jeopardy," the company contended in its brief. "The consideration of bids from union and non-union shops, which are not reviewed, could easily result in decisions adverse to the employer's interest."[16]

Despite the company's exertions, however, the success of the UAW organizing drive among the buyers reveals that a majority of them favored the collective security provided by a bargaining contract over the individualistic identity of management. In point of fact, their financial responsibilities and their constant interaction with managers notwithstanding, the employment conditions of the buyers differed little from those of organized white-collar workers. Like them, they were given three weeks of vacation once they had worked for the company for ten years, four after fifteen years, and five after twenty-five years. Their medical expenses, medical leaves, and life insurance were covered by the Prudential plan to which the company subscribed, and like the other white-collar employees they subscribed to a pension plan. In other words, they enjoyed no benefits in which either white-collar or blue-collar workers did not share in the divided welfare system that had developed in the postwar era. As for their pay, which ranged from $195 to $270 per week, it did not allow the buyers to claim a superior social status over white-collar and blue-collar employees. In a sense, Bell Aerospace thus symbolized the effects of the deradicalization of the labor movement's struggle since the 1940s, with the logic of security for which it had fought applying to a large number of blue-collar and white-collar workers alike.[17] But this deradicalization had a sharper edge too—because it encouraged the buyers not to identify as managers. Indeed, it is striking that that they did not feel compelled to have lunch in the managers' cafeteria—which the top managers strongly encouraged them to do—but usually joined the production workers in the main cafeteria.[18]

There was, however, an important difference between the buyers and the other white- and blue-collar workers employed by the company. Intent on making them professionals and managers in the full sense of the word, top managers used the provision of the Fair Labor and Standards Act excluding managers from its protection to refuse to pay them for overtime work. By contrast, engineers and technicians were paid time and a half for every hour they worked beyond the standard eight-hour day and forty-hour week. And it was precisely the question of overtime—along with the murky criteria governing the pay increases they could receive—that led the procurement buyers to seek the protection of the UAW. Moreover, when they prepared for and then led the negotiations over the amounts of large contracts, the buyers would travel far from Buffalo without being compensated for the time spent on the road.

Did Bell Aerospace open a Pandora's box when it agreed to bargain with the UAW over the status of its engineers and technicians? Company executives suggested this during the NLRB trial. By allowing these white-collar workers to embrace the collective practices of their blue-collar counterparts, the company's executives had eroded the respect for corporate authority that it needed from such workers. There indeed lay the significance of this localized challenge to managerial identity. If given the sanction of labor law, the decision of these buyers to claim the status of "employee" might undermine the foundations of the sociolegal levee built at midcentury to sustain managerial power, giving unionism greater legitimacy.

Labor law, however, was a serious obstacle. To hedge their contention that the procurement buyers were "managers" lying outside the purview of labor laws, Bell Aerospace executives relied on a long list of NLRB and court cases. Indeed, even before the adoption of the Taft-Hartley Act, the board differentiated systematically between managers and employees, explaining in *Ford Motor Company* in 1946 that "we have customarily excluded from bargaining units of rank and file workers executive employees who are in a position to formulate, determine, and effectuate management policies. These employees we have considered and still deem to be 'managerial,' in that they express and make operative the decisions of management."[19]

The categories that were then adopted to organize labor relations bore the impress of the Fordist regime in that they reflected the separation between planning and doing. In American enterprises geared toward mass production, the identity of middle managers was not at stake—they headed entire departments and made important decisions concerning the organization of work, the commercialization of products, and the company's financial strategies. As the NLRB's decision in the Ford case shows, manager and executive were then taken to be synonyms. Consequently, the NLRB had systematically classified engineers, chemists, and other professionals as "employees," precisely because they were not essential to the task of planning the company's production and future. Labor law thus acknowledged the difference between authority (the managers) and technological knowledge (professionals who were employees).

Such NLRB decisions had been made over corporate America's objections, and certainly had not obliterated the strong cultural forces weighing against white-collar unionism. Importantly, as we have seen, the logic of the distinction between planning and doing had prevailed even in the enactment of the Taft-Hartley Act. Congress excluded supervisors from the definition of "employee," thus extending the managerial exclusion to first-line foremanship: "The term 'supervisor' means any individual having authority, in the interest of the employer, to hire, transfer, suspend, lay off, recall, promote, discharge, assign, reward, or discipline other employees, or responsibly to direct them, or to adjust their grievances, or effectively to recommend such action if in connection with the foregoing the exercise of such authority is

not of a merely routine or clerical nature, but requires the use of independent judgment."[20] By way of contrast, the Senate rebuked the demands of
industrialists and prominent professional associations such as the National
Society of Professional Engineers, who sought to have professionals defined
as part of management. In its final version, the act protected professionals,
whom it defined as follows:

> 1. Any employee engaged in work (i) predominantly intellectual
> and varied in character as opposed to routine mental, manual,
> mechanical, or physical work; (ii) involving the consistent exercise
> of discretion and judgment in its performance; (iii) of such a
> character that the output produced or the results accomplished
> cannot be standardized in relation to a given period of time; (iv)
> requiring knowledge of an advanced type in a field of science of
> learning customarily acquired by a prolonged course of specialized
> intellectual instruction and study in administration or higher
> learning or a hospital.[21]

There was considerable overlap between the definition of professionalism
and the definitions of management and supervision provided by Congress
and the NLRB. Still, in the wake of the adoption of the Taft-Hartley Act, the
NLRB further elaborated on the classification of "manager" and "employee"
and put limits on companies' claims on the loyalty of their workers. In 1950
in the *New England Telephone* case, it ruled that workers in charge of leading
job interviews and recruiting new employees were indeed "managers" whose
membership in a union was incompatible with the fulfillment of their duties in the interest of the company. This "conflict of interest" test, however,
was not sufficient for sifting through all the potential managers, for many
of them did not take part in elaborating and carrying out the management
of the workforce. Indeed, following the Taft-Hartley Act, American companies made wide use of the title "manager," which became a weapon in the
fight against unions. After 1948, the ratio of the workforce that was classified by American companies as "supervisory" or "managerial" increased
substantially—a pattern that was not discernible in other countries such as
Germany and Sweden—which suggests that in the heyday of so-called labor-
management accord, the struggle for power between these entities did not
cease, but evolved into a less visible but equally important struggle over the
sociolegal notions defining the limits of each group.[22]

The board subsequently adopted a second test, the "discretionary power" test, to determine which workers were involved in formulating and implementing the objectives of the company employing them. At stake in this test was the discretion enjoyed by managers in making decisions. Thus, in 1963, the board ruled that workers who determined the prices of the products sold in a shop were not managers—they only carried out the directives formulated by their superiors.[23] Notably, this test allowed the board to firmly distinguish between the exercise of knowledge and true managerial prerogatives. In 1955, in *Westinghouse Electric Corporation*, the board decided that six engineers whose task was to determine whether a product was fit to be put on the market and at what price it should sell were not managers because the information they communicated to managers was the essence of their professional work.[24]

What the *Bell Aerospace* case revealed, however, was the organizational and technical evolution of American companies in the postwar era made it ever more difficult to distinguish between the exercise of authority characterizing managers and the exercise of knowledge that was embodied in any professional's work. At first blush the buyers' work was akin to that of many a professional insomuch as it was intellectual work, which was never routine, and required specific skills and training. They had to display the ability to make important decisions autonomously, and their position in the company's organization shows that they were not managers in the traditional sense of the word. None of them ran the Purchasing and Procurement Department, and it is significant that they worked under the supervision of eight supervisors whom the UAW did not seek to represent. Moreover, the autonomy of the buyers was only a partial one—they could commit the company to only small contracts, their decision to make or buy had to be validated by one of the supervisors, and even their lunch break was timed.

And yet there were other features in the buyers' work that suggested that buyers were managers. In assigning themselves cost-reduction objectives, the buyers acted as managers "making operative" the decisions of management. When they assembled a team to prepare the negotiation of a major contract, their task came close to Section 11, to "assign and responsibly direct." In short, any worker who enjoyed both autonomy and discretion on the job might have to give up the status of "employee."

Notably, what made the buyers' case so significant is that since the 1950s, knowledge workers had constituted the fastest growing group in the American workforce, an increase that came concurrently with the adoption of job-enrichment techniques advocated by theorists such as Chrys Argyris and Abraham Maslow, who suggested giving workers a measure of autonomy and discretion on the job to offset the debilitating consequences of Taylorism. Consequently, following Section 11 and the overall definition of supervisors and managers would inevitably put more and more workers out of the "employee" category and in the "management" one. A product of the mass-production enterprise that had budded before the Great Depression, the sociolegal categories "employee" and "managers" were now ill fitted to translate the new reality of industrial organization. At the very moment when the 1971 report *Work in America*, commissioned by Elliot Richardson, the secretary of HEW, denounced the "anachronism of Taylorism," the categories used to define the workforce and ascribe American workers a role and a social position were fast losing their social relevance.[25]

Here was the new frontier of labor progressives, for NLRB experts working within the framework of the sociology of labor established by Commons, who had always rejected class, were well positioned to take advantage of the erosion of the social structures produced by the industrial revolution.

Challenging Loyalty

In the 1960s the NLRB was no longer the storm center that it had been in the 1930s and 1940s. Certainly the agency, and unions in general, still counted determined opponents, such as the law professor Sylvester Petro, who published numerous books to advance the idea that labor law unfairly privileged unions at the expense of the freedom of workers. However, the combined impact of the Taft-Hartley amendments to the Wagner Act and the Republican nominations to the agency had largely eliminated the controversies that had animated the years during which the agency had thrown its weight behind the development of organized labor and particularly the CIO. The Eisenhower appointees to the board had redefined its role as that of a neutral agency with no vested interest in the outcome of labor conflicts. "Politics play a proper role in the enactment of laws, but politics have no place in their administration," estimated former corporate lawyer Guy Farmer, the chairman of the board. Philip Rodgers, another Eisenhower appointee, agreed that the NLRB's role was to see to the implementation of the law, not to seek to obtain "social, political or economic" results. Reflecting the fading political colors of the agency, Barry Goldwater, the libertarian conservative senator from Arizona, rejoiced in 1953 that the board was now committed to a "proper interpretation of the law." In James Gross's words, the "subversion" of American labor law was afoot, and the NLRB seemed both unable and unwilling to reclaim the mantle of social progress that it had once proudly displayed. When the NLRB tackled the *Bell Aerospace* case in 1970, however, three elements had fundamentally altered the political environment in which the board interpreted the law, giving the Progressive sociology of harmony through associational freedom a new lease on life.[26]

First was the Democrats' victory in the election of 1960, which brought a new generation of industrial pluralists to the board. There is no gainsaying, of course, that the 1960s brought a bittersweet harvest to American unions. Some of them, the UAW, for example, had provided useful groundwork in favor of the democratic candidate in the 1960 campaign, and Kennedy knew to tip his hat to labor in a speech delivered at Detroit on Labor Day, saying that unions were critical to the defense of the national interest. As for labor's hopes, they stemmed from the fact that in the two preceding years, the young senator had curried unions' favors by trying to use the impetus of labor reform brought by the McClellan Committee to amend the Taft-Hartley Act and make it easier for unions to sign collective bargaining contracts. Yet labor unions' political weight was less than their numerical strength might indicate. Even as liberalism ran at high tide, unions were unable to secure the repeal of the right to work provision of the Taft-Hartley Act—a clear sign of the influence that southern conservatives still wielded in the Democratic Party.

Even when the legislative process was closed for labor reform, the venue of administrative power still remained. As secretary of labor, Kennedy chose a well-known labor lawyer with whom he had collaborated in the Senate in the years 1958–1959, the United Steel Workers of America attorney Arthur Goldberg. Goldberg quickly convinced Kennedy to publish an executive order legalizing collective bargaining among federal employees, thus opening a new and important sociological horizon to American unions. Most important, Goldberg, before he left the Kennedy administration to join the Supreme Court in 1962, worked with James Landis on the list of candidates whom the president might nominate to the NLRB. A prominent liberal figure, Landis was a legal realist who had made a strong case for the development of administrative agencies in the 1930s, arguing that they were institutionally better fitted to defend the public interest than was Congress.[27] Landis's presence in the White House shows that there were in the halls of executive power many echoes of the New Deal. While the quest for industrial democracy had disappeared from the forceful social struggles led by the students riding south to force integration of public transportation, the modern liberal presidency still relied on the network of lawyers, economists, and theorists on which it had built its preeminence since the New Deal, and most important, its capacity to govern.[28]

President Kennedy did not have to wait long before he was first presented with an opportunity to stamp his mark on the NLRB. His nominee, Frank McCulloch, was a liberal whose personal career seemed to encapsulate the American liberal tradition. Kennedy had met McCulloch in Congress, where he worked as the legislative assistant to Paul Douglas, a prominent liberal senator who had taken an active role in New Deal politics in the 1930s. A 1930 graduate of Harvard Law School, McCulloch had first moved into social work, devoting his time to the Council for Social Action of the Congregational Christian Churches of America. McCulloch thus followed a family tradition—his mother, a suffragette, had studied with Jane Addams and spent long years working to uplift the poor. Then in 1946, McCulloch started working in the Senate, a job that he held alongside an appointment at Roosevelt University, where he taught industrial relations and created a program to train unionized workers.

Close on the heels of McCulloch's nomination, Kennedy nominated Gerald Brown. Trained as a historian in college, Brown studied economics in Chapel Hill with Harry Wolf, a former student of Harry M. Millis at Wisconsin. Under Wolf's aegis, Brown had written a master's thesis on the economic aspects of the Wagner Act. In 1938, he worked at the NLRB as a field examiner for the Atlanta regional board, which allowed him to take part in Operation Dixie—the unsuccessful large-scale organization drive launched by the CIO to break the hold of conservative democrats on the South. Brown was then promoted to director of the regional bureau of San Francisco, where he remained until his nomination. Like McCulloch, he was nominated for a second term in 1966.[29]

Kennedy's final nomination, by contrast, revealed the growing impact of the civil rights movement. The first African American to sit on the NLRB, Howard Jenkins was a moderate Republican who taught labor law at Howard University for ten years before joining the Department of Labor in 1956 as general counsel. Like that of Gerald Brown, Jenkins's career showed that the battles for racial and social inequality were not necessarily incompatible. While he was at the Department of Labor, Jenkins lent his legal abilities to the civil rights movement, but he also collaborated with Arthur Goldberg, who was then the attorney of the United Steel Workers of America.[30] Jenkins's nomination revealed the importance that political balance had acquired at the NLRB, and Johnson was careful not to upset this balance by nominating a Republican to the board in December 1964, Sam Zagoria. A journalist by training, Zagoria joined the *Washington Post* during World War II, and quickly evinced a strong interest for labor questions. Running against the tide of public opinion, which was then turning against unions, Zagoria became the head of the local section of the American Newspaper Guild, one of the few white-collar unions to thrive in the Popular Front culture of the New Deal, and then took a leave of absence to attend John Dunlop's classes at Harvard, where he fine-tuned his understanding of industrial pluralism. In 1955, Zagoria was hired as a legislative assistant to the Republican senator Clifford Case, and then he devoted much of his time to the investigations of the Labor and Public Welfare Committee, where he served as a precious link between Democrats such as Kennedy and liberal Republicans.[31]

Kennedy's and Johnson's nominations to the board thus demonstrate the bridges linking the intellectual and political liberal communities of the New Deal and of the Great Society. To be sure, industrial democracy had long disappeared from political debates, and the concept no longer animated the energies of youthful reformers. It remained in the guise of "industrial relations," which was a political culture, that is, a set of ideas whose influence was underwritten both by a social world made up of labor leaders, arbitrators, and professors and scholarly publications and by an institutional matrix protecting collective bargaining—the Industrial Relations Research Association, various academic programs, the NLRB, and the National Mediation Board, whose authority ensured the theory's social and political relevance.[32] Most important, the theory of industrial democracy had remained equally stable, as these experts conceived of labor relations in much the same way as their forebears. Democracy and cooperation were still the twin pillars of a policy aiming at promoting social peace. Taking stock of a decade of collective bargaining at the end of the 1960s, Gerald Brown thus extolled the philosophy that had developed at Wisconsin at the turn of the twentieth century in words that could have been used in the 1930s: "Collective bargaining as it has evolved in the United States is the best available method of resolving our industrial disputes consistent with our democratic system of free enterprise," he explained.[33]

These nominations led to the emergence of a new agenda at the NLRB, the second element fueling the rebirth of the struggle for harmony through collective bargaining. The strong intellectual and political ties between the Kennedy and Johnson appointees and the previous generation of industrial pluralists was manifested in a shared vision of the role of the NLRB, one fully in tune with the vision of reformers such as Leon Keyserling in the 1930s. Kennedy and Johnson appointed board members who argued that the mission of the NLRB was to *encourage* unionism because the public interest was vested in collective bargaining. These industrial pluralists thus remained wedded to the idea that the board should act like a legislator, not a judge. Rebuking the arguments advanced by conservatives since the 1940s, the chairman of the board, Frank McCulloch, denied that the general principles of adjudication of law should apply to the NLRB. Rather, McCulloch believed that the board was an agency in charge of promoting a right, and that to do so it had been given a wide mandate—to act on the preamble of the Wagner Act—a mandate typical of the policy-development mission usually given to administrative agencies. "The Board is not a court. The statute gives it affirmative authority which I would call *promotional* authority. It uses the words 'promote the practice of collective bargaining,'" Frank McCulloch later recalled.[34]

In the 1960s this perspective led to a jurisprudential activism symbolized by the board's fresh attitude toward unfair labor practices. In the *Plochman and Harrison* case, it ruled that the company's decision to show *And Women Must Weep*, a National Right to Work Committee film, was an unfair labor practice. The film told the story of an untruthful labor leader leading a strike that destroyed the local economy, plunging most workers into poverty.[35] The significance of the case did not simply stem from the fact that the drive to protect employer freedom of speech had fed the impetus to adopt the Taft-Hartley Act—in 1960 in California, employers had obtained the prosecution of a union for "libel by innuendo" after it had shown a controversial film titled *Poverty in the Valley of Plenty*.[36] Determined to bolster unions against corporate opposition, the board also reversed a 1953 decision to rule that if an unfair labor practice caused the defeat of a union in an NLRB election, the company should bargain with the union nonetheless. To cap it all, in *EX-Cell-O Corp.*, the Kennedy and Johnson appointees ruled that when a company refused to bargain in good faith, the collective bargaining contract should apply retroactively—any wage increase should apply to the period that had elapsed since the NLRB election.

Departing from the principles established by the Eisenhower board, the Kennedy-Johnson board sought to make labor law evolve congruently with American society and the economy to promote collective bargaining.[37] In a speech delivered at Washington University in 1964, Gerald Brown reminded his audience that the work done by the NLRB was part of the long institutional history of the theory of delegation. Like the Federal Trade Commission, the Interstate Commerce Commission, and the Fair Employment Practices Commission, the board sought to achieve a political and social objective—labor peace. The logic of delegation, Brown went on, was to rely on professional expertise, which meant in the case of the NLRB the capacity to understand the origins and meanings of social conflicts. "One doesn't become an expert in labor relations by merely reading records of cases involving unfair labor practices," Brown lectured. "The chief value of expertise is supposed to be flexibility in coping effectively with changing conditions." The idea of the social investigation had always been at the heart of the theory of collective bargaining—it had been developed in Wisconsin by Commons and his followers—and it clashed head-on with the idea that the board should behave like an neutral tribunal. But what is striking is that in 1964, the attendant theory of legal realism, one that had animated the reformist impulse of Progressives and New Dealers, remained at the heart of pluralist thinking and justified developing an industrial jurisprudence anew. Brown went on, "The development of life brings change and compels modification of many rules. . . . It was Oliver Wendell Holmes who said that 'the real justification for a rule of law is that it helps to bring about a social end which we desire.'"[38]

Delivered against the backdrop of the Supreme Court's increasing protection of racial equality, the speech must have struck a responsive chord, even if a strong anti-institutional attitude pervaded the youth, who were inclined, after C. Wright Mills, to see labor unions as an interest group resisting social change.[39] Indeed it is no surprise that Brown should have defended the board in front of students. But Brown's speech was more than a plea to remain relevant to the left—it reflected a fresh activism, a determination to remain abreast of current economic issues.

No case better exemplified the board's determination to adapt collective bargaining to changing conditions than *Fibreboard*. This case arose out of the decision made by a Californian company to subcontract the maintenance of its machinery, which had been performed by machinists affiliated with the United Steel Workers of America. The company made no secret of its motive, which was to save some $25,000 per year. To that effect, it had chosen a company that planned to use fewer machinists and to give them inferior fringe benefits than *Fibreboard*. In 1959, the Eisenhower appointees had agreed to this plan, but Brown and McCulloch expressed their opposition to the ruling as soon as they moved to the board. Working with John Fanning, the most liberal of the Eisenhower appointees, they reversed the 1959 ruling, arguing that subcontracting had become such an important feature of the nation's economic life that it should now be subject to collective bargaining.[40] The board confirmed its determination to fight emerging antiunion ploys when it ruled that a company had no right to close shop to avoid bargaining with a union.[41]

With decisions like these, it was no wonder that the 1960s were particularly difficult years for the agency. In similar fashion, the board's new activism coincided with the renewed corporate assault against unions, and companies sometimes refused to abide by the board's new decrees. Symbolized by J. P. Stevens's struggle against the board, this opposition reminds us that there were many tensions, as well as new challenges, in labor relations in the 1960s.[42] The battle over the legal definition of worker fit within a larger framework of perils and possibilities as businessmen and unions, labor experts, and other political elites debated the merits and future of the collective bargaining regime created in 1935.

Finally, it was the social context that nourished the pluralists' promotion of collective bargaining. In the 1960s, the new directions that collective bargaining should take were indicated by the new political struggles led by American youth. Chief among these was the fight for racial equality that had rocked the nation since the Montgomery movement in 1955. In 1964, the board adopted a new definition of the notion of *fair representation* in labor law in *Hughes Tool*, stating that unions that did not adequately represent the interests of African American workers were guilty of an unfair labor practice, but the board withheld its decision until the Civil Rights Act was adopted, lest it be used against the creation of the Equal Employment Opportunity Commission.[43] In the same fashion, Brown argued that the growing importance of environmental and consumer questions would require an evolution of collective bargaining and thus a possible redefinition of managerial prerogatives: "Workers and their unions have not gone into the questions of safety of products, fairness to consumers, pollution and such, and employers may assert unilateral control over such items as within their 'management rights,'" he noted. "But having observed some of the enthusiasm and vigor with which the young are tackling these environmental issues, I can only think some of this will spill over into collective bargaining."[44]

Beyond these immediate struggles, however, there was one issue that figured prominently in industrial pluralists' thinking, namely, white-collar unionism. According to Sam Zagoria, the budding white-collar movement, along with the shifting structures of the American economy, was the most significant feature of the economic environment in which the NLRB was to implement the theory of collective bargaining, and Zagoria went as far as organizing seminars at the board to convince his staff that they should work to adapt to these new conditions.[45] Soon enough, this concern was manifest in the board's evolving jurisprudence. The board first addressed the status of white-collar workers through the question of the size and scope of bargaining units. In 1944, it had ruled in the *Metropolitan Life* case that in the service industry no less than in the manufacturing one, bargaining units should be as large as possible—they should, the board then prescribed, gather all the workers of a company within a specific state. The rule made sense because in manufacturing, the mass-production economy literally "produced" a working class whose socioeconomic homogeneity underwrote the meaning of "employee," and whose interests were best defended with large units reinforcing the bargaining position of labor leaders. At the beginning of the 1960s, however, it was increasingly apparent that this rule had become an obstacle to the development of unionism among office employees, for unions encountered significant difficulties in gathering workers who did not share a work experience. In two important decisions handed down in 1961 and 1962, the board ruled that in the insurance and retail industries, bargaining units could represent groups of employees as small as a given store or a even a mere group of staff. "The realities were that the Board's decisions were frustrating the desires of employees to bargain collectively in those industries," Brown told a group of business and administration students in 1964. "Insurance agents and retail chain store employees have now been given the same rights as employees in other businesses."[46]

Such efforts take on their full meaning in the context of the sociological debate then raging about white-collar employees. While efforts to organize white-collar employees dated back to the early post–Civil War period, unionism really became significant outside of the blue-collar world after the 1930s. From the "unrest in odd places" that arose during the Great Depression to David Keefe's long exertions to organize the stock exchange workers in the 1940s, the creation of Engineers and Scientists of America (ESA) in 1953, the strikes of engineers at Westinghouse and General Electric, and the growth of public-sector employees in the 1960s, an arc of white-collar struggles seemed to suggest that unionism was poised to secure a foothold beyond the blue-collar world.[47] White-collar union membership had doubled in the 1940s, and increased from 1.4 million at the beginning of World War II to 2.75 million in 1960 and 3.2 million in 1968, at which point they represented 16 percent of all union members and 11.4 percent of white-collar employees. Pictorial representations also told a part of this cultural process, as the notion of the white-collar worker as "organization man" was challenged in comic books offering caricatures of office life with characters such as Mr. Dithers and Bugglebottom bossed around by gruff superiors.[48]

This was of course a modest pattern of growth, but it became a staple of the evolving labor economics expertise, filling hundreds of pages in labor relations and sociology publications. In a sense, the attention first stemmed from the high stakes that both corporate America and blue-collar unions discerned in the prospect of white-collar unionism. The former believed that the rise of unions in the office and the drawing room could be avoided if the mistakes made in the 1930s were not repeated. As early as 1957, the National Association of Manufacturers published booklets such as "Satisfying the Salaried Employee" and "Strengthening Ties with the Salaried Employee," which were designed to help their members adopt the right personnel policies, a practice that would last through the crisis of the 1970s, when some polls revealed that nearly half of all middle managers held favorable views of unions.[49] Unions, by contrast, looked with equanimity at these potential new members. Although they represented more than 30 percent of the workforce, American unions did not feel so secure that they could slight the prospect of recruiting professionals who had no historic ties to the picket lines, bloody strikes, and heroic moments that made up the labor lore. "The labor movement must break out of its 'blue collar shell' or face the prospect of becoming a declining numerical force," a research report of the AFL-CIO pithily explained in 1960. Indeed, by 1960 unions had started declining in absolute terms, and the changing composition of the workforce (white-collar workers composed the larger part of the workforce as early as 1960) was inauspicious for labor leaders.[50]

To labor economists, however, the white-collar union movement presented a challenge, to wit, understanding why a social group that had historically harbored a middle-class individualist mentality and always identified with management now seemed more and more willing to join unions. The challenge was most important because, as Clark Kerr, John Dunlop, Frederick Harbinson, and Charles Myers argued in 1955, managers and professionals were now an "economic resource," one that had become essential to economic growth.[51] David Moore and Richard Renck, two scholars associated with the Industrial Relations Center at the University of Chicago, agreed with the deans of the profession: "Because of the central position of technology in modern industry, it would seem that the professional employees, including engineers and natural scientists, should be a satisfied, well integrated group. Evidence . . . indicates that these employees tend to be chronically frustrated and dissatisfied."[52]

They answered this question within the framework of the dominant functionalist sociological school, emphasizing social roles and common values. Prominent in their analyses was the closing gap between white-collar workers' earnings and those of blue-collar workers, and, finally, their quest for security. Most important, however, is what Jack Barbash called the "socialization of the work situation" and what Clark Kerr and his colleagues called "the inevitable structuring of the managers and managed in the course of industrialization." In a way that somewhat anticipated Harry Braverman's work— albeit with a much different political flavor—they argued that as white-collar workers grew in numbers, professionals and technicians gradually lost their autonomy and felt the corrosive edge of the managerial imperative on their individuality. Thus in *The Scientist in American Industry*, a study of research scientists working in a laboratory, labor economist Simon Marcson estimated that the confrontation between traditional professionalism and industrial discipline was a source of strain to which managers were not alive.[53]

So far we are covering familiar ground, for these are the very dynamics that had led foremen to organize. There is, however, a fundamental difference between the two movements. The FAA emphatically contended that foremen were not managers. Indeed, they argued that they constituted a third group, supervision. By contrast, what most surfaced from the study of white-collar unionism was that in the 1960s, the social meaning of management was in a state of flux. Professionals needed to organize to defend themselves, but even as they responded to the allure of collective action, they did not shed their identity as managers. Thus airline pilots, who were 90 percent organized, claimed that they retained many of the basic managerial norms—an interest in the well-being of the company, a feeling of superiority to most blue-collar workers, an abiding individualism—none of which were incompatible with their decision to look after themselves as a group.[54] And in a pamphlet published to defend its choice to act as a labor union, ESA provided a rationale that was most germane to the case of Bell Aerospace buyers, and indeed to the future fate of labor in the United States:

> Are we really a part of management? Of course we are. At least
> we are in the sense that our work, our recommendations make

vital contributions to the operation of the company and to the
business decisions which must be made. However the shop
foreman, the bookkeeper, the plant guard, the shop worker
who institutes suggestions and the craftsman who takes pride
in his work all make vital contributions to the operation of the
company and assist top management in its job. Thus all are, their
way, a "part of management." The manager who proclaims that
"engineers are part of management" however, usually has another
thought in mind. He is thinking in terms of the "officer corps"
concept. Unconsciously or consciously the element which he is
emphasizing is that engineers should not be concerned about
their welfare and self interest. They should be confident that
management will take care of those matters adequately if not
handsomely.[55]

It seems hard to imagine a better case for the idea that the legal tension
between loyalty and unionism had run its course. Here lay a post-Fordist
definition of management, one that ESA defended because professional associations were not "so constructed as to be able to serve the interest of the
employed engineer in specific situations concerning his employment conditions."[56] Thus, from the white-collar struggle arose a legal question with
which industrial pluralists felt at ease—whether one could reconcile management and job conscious collective actions in labor relations. Soon this under-
taking would materialize in the case of the Bell Aerospace buyers, but first
it blossomed in an earlier case involving the rights at work of a man named
Jack Lenox.

An electrician employed as an adviser by a company selling electricity
in eastern Arkansas, Lenox seemed to be the perfect case in point to ease
the tension between unionism and loyalty that the Taft-Hartley Act had inserted into American labor law. A member of the International Brotherhood
of Electrical Workers (IBEW), he exemplified the question with which the
NLRB was faced—whether knowledge workers would enjoy the associational
freedom that had always characterized skilled work in America.

Lenox was employed by North Arkansas Electric, a Salem, Arkansas, company that employed fifty-five workers and was divided in seven branches.
Three bureaus were responsible for technical maintenance (Salem, Evening
Shade, Mountain Home), while the bulk of the work was divided into four
departments, management services, member services, office services, and

engineering services. Lenox worked in the member services of the Mountain Home bureau, were he was the only adviser. The other adviser worked for the Salem and Evening Shade bureaus.[57]

A member of the National Association of Electricity Inspectors, Lenox was not formally part of the company's management. The *manager* of the Mountain Home bureau was his supervisor. Yet he exercised numerous responsibilities—twice a year he attended a meeting with the general manager and the managers of each department, during which they discussed the development of the company's services and its overall strategy. Although he did not bear the title of manager, Lenox took part in these discussions as a technical advisor and made concrete suggestions as to the possible evolution of the company's rates. Once a year, he also took part in another meeting with the managers on the budget. He was also in charge of the company's advertisement strategy and controlled the use of money allocated to it. Finally, with these responsibilities came social responsibilities, as Lenox represented the company in the local meetings of the Rotary and Lions clubs.

Lenox's status in his company became contested in August 1966, when the IBEW launched an organizing drive among the company's workers. One of the managers then asked Lenox to remain neutral in the certification fight. "I considered him a management employee and part of the management team. I felt that as a member of management we had the right to ask him to remain neutral and not to take sides," the manager explained.[58] Indeed, North Arkansas managers were alive to Lenox's past as a member of the IBEW when he lived and worked in the North. In moving to Arkansas, Lenox had moved to a region where, in the words of James Gregory, "plain-folk Americanism"—a mixture of rugged individualism, independence, evangelicalism, and anticommunism—prevailed, leaving little room for the development of unions.[59] As Lenox explained, however, his reasons for leaving his union job and moving South had nothing to do with the union itself, and he quickly decided to join the organizing drive. On September 8, 1966, the union won the election organized by the NLRB. On the September 27, Lenox was fired, whereupon he petitioned the board, claiming North Arkansas was guilty of an unfair labor practice.[60]

Was Lenox an "employee" within the meaning of the Wagner Act? The board's decision reveals fully the problem raised by the case of knowledge workers. Lenox was not a manager in the traditional meaning of the word, but he did take part in formulating and effectuating his company's policies, and enjoyed discretion in doing so. According to Lowell Goerlich, the board's trial examiner, the discretionary power test was useless in the Lenox case. Accordingly, the board refused to classify Lenox as a manager. Without denying the importance of his responsibilities, board members argued that Lenox's autonomy and independence on the job were not wide enough to warrant his exclusion from the Wagner Act. His autonomy was limited by decisions made by the company's managers, and Lenox responded to a supervisor:

> The record is barren of any competent proof that Lenox exercised discretion *absent* any established policy or regulation of the Respondent. In fact the Responsibilities and Authorities established for electrification advisors in the position description provide that the electrification advisor "*within the limits of established policies, budget, legal requirements, and authority delegated by the Manager of Member Services assumes responsibilities and performs the following activities.*"[61]

To reach the conclusion that Lenox was an "employee" entitled to bargaining rights, the NLRB had thus modified its "discretionary power test" to resolve the tension between the exercise of authority and that of knowledge. The phrase "absent any established policy or regulation" indicated that regardless of their responsibilities, workers who did not work fully autonomously, workers who had supervisors, might not be classified as "managers" any longer. In a few words, the board provided a new definition of "employee," overturning a long line of precedents going back to the Wagner Act in order to allow the act to include the growing number of knowledge workers. Tellingly, the text of the decision highlighted the democratic ambition of its authors. "The Act is to be liberally and broadly construed to accomplish its purpose, among which are 'protecting the exercise of full freedom of association and of self organization,'" the decision said. "In that the rights provided to individuals by the Act are in the public interest, a deduction which denies an individual the protection of the Act ought to be avoided unless compelled by the clear language of the statute itself."[62]

Rebuking the board's democratic ambitions, the company refused to abide by the decision and sought redress in court. After three years of legal proceedings, in June 1969 the Court of Appeals for the Eighth Circuit handed down its decision. Reviewing the responsibilities held by Lenox, the court held that the NLRB's decision was untenable and reached the conclusion that the board members had sought to avoid; in light of the board's jurisprudence and the tests it had long developed to differentiate between managers and employees, Lenox indeed was a manager whose responsibilities were incompatible with unionism. Moreover, the court remanded the case to the board with what it called "specific instructions": "to determine whether or not the discharge of Lenox, as a 'managerial employee' was or was not violative of the Act."[63]

The court's message was clear: there was to be no progressive evolution of the concept of "employee." If the board wanted to reconsider its long-standing policy of excluding managers from the purview of the Wagner Act, it should do so openly. This, however, was less than a friendly invitation, for in asking the board to determine whether the decision to fire Lenox, a manager, constituted a violation of the act, the court launched a debate over the meaning of the supervisory clause of the Taft-Hartley Act and the idea that the loyal and effective representation of the employer was not fully compatible with the participation in a union.

The board's response came in August 1970. In its new decision, it officially abandoned the policy to exclude managerial employees, noting that "managerial employees, traditionally excluded from bargaining units because their interests are more aligned with management than with rank and file employees . . . might nevertheless be 'employees' within the meaning of the Act and entitled to the Act's protection."[64] Notably, this ruling was based on the decision to abandon the discretionary power test. From now on, only the "conflict of interest" test would be used. This was the most progressive interpretation of the act that the board could have given, and it left a serious dent in the doctrine of managerial loyalty. To be deprived of bargaining rights, a manager would have to be directly concerned with the management of the workforce. Since this was not Lenox's case, his dismissal was a violation of the Wagner Act. One year later, the NLRB applied this new reasoning in its decision regarding the procurement buyers employed by Bell Aerospace—although they were managers, they too were to enjoy the full protection of the law.

The Chameleon of Industrial Pluralism

This is not suggest to say that the labor experts working at the board in the 1960s and the early 1970s sought a radical transformation of the workplace that would thoroughly advance the cause of American workers and their quest for collective independence. As a number of historians and legal scholars have argued, industrial pluralism placed such an important emphasis on labor peace that its practitioners were sometimes willing to contemplate and resort to means to demobilize labor militancy, and one cannot appreciate the nature of the labor politics of these experts labor politics if one does not come to terms with their open rejection of class consciousness, which remained the basic feature of their approach to labor relations.[65]

In the 1960s and early 1970s, labor experts rejoiced at what they took to be the success of the project that the first generation of labor economists had started in the 1930s—to find an alternative to the class struggle arising from the workers' quest for economic independence. Thus, the most prominent of labor experts, John Dunlop, remarked, "Our collective bargaining system must be classed as one of the more successful distinctive American institutions. . . . The industrial working class has been assimilated into the mainstream of the community, and has altered to a degree the values and directions of the community, without disruptive conflict and alienation and with a stimulus to economic efficiency."[66] Defending the board against conservative criticism in 1971, Gerald Brown went Dunlop one better, arguing that "many scholars have remarked that the stabilizing and humanizing effect [of the NLRB] had provided suitable alternatives to the class struggle for reconciling conflicts of interests and consequently saved capitalism from the fate predicted by Marx and seen in Russia," a statement that faithfully echoed some of the arguments deployed in the 1930s to push for the adoption of the Wagner Act.

There were in such statements echoes of a kind of American exceptionalism that was fully in tune with the cult of consensus that characterized American society until the racial struggles of the 1960s, a consensus expressed in the dominant pluralism of the day. Symbolized by the work of Robert Dahl, a former advocate of planning, the idea that American society was best described as a "polyarchy" had become common coin, enveloping many a former leftist like Seymour Martin Lipset and Daniel Bell. In point of fact, industrial pluralists were at home in this deradicalized environment that celebrated consensus over strife. Indeed the idea of collective bargaining was fully compatible with the theory that the public interest was best served by the competition of various groups, which in turn implied that labor relations were thoroughly depoliticized. As historian Nelson Lichtenstein has argued, "Free collective bargaining was exactly that, which is why the AFL-CIO, the State Department, and the Voice of America hailed its depoliticized virtues around the globe."[67]

For industrial pluralists, then, the political culture of the midcentury, one largely influenced by the Cold War, did not stand in opposition to the reformist schemes of the Progressive Era. Rather, it reinforced their belief that collective bargaining promoted harmony by deflecting class feelings. To be sure, by the 1960s this achievement was itself contested, as a number of voices rose on the left to lament the growing political vapidity of organized labor. Collective bargaining was useless, such books and articles argued, because unions had lost the ability to project a political ambition. The energy was gone.[68] Yet labor experts were quick to dismiss these dissenting voices. Arthur Ross, who taught industrial relations at the University of California, delivered a sobering response, arguing that the critics would not be so disillusioned if they had not harbored "unwarranted illusions that the labor unions would bring about basic political and social changes in the United States." And Ross continued, "Really it is not surprising that unions have been absorbed into the fabric of a business economy, and that collective bargaining has become a business function devoid of preternatural significance."[69]

This context is important if we are to understand why and how it was possible to attempt to limit and reframe the conservative doctrine of loyalty. Moreover, it matters that to the pluralists, the structure of the workplace and social conflict at work were severed because of a variety of sociological factors that the literature on white-collar unionism in the 1950s and 1960s highlighted—while the main argument was that such unions were on the rise, it was expected that they would also fundamentally transform the political outlook of the existing labor unions, for white-collar employees elicited none of the concern for general social change that animated the radical moves of the 1930s. Rather, this literature emphasized the possibility to combine the technique of collective bargaining with a traditional white-collar ideology.

This was visible in the stance adopted by the ESA and the Air Line Pilots Association, but also in case studies such as Michael Harrington's lesser-known *The Retail Clerks* (1962). As Clark Kerr and colleagues argued, the key to understanding the white-collar worker in the postwar era was the growing tendency to organize "by occupation and skill"—a tendency that meant that the "ideological labor movements as we have known them will have passed."[70] The trend toward professionalism was indeed an object of interest to many sociologists at the time, and Arthur Ross, echoing the identity struggles of the day, used the phrase "professional mystique" to analyze the specificity of the outlook of most white-collar workers seeking to organize, while Bernard Goldstein saw in the development of nonaffiliated white-collar organizations the possible seedbed of a new "union center in the European sense," that is, "a federation of salaried employees, separate and distinct from the unions of production workers and skilled craftsmen"—which was precisely what the FAA had tried to do in the 1940s. All in all, white-collar unions evinced a job consciousness that cannot have taken the heirs of the Wisconsin school aback.[71]

While the new frontier NLRB was thus walking in the footsteps of William Leiserson and Harry Millis, there was one significant difference between this struggle for associational freedom and the previous one—the UAW was now thoroughly alive to the need to expand the realm of collective bargaining beyond the limits of blue-collar solidarity. In advancing this moderate vision of the postwar workplace, labor economists and the NLRB were fully in tune with the arguments marshaled by the UAW in its efforts to convince white-collar workers to join the union whose leaders had once been at the forefront of the critique of capitalism. "Your needs are different," a TOP leaflet explained, "and the UAW provides Special Solutions!" Among those were the promise to seal white-collar workers off from blue-collar members, to let them have their own membership meetings, their own bargaining committee, and specifically trained representatives. In a speech detailing the rationale behind the creation of TOP in 1965, Hubert Emerick did not try to hide the sociological gap separating most white-collar workers from their blue-collar counterparts. The fact remained, Emerick explained, that "a great deal of our failure stems from the idea that there are no differences in interests between the employer and the employee. . . . This conflict of interest is not subversive not immoral nor unethical. The theory of our constitutional form of government rests on the notion that the interests of the legislative, the executive and the judiciary may, and often do, conflict, and that this difference is good." What Marx had not brought about, then, Montesquieu and Madison could deliver—a fragmentation of the managerial ranks into a pluralist world of unions representing the collective interests of specific groups of managers.[72]

What, then, should we make of the pluralists' effort to change the meaning of the categories "employee" and "manager"? As we have seen, the case of foremen in the 1940s showed that even a moderate and pragmatic development akin to the creation of professionally oriented unions such as the organizations of "cadres" in France implied a definition of the social meaning of work that fully departed from the managerial book, which stressed that unionism was incompatible with self-advancement in occupations and jobs that involved more than soulless labor. And conservatives were not about to give up on this cherished ideal. Here, indeed, lay the radical edge of industrial pluralism, an edge that mattered even more than in the 1940s, when William Leiserson, Harry Millis, and Paul Herzog had labored to bring foremen under the purview of the Wagner Act. Industrial pluralists did not argue that conflict at work was dysfunctional, but only that it could be managed and channeled if the employment relationship was democratic. They forcefully reaffirmed the idea that principles guiding collective bargaining social justice and democracy remained relevant as long the as the employment relationship existed. As McCulloch explained at the turn of the 1970s, no return to the free labor doctrine was acceptable: "That's the whole idea. That the individual will not be subject to the whim of employers, but will be protected by a collective grouping which will serve the purpose of mutual aid and protection. . . . I believe the social conditions—the need for employees to have a more effective voice through their collective operations in a union—are still great."[73] The use of the word "individual" encapsulated the protean character of industrial pluralism, for while it entailed a rejection of class consciousness of the kind expressed in many strikes organized in the 1960s in the United States and Europe, it also reaffirmed the asymmetrical nature of the employment relationship. Both McCulloch and Brown insisted that no individual could be expected to deal with his or her employer alone, and that in a democracy, workers should voluntarily agree to their employment conditions.[74] Moreover, it was precisely this belief in the need to bolster the position of the "individual" at work that led industrial pluralists to advocate the development of unionism in the white-collar and managerial world. Thus Jack Barbash, who taught industrial relations at the University of Wisconsin, noted that for professional workers, "the character of the work makes little difference whether problems exist between the employee and the employer . . . there are essential differences of interests between those who are employed and those who employ."[75] Indeed, it was all the easier to contemplate such a development that the dynamics of labor relations did not entail that white-collar and blue-collar workers be included in large bargaining units. "In this pluralistic society, we will continue to have many forms of companies and unions, different types of collective bargaining in different units," Brown explained.[76]

Interestingly, in making this claim industrial pluralists did not simply strive to reaffirm the significance of the New Deal experience, they also derived their energy and self-confidence from the social and political context of the postwar era, especially the revolt against structures of authority that characterized the struggles of that time.[77] In this respect it was no happenstance that Clark Kerr was the president of the University of California just as it dealt with the question of student democracy, for Kerr believed that he could mediate social relations on campus to achieve durable institutional peace and progress. Similarly, at the end of the decade, Gerald Brown sanguinely predicted the extension of the principles of collective bargaining to new areas of society such as farmer and agricultural employee relations, government and public employee relations, professional teams and athletes, landlords and tenants, universities and students. Brown saw in all these current conflicts the need for a process whereby negotiation would make an agreement possible. Collective bargaining thus "offered the hope" in Brown's words, that the country's most urgent social problems would be solved reasonably and that demonstrations and violence would make way to social peace. Brown looked with such optimism at the future of collective bargaining that he believed that it might even require a new name.[78]

The promotion of white-collar and managerial unionism was thus fully compatible with the disappearance of the labor question. This irony had been noticed as early as 1948 by the weekly conservative *Business Week* in an article outlining the new contours of the struggle between unions and corporations: "The logic behind [the Taft-Hartley Act] might be that unions had been put in their place, but it flatly affirms that they do have a place. The matter of respectability can be weighty to an office worker out of all proportion to how it would bear on a factory hand."[79] In an ironic twist of history, then, the pluralist idea that the public interest lay in the synthesis of several competing interests was fully in tune with the process of negotiation that labor experts advocated, and it thus became the best argument against the idea that unionism made sense only in the Fordist context of manual, blue-collar work. As Jack Barbash explained, "The essence of democratic, pluralistic society as distinguished from monolithic mass society is the existence of self-governing groups which can have influence on things that matter to them. I can see no good reason why professional employees ought not to have this opportunity for self-government free from their own indulging myths and from myths of management's making."[80] Chameleon-like, industrial pluralism appears bland against the grand reformist schemes 1930s, but in view of the stakes inherent in the definition of "employee" and "manager," in a context of growing anti-unionism it takes much brighter colors. Just as corporate America, which had never accepted the basic premise of unionism, was getting ready to launch a full-scale attack on the New Deal collective bargaining regime, the industrial pluralists' promotion of an individual right to organize that should accrue to any person working for wages or a salary offered important protection. The ideology of social harmony was as important to the defense of unionism in the 1960s and 1970s as it had been fifty or sixty years earlier.

Yet there was one fundamental difference between political pluralism and collective bargaining. Coinciding with the rediscovery of Alexis de Tocqueville's *Democracy in America*, the rise of pluralism was premised on freedom of association. Tellingly, in the early 1960s the Supreme Court had reinforced this right by protecting the activities of the NAACP.[81] By contrast, notwithstanding the union leaders' and the board members' rhapsodic descriptions of the corporation as a polity, the right to organize was nowhere to be found in the jurisprudence protecting freedom of association and individual rights. As we saw in Chapter 2, the law had not been built to protect workers as citizens, but rather to give the federal government the administrative means to foster social harmony, and the definition of the worker had always been subservient to that policy. It remained to be seen whether pluralists would be able to transcend such limitations.

The Limits of Labor Liberalism

In arguing that Bell Aerospace buyers were "managers" who should be allowed to organize because they were did not take part in the formulation of the labor policies of the company, the board and its new general counsel, Peter G. Nash, hoped to rely partly on the oddest of precedents: *ILGWU v. NLRB* (1964). The case arose out of the organizing wind that blew through union business agents in the late 1950s and early 1960s. Most unions agreed to bargain with their employees, but the International Ladies Garment Workers Union (ILGWU) took a different route. Seeking to chastise its organizers for placing their own interests above the cause defended by the union, the ILGWU argued that it need not bargain with its business agents because they were "managers," not "employees." The board decided against the union, and the Court of Appeals for the Second Circuit ruled that in spite of the skill and independent judgment required from union agents, they should not be classified as "managers" because they followed and applied the policy set by the union.[82]

Yet as a precedent, the case was a mixture of good and bad. On the one hand, pointing to a case decided by the court prior to the board's decision to alter its policy to exclude managerial employees was a way to downplay the importance of the decision to shift course and focus on the criteria defining the workers' jobs. The board could thus hope to demonstrate that in the absence of a clear conflict of interest, protecting the freedom to organize of a worker made sense regardless of his or her title. But there was also a sobering feature in the ILGWU's battle against the bargaining rights of its own staff—in fighting this battle, one of the unions that had engineered the move toward industrial democracy proved willing to contribute to a body of law restricting the right to organize. Considering the jurisprudential logic of law, this was a sign of the growing entrenchment and separation of the categories of managers and employees as social entities spelling rights at work. The union should have shuddered at that, but it did not.

The Supreme Court handed down its decision in the *Bell Aerospace* case on April 23, 1974. The ruling was a defeat for the NLRB, but also for the solicitor general, Erwin Griswold, who had in this case adopted a progressive position, asking the Court not to deprive all managerial employees of bargaining rights. Indeed the Court decided that all managers, regardless of their responsibilities, should be assimilated to "employers" in the collective bargaining process. Furthermore, the Court chastised the board for resorting to "rule making" in *North Arkansas* and *Bell Aerospace* and trying to effect a major change in labor relations. Ruling that the company was under no obligation to bargain with its buyers, the majority of the Court was composed of the conservative justices nominated by Richard Nixon, William Rehnquist, Burger, and Lewis Powell, but also of William O. Douglas and Harry Blackmun, two figureheads of legal liberalism.[83]

The majority opinion, drafted by Lewis Powell, reflected the lowly institutional position of the NLRB. Board members had taken heart from the Court's approval of their decision to facilitate organizing in the insurance industry in the *Metropolitan Life* case (1965). In this case, it had been acknowledged that the board could "depart from precedent." But oral arguments in *Bell Aerospace* must have dashed these hopes, for they mostly focused on the board's authority to depart from the policy to exclude managers, rather than on the rationale of the board's main argument—that contrary to the claims of the company's executives there was no "community of interest" between them and the buyers. Indeed even in the majority opinion Powell ignored whatever considerations may have led the board to reconsider its policy to exclude managers from collective bargaining. Far from trying to reconcile the legal norm with social reality, Powell focused on the original intent of the drafters of the Taft-Hartley and Wagner Acts. In a memorandum sent to his brethren in March 1974, Powell explained that the historical research he had conducted had convinced him that the congressional intent was indeed to exclude managers from the protection of the act. In no way could the NLRB circumvent this original design as it had in its *North Arkansas* decision.[84] Indeed, the only element qualifying the severity of the ruling was the Court's decision to re-mand the case to the NLRB so that the board would decide whether the buy-ers were indeed "managerial."[85]

The weakness of the board in this debate over congressional intent was pat-ent, and it largely symbolized the growing suspicion with which courts had looked at administrative agencies in the postwar era. As we have seen, faith in the superior power of expertise to achieve social reform through objective ad-ministrative rule making had informed much of the New Deal and animated a generation of labor liberals, foremost among whom were James Landis and William O. Douglas. But the legitimacy of expertise had largely faded. Agency capture had belied hopes for neutrality, while the reliance on expertise of the fascist and Nazi regimes had deprived the theory of the legitimacy it once had. By the 1960s, intellectuals like Louis Jaffe and Theodore Lowi denounced the "illusion of ideal administration" and the congressional practice of delegation. Democracy did not require expertise; on the contrary, it required participa-tion. Indeed, a whole generation of students could only agree.[86]

Compounding the board's weakness was the lack of a strong social move-ment to bolster its new reading of the social meaning of management. As we have seen, in the 1940s, the changing definition of "employee" had been forged within the framework of a dialogue involving statist agencies and fore-men pushing for change from the bottom up. By contrast, in the 1960s and early 1970s, the white-collar movement lacked a strong power base shoring up the social vision advanced by labor economists. Not only did this orga-nizing drive take place against a background of growing antiunionism, but companies easily thwarted unions by granting professional and managerial employees "tandem increases" making the unions unappealing. And profes-sional societies such as the National Society of Professional Engineers ham-pered the unionization effort with the creation of "sounding boards" meant to bring professional employees and managers closer together. Significantly, as in the case of General Electric, such sounding boards grouped all employed engineers, including those at all levels of management.[87]

Consequently, the returns of NLRB elections in the 1960s tell a sober-ing story—the elections for white-collar units organized from January to September 1960 resulted in sixty-one victories and sixty defeats for unions, which thus recruited over 2,220 workers and failed to attract another 3,910. In 1965, the UAW TOP was involved in seventy elections, winning forty of them and gaining 3,418 members. In the 1970s, elections involving units of engineers of 100 or more mostly resulted in defeats for unions, which lost fourteen elections out of eighteen. A symbol of the white-collar promise in the 1950, the ESA by the end of the 1960s was lurching toward a rapid death, its members unable to come to an agreement on whether the union should affiliate with the CIO or even let in technicians. There were, of course, strong white-collar unions such as the American Federation of State, County and Municipal Employees (AFSCME), the American Federation of Teachers (AFT), the Professional Air Traffic Controllers, and the Air Line Pilots Association, but overall the movement did not come close to providing the critical mass that experts need to weigh on the evolution of social policies.[88]

Penned as it was from a representative of the conservative establishment of Virginia, the majority opinion in *Bell Aerospace* was hardly surprising— Nixon, after all, had made original intent a litmus test in the selection of his Supreme Court nominees. Lewis F. Powell exemplified Nixon's determination to alter the course of the Supreme Court. Born in 1907 to a distinguished Virginia family, Powell studied law in Virginia at Washington and Lee University before spending a year at Harvard Law School, where he received his LLM, but he was not fully swayed by the teaching of Frankfurter and Roscoe Pound. A respected jurist and a well-known opponent of attempts to preserve segregation in his home state, Powell was a conservative in the mold of the new right when it came to economic questions. Indeed, Powell went on to become a corporate attorney and made his mark among conservatives by drafting a policy memo for the director of the U.S. Chamber of Commerce in 1971, a few months before his nomination. In what is known as the "Powell manifesto," the Richmond attorney warned against the continuous diminution of freedom in the United States: "No thoughtful person can question that the American System is under attack. . . . The assault on the free enterprise is broad-based and consistently pursued. It is gaining momentum and converts."[89] The memo rang with new right intellectual overtones (Powell quoted Milton Friedman and William F. Buckley), but it was meant to provide concrete guidelines. Powell called on conservatives to finance campaigns to regain control of crucial political levers such as universities, the media, and the courts. Clearly, the man who argued that the "freedom of both business and labor" had been "seriously impaired" was unlikely to sanction the unionization of managers.[90]

More intriguing, however, is William O. Douglas's response to the letter sent by his fellow justice, for Douglas assured Powell that he would side with him during the conference vote. To understand why Douglas and even Blackmun, two of the main engines of the Court's activism in the constitutional interpretation of individual rights, rebuked the NLRB's most innovative decision, one needs to turn to Powell's opinion, one that must have elicited much satisfaction in Douglas. Indeed, the opinion did not endorse the complaints of the new right ideologues who had inspired Powell's manifesto. Rather, it largely endorsed the arguments deployed by the great liberal jurist in his dissent in the *Packard v. NLRB* case in 1947.[91]

A conservative jurist like Lewis Powell, who had always been removed from the liberal policy networks that had grown dominant since the New Deal, was unlikely to seek much support in an opinion authored thirty years earlier. Powell might have been content with writing an opinion overturning the board's decision in *Bell Aerospace* on the grounds that it conflicted with the intent of Congress. But Powell was keenly interested in Douglas's dissenting opinion because he wanted to write his opinion within the framework of the history of industrial democracy.

William Orville Douglas was no stranger to that tradition. Born in Minnesota in 1898, this Presbyterian grew up in poverty but still managed to combine work and academic studies. A stellar student, he graduated from the Columbia Law School in 1923, where he imbibed many of the reformist schemes that underwrote the adoption of the Wagner Act—institutional economics and legal realism. After a brief teaching stint at Columbia, he earned an appointment at Yale Law School, the seedbed of legal realism, where he taught until 1934. At that time, like many lawyers, he moved to Washington, where he became one of the keystones of the New Deal. Nominated chairman of the Securities and Exchange Commission in 1937, Douglas's position in the liberal policy community was prominent enough—he was close to Felix Frankfurter, Isador Lubin, and Harold Ickes—that he was appointed by Roosevelt to the Supreme Court in 1939, after the debacle of the Court Packing Plan, when the president needed to send the most trustworthy advocates of American liberalism to the high bench.[92]

Most important, Douglas was also very close to the labor movement, as was evidenced by his participation in the Tenth Annual Convention of the CIO in 1948. While unions were under attack from conservatives and faced an uncertain future as the Cold War dawned, the Supreme Court justice urged CIO leaders to play the same role in peacetime as they had during the conflict. Theirs was a most important economic and political contribution, Douglas explained: "Labor's role in our national progress is unique and paramount. It is Labor, organized and independent labor that can supply much of the leadership, energy, and motive power which we need today."[93]

Douglas remained an adamant supporter of labor unions throughout his career on the bench, relentlessly reminding companies of their social obligations. But Douglas also used the authority vested in him to outline the limits of industrial democracy. And it was precisely those limits that attracted Powell's attention. Pointedly, two elements in Douglas's dissenting opinion were relevant to Powell's design. First was the idea that legitimizing collective bargaining by foremen was tantamount to subverting the dynamics of labor relations, a point that Powell readily endorsed in *Bell Aerospace*, quoting Douglas:

> The present decision . . . tends to obliterate the line between management and labor. It lends the sanctions of federal law to unionization at all levels of the industrial hierarchy. It tends to emphasize that the basic opposing forces in industry are not management and labor but the operating group on the one hand and the stockholder on the other. The industrial problem as so defined comes down to a contest over the fair division of the gross receipts of industry between these two groups. The struggle for control or power between management and labor becomes secondary to a growing unity in their common demands on ownership.[94]

What Douglas had argued in effect was that allowing foremen to organize would pave the way for a democratic regulation of productive property that would subvert capitalism by placing the democratic ideal above the sanctity of property on which the capitalist system had heretofore relied.[95] As we have seen, in 1947 Douglas's dissenting opinion embodied the "end of reform" analyzed by Alan Brinkley, for his defense of management stood squarely against the more reformist vision laid out by Adolph Berle and Gardiner Means in their 1932 opus, *The Modern Corporation and Private Property*, in which they exposed the unaccountability of managerial circles to society as a whole. This idea had not died, cropping up in various guises in the work of James Burnham and John. K. Galbraith, but in the 1970s it was a more recent theory that seemed to give the unionization of professionals and technicians classified as "managers" its full political meaning. The theory of a "postindustrial society" had blossomed, and with it the idea that science and technology were potential "social" resources, removed from the dynamics of the market, and that those social sources could give rise to a fresh democratic impetus.

While they did not claim to advance such ideas, board members neverthe-less indirectly favored them. In 1970, the NLRB had revised and extended its jurisdiction to the very locus of the production of knowledge, university campuses, helping the American Association of University Professors and the AFT (which held different political views) to organize sundry campuses throughout the nation.[96]

But the Supreme Court had no taste for this democratic potential, and it soon took a strong stance against unionized faculties.[97] There again it was Justice Powell who led the charge, this time rejecting the NLRB's argument that the duties and responsibilities of the faculty of Yeshiva University—course selection, deciding course offerings, teaching methods, grading policies, and the number of students admitted—were all part of the routine discharge of their professional duties, that is, they were not exercised in the employer's interest and properly fell within the provision of the Taft-Hartley Act protection of professionals.

To Powell, however, there was no difference between university professors and high-grade managers in a private company. "To the extent the indus-trial analogy applies," Powell explained, "the faculty determines within each school the product to be produced, the terms on which it will be offered, and the customers who will be served." Powell never explained why the industrial analogy was apposite and why the unionization of faculty staff constituted a threat of "divided loyalty" for the university. As William J. Brennan—one of the architects of the Warren Court's liberal jurisprudence—noted in dissent, the idea that scholars' competence depended on their undivided loyalty to their employer actually put a serious dent in the concept of academic free-dom.[98] But Powell, like many conservatives in the 1970s, had identified the university as a key element in the liberals' ability to labor American culture, and he was not about to sanction its unionization. In *Yeshiva*, the Court im-posed the managerial exclusion where it least belonged, turning the univer-sity into a laboratory for conservatives seeking to make ever greater numbers of workers dependent on the goodwill of employers and the vagaries of the market. Years later, the Bush NLRB followed in Powell's footsteps by ruling that graduate teaching assistants and research assistants at Brown University were not "employees" but "students" because teaching those classes was sim-ply part of their academic training. Yet if the board had followed the tortuous "industrial analogy" that led Powell to characterize scholars as managers be-cause of their responsibilities, it should have logically concluded that teach-ing assistants and research assistants were, by contrast, workers. At least hundreds of thousands of young Americans each year would have been provided with an important opportunity to reflect on the links between democracy and work.[99] To paraphrase the great Oliver Wendell Holmes, "the life of the [conservative] law has not been logic."

Quite beyond the struggle against liberal academia, *Yeshiva* partook of the conservative strategy to reinforce the managerial exclusion. To the Court, unionizing management was unthinkable because it ran straight into the principle of "entrepreneurial control," a phrase Douglas had used in his dissent in *Fibreboard*, echoing a principle that many industrial pluralists had expressed since the beginning of the struggle for industrial democracy during the Progressive Era—that the logic of democracy stopped at the door of free enterprise, which it did not fundamentally challenge. By way of contrast, the view advanced by the NLRB in the 1940s and 1960s was that the right to organize was an expression of the democratic ideal, one essential in making the worker a citizen worker. In this perspective there could be no sociological limits to the meaning of "employee," which was the industrial equivalent of the citizenry: "The essence of democracy has been described as the participation of every mature individual in the formation of the values and institutions which regulate men living together. This agency has contributed much in this direction, and I am proud to have been a small part of it," Brown explained as his first tenure at the board ended in 1966.[100]

But if American workers were not citizen workers, what then was an "employee"? Against the reformist design of the board, Powell, Blackmun, and Douglas now marshaled a historicized vision of the right to organize and the policy on which it rested. According to them, the logic of collective bargaining was not to transcend the structure and dynamics of the modern enterprise, but simply to remedy the most nefarious social effects of capitalism. Quoting Louis D. Brandeis, the Supreme Court justice and early advocate of both industrial democracy and Taylorism, Douglas explained in 1947 that the employer's quest to attain the greatest productivity possible was a legitimate one, but should be pursued through a "narrowing of the gap between management and labor." Collective bargaining, Douglas argued, was a "measure of therapeutic value," and the right to organize, like all rights, was a means to a social and economic end. In protecting workers and freeing them from foremen's and managers' arbitrary rule and favoring cooperation in its stead, it had fulfilled this objective.[101]

Hence Douglas did not subscribe to the rights-based vision of industrial harmony propounded by the pluralists, who saw associational freedom as an unmitigated good. Rather, he defended a vision of industrial harmony through unionism that was anchored in the Progressive search for order. To him the Wagner Act did not protect a political right, but an economic right that the federal government bestowed on a social group whose limits were defined according the objectives of the law—and this goal was really to make capitalism socially acceptable. There was no better guide to this perspective than Douglas's own dissenting opinion in *Machinists v. Street* (1961), where the liberal icon argued pointedly that "collective bargaining is a remedy for some of the problems created by the modern factory conditions."[102] Accordingly, in *Bell Aerospace* Powell concluded, with Douglas, that the Wagner Act applied only to "laborers."

As in the 1940s, American liberals were thus the most reliable purveyors of the conservative doctrine of managerial loyalty. In an irony of history, legal realism had come full circle in the labor field, leaving both its advocates and conservatives on the high bench as common laborers crafting their own, conservative definition of the "postindustrial society," one that easily bested Daniel Bell's, if only because it enjoyed the cultural authority of law.

The New Frontier That Was Not

The movement of Bell Aerospace buyers for recognition was brought to a successful end on June 6, 1976, almost six years after it began. In the end, the power of collective pressure proved too strong for the company. One year after the Court's decision, the board ruled that the buyers were not managers but employees, a ruling the company decided it could not afford to appeal to the Supreme Court. When the UAW announced that if the buyers were not given a contract, all the employees of Local 1286 would go on strike—planners, planning engineers, estimators, mold loftsmen, who could not be replaced easily—the company relented and agreed to bargain. As a result, the buyers obtained the full extent of security at work—an automatic progression of $5 every six months and a $1,500 life insurance policy after retirement were provided, overtime was equalized, the company agreed to shoulder the cost of dependent coverage, and, most important, seniority now applied to layoffs.[103]

It was, as a UAW representative explained, "all in all a fine job," in light of the company's determination to treat the buyers as managerial employees. But the fate of the buyers was no longer on the same course as that of the labor movement. For in *Bell Aerospace*, some of the justices who were so deeply involved in the protection of individual rights ruled that the right to organize, as protected by the Wagner Act, was nothing more than a historically situated effort at social cohesion that was bound to run its course as the laborers it was designed to protect declined in numbers. As a result, instead of adapting the labor relations law to an emerging post-Fordist contest, the Court protected the sociological and cultural integrity of management by deciding that workers who "formulate, determine, and effectuate management policies" have duties incompatible with the exercise of the democratic right to unionize.

The making of the Wagner Act as a law that protected "employees" rather than citizens thus cast an increasingly long shadow over the evolution of the labor movement. For the second time, industrial pluralists had sought in vain to transcend the sociological limits of the labor movement, and for the second time businessmen and conservatives had been able to oppose this attempt by waging an important legal and cultural battle over the legal definition of the worker. Yet this definition would remain contested beyond the conservative victory in cases like *Bell Aerospace* and *Yeshiva*. By the 1970s, American liberalism as a whole was running out of breath: what with union workers falling prey to conservative rhetoric in presidential elections and an economic crisis delegitimizing Keynesianism, there was little hope that beyond the NLRB, the liberal community would muster the strength to rebuild the legal definition of the worker and anchor it in democratic principles. In *Bell Aerospace*, the Court thus laid the legal groundwork for a post-Fordist economy in which the work setting was the place where two rival social identities would be distributed, with "managers" growing in numbers, and bidding farewell to the security attending the status of "employee." Indeed, as a management consultant noted in the early 1970s, the question of whether a worker was a "supervisor" was increasingly litigated.[104] It was at this point that the conservative ascendency gave company executives and top managers what they still lacked in the 1970s to whittle the legal definition of the worker further away—Republican victories at the polls and majorities on the Supreme Court and the NLRB.

CHAPTER 7

The Wages of Textualism

SOME controversies are carefully planned and crafted from below by activists and organizations seeking to change the established legal order. Others happen largely in spite of them. Glenn Moore, a rehabilitation counselor who worked hard in the fall of 1996 to organize the workers employed by Caney Creek, a mental health institution in Kentucky, could not have anticipated that his efforts would eventually lead to hearings inside the hallowed marble temple of justice in Washington, D.C. Indeed, none of the elements that go into a classic Supreme Court case seemed to be present in Moore's struggle against the management of the psychiatric rehabilitation facility. The issues that stood at the heart of the dispute were fairly common—they included difficult working conditions, low pay, and insufficient staff. Equally common was the company's lack of rules regarding pay increases. Caney Creek workers actually felt overly dependent on the performance evaluations drafted by the two supervisors of the facility—a unit and a nursing coordinator. To help Caney Creek workers regain a voice and improve their lot, Glenn Moore contacted the local Carpenters Union and filed a petition for the recognition of one large bargaining unit including kitchen and maintenance workers, recreation assistants, rehabilitation assistants, rehabilitation counselors, one licensed practical nurse (LPN) and six registered nurses (RNs). The unit reflected the strong potential for organization that lies in the service industry—there were no blue-collar workers at Caney Creek, but the employees faced problems American workers had struggled with for decades. As for Glenn Moore, who was fired in March 1997, his fate mirrored that of large numbers of workers trying to use their democratic right to unionize.[1]

Its low profile notwithstanding, *Kentucky River* (named for the corporate parent of the Caney Creek facility) was the case that the Supreme Court chose to review once more the NLRB's definition of "employee." This was a victory for the management of Caney Creek, which from the beginning refused to bargain with the union on the grounds that many of the workers it sought to include in the bargaining unit—registered nurses in particular—were not "employees" for the purposes of the Wagner Act, but "supervisors" with no substantive legal rights to organize. Like dozens of hospital managers faced with an increasingly militant nursing workforce, they contended that nurses, who direct other health care workers, are no different from the industrial foremen that Congress excluded from the Wagner Act in 1947.

Since its adoption in 1947 to thwart foremen's unionism, the supervisory clause had rarely made the headlines, its implementation removed from larger struggles over power in the workplace. But the momentum acquired by nurses unions in the 1980s and 1990s largely brought it back into the spotlight. Like public employees, nurses have stood for over twenty years at the forefront of the labor movement, defending both their personal interests as workers and a progressive, patient-oriented vision of health care that is profoundly at odds with the logic of managed care. As they became organized and political, they found their ability to articulate a language of economic dissent increasingly challenged by managers hoping to stymie their movement by waging a legal battle similar to the one General Motors had fought in the 1940s—a war to force business values on a stratum of workers seen as key to preserving loyalty to managerial power.

The militancy of nurses and the adamant opposition of hospital executives to unionism thus lent new urgency to the question that had stood at the heart of *Bell Aerospace* and *Yeshiva*, to wit, the degree to which the Wagner Act covers knowledge workers who can also be said to have responsibilities aligning them with management. Quite apart from the politics of health care, nurses are in many ways the ideal type of the worker on whom the American economy increasingly relies—the salaried semiprofessional or professional who brings the expertise necessary to complete a task and uses his or her knowledge to direct the manner in which other employees will accomplish it. Today such workers compose a third of the workforce, and in the 1990s and 2000s, the contours of their legal rights remained contested.

Nurse unionism, because of its success, thus came to be the very battleground of the conservative struggle to write and define large numbers of American workers out of legal existence. In their case, however, the jurisprudence established in *Bell Aerospace* and *Yeshiva* was not enough to sustain business claims to managerial loyalty, for in fact, nurses have no real managerial responsibilities—they do not set hospital labor policies, they neither hire nor fire, and they can in no way commit a hospital's financial responsibility. To press their claims, antiunion hospital executives relied explicitly on the text of the 1947 supervisory exemption to argue that nurses are the functional equivalent of industrial foremen. Textualism, the notion that legislative and constitutional texts should be interpreted literally, became the conservatives' best weapon against the right to organize.

This final chapter thus takes the history of the legal construction of the worker back to the point where this book started it—the *Kentucky River* cases. It chronicles the rise of nurse unionism and analyzes its political dynamics. It then moves on to show that the postindustrial reading of the Wagner Act— the notion that its framework is ill-adapted to the workers of the knowledge economy—is largely a conservative one, and that it is the product of business hegemony over labor law. Through the 1990s, progressive nominees on the NLRB tried to protect the bargaining rights of nurses and even tried to reaffirm the old ideal of social harmony through collective bargaining. This progressive definition of the modern employee, however, was severely rejected by the Supreme Court, which in *Kentucky River* emphasized that the NLRB could pursue no social end—it must be bound by the very words of the statute, and should instead develop a definition of "employee" fitting the words and syntax of the text, whatever the number of workers who might lose their bargaining rights. By 2006, the Republican appointees to the board had taken the Court at its word. In the *Kentucky River* cases, they used phrases inherited such as "responsibly direct" and "assign," to take bargaining rights from millions in the name of managerial loyalty.

"The Last Authoritarian Bulwark"

That nurses today should find themselves at the center of the debates of the definition of "employee" can seem surprising or even paradoxical. Members of an occupation dominated by a heightened, middle-class sense of professionalism long promoted by the American Nurses Association (ANA), nurses have elicited none of the interest that nineteenth-century artisans or twentieth-century automobile workers aroused among historians seeking to understand the making and unmaking of the American working class. Yet nurses are indeed central to the recent history of American labor for two reasons. First, nurses' work culture was never thoroughly congruent with the professional ideal—indeed it was during the years when the ANA enjoyed a virtual monopoly on the representation of nurses that collective bargaining became an established practice in American hospitals. Second, nurses unions rose significantly after 1974, when Congress adopted an amendment extending the protection of the Wagner Act to workers employed in what one nurse in 1960 called "the last bulwark to in our society to retain authoritarian administration": like public employees, nurses were the last workers in America to benefit from the century-old Progressive ideal of a democratized workplace.[2]

Although nurse unionism still awaits a sustained historical treatment, it is possible to provide a brief sketch of the process that led nurses to militancy. The first attempts to unionize nurses took place in the tumultuous 1930s. Like teaching and engineering, nursing was one of the "odd places" where unrest developed alongside the factory world.[3] By 1939, the CIO had established locals in nine states and had recruited significant numbers of nurses in New York, Seattle, and San Francisco. Yet prejudice against both collective bargaining as it was practiced by unions and their largely ethnic membership usually represented obstacles to the organization of this white-collar workforce. While the CIO's forays into health care did send ripples through the ANA, leading it to evolve into a bargaining agency capable of addressing the demands of discontented nurses, the ANA continued to insist on separating the "professional negotiations" it sought to develop from regular unionism. In 1946, seizing on the zeitgeist, it published an "economic security program" that included paid vacations and health insurance, among other personnel policies, but also pointed to its social conservatism, explaining that "collective bargaining is not to be confused with unionism."[4]

However, it would take long years before the nurses' quest for economic security bore fruit. During the 1940s, only seven states had established collective bargaining programs for nurses. In spite of its postwar no-strike pledge, the ANA's impetus was thwarted in 1947 by the Taft-Hartley exemption of nonprofit hospitals from the NLRA, which reaffirmed the old vision of nursing as a charitable, benevolent activity. As a result, its state divisions were able to negotiate only a handful of agreements in the postwar era. By 1960, the ANA claimed a paltry seventy-five agreements involving 115 institutions and covering eight thousand nurses, that is, about 1.5 percent of the half million professional nurses in the United States at the time. Blue-collar labor unions seeking to represent nurses fared little better and were unable to expand beyond the bases established during the heady days of Great Depression.[5]

Yet nurse unionism did not remain dormant for long. The main paradox of the Taft-Hartley Act was that it took nurses out of the umbrella of labor law at the very moment when private duty declined and hospitals increasingly represented the main postgraduate venue for nurses. By the 1950s, a majority of nurses were employed in nonprofit hospitals, a setting that provided mixed blessings. On the one hand, the rationalization of hospital work cut against the nurses' craft culture, and the pay and working conditions of nurses did not support claims to a white-collar social status. On the other hand, the hospital ward provided aggrieved nurses with the actual possibility of engaging in collective activity and developing a collective consciousness— very much like the modern factory floor, which brought workers together and thus facilitated the emergence of class actions. With the growing shortage of nurses in postwar America reinforcing their power and scientific advances vindicating their claims to professionalism, nurses gradually developed an appreciation for traditional collective action. "A nurse's place is in her Union," read nurses' T-shirts during demonstrations held in Washington, D.C., in the 1960s. By 1968, the ANA had renounced its no-strike pledge, and soon it was lobbying Congress for a legislative amendment bringing nurses back into the Wagner Act. In the modern hospital environment, it seemed, the traditional antiunion professional stance was detrimental to nurses' interests.[6]

The strikes that shook the Bay Area during the first half of 1966 exemplified this growing unrest. In the area's sixty-three hospitals, the median monthly wage was $505, when production workers averaged $502. Combined with poor working conditions, such low pay led some 60 percent of nurses each year to quit their jobs—there were about 119,000 professional nurses in and around San Francisco, but only 56,000 were employed as such. However, the growing nursing shortage did not convince hospital managements to bargain with the California Nurses Association—they held back for over six months when a wave of picketing and mass resignations (more than 2,000 nurses submitted their resignation) forced their hands. In the end, the nurses won pay increases of as much as $130 a month, better insurance, and better pay for night shifts. Commenting on the momentum of the nurses' movement, a commentator noted somewhat ironically that "Florence Nightingale is all of a sudden sounding like Samuel Gompers."[7]

Whether the movement grew because of its business unionist ends is unclear, but it was no doubt developing, and largely fit within the broader movement of sanitation workers, teachers, and government workers that promised to sustain unionism beyond the confines of the blue-collar factory.[8] In 1967 the ANA claimed to have signed 166 collective bargaining agreements cover-ing over twenty thousand nurses. To be sure, this meant that the immense majority of hospitals in the country still had no agreement with their nursing personnel, but the movement was gaining both geographic and numerical strength—that same year, the ANA also reported union recognition battles involving seventy-five thousand nurses in forty-three different states. Labor unions such as the Service Employees International Union (SEIU) now moved aggressively to represent both nurses and physicians and joined the ANA in lobbying Congress for a legislative amendment to the Wagner Act.[9]

It was at that point that the NLRB, whose members, particularly Sam Zagoria, John Fanning, Gerald Brown, and Frank McCulloch, largely sup-ported the emergence of white-collar unionism, asserted the agency's jurisdiction over proprietary—that is, for-profit—hospitals, thus lending ad-ditional legitimacy to nurses' claims for equal treatment and opportunity. To the members of the board, what with the growth of medical insurance, the rising costs of health care, and the adoption of Medicare, it was no longer possible to argue that hospitals were charitable or local commercial activities or had no impact on interstate commerce. Like white-collar unionism, health care was thus to become the new frontier of industrial democracy, and the government's intervention in that realm would offer both a peaceful resolu-tion of labor disputes and a degree of economic justice.[10]

By 1972, national sentiment on this question had evolved enough for the House to pass a bill bringing all of the health care industry, including non-profit hospitals—which the board's 1967 decision had not affected—within the purview of the Wagner Act.[11] An important element in this respect was the increasing number of labor conflicts that now disrupted the delivery of care. According to the Bureau of Labor Statistics, work stoppages had in-creased sharply in the health care sector in the 1960s, going from six in 1962 to a peak of seventy-five in 1970, with over half of the conflicts occurring in private and public hospitals.[12]

However, there was no dearth of similar arguments against nurse unionism, and it took an additional two years of hearings and lobbying before the Senate voted on a similar bill. The Chamber of Commerce, the American Hospital Association (AHA), and other assorted conservative organizations such as the National Right to Work Committee opposed the extension, contending that unions did not belong in an environment oriented toward providing medical care. Conservatives contended that collective bargaining entailed the right to strike and that strikes and pickets would in turn jeopardize Americans' access to medical care. "The prospect of a hospital being turned into a morgue is all too real," argued the Chamber of Commerce, while the AHA called on Congress to treat nurses like policemen and firefighters—public employees whose rights to strike were denied because of public safety concerns.[13]

Yet nurses unions were able to prevail over this concerted opposition. Strikingly, the promotion of collective bargaining was couched in words that Wisconsin labor economists such as John R. Commons would have understood, for it was premised on the idea that given adequate institutions, nurses and managers would negotiate and cooperate, not fight. The growing number of strikes, union leaders contended, were actually recognition strikes that simply reflected the lack of a mechanism to solve the conflicts between nurses and hospital managements. George Hardy, the president of SEIU, argued that "coverage under the provisions of the NLRA would provide a peaceful method for employees to obtain recognition from their employer," while Mike McDermott, a local union leader, contended that "employees of nonprofit hospitals should no longer be excluded from the act. It is the cornerstone of our industrial democracy. It provides a meaningful alternative to the strike for non-profit hospital employees who want union representation, and most important, it works."[14]

Echoes of the Progressive faith in social harmony through collective bargaining also rang in the Senate report, which noted that "the exemption . . . had resulted in numerous instances of recognition strikes and picketing," and expressed the hope that "coverage under the Act should completely eliminate the need for such activity, since the procedures of the Act will be available to resolve organizational and recognition disputes."[15] It was an added benefit to the cause that members of Congress were concerned with the low wages and the poor working conditions of the health care industry. Of particular importance was the testimony of SEIU's Joseph Murphy, according to whom between 1968 and 1973, the wages of nonsupervisory hospital workers had increased by 43 percent, while the consumer price index of hospital rates increased by 66 percent. In similar fashion, the Communication Workers of America indicated that the average income for all hospital employees, including doctors, was a paltry $5,290 in 1970.[16] Congress reasoned that improved standards of living for nurses would lead to higher morale and better hospital care.

Even as American liberalism entered a period of crisis, it was the continued relevance of one of its most important tenets that made one last extension of the principles of the Wagner Act palatable to a majority in Congress. As Nixon's secretary of labor, James Hodgson, noted in support of the bill, "in many instances, lack of ground rules for union recognition and collective bargaining in this sector has resulted in uncontrolled tests of strength in which the public as well as the parties suffer heavily. These issues will continue to arise, probably with increasing frequency. It is far better that they should be resolved through the orderly procedures of the NLRA than through bitter and wasteful confrontations."[17]

Indeed, it is remarkable that that the ANA, SEIU, and assorted organizations were able to pressure Congress into giving them what it refused to grant public employees—full collective bargaining rights. In the early 1970s, the staggering number of public employment strikes—which reached an astonishing 478 conflicts in 1975—had led to Congressman Clay's National Public Employees Relations Bill, which sought to bring all local and federal public employees under the purview of a collective bargaining regime similar to the one created by the Wagner Act. Notably, the gains of the Democratic Party in the senatorial elections in 1974 seemed to have opened the door for it. However, what with the relentless opposition of the right to work community and the pressure exerted on national and local government budgets by the fiscal crisis, this ambitious project fell through. The idea that governments are fundamentally different from companies and should not be forced to bargain with unions prevailed.[18]

In fact, the congressional hearings reveal that the standards of patient care—and the need for its permanent availability—were crucial to the legislative success of the nurses' movement in 1974. Advocates of the bill insisted that collective bargaining in the health care industry would not simply protect patients by removing the threat of strikes; it would also elevate the quality of care by enhancing the working conditions of many nurses, thus bringing down their staggering turnover rates, which sometimes reached 1,500 percent.[19] "Indeed it can be argued that when hospital employees are unionized . . . and able to act as true partners with management in the provision of good patient care, the result is better job stability and security than is possible without such collective bargaining arrangements," an SEIU representative explained.[20] Along with the Progressive quest for social cohesion, the 1974 amendments to the NLRA thus suggest how important it is for workers to tie their own fate to a vision of the public interest. In this respect, nurses were—and, as we will see, still are—quite exceptional.

Original Intent: Nurses as Employees

Conservatives have long prized the doctrine of original intent in legal and constitutional debates. Yet in this case original intent does not bolster the business battle to secure a spacious application of the notion of managerial loyalty. Indeed, when Congress debated the extension of the NLRA to the health care industry, the supervisory exclusion was already a salient question. Before the 1974 extension, the ANA had sought to include all nurses in its bargaining agreements, including nurses with the title of "supervisor"— typically "head nurses" overseeing the nursing unit in a traditional hospital. Like the AFL of old—which represented foremen because they belonged to the same craft as other skilled workers—the ANA suggested that bargaining units should be organized on the basis of the knowledge.[21] From 1967 to 1973, in decisions involving proprietary hospitals, the NLRB regularly found that— contrary to hospital management's arguments—nurses were not supervisors unless they were vested with "true supervisory powers," such as the power to hire and fire or the power to recommend discharge or wage increases.[22]

Moreover, no state law considered RNs as "supervisors" for collective bargaining purposes. In Washington, the definition of "supervisor" was amended to specify that a "supervisor includes registered nurses only if administrative supervision is his or her primary duty and activity." In Massachusetts, the State Labor Relations Commission ruled in 1965 that supervisors and head nurses should be included in the bargaining unit. In New York, the Labor Relations Board held in 1967 that supervisory nurses should have a bargaining unit of their own, but could be represented by the same association as the staff nurses.[23] In public employment, a similar debate took place, as the ANA skirmished with the city of New York over the definition of managerial employees very early on, and in 1969 President Nixon signed Executive Order 11491, which outlawed supervisory unionism in the hospitals run by the Veterans Administration, ending the agency's practice of allowing each hospital management to whether to include head nurses in the bargaining unit.[24] All in all, in the hospital setting the line separating "employees" from "supervisors" was still largely contested, but it clearly hovered at some level above the ranks of RNs.

Still, early attempts to classify nurses as "supervisors" convinced ANA leaders that the supervisory extension represented a threat to their organizing capability and they came to the congressional hearings over the extension of the NLRA with a definite legislative agenda—amending the Taft-Hartley definition of supervisor to include all health care professionals. A mechanical translation of the concept of "supervisor" in the hospital setting, they argued, would defeat the purposes of the extension sought by a majority of the members of Congress.[25]

Like interns and residents, who also feared being misclassified as "super-visors," nurses argued that the concept of "supervisor" had no bearing in the hospital environment, which was not designed to maximize profit but to provide the best care possible. The hospital, they argued, is a mix of two authority systems, the bureaucratic and the professional.[26] Nurses and residents used independent judgment in their work because state licensure laws required them to do so, not because of management policy. Unlike the foremen at issue in *Packard*, they argued, they had no managerial prerogatives such as the right to hire, fire, promote, and discharge, or even the right to make recommendations in these matters. ANA leaders emphatically insisted that when they directed other employees they only did so incidentally to their work as professionals: "Whatever transitory or limited authority nurses have over other employees is often not supervisory but rather a *manifestation of the professional role* in the nursing care of patients. A registered nurse who leads subprofessional employees should not be considered a supervisor any more than a doctor should be considered a supervisor because nurses respond to his direction, or an attorney should be considered a supervisor because a sec-retarial staff is available to work with him."[27]

The ANA had a point when it argued that nurses had nothing in common with Packard foremen. The Fordist system, which relied on engineering skills for the planning and conception of production, had turned the modern fac-tory into a giant arm carrying out management's production plan. Discipline was the essence of the relationship between workers and foremen, because the latter were expected to maintain the former's adherence/obedience to the manager's goals, and, as we have seen, it was from this need for industrial discipline that the tension between unionism and loyalty sprang in the case of foremen. Nurses, however, were closer to the social figure that Taylorism had all but obliterated from the industrial landscape—the independent skilled worker. Indeed, at the beginning of each shift, nurses typically decide that one of them is going to take "charge," that is, organize the work, assign pa-tients, and oversee the delivery of care. Even when they "take charge," how-ever, nurses have patients of their own. The "charge" responsibility is taken on a rotating basis, a reflection of the nurses' professional culture.[28]

Indeed, the ANA claimed, nurses exercised their autonomy and direction only in the interest of the patient, not financial profit. They were "patient care coordinators," "evaluating whether good or adequate care is being given by others, whether medical directives are being carried out properly and whether records are adequately maintained within the unit so that continuity

of patient care can go on despite the shifts in personnel."[29] The ANA clearly
worried that for lack of recognition of the difference between a foreman and a
nurse, the rights of nurses would likely be jeopardized, particularly in hospitals using the team concept to organize small independent groups of workers
devoted to a specific kind of care.[30] In a harbinger of future developments,
the ANA claimed that under current labor law, hospital managements would
have an incentive to "encumber registered nurses with whatever regalia" to
avoid bargaining with them.

Other union leaders, no doubt aware of the sensitivity of the supervisory
question, adopted a careful, noncommittal position that reflected their un-
willingness to jeopardize a major policy breakthrough by opening a legal
Pandora's box. "We are most anxious to see this bill passed," said Lester Asher,
the counsel of the SEIU. "With respect to the supervisor problem, we neither
favor nor oppose it. . . . We would just like to get something out as quickly as
possible. . . . I fear that if you open up the statute with respect to the issue of
interns and supervisors, you will be deluged with requests for similar exemp-
tions for other occupations where lines of supervision are extremely close."
Seeking to strike a moderate note, SEIU leaders said they would be content
with leaving the NLRB making decisions on a case-by-case basis.[31]

As for the AHA and other hospital management associations, they rallied
behind an alternative bill supported by Senator Taft, one that purported to
address a different problem—the potentially excessive number of collective
bargaining units that might be created to represent health care employees
(which would multiply the possibilities for conflict and sympathy strikes).
Rather cleverly, this bill divided the social world of hospitals into four groups,
namely, professionals, technicians, clerical employees, and service and
maintenance employees. Although they represented over 20 percent of the
workforce in hospitals, the nurses' voices would thus be diluted in the "professional" group, a much broader—and much more masculine—category.[32]
Nurses would thus be returned to their erstwhile social status as the "physician's hand," and would be encouraged by law to identify with doctors and
managers instead of providing a nurse-defined view of the job that would
challenge administrative control.

While members of Congress were aware of the need to limit the number of
bargaining units, the law that was eventually adopted largely allowed nurses
to stake their claims as an independent and distinct group of workers. It did
not, however, include an amendment to the supervisory exemption for the
health care industry. Yet this does not mean that members of Congress did not

want nurses to be classified as "employees" when the law was implemented. Indeed, what the reports submitted by the special committees in the House and in the Senate demonstrate is that the congressional intent was clearly to *include*, not *exclude*, RNs in the category "employee" and that an amendment to the NLRA was not necessary for that. In light of the current debate, it is worth quoting from them.

In 1972, after the first hearings, the House report came out strongly against the idea that RNs were supervisors: "Your committee's intent in extending NLRA coverage to non-profit hospitals is that nurses as well as all other hospital employees enjoy the rights guaranteed to other employees covered by the Act, and it is your committee's view that nurses with only nominal supervisory duties should not be considered as 'supervisors' within the meaning of the NLRA."[33] In 1974, the Senate report came to the same conclusion, and clearly supported the notion that direction of employees when exercised in the interest of the patient did not mean that a worker should be classified as a supervisor:

> Various organizations representing health care professionals have urged an amendment to Section 2(11) of the Act so as to exclude such professionals from the definition of "supervisor" . . . the proposed amendment is unnecessary because of existing board decisions. The Committee notes that the Board has carefully avoided applying the definition of "supervisor" to a healthcare professional who gives direction to other employees in the exercise of professional judgment, *which direction is incidental to the professional's treatment of patients and is thus not the exercise of supervisory authority in the interest of the employer.* The Committee expects the Board to continue evaluating the facts of each case in this manner when making determinations.[34]

The distinction between responsibilities exercised "in the interest of the employer" and those "in the interest of the patient" was an important limit set on the notion of worker loyalty. Indeed, in the jurisprudence it had developed since 1967, the NLRB had firmly established the principle that nurses' duties with regard to lesser-skilled health care workers and their authority over them derived only from their technical knowledge and could not be seen as a manifestation of a supervisory authority as defined in Taft-Hartley. Congress expected the NLRB to continue to identify "employees" and "supervisors" based on this rationale, a policy the board followed after 1974, and even formalized when it published three consecutive rules (1987, 1988, 1989) mandating the creation of separate bargaining units for RNs and ending managerial attempts to dilute nurses' voices in broader units.[35] Most important, the Supreme Court explicitly approved of the board's policy in a footnote to its *Yeshiva* decision in 1980.[36]

No Original Intent: The Worker as Text

Hospital managements, however, willfully ceded very little ground to unions. Far from subscribing to the Progressive theory of harmony in the workplace, they perceived unions as threats for their authority over the hospital ward. As two directors of personnel associated with the AHA explained in 1976, in the aftermath of the amendments bringing hospitals within the protective framework of the NLRA, "We are beginning to realize that as managers, we may not be totally in command of things in the years ahead. Our voice grows weaker as one analyzes the implications of the 1974 NLRA amendments may have on the future of the heath care industry. Control of the work by the worker lends itself to the total control of the hospital. Lose control of the worker, lose control of the work, and you've lost control of your total management system."[37]

This was largely reminiscent of the laments of automobile executives opposing foremen's unions, but in the 1970s the context of labor relations was changing and antiunionism was increasingly visible. In fact, celebrations of the virtues of the postwar labor-management accord had probably always been as much a way to discredit right-wing criticism of the Wagner Act as an accurate description of the state of labor relations, but by the late 1970s, the political ground was shifting for unions and their allies. Douglas Fraser's 1978 decision to resign from the Labor Management Group was an important signpost suggesting that such celebrations were no longer in order.[38]

A manual published in 1976, *The Union Epidemic: A Prescription for Supervisors*, provides additional insight into this steadfast resistance.[39] A clarion call to all managers to get their house in order to stop the "threat of the union disease," the book also brimmed over with the antiunion clichés that the libertarian right was then putting forth with increasing frequency. The authors did not simply call on the loyalty of supervisors to establish stable labor relations typical of the midcentury factory; rather, they insisted that labor law "recognizes that a supervisors are an employer's best weapon to resist the union attempt." During an organizational drive, they explained, the role of supervisors was to "maintain control and discipline," and be ready to discharge the workers who failed to comply with company rules. This call did not go unheeded, and as early as 1981 union leaders complained about the intensive use of antiunion consultants in the health care industry.[40]

Most important, the authors of *Union Epidemic* identified the construction of workers as "employees" or "supervisors" as being critical to building the hospital's line of defense against unions and insisted that many nurses, particularly charge nurses, fell in a gray legal area because of their duties. For antiunion managements, law was to be as much a place of conflict as the hospital ward, and while the use of antiunion consultants was gaining currency, management hired lawyers to replicate the legal battle for loyalty that had resulted in the exclusion of foremen in 1947. As early as 1979, Herbert Melnick, of the Modern Management antiunion firm, related the defeat of a union campaign to teach the participants of a seminar on union avoidance how to use the supervisory exclusion to their advantage: "We got every single nurse excluded as a supervisor, every licensed practical nurse as a supervisor. And that's how we won it. Otherwise, if you went by the election there was no question. [The union] had 90% of the people signed up. ... But you have to be prepared—you have to structure it now. And one way to do it is to get those people and say "you are a supervisor." . . . Give them the job description and let them sign for it. Papers impress the government more than anything else."[41]

Still, given the history of the 1974 amendments, the business struggle for loyalty would not have been successful without the rise in conservative legal circles of a new interpretative methodology, namely, textualism. Textualism, indeed, is the main conservative contribution to the theory of judicial review. According to its main proponents, Justices Antonin Scalia and Clarence Thomas, there is no need for an agency or a court to delve into the legislative history of a statute it must enforce or to consider the potential social effects of statutory interpretation before adjudicating a case, because doing so is futile. According to textualists, not only is it impossible to reconstruct the intent of the legislator, but the meaning of a text is autonomous and can indeed be different from the intent of its author. Consequently, the plain meaning of the text of a legislation should be given effect, which means that the agency must focus on the words themselves, on syntax and on relationships between different parts of the statute.[42]

Textualism made it possible for conservatives to overcome the main obstacle to the notion that RNs should be classified as "managers"—the notion that they exercise their responsibilities in the interest of the patient, not the employer. By the early 1990s, the Sixth Circuit had taken the lead in propounding this jurisprudential turn with a reasoning that was strangely reminiscent of Powell's "industrial analogy" in *Yeshiva*. "As a matter of economics," the Sixth Circuit Court explained in the 1992 case *Beverly Enterprises*, the patients are the employer's customers, and it's in the employer's interest to serve them well." The plain meaning of the statute—one that, interestingly, the court took to be basic laissez-faire values—thus indicated that there could be no logical distinction between responsibilities exercised in the interest of the patient (opening to "employee" status) and responsibilities exercised in the interest of the employer (mandating "supervisory" status). In a thorough rejection of the idea of legislative intent, the Sixth Circuit went on to note that the NLRB exceeded its authority when it tried to protect the bargaining rights of professionals such as RNs: "It is up to Congress to carve out an exception for the health care field, including nurses, should Congress wish for Nurses not to be deemed supervisors," the court ominously noted.[43]

Notably, by 1994, this viewpoint was endorsed in by the Supreme Court in *Health Care & Retirement Corp.*, a case that bore on the status of three LPNs who had been disciplined for their "uncooperative attitude"—they assisted nurses' aides in an organizing drive—and had filed a complaint for unfair labor practice. The board first ruled that their dismissal indeed constituted an "unfair labor practice," but the employer had challenged this ruling in court on the grounds that the LPNs were "supervisors" because their duties included ensuring adequate staffing, making daily work assignments, and monitoring aides' work to ensure proper performance (counseling and disciplining aides). The board had countered that these duties were not carried out "in the interest of the employer" because they stemmed from the nurses' knowledge and their license. The Supreme Court disagreed, insisting that the "ordinary meaning" of the phrase "in the interest of the employer" led to the logical conclusion that all professional work is necessarily "in the interest of the employer" and that the board's reliance on this rationale was a "false dichotomy." Dismissing evidence of congressional intent such as the 1974 Senate report as "isolated statements," the Court criticized the board for being indifferent to other parts of the text of the statute, particularly the section saying that a person who "responsibly directs" coworkers is a supervisor, which it accused the board to have made "meaningless." "The Statute must control the Board's decisions, not the other way around," the Court lectured, insisting that the days of legal realism were over: textualism, not legal realism, was to control the definition of the worker in American law.[44]

Written by Anthony Kennedy for a majority composed of Sandra Day
O'Connor, William Rehnquist, Antonin Scalia, and Clarence Thomas—all
appointees of Ronald Reagan and George H. W. Bush—the Supreme Court's
decision in *Health Care & Retirement Corp. v. NLRB* thus reflected the growing impact of the rightward shift of the country on labor law. Tellingly, the
Court was badly divided, with Justice Ginsburg writing a dissent (joined by
Justices Blackmun, Stevens, and Souter) in which she faulted the majority for
denying that there is an inherent tension in the act between the exclusion of
supervisors who owe a duty of loyalty to their employer and the protection
of professionals whose rights are explicitly protected. Indeed, in both cases
the act defines them as individuals directing others. Warning that the present
decision made the protection of professionals "meaningless," Ginsburg cited
a host of workers whose rights had been upheld by the board but now seemed
to be at risk: the list ran from newspapers editors assigning and editing articles to lawyers serving as unit heads, including project engineers, project
architects, catalog librarians, and senior social workers supervising others.[45]

Harmony Redux?

In retrospect, however, the most striking element in the 1994 *Health Care*
decision was that it was handed down at a time when the old ideal of cooperation and mutual interests between employers and workers had regained a salient place at the forefront of the political debate over labor law. Since the late
1980s, a number of pundits and experts on both the business and academic
sides had been advocating new forms of management known as "employee
involvement" or "employee participation plans" to improve productivity and
quality. Indeed, for close to twenty years the American economy had seemed
at pains to compete with its foremost competitors, Germany and Japan, with
their work councils and team concepts that seemed more efficient than gritty
Taylorist labor relations to generate productivity. If American workers were
likewise allowed to participate in planning, it was believed, production would
be more flexible and more responsive to market demand, making U.S. companies more productive. The future lay in a system in which the separation
erected by Taylorism between management and workers would disappear.[46]

The members of the Commission on the Future of Worker Management
Relations, created by Bill Clinton in 1993, endorsed these ideas in a widely
publicized report calling for an evolution of labor law that would accommodate the idea that unionism should no longer be adversarial, but

collaborative, which in effect meant removing the Wagner Act's Section 8a(2) ban on company unions and shop committees in order to allow for localized and particularistic forms of collaborations and bargaining within American companies. This change in the legal representation of workers' rights reflected an important evolution in progressive attitudes toward unionism and collective bargaining. No longer did labor law need to reflect the varying interests of two social entities management and labor—in this new post-Fordist era, "empowered employees" would work in unison with employers to compete in the marketplace. Through quality circles, teamwork, and labor-management committees, mutual respect could be restored to the American workplace.[47]

That a fresh vision of the worker underwrote the drift of this reform is visible in the participation of the labor-oriented members of the Dunlop Commission; for them employee participation plans promised more than added competitiveness—they would usher in no less than a new era in the history of labor relations. As Paul Weiler explained, a more democratic, flexible unionism would emerge out of the ashes of the old bureaucratic AFL-CIO industrial unions that once dominated the pattern-setting contracts typical of the midcentury period. Meanwhile, the cultural gap between managers and workers would be bridged for good because the workers would now derive much satisfaction from the fact that their jobs had been "enriched" with true content, requiring them to provide creative input. Given the disappearance of the ideo-typical militant worker, Charles Hecksher argued, it had become necessary to devise a system of labor relations that, instead of fostering industrial peace, would accommodate the wishes of a growing numbers of professionals and semiprofessionals on whose skills the economy increasingly relied, and who felt at odds with traditional unions. Oddly, the Dunlop Commission thus reaffirmed the old Progressive idea that institutions could be used to produce new social norms. And as in the early years of the twentieth century, when John R. Commons and his students developed industrial pluralism, cooperation and partnerships were the norms necessary to produce the high performance necessary in a globalized economy.[48]

What of the tension between unionism and loyalty? Naturally, this new cooperative framework devalued the very premise of the managerial and supervisory exclusions in labor law—the notion that companies were entitled to the undivided loyalty of their representatives because collective bargaining relied on the conflict of interests between workers and managers.[49] Notably, General Motors, which had once insisted on the sharp difference between management and workers to justify the supervisory exemption, now claimed that at its Fort Wayne, Indiana, plant, where the team concept had been implemented, there were no longer any workers and bosses, just "associates" and "advisors."[50] Seen from this perspective, it was possible to envision the end of the tension between unionism and loyalty that had structured labor law since 1947, for the distinction between "supervisors" and "employee" in the implementation of the Wagner Act no longer made sense and should be repealed indeed. As the ACLU's Lewis Maltby explained to the commission,

> Given the way industry is involving employees in day to day operations, it won't be long before everyone is a supervisor under the NLRA, and no one has a theoretical right to join a union. The key to this change is eliminating the exception for supervisors under the NLRA, and modifying the exception for managers. While supervisors and managers owe their employer a duty of loyalty, that does not distinguish them from other employees. What does distinguish some senior executives is that they have significant individual bargaining power, and do not need collective bargaining to protect their interests. Rewriting the management exclusion around this concept would protect the legitimate interests of employers without denying the right to join a union to those who need it.[51]

The Dunlop Report proceeded to openly criticize the Supreme Court for creating the managerial exception in *Bell Aerospace* and *Yeshiva* and expanding the supervisory exception in *Health Care*. "These Supreme Court cases fail to take into account the degree to which supervisory and managerial tasks have been diffused throughout the workforce in American firms," the report noted. "As a result of the Court's interpretation, thousands of rank and file employees have lost or may lose their collective bargaining rights." To remedy this problem, it called for a mild amendment to the NLRA, one that would still keep out statutory supervisors (who are in charge or hiring, firing, or disciplining) and persons who are "near the top of the managerial structure, who have substantial individual discretion to set major company policy," while "members of work teams" and "professionals and paraprofessionals who direct less skilled workers" would now be classified as "employees."[52] Clearly, the commission suggested that it made no sense to ask workers to choose between workplace cooperation and taking advantage of their bargaining rights under the NLRA.

By the late 1990s, however, progressives were in no position to challenge conservative nostrums on labor law, particularly the managerial exclusion. Corporate America did not view *Health Care & Retirement Corp.* in the same light, if only because businessmen and top managers prized its main holding—that the distinction between professional and business values on which the board had relied was unacceptable. Moreover, in a review of the case, a corporate labor lawyer explained that the very essence of the total quality movement and more generally the development of new managerial forms was to bring business values and technical knowledge in lockstep: "If Secretary Reich and his cohort, NLRB Chair Gould, truly desire the 'high performance' workplace of which they regularly speak, they will adhere to the Court's view in health care," he explained.[53] The author went on to consider whether the focus on total quality was "incompatible with unionism," and suggested that amending the NLRA was not necessary—if a self-directed work team was not a "labor organization" under the NLRA, then quite simply the workers involved in them should all be classified as "managers." To reach a postindustrial world devoid of militant workers, all one had to do was to let the Fordist categories inscribed in U.S. labor law run their course and die under the caring hand of conservative justices.

Caught in the conflicting winds of progressive and conservative readings of employee involvement and job enrichment, the Dunlop Report soon became a dead letter. The Republican victory in 1994 further doomed any attempt at labor reform. In fact, Congress did pass the TEAM Act, which only amended the NLRA to allow employee participation committees. The act was in turn promptly vetoed by Clinton, who suggested perfunctorily that "it would undermine the collective bargaining system that has served the country so well for many decades." Of course, by then the union movement had reached an all-time low and had almost reverted to its pre–New Deal levels, and in many industrial fields collective bargaining was only a memory. Corporate America was content to limit itself to its—largely successful—antiunion agenda, and with the solid economic growth of the late 1990s, its interest in this reform of Section 8a(2) largely declined. If there was a new emphasis on partnership and shared values between workers and managers, it came from citadels of the antiunion struggle such as Wal-Mart, which referred to its employees as "associates" and cultivated their loyalty by affirming shared conservative social values, and left it to its top managers and engineers to organize the work process.[54]

Collision Course: Nurse Unions and
the Politics of Health Care

For nurses, this stalemate has had significant consequences. On the one hand unions of nurses have made significant progress. In 2009, the creation of the National Nurses United Union, which is affiliated with the AFL-CIO, confirmed the changing character of nurses' professional identity. To be sure, as a number of commentators have noticed, the quest for professionalism is still an obstacle—many RNs remain reluctant to join a union because they do not think that it is compatible with their commitment to patients. Yet today unions represent nearly 20 percent of all RNs in the country, a figure that reflects the relevance of unionism in the contemporary post-Fordist workplace. Indeed, nurses today are not unlike the industrial workers of the 1930s who chafed under the autocratic management of the large corporations that dominated most industries and justified calls for industrial democracy. For one thing, the health care industry differs from others insomuch as there are no real alternatives for workers dissatisfied with their job—hospitals hold a "monopsony" power that has allowed them to keep wages down: from 1992 to 2002, wages for the labor force increased by 6.8 percent, while wages for RNs increased by only 3.3 percent. Notably, the wages of less-skilled hospital workers are so low that in 2004 *Business Week* chose the picture of a nursing aide earning $9 an hour to illustrate a story on the growing problem of the working poor in industrial America.[55]

Although nurses usually do not join unions that seek to represent all health care workers on the model of industrial unionism, they do derive substantial benefits from collective bargaining. On average, they earn almost $3 (more than 10 percent) more per hour than nonunionized nurses. Furthermore, in metropolitan areas where union density is high enough, collective bargaining contracts have an effect on the local labor market as a whole. According to a recent study, in areas where unionization exceeds 50 percent, hourly wages are $7 higher than in areas with fewer union members. Along with their compensation, nurses typically bargain over health care benefits and seek to protect their employment from mergers.[56]

The reach of collective bargaining agreements, of course, is much longer than the bread-and-butter question of wages. In similar fashion to the contracts established in the heyday of Fordist mass production, RNs negotiate working rules that limit management's ability to change their work assignments arbitrarily. Typical provisions eliminate or limit overtime requirements as well as "floating"—the sudden reassignment of a nurse to a different

unit for a determined amount of time—and "detailing"—the reassignment
of a nurse for an unspecified length of time. Contracts also typically include
staffing requirements, known as "nurse to patient ratios" and offer some degree of protection against the most taxing effects of what remains physically
demanding labor. Nurses make up an aging workforce, and yet they spend
long hours standing, walking, and moving patients around. "No single lifts"
provisions—meaning that nurses will not be required to move or reposition a
patient alone—testify to the need to protect the body as much as the pocketbook, for the incidence of back injuries in nursing exceeds that in construction and mining. Indeed, nursing is a dangerous activity: in 2010, the rate for
occupational injuries and illnesses for hospital employees was 6.5 per 100,
workers as opposed to 3.4 in all private-sector industries and 3.9 in manufacturing. Each year, nurses account for over 40 percent of needle stick injuries,
which expose them and their patients to HIV and hepatitis. Such hazards do
not simply discount claims that unions are not needed in the service, postindustrial economy; they also account for the high dissatisfaction rates among
nurses, and in particular the high turnover in acute care hospitals, which exceeds 20 percent and reaches a staggering 48 percent in nursing homes.[57]

Given these elements, the difficulties faced by nurses in joining unions and
signing collective bargaining agreements ameliorating their working conditions can be surprising. Nurses might, after all, be in high demand and short
supply. In 2009, the Bureau of Labor Statistics projected that over half a million new RN positions would be created through 2018 to respond to the rising
demand for care that both demographics and health care reform will generate. Yet the national RN vacancy rate was already 8 percent in 2007, and
nursing schools do not produce enough graduates each year. Although the
recession has eased the shortage, experts believe that some 265,000 nurses
will be missing in 2025.[58] Obviously, nurses should be in a good position to
bargain for better working conditions.

Yet, as we have seen, from the beginning nurse unions were faced with
managements fretting over their possible loss of authority over the hospital
wards, and the stakes involved in this battle for control of the care floor have
only grown with the changing politics and economics of health care since the
1980s and the emergence of managed care. Relying on cost-control strategies
such as mergers of hospitals and the reorganization of health care work, managed care is precisely designed to force a reduced number of nurses to care
for a larger number of patients who are likelier to have serious conditions.
Indeed, HMOs now seek to allow only the most seriously ill patients to go to

the hospital. To achieve this organizational goal, managed care has brought a rationalization of nurses' work that shows that Taylorist principles are very much alive in today's workplace. Indeed, one can't understand the debate over nurses unions and the business struggle for nurses' loyalty unless one comes to grips with the heart of the matter: a battle over the control of the work process.

As the author Suzanne Gordon explains, the process whereby bottom-line financial concerns resulted in a "mangling" of medical care started with the reform of Medicare in 1983. Instead of reimbursing a hospital for the cost of an individual's stay, Medicare shifted to a prospective payment system relying on "DRG"—diagnosis related group. To each illness or procedure (hip replacement, for example), Medicare now assigned an average length of hospital stay and a corresponding sum. If an individual's treatment exceeded what the DRG planned for, the cost was to be borne by the hospital alone. By contrast, if the illness was cured or the procedure done quicker than what the DRG planned for, the hospital could keep the money that had been saved. The move to DRG-based reimbursement introduced the industrial logic of "throughput" into the world of health care. By the 1990s, as hospitals competed for managed care contracts, they moved to further cut the length of stays and outsource patients who did not need acute care. For nurses, this has meant both a steady increase in patients with critical conditions and an increasing number of incoming patients during any given shift.[59]

To deliver quicker and cheaper medical care, hospitals have not simply required nurses to do fast work with patients with acute needs. They have also directly aimed at the size of nursing staffs because nurses constitute the largest component of the workforce in what remains a labor-intensive industry. To cut back on staffing, they hired consultants telling them how to gain a firm grasp of the very process of care delivering. Such consultants brought a number of processes that turned nursing into measurable industrial labor. First, hospitals have used "patient acuity systems," that is, computerized programs telling the managers of the hospital how many nurses and nursing aides are needed on a given shift based on the condition and illness of the incoming patients. To predict the labor hours that will be needed, these programs use a modern version of the time studies done by engineers—they are based on an estimate of the time that each medical procedure requires. Furthermore, consultants gather data on the time devoted to nursing care in different hospitals and use the most efficient one as a "benchmark" for others to follow. As early as 1994, the consultant group American Practice Management boasted that since 1987 it had helped hospitals save $1 billion in expenses, mostly through reductions in nursing care hours.[60]

But the rationalization preached by consultants went further still, and extended to a thorough reorganization of services to reach a kind of continuous production needed to make managed care possible. As one consultant explained, "[We need to make] a fundamental shift in thinking from how to best provide a wide variety of independent services to how to effectively combine individual service components into an integrated health experience. Or, in other words, how can we create mini-assembly lines containing as many of the resources as needed to achieve a patient's desired outcome."[61]

The result of this ambition was "patient-focused care," an attempt to map the trajectory of a patient afflicted with a specific condition or illness so as to make the treatment a swift continuous process. Like the auto workers producing the Model T in the early days of the industrial era, the work of nurses is thus standardized: the pathway of an individual patient through his or her treatment is charted so that nurses are told what needs to be done and how long it takes to do it. Since 2006, as federal reimbursement for Medicare and Medicaid has been tied to patient satisfaction, hospitals have even used "rounding" and "scripting" to reduce nurses' autonomy even further. "Rounding" implies that nurses will make rounds on their patients to make sure that all their needs are met—even fluffing a pillow—instead of prioritizing their visits based on the conditions of patients. As for scripting, it literally involves suppressing the nurse's own voice by telling him or her exactly what to say in specific situations, so as to make sure that the patient's "experience" is the best one. No longer under the workman's cap, the manager now sits inside a laminated card telling nurses what words they must use with a patient while treating him or her in a hurry.[62]

Consultants and hospital executives deny that market-driven managed care erodes the standard of nursing. Rather, they claim that the changes they have pushed through in the past two decades can offer nurses the opportunity to gain what they have long been seeking—the social recognition that comes with professionalism. Indeed, reductions in nurse staffing—hospitals have lost up to 12 percent of their nurses annually—have been possible because an increasing number of less qualified personnel, such as LPNs and nursing aides, have been hired to work with them, doing many tasks that used to be done by RNs themselves. According to consultants, nurses should therefore now conceive of themselves as "managers of care," rather than actual doers. The traditional bedside nurse should thus make way for a coordinator of the activities that make an individual patient's health care experience.

Loyalty to Whom?

Yet the loyalty of nurses has proven fairly hard to cultivate. Indeed, hospital managements have stumbled on an obstacle that did not exist in the case of industrial foremen, Bell Aerospace buyers, or university professors. Like doctors, nurses have a privileged relationship to their patients, and it is to them that their loyalty is directed. Many nurses have resisted the conservative, individualistic appeal of this managerialism because they derive much of their occupational identity from the license that allows them to practice, not from the HMO that employs them. Indeed, it is precisely on the system of licensure that managed care's assault on nursing skills has foundered—many nurses argue that managed care is a drive to the bottom that puts patients at risk and thwarts their ability to fulfill the responsibilities for which they are licensed. In point of fact, it is precisely this system of licensure that has led nurses to reject emphatically that they are arms of management on the hospital floor. "I have a license from the State of Massachusetts to maintain a certain practice," RN Sandy Eaton remarked during the hearings organized by the NLRB in 2003. "What do you think about that?"[63]

Research suggests that the primary motive of nurses when they organize is not wages, but the quality of patient care. Indeed, organized nurses see themselves as the only countervailing force to a for-profit model that degrades the standard of care. "For many of us, it's the only way we can stay in the profession," a nurse remarked.[64] This is why in health care conflicts between workers and management have come back with a vengeance. While nurses are pushed to run patients through the system as quickly as possible, unions insist that the nurses' responsibility must go to protecting the interests of the patients, not those of the HMOs with which their hospital is under contract. Yet at the end of the 1990s, as many nurses unions were breaking away from the ANA, there was increased awareness of the dangers caused by the reduction in the nursing workforce. In 1999, the Institute of Medicine published "To Err Is Human," a widely discussed study that concluded that up ninety-eight thousand people died each year of accidental injuries in American hospitals. In 2002, another influential study published in the *Journal of the American Medical Association* contended that "the odds of patient mortality increased by 7 percent for every additional patient in the average nurse's workload in the hospital."[65] Meanwhile studies released by unions and other organizations revealed that a majority of nurses felt they were understaffed and, as a result, unable to provide patient care on a timely basis.[66]

Emerging as patient advocates, nurses unions have opposed the worst effects of managed care by negotiating contracts that explicitly protect their professional identity. For example, in 1994 the California Nurses Association signed a contract stipulating that "the medical center and nurses are committed to the highest levels of patient care in terms of the patient's health and safety. Accordingly, the parties agree that the nurse shall not practice, nor shall the nurse be required to practice, in any manner which is inconsistent with the above or which places the nurse's license in jeopardy."[67] Other typical provisions tried early on in California include watchdog committees that conduct investigations on the quality of care at a given facility and then provide this confidential information to nurses, who can then take action to request a change in the staffing or organization of work.

Managements have not taken such action lightly. In 2008, the Court of Appeals for the Ninth Circuit passed on the case of RNs who were fired for wearing union buttons that read "staffing crisis—nursing shortage—medical errors—real solutions" or "nurses demand safe staffing." Reversing the Bush appointees on the NLRB, the court found that the decision to fire the nurses did constitute an unfair labor practice. A few years earlier, another federal court had sustained the board's decision that RNs could not be prevented from wearing "no FOT" (forced overtime) union buttons simply because this might cause concern among the patients.[68] Labor law is also crucial to protect the nurses' ability to advocate the patients' interests even when RNs are not organized. In 1995, it was through the venue of the NLRB's protection against unfair labor practices that Barry Adams—an RN who was fired by his Boston hospital after he called his managers' attention to the inordinate incidence of deaths in the hospital—was able to make a case that led to the adoption of Massachusetts's whistleblower law.[69]

Overall, however, nurses unions have become political to obtain recognition of their problem. Eschewing the apolitical voluntarism that has often characterized skilled unions, they have been lobbying for laws mandating adequate nurse-to-patient ratios that cut directly against the grain of managed care. The first one, which was adopted in California in 1998, is a one to five ratio in medical and surgical units and a one to four ratio in special units, but the law remained in doubt until 2005, when voters refused to gut them in a referendum backed by the probusiness agenda of the Schwarzenegger administration (voters were also asked to require public unions to get written consent from members before spending dues money for political purposes).[70] Moreover, nurses unions such as National Nurses United actively promoted health care reform after the election of Barack Obama.[71]

Nurses' ability to voice a language of economic dissent and to offer alternatives to market-driven health care thus sits at the very roots of the ongoing attempt to deprive them of their right to organize and corral them in the managerial realm. While nurses have strongly asserted their professional identity and values, contending that these are profoundly distinct from the business values that prevail in hospital managements, conservatives have waged their battle for loyalty by countering that the text of the supervisory exclusion adopted in 1947 does not allow for such a distinction, hoping that the courts might lead the NLRB to forego attempts to protect the freedom of association of nurses.

Kentucky River

It was at this point that Glenn Moore's efforts to organize the workers of the Caney Creek mental facility in Kentucky in the fall 1996 became central to the business struggle for loyalty. In fact, it was the NLRB that selected the *Kentucky River* case as one it could possibly win at the Supreme Court to mitigate the potential effects of the 1994 *Health Care & Retirement Corp.* decision. Unlike hospital nurses, the RNs at this mental rehabilitation facility had very few of the indicia susceptible to justify making them "supervisors," and, as we have seen, they were not essential to the bargaining unit and the struggle going on at the Caney Creek facility.[72]

For the board, this seemed a good case to test the standard it had developed to mitigate the effects of the 1994 *Health Care & Retirement Corp.* decision— "independent judgment."[73] In 1996, in *Providence Hospital*, the board used this new test to adjudicate a dispute that encapsulated the debate over "employee." At stake was the victory of the Alaska Nurses Association, which had won an election to represent more than seven hundred nurses at one of the six acute care centers operated by Providence in Anchorage. But the employer held that all the RNs who functioned even part-time as "charge nurses"—as many as 25 percent of the RNs—were supervisors. Without those votes, the union lost the election.[74] The board ruled that charge nurses who assigned nurses to patients and could require them to work overtime were "employees" not "supervisors" because the "independent judgment" they used to direct other employees was of a professional, not managerial nature, and then instructed all the "regions" to follow this case in all the cases adjudicated at the local level.[75]

This new policy had largely increased the political and legal pressure bearing on the agency. In a well-publicized memo titled "Where Have All the Supervisors Gone?" the corporate lawyer Roger King accused the agency of deliberately flouting congressional intent. As for the courts that disagreed with the board's analysis—the Sixth and the Fourth Circuit Courts particularly—they now couched their rebuttals of the board's jurisprudence in harsh language. Beyond the technicalities of statutory interpretation, it was the political legitimacy of the agency that Congress had created to implement the Wagner Act that was at stake in *Kentucky River*.[76]

Released in 2000, the *Kentucky* decision handed the board yet another stern rebuke. Writing for a small majority, Justice Scalia explained that the board's attempt to distinguish between two types of "independent judgment"—professional and managerial—was unacceptable because the statute actually left no room for a distinction based on the nature of independent judgment. "What supervisory judgment worth exercising . . . does not rest on 'professional or technical skill or experience?'" he asked. Once again, the Court found fault with the board's attempt to ignore the text of the statute and accused it of reading the phrase "responsibly direct" out of the statute. Indeed, the majority opinion denounced the board's "running struggle" to limit the impact of the supervisory exclusion, noting that it was "presumably driven by the policy concern that otherwise the proper labor-management balance will be disrupted."[77]

Afterward, the counsel for *Kentucky River* hailed the Court's decision, saying that "textualism saved the supervisory exemption."[78] True, but in fact, it seems difficult to think of another area of law where the Supreme Court has gone to such great lengths to deny a federal agency the right to carry out the role that Congress has bestowed upon it—implementing a statute and giving concrete effect to the legislators' intent, which is to promote the right to organize and collective bargaining. Indeed, it is striking that in both *Health Care* and *Kentucky River*, the Court broke with the framework it established at the beginning of the 1980s to guide judicial review of agency work. According to this framework, if the intent of Congress is clear, the courts must make sure that the agency has followed this intent. If congressional intent is ambiguous or unknown, then the agency must provide a "reasonable" interpretation of the statute: in other words, the Court recognized that administrative agencies must often make policy choices to which courts must defer as long as they are based on permissible constructions of laws.[79] Yet in *Health Care* and *Kentucky* the Court jettisoned this policy of judicial restraint to make sure, as the Court itself admitted in *Kentucky*, "that supervisors will not be eliminated from the Act."[80] In this case, textualism obviously allowed the Court to justify favoring the presumed intent of Taft-Hartley—to protect managerial prerogatives— over the intent of legislators in the 1974 amendments, and the result is a juris- prudence that disembodies the worker into textual fragments.

Kentucky River also marked the defeat of the board's last attempt to craft a socially meaningful definition of "employee," one that would limit the impact of the doctrine of loyalty over the right to organize. Soon after the decision was rendered, the 2000 elections changed the institutional dynamics of the debate by allowing Republicans to make nominations to the NLRB. The ef- fects of this change were evident when, in 2003, the board announced that it would hold hearings to devise a new definition of "employee" and "supervi- sor." A treasure trove for textualists, the list of questions then published by the board for the participants was a sign of the growing disjunction between the legal definition of the worker and the social world:

1. The difference between "assigning" and "directing."
2. The meaning of the word "responsibly" in the statutory phrase "responsibly direct."
3. The distinction between directing "the manner of others' perfor- mance of discrete tasks" and "directing other employees."
4. The significance of schedules that rotate employees in and out of supervisory positions.
5. The meaning of "independent judgment."[81]

Three years later, a spirit of strained anxiety pervaded the ranks of pro- gressives and labor activists as the board's decision in the *Kentucky River* cases—three cases in which the board would provide a new definition of "employee"—was pending. A study published by the Economic Policy Institute (EPI) the same month compounded this feeling of urgency: using official data provided by the Bureau of Labor Statistics, the EPI found that some eight million workers were to lose bargaining rights if the board re- stricted the definition of "employee" to exclude charge nurses.[82] In mid-July, nurses unions and the AFL-CIO teamed up to organize a "week of protest" throughout the nation. In twenty-one American cities, workers denounced the antilabor policies of the Bush administration and called on the NLRB to stop "rolling back workers' rights."

The demonstrations did not necessarily make the national headlines, but in a context of staunch antiunionism, when so few workers were able to organize, they demonstrated the centrality of the struggle against business hegemony over labor law for American workers hoping to revive a democratic movement. As for hospitals, they were so eager for the board's decision that they sometimes anticipated it: the Virginia Mason Medical Center in Seattle, Washington, countered an organizing drive by the Washington State Nurses Association by relabeling six hundred RNs as "supervisors" even before the decision was announced.[83]

The trio of decisions that the board published on September 29, 2006, largely confirmed these fears. First came *Oakwood Care Inc.*, a case that mattered enormously because it seemed to symbolize the promise that the old industrial unionism would somehow gain a new lease on life in the new workplace. At Oakwood Heritage hospital in Taylor, Michigan, the UAW led an organizing drive among 220 RNs, many of whom acted as "charge nurses" on a regular basis. This meant that they were responsible for overseeing the patient care unit, meeting with doctors and relatives of patients, assigning patients to RNs, and dealing with unusual incidents. None of them, however, dealt with the grievances of nurses or had the authority to assign them to shifts—such were responsibilities of the clinical managers. Twelve nurses were permanent "charge" nurses, while some 112 rotated to take charge. All earned an additional $1.50 an hour when they assumed this duty. When the UAW filed for a certification election in 2002, it sought to represent all the RNs, and the local NLRB ruled that the nurses were not supervisors.

The hospital management, however, countered by contending that none of its clinical managers were involved in the day-to-day supervision of the hospital units. Executives also insisted that "on any given day, while clinical managers and assistant clinical managers are busy attending to the administrative concerns of their multiple units, charge nurses are responsible for ensuring the proper functioning of their individual nursing units." Why this responsibility should be incompatible with unionism, the hospital never said, but it sought to exclude all its RNs on the basis of their rotating charge responsibilities.[84]

In *Oakwood*, the board did not go as far, as it held that only the twelve permanent charge nurses were "supervisors." Still, in engaging in the textualist analysis called for by the Supreme Court, it outlined a new standard for assessing "employees" and "supervisors" that confirmed many of the progressives' and labor activists' worst fears—more than a decision in the instant case, the board opened the door to the industrial disenfranchisement of many workers. First, the board defined "to assign" as "designating an employee to a place . . . appointing an employee to a time . . . or giving significant overall duties, i.e. tasks, to an employee." In the health care context, this meant that a nurse assigning other nurses or aides to patients would be a "supervisor." However, the board ruled that to "assign" did not include the directing of another nurse or aide to perform a discrete task such as "the charge nurse ordering an LPN to give a sedative to a patient."[85] The definition of "assign" thus left the door ajar for nurses hoping to remain beyond the reach of managerial loyalty.

But the board slammed it closed when it defined "responsibly direct" and "independent judgment." First, it held that "to direct" included even ordering an employee to perform a "single, discrete task." All an employer had to do to classify a worker as a supervisor then was to hold him or her "responsible" for this "direction," which meant that the person "must be accountable for the performance of the task by the other, such that some adverse consequences may befall the one providing the oversight if the tasks performed . . . are not performed properly."[86] Second, according to the board, "independent judgment" meant that anyone who did not follow "detailed instructions" in directing other employees used independent judgment. For nurses, this meant that "if the registered nurse weighs the individual condition and needs of a patient against the skills or special training of available nursing personnel, the nurse's assignment involves the exercise of independent judgment."

Finally, and most important, the NLRB held that if a worker spends a "regular and substantial" portion of his or her work performing the supervisory functions outlined above, he or she must be classified as a supervisor. There again was much for employers to rejoice. The board defined "regular" as being "according to pattern or schedule," and held that "substantial" meant that the person performed duties for as little as 10 to 15 percent of his or her total work time supervising. As the dissent written by members Liebman and Walsh noted, the decision threatened to "create a new class of workers under Federal Labor law: workers who have neither the genuine prerogatives of management, nor the statutory rights of ordinary employees."[87]

The Old Is Dying . . .

The *Kentucky River* cases elicited a chorus of outraged responses. In fact, rarely had an NLRB decision elicited so much attention in the media and the political sphere. Ranging from humorist Stephen Colbert to author Steven Greenhouse, from Edward Kennedy to Howard Dean and Harry Reid, a large number of progressive and Democratic voices joined AFL-CIO leader John Sweeney in lambasting the agency for its biased decision. "Disgrace is the only word that describes your decision," wrote a bitter Larry Cohen, the president of the Communication Workers of America, to NLRB chairman Robert Battista. At a time when labor unions were gearing up to fight for the Employee Free Choice Act (EFCA), the board's decision was a potent symbol of the determination of the American right to oppose unionism, and an eloquent demonstration of its hegemony over labor law.[88]

Five years later, assessing the effects of the decision remains an elusive task, particularly because union membership rates have dropped to new lows in the private sector. On the one hand, it is clear that the controversy has died down, and that unions do not believe the *Oakwood* decision has seriously affected them yet. This is owed to the fact that in industries with well-established labor relations, such as the automobile sector, it has not been used by companies against unions. In the health care industry, the impact of the decision has been somewhat blunted because in many cases, unions such as National Nurses United have been strong enough to force a local management to include all RNs in the unit—whether they may be "supervisors" in the eyes of the law or not.[89]

Yet it seems also clear that it is in new organizing situations, and in health care, where the union does not enjoy broad following, that the main effects of the *Oakwood* case will be visible. Not only will employers use it as an efficient delaying tactic, leading to lengthy hearings and appeals before the legal status of the individuals at issue becomes clear, but quite simply the *Oakwood* case puts unions in a catch-22. If they include potential "supervisors" in their organizing effort and win the election, the results of the election could be thrown out because they were not free of employer domination. If unions choose to be on the safe side and exclude those workers, then they might simply deprive themselves of much-needed energy and lose the election. The combined facts that nurse unions have hardly made any numerical headway in ten years and that there has been a steady decline of board cases dealing with the supervisory issue bode no promise for the future, especially if one keeps in mind that the *Oakwood* decision gives employers a blueprint to secure the classification of many workers as "supervisors."[90]

Along with their impact, the *Kentucky River* cases should be seen as the product of a multidecade struggle for the defense of managerial loyalty. By

2007, the success of this struggle seemed to threaten the rights of so many workers in America that it seemed to be the perfect illustration of Antonio Gramsci's dictum that "the crisis consists precisely in the fact that the old is dying and the new cannot be born; in this interregnum a great variety of morbid symptoms appear."[91] The *Kentucky River* decision and its legal progeny were one such morbid symptom. The decision signaled the death of the faith in social harmony that had given birth to the New Deal labor regime and sustained efforts to improve and enhance the lot of workers throughout much of the twentieth century.

EPILOGUE
Looking for Respect

THE paradox of the *Kentucky River* cases was that they put the topic of labor law back in the congressional limelight. On May 8, 2007, speaking in Congress in favor of the Re-Empowerment of Skilled, Professional Employees and Construction Tradeworkers (RESPECT) Act, the labor lawyer Sarah Fox expressed a hope shared by many labor progressives in the waning days of the Bush administration—that having regained a majority in Congress, Democrats would now address some of the most salient legal obstacles to the organization of workers in the United States, including the legal definition of the worker:

> Thanks to the work of the Chairman and others, and with the
> passage of the Employee Free Choice Act in the House, for the
> first time in a very long time we are seeing the beginnings of
> a national conversation about reform of our labor law to meet
> the desires of workers in the 21st century who want and need
> collective bargaining as a means to achieve individual opportunity,
> restore economic fairness, and rebuild America's middle class.
> And one of the areas most in need of reform is the statutory
> definition of supervisor, which was added in 1947.[1]

"Clearly this will not be an uncontroversial proposition," Democratic Congressman Robert E. Andrews noted about the RESPECT Act, which would have legislatively overruled the NLRB's latest decisions in the *Kentucky River* cases by removing the terms "responsibly direct" and "assign" from the statutory definition of supervisor and by specifying that to be classified as a supervisor, a worker must exercise supervisory duties at least 50 percent of the time.[2] Indeed, the short duration of the hearings, which lasted only one day, and the small number of witnesses suggested that pushing the law through would be no easy task. Still, in 2007, a number of factors seemed indeed to suggest that the political context had changed, making a debate over the relationship between workplace democracy and economic justice possible.

First, there was the growing perception of a deeply entrenched social inequality in America, which made the task of rebuilding the "middle class" very urgent in the minds of most progressives. This urgency was in turn compounded by the frustration of union leaders at the ineffectual character of the Wagner Act, which many workers and unions now circumvented because its cumbersome procedure afforded no meaningful protection. Finally, with the controversial debate over EFCA, which the House had passed in March 2007, both Democrats and labor progressives had shown their enduring faith in the basic notion that workplace democracy and economic justice are closely intertwined. In 2008, the advocacy organization American Rights at Work even sounded a sanguine note, suggesting in a report titled "The Haves and the Have Nots" that any attempt to foster economic justice would include a reappraisal of the way American labor law conceives of workers: "With the election of a pro-worker president and greater pro-worker majorities in Congress, the political conditions are ripe for addressing the problem of a diminishing population of workers with protected union rights. Congress could clarify or expand the definition of "employee" under the National Labor Relations Act (NLRA) to better reflect the realities of today's workforce."[3] In retrospect, it is striking that such hopes, however modest they may have been, were ill founded. The continuing faith of labor progressives in the Wagner Act's lofty ideals was not translated into significant political action. The Obama administration quickly decided to spend its political capital on health care reform, and like "second-tier" reforms such as immigration, both EFCA and the RESPECT Act fell by the wayside.[4] Still, as this historical inquiry comes to a close, it is worth reflecting on the arguments made at that time.

At the heart of this progressive call for the RESPECT Act was the theory of the "aging" of labor law. According to this view, the Wagner Act has become an antique statute. As the legal scholar Cynthia Estlund has argued, "The core of American labor law has essentially been sealed off—to a remarkably complete extent and for a remarkably long time—from both democratic revision and renewal and from experimentation and innovation. The basic statutory language, and many of the intermediate level principles and procedures though which the essentials of self organization and collective bargaining are put into practice, have been nearly frozen, or ossified, for over fifty years."[5] In part this "aging" is owed the political and judicial constraints under which the NLRB has functioned over the past thirty years, particularly those owing to the conservative revolution. Nevertheless, scholars have also insisted that the framework of the act is no longer adapted to the contemporary economic environment because the workplace for which it was designed—the Fordist workplace—no longer exists.[6] Seen from this perspective, the exclusion of supervisors and managers no longer makes sense because in the modern workplace there is no longer a sharp divide between the task of conception and the task of execution—indeed, boundaries between the two groups have increasingly blurred. Yet, because that divide is still embedded in the law, a large number of workers are deprived of their bargaining rights although they have nothing in common with the foremen who were the main target of the supervisory exemption in 1947. While the Fordist system of mass production in which the exclusion found its technical meaning has all but disappeared, today a growing number of workers, particularly semiprofessionals and knowledge workers, fall in a gray area between the categories that structured the midcentury workplace—labor and management. New management techniques such as job enrichment and teamwork also seem incompatible with the supervisory exclusion. As a result, as Sarah Fox argued, the time has come to deal with the tension that exists between the act's explicit protection of the right to organize of white-collar professionals and its exclusion of "supervisors" who are expected to exert a form of authority over others.[7]

As this book has shown, there is much to be said for this theory—the debates over procurement buyers employed at Bell Aerospace in the 1970s, over university professors, and more recently over nurses exemplify the problems identified by proponents of the RESPECT Act. Because of this changing work environment, as time wore on, labor experts found it ever harder to apply the principles of the Wagner Act, which were designed to respond to the Fordist workplace. Moreover, these difficulties have indeed been compounded by the increasing reluctance of the courts to allow the NLRB the flexibility and autonomy it needs to address the needs of workers in the new workplace. In this respect, predictions that the law will be increasingly irrelevant to the needs of workers are well grounded.

Yet implicit in this approach to the crisis of labor law is a technological determinism that tends to deemphasize the thoroughly political character of debates over the legal definition of the worker and to mask the democratic deficiencies of the old order. Indeed, the exclusion of "supervisors" and managers from collective bargaining in 1947 was an alignment of technology and conservative political culture. It was the product of a bitter war to protect managerial values and secure the loyalty of workers who were not bound by authority of the machines on the assembly line. By focusing on its apparent anachronism and lack of clarity in the contemporary workplace, we risk naturalizing the main rationale for this exclusion—that unionism is incompatible with the faithful performance of duty.

The RESPECT Act was illustrative of such limits. By removing the terms "assign" and "responsibly direct" from the definition of supervisor, and by stipulating that to be classified as a supervisor, a worker must exercise supervisory duties at least 50 percent of the time, the law would no doubt have assuaged the fears of nurses, construction workers, and others who seemed to lose the most from the NLRB's 2006 decisions. But in doing so, the bill would also have bolstered the notion that the right to organize is not a universal one. Indeed, the proponents of the act often referred to the opinion of the dissenters in the 2006 *Oakwood* case, saying the decision had created "a new class of workers under federal labor law: workers who have neither the genuine prerogatives of management, nor the statutory rights of ordinary employees."[8] Notably, Senator Dodd, the sponsor of the bill in the upper chamber, contended that it would restore the definition of the worker as defined in the Taft-Hartley Act, a "sensible precedent." AFSCME leaders echoed this sentiment, stating that "these changes would respect the original intent of Congress"—rarely had the Taft-Hartley Act cut such a progressive figure on the political horizon.[9]

Thus, for all the talk about freedom of association and human rights, there was no attempt to challenge the managerial exclusion head-on. Rather, Congressman Andrews explained at the outset, the law reaffirmed that there were "people who are part of management, who are supervisors, and for whose divided loyalties would never make it possible to be both in a union and representing the employer."[10]

Yet there is no more reason to argue that the democratic right to organize should be limited to workers with low responsibility levels than to suggest that the right to vote should be limited to property holders. In both cases, these restrictions suggest that that there is a deep-seated ambivalence about the right at stake.[11] In fact, the historical relationship between those two conservative fears may be more significant than we think. As a number of scholars have shown, during the Gilded Age and the early twentieth century, businessmen and upper-class Americans were worried about the potential consequences of the working-class vote on their domination of politics. Particularly irksome to them was the possibility of higher taxes, which they saw as a threat hanging on both their property and the country's prosperity.[12] Efforts to prevent a liberal upsurge at the polls failed, and by the 1940s workers had largely asserted their electoral power and now bolstered the New Deal coalition. By then, however, the struggle over American democracy had taken a new form. With foremen organizing, businessmen once again sought to limit the extension of the democratic principle along a participatory axis, arguing that an expansive vision of industrial democracy in which every employee had a voice would threaten capitalism. Hence, from the 1940s onward, the concept of "loyalty" became the bulwark protecting the hegemony of the business world against the encroachment of freedom of association.

In point of fact, business executives and conservative think tanks shared none of the interest of the sponsors of the bill in the original intent of Congress in Taft-Hartley. Rather, they united against the prospect of a return to that "sensible precedent." "This far reaching change would upset the long established balanced between labor and management in the workplace," the Heritage Foundation explained in a memo opposing the law; "in order to run effectively, a company needs the undivided loyalty of its management."[13] The National Association of Manufacturers (NAM) echoed this sentiment, suggesting unionization of workers above the rank and file would foment discord among "employee classes": "A successful business depends upon a united workforce, including supervisors whose primary role is to manage employees and operations of behalf of employers. The NAM strongly opposes the proposed RESPECT Act, which would undermine this foundation from which positive employer-employee relationships are developed and established."[14]

In fact, in 2007 business associations could no longer invoke the threat of a rank-and-file takeover of the plants or even a lack of discipline, as they had in the 1940s when opposing the foremen's unions. Yet they insisted that participation in a union was not compatible with the exercise of duties and responsibilities. According to the National Association of Waterfront Employers, for example, unionism among low-level supervisors would be detrimental to the safety and efficiency of dockers: "Ship superintendents are essential to carrying out the expert performance required of a stevedore company and are placed on the vessel to ensure that cargo handling operations are conducted in a safe and efficient manner. This can only be achieved with the undivided loyalty of the ship superintendent to his/her MTP stevedore employer, and not by splitting the superintendent's loyalties between his/her employer and his/her union."[15] In similar fashion, the attorney Roger King—a noted conservative expert on labor law—suggested in his statement that without full control of their supervisors, companies would be unable to secure compliance with OSHA regulations and other important labor laws such as the Fair Labor Standards Act. Why unions would seek to thwart the enforcement of legislation designed to protect workers, King never said, but all the same, his statement reflected corporate confidence in the strength of the loyalty argument they had built over seventy years.[16]

More than the ossification of labor law, it is this successful struggle for loyalty that this book has traced, a struggle that demonstrates dramatically the power of business elites in making their vision of unionism *the* vision that has been adopted in American law. The consequences of this hegemony are threefold. First, today managers and supervisors—some thirteen million workers—compose the largest group of workers excluded from the protection of the Wagner Act, and the number of people whose duties straddle the line between professional and supervisory duties and are thus potential "managers" for the purposes of the Wagner Act is much higher, probably more than 20 percent of the workforce.[17]

The importance of this exclusion, however, goes well beyond the number of workers who do not have a voice at work. For corporate America, it was an ideological marker that partly delegitimized the labor movement and the labor unions by suggesting that market freedom is not totally compatible with unionism—according to conservatives, businesses need a reliable cadre of managers on whom they can count to design and carry out market strategies of growth and profits. The supervisory exclusion suggests that the *agents* of free enterprise cannot and should not be allowed to organize, and that this democratic freedom should be limited to the "employees" of free enterprise, that is, those who are "used" and exert little influence over the final result.

Most important, in securing the "loyalty" of managers and supervisors, businessmen have done more than imprint their values on the labor law; they have also secured the ability to use supervisors against rank-and-file unions. As a union organizer noted in 1979, "Supervisors are made to feel that his or her own personal worth, loyalty to the institution, and future depend on how many 'no' votes he or she can produce."[18] "Supervisors constitute management's most important asset and are vital to combating attempts at unionization," noted a corporate attorney in 1981.[19] A mere look at the sundry publications aimed at antiunion campaigns by labor experts such as Alfred T. Maria suggests the extent to which companies have been able to use managers and frontline supervisors as the functional equivalent of the union organizer.[20] There again, the law has been most supportive—it is legal for top managers to ask supervisors to contribute to defeating a unionization drive, and even to tell them that they might lose their jobs if they fail to do so. In fact, one may argue that the entire American working class was defeated when supervisors and managers were framed and defined as being impervious to freedom of association and collective bargaining.

"Progressives in the United States need an ideological offensive against the anti-union right, one that puts the idea of workers' rights at the center of liberalism and democracy," the historian Nelson Lichtenstein noted in 2008.[21] Other scholars, arguing along the same lines, have contended that the right to organize should be a civil right protected by Title VII of the 1964 Civil Rights Act. Yet no such effort will be successful without challenging directly the definition of the workers whose rights are protected. Today's progressives may thus find the earlier efforts of industrial pluralists worth pondering, if only because these efforts show that the expansion of the right to organize is far from being incompatible with the American disposition. Industrial pluralists were not steeped in socialist culture—indeed, they had largely abandoned the labor metaphysic. Nonetheless their language of social harmony through democracy—one inherited from the Wisconsin school pioneered by Commons—was a radical one, for it denied the validity of the loyalty argument. In rejecting class consciousness and pushing for an expansive vision of workplace democracy at the same time, what industrial pluralists offered was a postindustrial vision of labor relations that today could be quite useful to all progressives seeking to remedy the "aging" of American labor law and rebuild a legal framework for economic justice.

NOTES

Introduction

1. The phrase "*Kentucky River* cases" is commonly used to refer to three National Labor Relations Board (NLRB) decisions (*Oakwood Healthcare Inc.*, 348 NLRB no. 37, *Golden Crest Healthcare Center*, 348 NLRB no. 39, and *Croft Metals, Inc.*, 348 NLRB no. 38) handed down on September 29, 2006, in response to the Supreme Court ruling in *NLRB v. Kentucky River Community Care*, 532 U.S. 706 (2001). *Oakwood*—the main case—bore upon the UAW's organizing drive at a hospital in Detroit, where over 180 nurses took turns in "taking charge"—assigning patients to one another and monitoring the patients. For a greater description of the charge nurse system, see Chapter 7 of this study.

2. Nancy Pelosi, "NLRB Rulings Are a Ruthless Attack on American Workers" (press release, October 5, 2006). On the social protests generated by the NLRB decision, see James Parks, "Workers Have Had Enough," AFL-CIO NOW blog, July 14, 2006.

3. Cheryl Johnson is quoted in James Parks, "NLRB Decision Affecting Eight Million Workers Could Happen Any Day," AFL-CIO NOW blog, September 25, 2006.

4. "Supervisor in Name Only: Union Rights of Eight Million Workers at Stake in Labor Ruling" (EPI issue brief 225), http://www.epi.org/publication/ib225/. The complaint filed with the ILO is available on the AFL-CIO website, http://www.aflcio.org. The Freedom of Association and Right to Organise, convention 87 of the ILO, stipulates that "workers without distinctions whatsoever" shall have the right to join a union. In fact, however, the United States has never ratified convention 87, which was adopted in 1948, nor the Right to Organize and Collective Bargaining Convention 98, which was adopted in 1949. For the U.S. government's response and the ILO's recommendations, see case 2524, "Complaint Against the Government of the United States Presented by the American Federation of Labor and the Congress of Industrial Relations," in *349th Report of the Committee on Freedom of Association* (New York: International Labour Organization, March 2008), 794–858.

5. Today workers classified as "supervisors" and "managers" compose the largest group of workers excluded from the protection of the law, that is, some thirteen million workers. Yet the number of professionals who might fall within the purview of the supervisory exception is probably well over 20 percent of the workforce; see Charles Hecksher, *The New Unionism* (Ithaca: Cornell University Press, 1994), 68–69. There is of course a large amount of literature covering the history of industrial democracy, but this historiography has largely ignored the question of the definition of workers. Sociologists have recently noted the importance of this question; see the special issue "Constructing Workers: Working Class Formation Under Neoliberalism," *Qualitative Sociology* 30, no. 4 (2007).

6. On the history of the master and servant doctrine, see Robert Steinfeld, *The Invention of Free Labor: The Employment Relation in English and American Law and Culture, 1350–1870* (Chapel Hill: University of North Carolina Press, 1991); and Christopher Tomlins, *Law, Labor and Ideology in the Early American Republic* (New York: Cambridge University Press, 1993).

7. In thinking about conservatism, I benefitted from Corey Robin's *The Reactionary Mind: Conservatism from Edmund Burke to Sarah Palin* (New York: Oxford University Press, 2011). Unlike recent authors on the topic, Robin believes not only that conservative ideas can be traced back to the eighteenth century, but also that conservatism is first and foremost an opposition to the democratization of social structures. As reviewers have noted, Robin's analysis of the conservative response to the democratic impulse leaves many questions unsolved, but it is useful nonetheless.

8. On the need to reframe twentieth-century political history as the history of democracy rather than liberalism, see James Klopenberg, "From Hartz to Tocqueville: Shifting the Focus from Liberalism to Democracy in America," in *The Democratic Experiment: New Directions in American Political History*, ed. Meg Jacobs, William J. Novak, and Julian Zelizer (Princeton: Princeton University Press, 2003), 350–400.

9. See Alfred T. Chandler, *The Visible Hand* (Cambridge, Mass.: Harvard University Press, 1977).

10. The phrase "moments of madness" and the sentence that follows it are taken from Aristide Zolberg, "Moments of Madness," *Politics and Society* 2 (1972): 83–207.

11. James Atleson, *Values and Assumptions in American Labor Law* (Amherst: University of Massachusetts Press, 1983). See also his "Confronting Judicial Values: Rewriting the Law of Work in a Common Law System," *Buffalo Law Review* 45 (1997): 435–456.

12. For work laying out this perspective in detail, see David Brody's classic essay, "Workplace Contractualism," in *Industrial Democracy in America: The Ambiguous Promise*, ed. Howell Harris and Nelson Lichtenstein (New York: Cambridge University Press, 1993); Jack Metzgar, *Striking Steel: Solidarity Remembered* (Philadelphia: Temple University Press, 2000); Daniel J. Clark, *Like Night and Day* (Chapel Hill: University of North Carolina Press, 1997); and Nelson Lichtenstein, *State of the Union* (Princeton: Princeton University Press, 2002), chap. 1.

13. Quoted in Margo Anderson, "The Language of Class in 20th Century America," *Social Science History* 13, no. 4 (Winter 1988): 349–375, 349.

14. See Joël Colton, *Léon Blum: Humanist in Politics* (New York: Knopf, 1966), 186; and John Morton Blum, *From the Morgenthau Diaries* (Boston: Houghton Mifflin, 1959), 163.

15. For the classical statement on American exceptionalism, see Werner Sombart, *Why Is There No Socialism in America?* (1907; repr., White Plains, N.Y.: M.E. Sharpe, 1976). For a more recent attempt to tackle this question, see Jean Heffer, ed., *Pourquoi n'y a-t-il pas de socialisme aux Etats-Unis?* (Paris: EHESS, 1984). On the "new Labor history," see David Brody, "The Old Labor History and the New: In Search of an American Working Class," *Labor History* 20 (Winter 1979): 11–26. On the railroad strikes of 1877, see David Stowell, *The Great Strikes of 1877* (Urbana: University of Illinois Press, 2008). On the Lordstown Strike, see Jefferson Cowie, *Stayin' Alive: The 1970s and the Last Days of the Working Class* (New York: New Press, 2011).

16. In conceiving of this investigation on the language of harmony, I largely benefited from Martin J. Burke's wonderful *The Conundrum of Class: Public Discourse on the Social Order in America* (Chicago: University of Chicago Press, 1995). See also Wendy Wall, *Inventing the American Way: The Politics of Consensus from the New Deal to the Civil Rights Movement* (New York: Oxford University Press, 2008); and Olivier Zunz, *The American Century* (Chicago: University of Chicago Press, 1998).

17. Lichtenstein, *State of the Union*, 35–36, 148–156; and Christopher Tomlins, *The State and the Unions* (New York: Cambridge University Press, 1986). A student of Gabriel Kolko, Tomlins suggested that the Wagner Act was yet another element in an organizational synthesis that created the institutions necessary to make modern capitalism manageable. But the constant intervention of the government in labor disputes and its constant emphasis on bargaining was an unmitigated bane

on the labor movement, one had drew the sap out of it and deprived it of the means to defend itself against conservative backlash. I deal with this historiography at greater length in the introduction to Chapter 5 of this study.

18. Paul Goodman, *Growing Up Absurd* (New York: Vintage, 1962), quoted in Kevin Mattson, *Intellectuals in Action: The Origins of the New Left and Radical Liberalism* (University Park: Pennsylvania State University Press, 2003), 1.

Chapter 1. The "Employé"

1. Richard McMurtrie, "The Legal Rights and Duties of Employers and Employed, as Affecting the Interests of the Public," *American Law Register and Review* 41, no. 5 (May 1893): 421–437, esp. 421–423.

2. *Vane v. Newcombe*, 132 U.S. 220 (1889), 221.

3. On the composition of the American workforce at the end of the nineteenth century, see David Montgomery, *The Fall of the House of Labor* (New York: Cambridge University Press, 1987), chaps. 1–3.

4. *Vane v. Newcombe*, 220–227.

5. Henry Farnam and Clive Day, *Chapters in the History of Social Legislation in the United States to 1860* (New York: Lawbook Exchange, 2000), 152, passim. The Populist Platform was particularly successful in Ohio, where, according to an observer, one could "get a taste of that which Populism, in all its vagaries, never dared to dream." See C. L. Martzolff, "Recent Ohio Legislation Confirming to the Constitution," *American Political Science Review* 7, no. 4 (November 1913): 639–647, 639. A lien section was included in the constitution adopted in Ohio in 1912. See C. L. Martzolff, "Ohio: Changes in the Constitution," *American Political Science Review* 6, no. 4 (November 1912): 573–576. In an article dealing with Progressivism in the South, however, Arthur Link noted that in Texas as early as 1892, the Populist Platform included a mechanics' lien law, along with an eight-hour day. See Arthur Link, "The Progressive Movement in the South, 1870–1914," in *Myth and Southern History*, vol. 2, ed. Nicholas Cords and Partrick Gerster (Urbana: University of Illinois Press, 1989), 64.

6. *Vane v. Newcombe*, 223.

7. *Vane v. Newcombe*, 227–229.

8. *Water Company v. Ware*, 16 Wallace 566 (1872). The company, which was to lay water pipes in the city of St. Paul, had agreed to "be responsible for all damages which may occur by reason of the neglect of their employés on the premises," and so was held responsible for the injuries sustained by one Ware, whose horse had been frightened by a blast as he rode down a street where excavation work was done by a subcontractor of the company.

9. *Gurney v. Atlantic & Great Western Railroad*, 58 N.Y. 358 (1874). By contrast, in *Wakefield v. Fargo*, 90 N.Y. 213 (1882), it was held that a statute making stockholders of a corporation "liable for all debts that may be due and owing to their laborers, servants, and apprentices for services performed for such corporation" did not include a bookkeeper or a general manager. Commenting on this case in *Vane v. Newcombe*, the Court explained, "The view taken by the court was that the services referred to were menial or manual services; that he who performed them must be of a class who usually looked to the reward of a day's labor or service for immediate or present support . . . one who was responsible for no independent action, but who did a day's work or a stated job under the direction of a Superior." *Vane v. Newcombe*, 236.

10. *Ritter v. State*, 111 Ind. 324 (1887), 502; *State v. Sarlls*, 135 Ind. 195 (1893), 1130.

11. I make this point in qualification of the argument presented by Tomlins in *Law, Labor and Ideology*, 217–292, 219. Tomlins refers to the law treatise written by one Walker in 1837, in which the author argues, "We understand by relations of master and servant, nothing, more or less, than that of *employer* and *employed*."

12. James Schouler, *A Treatise on the Law of Domestic Relations* (1895), 3, 744; Irving Browne,

Elements of the Law of Domestic Relations and Employer and Employed (1890), 123–124, quoted in Mary Ann Glendon and Edward L. Rev, "Changes in the Bonding of the Employment Relationship," *Boston College Law Review* 20, no. 3 (1979): 457.

13. The miners' law was adopted in 1879 and the mechanics' lien law in 1881; see *Vane v. Newcombe*, majority opinion, 234–235.

14. *Vane v. Newcombe*, 233–235.

15. Jay Feinman, "The Development of the At-Will Rule," *American Journal of Legal History* 20, no. 2 (1976): 118.

16. *Louisville, Evansville and St Louis Railroad Co v. Wilson*, 138 U.S. 501 (1891), 501–503, 506–507. On the highly competitive context of the railroad industry, see Chandler's classic text, *Visible Hand*, 122–144.

17. On the history of the Supreme Court and the judiciary at the time, see Alpheus T. Mason, *The Supreme Court from Taft to Burger* (Baton Rouge: Louisiana State University Press, 1979), 22–27. *Louisville v. Wilson*, 505.

18. *Finance Co. of Pennsylvania, et al. v. Charleston C. & C.R. Co. et al.*, 52 Fed. 527 (1892).

19. *Black's Law Dictionary*, 2nd ed. (1910), s.v. "employé."

20. The literature on this question is huge. For my understanding of this period, I have relied on Harry L. Watson, *Liberty and Power* (New York: Hill and Wang, 1990); Richard Stott, "Artisans and Capitalist Development," *Journal of the Early Republic* 16, no. 2 (Summer 1996): 257–271; Bruce Laurie, *Working People of Philadelphia* (Philadelphia: Temple University Press, 1980); Sean Wilentz, *Chants Democratic* (New York: Oxford University Press, 1984); Alan Dawley, *Class and Community in Lynn* (Cambridge, Mass.: Harvard University Press, 1976); Philip Foner, *History of the Labor Movement in the United States*, vol. 1 (1947; repr., New York: International Publishers, 1975); Eric Foner, *The Story of American Freedom* (New York: Norton, 1998).

21. *Webster's Dictionary* (Springfield, Mass.: H.S. Taylor's Steam Power Press, 1849), S.V. "employ."

22. *Eleventh Census of the Population, 1890*, vol. 6 (Washington, D.C.: GPO, 1895), 13. Note that the report actually provided two different numbers for the year 1890 because of a changing methodology.

23. On white-collar workers, see Olivier Zunz, *Making America Corporate* (Chicago: University of Chicago Press, 1990). On tramping, see Alex Keyssar, *Out of Work: The First Century of Unemployment in Massachusetts* (New York: Cambridge University Press, 1986); and E. H. Monkonnen, ed., *Walking to Work: Tramps in America, 1790–1920* (Lincoln: University of Nebraska Press, 1984). See also David Montgomery, "The Common Laborer," in *The Fall of the House of Labor* (New York: Cambridge University Press, 1989).

24. See Stuart Blumin, *The Emergence of the Middle Class: Social Experience in the American City, 1760–1900* (New York: Cambridge University Press, 1989).

25. *Centennial Dictionary* (1890), s.v. "employé."

26. Ibid., s.v. "employ."

27. *Vane v. Newcombe*, "Argument for Appellant," 231.

28. Louis Guyot, another advocate of liberalism, suggested getting rid of the term "patron," which, according to him, "implied the superiority of the one who pays for work over the one who performs it, which is a remnant from a feudal psychology"; see Jacques Le Goff, *Du silence à la parole* (Rennes: Presses Universitaires de Rennes, 1994), 78. This is why liberals with a social bent such as Paul Leroy Beaulieu, who did not divorce capitalism from social ethics, lamented the rise of the term.

29. This anecdote was actually first told by Daniel Defoe. See E. P. Thompson, *Customs in Common: Studies in Popular Traditional Culture* (New York: New Press, 1991), 84; and Christopher Tomlins, "Subordination, Authority, Law: Subjects in Labor History," *International Labor and Working Class History* 47 (Spring 1995): 56–90. Tomlins takes issue with E. P. Thompson, who argued that the master and servant model of discipline had disappeared for good, but had been

replaced by factory discipline. Tomlins argues that starting with the Woolen Manufactures Act of 1725, Parliament adopted a series of laws restoring the duty of service.

30. Tomlins, "Subordination, Authority, Law," 75.

31. In England, the Master and Servant Law was abolished by the Conspiracy and Protection of Property Act of 1875. By then, an increasing number of people believed the criminal sanctions that the Master and Servant Law provided against recalcitrant workers were unfair, since it was nearly impossible for servants to enforce any of the civil penalties the law allowed for masters who did not fulfill their responsibilities. See Wanjiru Noya, *Property in Work: The Anglo-American Employment Relationship* (Burlington, Vt.: Ashgate, 1988), 27–28. This paragraph largely relies on Simon Deakin, "The Contract of Employment: A Study in Legal Evolution" (University of Cambridge Working Paper No. 203, ESRC Centre for Business Research), http://www.cbr.cam.ac.uk/pdf/WP203.pdf; and Simon Deakin and Frank Wilkinson, *The Law of the Labour Market: Industrialization, Employment and Legal Evolution* (Oxford: Oxford University Press, 2005), 61–74, 86–100. On the evolution of the franchise in England, see John Cannon, *Parliamentary Reform* (Cambridge: Cambridge University Press, 1980); and Michael G. Brock, *The Great Reform Act* (London: Hutchinson, 1973).

32. Steinfeld, *Invention of Free Labor*.

33. *Philadelphia Ledger*, February 2, 1849, quoted in John R. Commons et al., *History of Labor in the United States* (New York: Macmillan, 1918), vol. 1, 603.

34. Quoted in Steinfeld, *Invention of Free Labor*, 15.

35. "Employee Not Employe," *New York Times*, September 30, 1894.

36. Karl Marx, *Capital: A Critique of Political Economy,* vol. 1, trans. Ben Fowkes (New York: Vintage, 1977), 280.

37. Henry C. Carey, *Principles of Social Science*, vol. 3 (Philadelphia: J.B. Lippincott, 1858), 102; Rodney Morrison, "Henry Charles Carey and American Economic Development," *Transactions of the American Philosophical Society* 76 (1986): 24. Michael Perelman, "Political Economy and the Press: Karl Marx and Henry C. Carey at the *New York Tribune*," in *Marx's Crises Theory* (New York: Praeger, 1989), 10–26.

38. Richard Grant White, "Social Distinctions in America," *North American Review* 137, no. 322 (September 1883): 231–247, 233. On the use of the phrase "distinction of employments," see Burke, *Conundrum of Class*, 188–119. I have greatly benefited from Burke's analysis, on which this paragraph relies heavily.

39. This point is made at great length by William Forbath, "The Ambiguities of Free Labor: Labor and the Law in the Gilded Age," *Wisconsin Law Review* (July 1985): 767–814; and by Eric Foner, "The Meaning of Freedom in an Age of Emancipation," *Journal of American History* 81, no. 2 (September 1994): 435–460. I am indebted to both of them for my understanding of the history of free labor in America, particularly the two strands of it after the Civil War.

40. Schouler, *Treatise on the Law of Domestic Relations*, 7 (in introduction). It is actually quite difficult to tell at what point in the nineteenth century the terms "master" and "servant" fell into disrepute. John Bristed, an American lawyer, argued as early as 1818 that "there is no such thing as master and servant in this country . . . indeed, the name is not permitted." "Servitude, strictly so called, does not exist in this country," the legal scholar Thomas Walker wrote in 1837. "We understand by the relation of master and servant nothing, more or less, than that of the employer and the employed." See Christopher Tomlins, "The Ties That Bind: Master and Servant in Massachusetts, 1800–1850," *Labor History* 30, no. 2 (1989): 193–227, 216.

41. On the emergence of the word "help" as opposed to "servant," see David Rodiger, *The Wages of Whiteness* (New York: Verso, 1999); and Albert Matthews, "The Terms Hired Man and Help," in *Publications of the Colonial Society of Massachusetts*, vol. 5 (Cambridge, Mass.: John Wilson, 1900), 225–254.

42. On the "entire contract" rule, see Karen Orren, *Belated Feudalism* (New York: Cambridge University Press, 1992), 84–85.

43. Tomlins, "Ties That Bind" and *Law, Labor and Ideology*, 259–293; as well as Orren, *Belated Feudalism*; and the response offered by David Montgomery in *Citizen Worker* (New York: Cambridge University Press, 1994). Montgomery argues that claims that a "feudal" system of labor relations still obtained in the nineteenth century are overwrought and ignore the significant differences between the rights of American workers and those of their European counterparts, for example, Belgian workers still required to carry a *livret*. On judicial opposition to labor unions, see Victoria Hattam, *Labor Visions and State Power* (Princeton: Princeton University Press, 1993), who focuses on charges of conspiracy as the main device against unions in the 1870s and 1880s; William Forbath, *Law and the Shaping of the American Labor Movement* (Cambridge, Mass.: Harvard University Press, 1991), who sees judicial opposition at its apex in the 1890s to 1920s, when the courts used the Sherman antitrust act against unions. Both, however, contend that this judicial hostility produced the voluntarism that characterized the AFL.

44. Orren, *Belated Feudalism*, 183–184; and Theresa Ann Case, *The Great Southwest Railroad Strike and Free Labor* (College Station: Texas A&M University Press, 2010), 106. The absence of unions notwithstanding, in fact the question of loyalty continued to nag employers, pushing them to experiment with a host of strategies that went from creating industrial villages such as Pullman town in the 1890s to establishing progressive welfare capitalist practices in the 1920s.

45. The notion that Gilded Age judges actually relied on a political tradition of free labor and equal rights that hearkened back to Jacksonian and even Jeffersonian America is a staple of the revisionist account of "Lochnerian jurisprudence" and its origins. Alan Jones, for example has shown that the defense of the right of property put forward by Cooley in his *Treatise on Constitutional Limitations* was imbued with a large amount of nostalgia for a Jeffersonian, preindustrial world. See Alan Jones, "Thomas M. Cooley and Laissez-Faire Constitutionalism: A Reconsideration," *Journal of American History* 53 (1967): 751–771; as well as Charles McCurdy, "Justice Field and the Jurisprudence of Government-Business Relations: Some Parameters of Laissez-Faire Constitutionalism," *Journal of American History* 61 (1975): 970–1005; and Howard Gillman, *The Constitution Besieged: The Rise & Demise of Lochner Era Police Powers Jurisprudence* (Durham, N.C.: Duke University Press, 1992), 19–75. In an important article, however, William Forbath has shown that the meaning of the free labor tradition was profoundly contested in the post–Civil War era. One vision of free labor, stemming both from the language of abolitionism and the Jacksonian fear of monopolies, emphasized the right to sell one's labor free from governmental constraints. By contrast, labor leaders fretted about the social consequences of this freedom, which they deemed to be incompatible with republican principles of dignity and independence. As a result, although it was derived from the same principles, the labor critique of capitalism was at odds with the liberal doctrine of the judges. See Forbath, "Ambiguities of Free Labor." As the last section of this chapter suggests, I am in full agreement with this argument.

46. *Scranton Times*, December 31, 1873, quoted in Herbert Gutman, "Trouble on the Railroads, 1873–1874: Prelude to the 1877 Crisis?" *Labor History* 2 (1961): 253.

47. Quoted in Melvyn Dubofsky, *The State and Labor in Modern America* (Chapel Hill: University of North Carolina Press, 1994), 18.

48. *Jordan v. State*, quoted in Marc Linder, *The Employment Relationship in Anglo-American Law* (Westport, Conn.: Greenwood, 1989), 121.

49. This paragraph relies on the wonderful analysis offered by Burke, *Conundrum of Class*, 153.

50. William Graham Sumner, *What Social Classes Owe Each Other* (1883; repr., Los Angeles: Pamphleteers, 2008), 71–76.

51. George McNeill, *The Labor Movement: The Problem of Today* (1887; repr., New York: Kelley, 1971), 480.

52. Ibid., iv.

53. For the Knights of Labor, I have relied on Leon Fink, *Workingmen's Democracy, The Knights of Labor and American Politics* (Urbana: University of Illinois Press, 1984); and Richard Schneirov,

Labor and Urban Politics: Class Conflict and the Origins of Modern Liberalism in Chicago, 1867–1897 (Urbana: University of Illinois Press, 1998).

54. Henry George, *Progress and Poverty* (San Francisco: Hinton, 1879).

55. McNeill, *Labor Movement*, 484.

56. Ibid., 479.

57. On the 1896 election, see Michael Kazin's biography of William Jennings Bryan, *A Godly Hero* (New York: Knopf, 2006), in which he argues that while Bryan lost, he remade the Democratic Party into a party of social reform.

Chapter 2. Struggling Against Class

1. Bureau of Labor Statistics of Illinois, "The Sweating System in Chicago," in *Seventh Biennial Report* (Springfield, Ill.: H. K. Rokker 1893), 361; "Florence Kelley's Testimony on the Sweating System," in *Report and Findings of the Joint Committee to Investigate the "Sweat Shop" System* (Springfield, Ill.: H. K. Rokker, 1893), 135.

2. Robert Hunter, *Poverty: Social Conscience in the Progressive Era*, ed. Peter d'A. Jones (1901; repr., New York: Harper, 1965). Noted Hunter, "I am reminded now of a vagrant whom I knew well and for many years believed to be sincerely trying to become 'a man,' as we used to say. He has turned up wherever I have happened to be—in Chicago or New York. He has always looked me up, and together we have conspired to overcome his vagrant instincts. We have always failed, and after a few weeks' work Jerry disappears, and I know what has become of him. At last, in his case as in many others, I have become convinced that he is more satisfied and content with the life of a vagrant than with the miserable lot of an unskilled, underpaid workman." On nineteenth-century repression of vagrancy, see Amy Dru Stanley, "Beggars Can't Be Choosers," *Journal of American History* 78, no. 4 (March 1992): 1265–1293.

3. See Jennifer Klein, *For All These Rights: Business, Labor and the Shaping of the America's Public-Private Welfare State* (Princeton: Princeton University Press, 2003); Meg Jacobs, *Pocketbook Politics* (Princeton: Princeton University Press, 2005); Foner, *Story of American Freedom*, 139–219.

4. Florence Kelley, as quoted in Michael Kazin, *American Dreamers: How the Left Changed a Nation* (New York: Knopf, 2012), 68.

5. The argument that I make in the following lines is also made much more fully by Shelton Stromquist in *Reinventing the People: The Progressive Movement, the Class Problem, and the Origins of Modern Liberalism* (Urbana: University of Illinois Press, 2006).

6. Jane Addams, "Trade Unions and Public Duty," *American Journal of Sociology* 4, no. 4 (January 1899): 448–462, 448. Addams also quoted Comte, who famously interpreted the French Revolution as the product of a social breakdown.

7. Ibid., 461; and Jane Addams, "The Settlement as a Factor in the Labor Movement," in *Hull House Maps and Papers: A Presentation of Nationalities and Wages in a Congested District of Chicago, Together with Comments and Essays on Problems Growing Out of Social Conditions* (New York: Thomas Crowell, 1895), 183–204.

8. Doug Rossinow, *Visions of Progress: The Left-Led Tradition in America* (Philadelphia: University of Pennsylvania Press, 2007), chap. 1. Note however the difference between Rossinow and Stromquist: Stromquist emphasizes more strongly the opposition of Progressives to class, while Rossinow puts more emphasis on the collaboration of the left and Progressives, which he sees as a kind of matrix for New Deal reforms. Basically Stromquist thinks that Progressives held fast to a kind of Lincolnesque ideal, while Rossinow sees them as the engine of something close to an American Fabianism.

9. On the idea of "issue politics" as applied to the Progressive Era, see Daniel Rodgers, "In Search of Progressivism," *Reviews in American History* 10 (1982): 117.

10. The background information on the *Lochner* case is derived from Paul Kens, *Lochner v.*

New York: Economic Regulation on Trial (Lawrence: University Press of Kansas, 1998); David E. Bernstein, "*Lochner v. New York*: A Centennial Perspective," *Washington University Law Quarterly* 85, no. 5 (2005): 1469–1528; and Peter H. Irons, *A People's History of the Supreme Court* (New York: Penguin, 1999), 254–256.

11. For the text of the law, see Kens, *Lochner v. New York,* Appendix B, 169–170.

12. Bernstein, "*Lochner v. New York,*" 1482.

13. *Muller v. Oregon*, 208 U.S. 412 (1908).

14. Charles R. Henderson, *Industrial Insurance in the United States* (Chicago: University of Chicago Press, 1909), 44, quoted in John F. Witt, "The Transformation of Work and the Law of Workplace Accidents," *Yale Law Journal* 107, no. 5 (1998): 1467–1502, 1488. On factory legislation, see Daniel Nelson, *Managers and Workers: The Origins of the New Factory System in the United States, 1880–1920* (Madison: University of Wisconsin Press, 1975), 122–140.

15. Léon Bourgeois, *La solidarité* (Paris: Armand Colin, 1896).

16. This account of solidarism relies on Le Goff, *Du silence à la parole*, 254–257; Judith Stone, *The Search for Social Peace: Reform Legislation in France, 1890–1914* (Albany: State University of New York Press, 1985), 25–54; Janet Horne, *A Social Laboratory for Modern France* (Durham, N.C.: Duke University Press, 2002), 9–10, 118–120.

17. See, e.g., Célestin Bouglé, *Solidarisme et Libéralisme* (Paris: Rieder, 1904), 113–114.

18. Thierry Pilon and François Vatin, "Retour sur la question salariale," *Histoire et Sociétés* no. 1 (1er trimestre 2002): 95–96; Le Goff, *Du silence à la parole*; Alain Cottereau, "Droit et bon droit," *Annales* 57, no. 6 (2002): 1521–1557.

19. For the notion that in the American polity all powers are involved in a "constitutional dialogue" with the courts, I have relied on Neal Devins, *Shaping Constitutional Values: Elected Government, the Supreme Court and the Abortion Debate* (Baltimore: Johns Hopkins University Press, 1996*).* See also William Forbath, "The Long Life of Liberal America," *Law and History Review* 24, no. 1 (Spring 2006): 179–192.

20. *Ritchie v. People*, 155 Ill. 98 (1895), "Brief for Appellant," 19, passim. The brief clearly called on the Illinois Supreme Court to use the Fourteenth Amendment to invalidate the law and pointed, among others, to the infamous *Godcharles v. Wingeman* decision, in which a tribunal invalidated a law prohibiting payment in any means other than money. By "substantive," jurists mean that the due process clause referred not simply to a process, but also to a number of specific rights, foremost among which was the right to property.

21. *Ritchie v. People*. On the public/private distinction, see Morton Horwitz, "The History of the Public Private Distinction," *University of Pennsylvania Law Review* 130, no. 6 (June 1982): 1423–1428; and Barry Cushman, *Rethinking the New Deal Court: The Structure of a Constitutional Revolution* (New York: Oxford University Press, 1998), 47–48.

22. This doctrine was first highlighted in Justice Field's dissent in the 1876 *Slaughterhouse Cases*, and by 1897 the U.S. Supreme Court had endorsed the main lines of the freedom of contract argument. See Irons, *People's History*, 248–249.

23. Bernstein, "*Lochner v. New York,*" 1486, on whom this paragraph relies heavily; Irons, *People's History*, 255.

24. *Lochner v. New York,* 198 U.S. 45 (1905), 54. The background information on this case is derived from Bernstein, "*Lochner v. New York,*" 1493–1496.

25. *Otis v. Parker*, 187 U.S. 606 (1903), 609. The similarities between Holmes's opinions in *Otis* and *Lochner* are highlighted by Edward G. White, *Justice Holmes: Law and the Inner Self* (New York: Oxford University Press, 1995), 326–327.

26. Roscoe Pound, "Liberty of Contract," *Harvard Law Review* 18, no. 7 (1909): 454–487, 454. For an additional indictment of the idea of liberty of contract, see Josephine Goldmark, *Fatigue and Efficiency: A Study in Industry* (New York: Russell Sage, 1912).

27. *Adair v. U.S.*, 208 U.S. 161 (1908), 174–175; Thomas M. Cooley, *A Treatise on the Limitations Which Rest upon the Legislative Power of the States of the Union* (Boston: Little, Brown, 1878).

28. See *Lochner v. New York*, 64. For the biography of Peckham, see Irons, *People's History*, 255. On David Brewer, see Mason, *Supreme Court*, 23–27; and Robert A. Burt, *The Constitution in Conflict* (Cambridge, Mass.: Harvard University Press, 1995), 245–253.

29. See, e.g., Gillman, *Constitution Besieged*; Howard Gillman, "Delochnerizing Lochner," *Boston Law Review* 85 (2005): 859–865; and Michael J. Phillips, *The Lochner Court, Myth and Reality* (New York: Praeger, 2001). According to Morton Keller, the Court actually validated 93 percent of such laws between 1887 and 1901 and 76 percent between 1901 and 1910. See his *Affairs of State: Public Life in Nineteenth Century America* (Cambridge, Mass.: Harvard University Press, 1977), 369. Melvyn Urofsky challenged the idea that the judiciary opposed social legislation in "State Courts and Protective Legislation in the Progressive Era: A Reevaluation," *Journal of American History* 72 (June 1985): 63–91. See also note 45 in Chapter 1.

30. My emphasis. *Coppage v. Kansas*, 236 U.S. 1, 17.

31. For my understanding of the history of the at-will rule, I have relied on Katherine van Wezel Stone, "Revisiting the At-Will Employment Doctrine: Imposed Terms, Implied Terms, and the Normative World of the Workplace," *Industrial Law Journal* 36, no. 1 (March 2007): 84–101.

32. John Marshall Harlan, dissenting opinion, *Lochner v. New York*, 69–72. This became standard practice for Supreme Court justices. See for example the majority opinion in *Bunting v. Oregon*, 243 U.S. 426 (1917).

33. In his *History of American Law*, 2nd ed. (New York: Simon & Schuster, 1985), Lawrence M. Friedman noted that the case stood "perilously close to the legal frontier," 563. Yet, the case may have been an expression of what William Novak has called a "well regulated society," in *The People's Welfare: Law and Regulation in 19th Century America* (Chapel Hill: University of North Carolina Press, 1996), which denies that the United States was a stateless society in the nineteenth century and argues not only that regulation was acceptable if it led to social order and the protection of the public's welfare, but also that it was "overwhelming" enough to conclude that "private rights were subject to public objectives" (235–236). *Holden v. Hardy*, 169 U.S. 366, 397.

34. *Chicago Burlington Quincy Railroad Co v. McGuire*, 219 U.S. 549 (1911). A few months later, in *Baltimore & Ohio v. ICC*, 221 U.S. 612 (1911), the Court argued that Congress could regulate the working hours of railroad employees even if the regulation applied to companies that were engaged in intrastate business as well. Again, what mattered primarily to the Court was the rationale behind the regulation—it was well accepted, the judges contended, that in the railroad industry hours of labor were tightly linked to efficiency.

35. *Bunting v. Oregon*.

36. *Miller v. Wilson*, 236 U.S. 373 (1915), 382.

37. The case was *Hawley v. Walker*, 232 U.S. 718 (1914).

38. See James Henretta, "Charles Evans Hughes and the Strange Death of Liberal America," *Law and History Review* 24, no. 1 (Spring 2006): 121. The following biographical sketch of Hughes heavily relies on Henretta's convincing argument.

39. Ibid., 136.

40. *Miller v. Wilson*, 384.

41. See Robert Wiebe's classic *The Search for Order* (New York: Hill and Wang), 1966.

42. On industrial democracy, see Chapter 3 of this book, as well as Joseph A. McCartin, *Labor's Great War* (Chapel Hill: University of North Carolina Press, 1998); and Harris and Lichtenstein, *Industrial Democracy in America*.

43. Two scholars making this argument are Lizabeth Cohen, *Making a New Deal* (New York: Cambridge University Press, 1991); and Lichtenstein, *State of the Union*, 20–53.

44. The idea that the New Deal was not born of the death of orthodox liberalism in America but was rather the product of a "half century of conflict and accommodation between old liberalism and New liberalism," with remnants of the old visible in the American welfare state is expounded on a broader scale in Forbath, "Long Life." In "The Hughes Court and Constitutional Consultation," *Journal of Supreme Court History* 23, no. 1 (1998): 79–111, Barry Cushman makes a similar

argument about the laws that were validated by the Court in the late 1930s—to wit, that they were the product of a dialogue rather than a conflict and rupture. Cushman, however, mostly deals with policy areas in which the Court first struck down legislation and does not address the question of the Wagner Act.

45. Dubofsky, *State and Labor*, 126. Historians have often stressed the discontinuities between the Progressive Era and the New Deal. The difference was stressed very early on in Irving Bernstein's accounts and in accounts of the CIO, such as Robert Zieger's *The CIO, 1935-1955* (Chapel Hill: University of North Carolina Press, 1994), but it figures prominently in Cohen, *Making a New Deal*. More recently, historians have emphasized continuities between the two periods; see especially McCartin, *Labor's Great War*.

46. The history of railroad conflicts is neatly summarized in Dubofsky, *State and Labor*, 8-21. On the Railway Labor Act itself, see Ruth O'Brien, *Workers' Paradox: The Republican Origins of New Deal Labor Policy* (Chapel Hill: University of North Carolina Press, 1998), 63-147; and Dubofsky, *State and Labor*, 8-101.

47. *Texas & New Orleans Railway Co. v. Brotherhood of Railway & Steamship Clerks*, 281 U.S. 548 (1930). See also Irving Bernstein, *The Lean Years: A History of the American Worker, 1920-1933* (Boston: Houghton Mifflin, 1972), 215-220.

48. *Texas & New Orleans v. Brotherhood*, 556-559.

49. *American Steel Foundries v. Tri City Central Trade Council*, 257 U.S. 184 (1921), 209.

50. *Texas & New Orleans v. Brotherhood*, 570. *Coppage v. Kansas*, 32.

51. "Due Process and the Employment Contract," *Harvard Law Review* 44, no. 8 (June 1931): 1287-1291, 1291.

52. Edward Berman, "The Supreme Court Interprets the Railway Labor Act," *American Economic Review* 20 (1930): 638. Indeed, Berman rejected the possibility that the *Texas* decision might be compatible with the *Adair* or *Coppage* decisions and concluded instead that the Court had taken an important step forward in deciding that the social harm involved in restricting the carrier's freedom of contract was more than offset by the social benefit secured by the law.

53. Works published by advocates of planning include Charles Beard, "A Five Year Plan for America," *Forum*, July 1931; Charles Beard, ed., *America Faces the Future* (Boston: Houghton Mifflin, 1932); George Soule, "Hard-Boiled Radicalism," *New Republic* 65 (January 1931): 261-265; and Rexford Tugwell, *Industrial Discipline and the Governmental Arts* (New York: Columbia University Press, 1933). The best account of the talk over planning is in Ellis Hawley, *The New Deal and the Problem of Monopoly* (Princeton: Princeton University Press, 1966); see also Robert Westbrook, "Tribune of the Technostructure: The Popular Economics of Stuart Chase," *American Quarterly* 32, no. 4 (Autumn 1980): 387-408. For a good history of the "postcapitalist" ideal, see Howard Brick, "The Postcapitalist Vision in Twentieth Century American Social Thought," in *American Capitalism: Social Thought and Practice*, ed. Nelson Lichtenstein (Philadelphia: University of Pennsylvania Press, 2006), 30-35.

54. The "urban liberalism" of Robert Wagner is analyzed in Joseph Hutmacher, *Senator Robert F. Wagner and the Rise of Urban Liberalism* (New York: Atheneum, 1968). For a study of the "new unionism" in the textile industry, see Steven Fraser, *Labor Will Rule: Sidney Hillman and the Rise of American Labor* (Ithaca: Cornell University Press, 1991). On the mine workers' efforts to ease the transition of the mining sector from its nineteenth-century organization to a more profitable one, see David Brody, "Market Unionism in America: The Case of Coal," in *In Labor's Cause* (New York: Oxford University Press, 1993), 131-174; and C. K. McFarland, *Roosevelt, Lewis, and the New Deal, 1933-1940* (Fort Worth, Tex.: Texas Christian University Press), 15-19.

55. Labor organizations marched in strides in the mining, textile, and construction industries, while militancy reached levels unseen since 1921. In 1933 alone, the AFL added 500,000 members to its existing ranks. The number of man-days lost to strikes in the second half of 1934 was four times higher than during the first half: 2.4 million as compared to 600,000. The AFL would add another 400,000 members, but its craft organization was ill fitted to the task of organizing indus-

trial workers. As a result, many workers who would have wanted to join unions could not do so in 1933 and 1934. See Dubofsky, *State and Labor,* 107–136.

56. Louis Stark, "Cars and the Men," *Survey Graphic,* April 1935.

57. Dubofsky, *State and Labor,* 77.

58. These figures come from Melvyn Dubofsky, "Not So Turbulent Years: Another Look at the 1930s," *Amerikastudien* 24 (1979): 5–20. Dubofsky offers a subtle perspective, arguing that the strikes were not so overwhelming, given that 93 percent of the workers did not take part in them in 1934 or 1937. Consequently, he argues, one should differentiate between the reality of the class struggle and "[w]orkers fully aware as a class of their role." By contrast, a new left perspective still holds that the 1930s was a time of a missed opportunity; see Staughton Lynd, ed., *We Are All Leaders: The Alternative Unionism of the 1930s* (Urbana: University of Illinois Press, 1996). On the textile strike and Francis Biddle's disenchantment, see Eric Leif Davin, "The Defeat of the Labor Party Idea," in Lynd, *We Are All Leaders,* 125–127.

59. Testimony of Senator Patrick J. Boland, February 20, 1935, in *Legislative History of the National Labor Relations Act,* 2 (Washington, D.C.: GPO, 1949), 2430; Testimony of Francis Haas, March 15, 1934, in *Legislative History of the National Labor Relations Act,* 1: 145.

60. Robert F. Wagner, May 15, 1935, *Congressional Record,* 74th Congress, 1st Session, 7565, quoted in Leon Keyserling, "Why the Wagner Act?" in *The Wagner Act: After Ten Years,* ed. Louis Silverberg (Washington, D.C.: BNA, 1945), 14.

61. As Francis Biddle noted, "The right to work, the freedom of contract, the tradition of the rugged individual with a door open to his future if he could but apply himself, and take what was offered—these phrases lost their reality in a world in which the labor market was choked with a fluid and floating surplus, where industry dictated the contract, and the worker took it, or starved; where the individual to make his ruggedness effective must combine and act thus in combination"; see William Green et al., *Labor's Charter of Rights* (Washington, D.C.: American Federation of Labor, 1935), 49, Leon Keyserling Papers, Georgetown Library, box 1, folder 2.

62. Harry M. Millis, testimony on the bill, reprinted in Green et al., *Labor's Charter of Rights,* 45; Robert Wagner, 78 *Congressional Record,* 3679, reprinted in *Legislative History of the National Labor Relations Act,* 1:20.

63. James Gray Pope, "Labor's Constitution of Freedom," *Yale Law Journal* 106 (1997): 941–1031. Pope shows that the AFL's Andrew Furuseth argued that the protection of the right to organize should be based on the Thirteenth Amendment's prohibition of "involuntary servitude."

64. Wagner, testimony in Congress, reprinted in Green et al., *Labor's Charter of Rights,* 9. Statement of Robert Hale on S. 2926, in *Legislative History of the National Labor Relations Act,* 82. Francis Biddle referred to the *Texas* case in his testimony on S. 2926 and H.R. 6288, see the memorandum he prepared for it, "Policy of Industrial Recovery Records of the National Labor Relations Board," 6, Committee Management Files (CMF), Record Group (RG) 25, National Archives, box 4.

65. Statement of Francis J. Haas, *Legislative History of the National Labor Relations Act,* 116. Francis Biddle thus asked members of Congress to contemplate the notion that "[w]e no longer conceive of labor organizations as conspiracies, for the evil of conspiracy is the end sought, and the end sought—to improve conditions of life—does not now, in our minds, interfere with the inherited scriptural tradition to keep the poor always with us"; see his testimony reprinted in Green et al., *Labor's Charter of Rights,* 49.

66. For statistics on the NLRB, see hearings on S. 2926, *Legislative History of the National Labor Relations Act,* 40–48. Testimony of William Green on S. 2926, 110, quoted in James Pope, "The Thirteenth Amendment versus the Commerce Clause: Labor and the Shaping of American Constitutional Law, 1921–1957," *Columbia Law Review* 102, no. 1 (January 2002): 1–122, 59.

67. "Third draft," Keyserling Papers, file 18, box 1. By 1932, Rexford Tugwell, Leon Keyserling's economics teacher at Columbia University, urged FDR to understand that contrary to what the business sector argued, the crisis did not stem from overconsumption, but rather from "underconsumption," that is, top industrial managers' failure to pass on to workers a sufficient share of the

proceeds of the productivity gains of the 1920s. See David M. Kennedy, *Freedom from Fear* (New York: Oxford University Press, 1999), 122. For the importance of what some economists called "underdemand" to the adoption of the NIRA, see Charles Dearing et al., *The ABC of the NIRA* (Washington, D.C.: Brookings Institution, 1934). See also Kenneth Casebeer, "Holder of the Pen: An Interview with Leon Keyserling on Drafting the Wagner Act," *University of Miami Law Review* 42 (November 1987): 300–301, 313; oral interview of Leon Keyserling, May 3, 1971, 8–9, Truman Library; Keyserling, "Why the Wagner Act?" 7–12.

68. Jacobs, *Pocketbook Politics*.

69. John Lonsdale, "The Period of Adjustment," *American Bankers Association Journal* (October 1930): 267, quoted in Maurice Leven, Harold Moulton, and Clark Warburton, *America's Capacity to Consume* (Washington, D.C.: Brookings Institution, 1934), 116. The reference to the $2,500 threshold is at 119–121.

70. Interestingly, support along the same lines also came from the AFL, which no longer wanted "the earth and fullness thereof." As William Green argued, "If the largest groups of consumers—the wage earners—make more than 66 percent of the purchases in retail markets—if they were in a position to maintain their incomes at a level that would absorb the output of industry, we would have operating a condition essential for balance in distribution and regularity in production. That condition is that workers be given industrial status that makes possible bargaining equal to their employers." See testimony of William Green, *Legislative History of the National Labor Relations Act*, 98. These arguments and figures were probably most important in the effort to discredit the idea that company unions could play the role that New Dealers envisaged. As Wagner noted, in December 1934 wages were only at 60 percent of their 1926 level, whereas dividend and interest payments stood at 150 percent of their level the same year. Total wages had risen by 28 percent since 1932, while the increase in the profits of the 840 largest companies in the United States was 42 percent from 1933 to 1934. See *Congressional Record*, 74th Congress, 1st Session, May 15, 1935, 7568.

71. *NLRB v. Jones and Laughlin Steel Corporation*, 301 U.S. 1 (1937), 33.

72. Ibid., 37.

73. Ibid., 41.

74. There has been serious debate as to the way the *Jones and Laughlin* decision should be interpreted. One school, led by scholars such as Cushman in *Rethinking the New Deal Court* and G. Edward White in *The Constitution and the New Deal* (Cambridge, Mass.: Harvard University Press, 2000), offers an internalist analysis that denies that there was a constitutional revolution in 1937. The other school, best represented by the work of William Leuchtenburg in *The Supreme Court Reborn: The Constitutional Revolution in the Age of Roosevelt* (New York: Oxford University Press, 1995); and Bruce Ackerman, *We the People: Vol. 1, Foundations* (Cambridge, Mass.: Harvard University Press, 1991) emphasizes the social and institutional dynamics that led to the Court's abrupt change of course. One account of this debate is Laura Kalman, "The Constitution, The Supreme Court, and the New Deal," *American Historical Review*, 110, no. 4 (October 2005): 1052–1080. My account here does not take sides in this debate, since my aim is only to understand what institutional dynamics (as well as social ones) informed labor reformers' thinking about the working class and its representation.

75. On this question, see Ellen Dannin, "Not a Limited, Confined Private Matter—Who Is an 'Employee' Under the National Labor Relations Act," *Labor Law Journal* 59 (2008): 5–15.

76. *Phelps Dodge Corp. v. NLRB*, 313 U.S. 177 (1941), 192–93. As Dannin notes, in 1947, the National Labor Relations Board cited the decision, explaining that the definition of employee "is broad enough to include members of the working class generally" and that to limit protection "only to employees of a particular employer, would permit employers to discriminate with impunity against other members of the working class, and would serve as a powerful deterrent against free recourse to Board processes." Dannin, "Not a Limited, Confined Private Matter," 8.

77. See Cohen, *Making a New Deal*.

78. This paragraph relies on Sean Farhang and Ira Kaltznelson, "The Southern Imposition:

Congress and Labor in the New Deal and Fair Deal," *Studies in American Political Development* 19 (Spring 2005): 12–14. There is very little archival material to trace the political history of this change. Notably the Wagner Archives are quite poor in this regard, although they contain a letter sent by Harvard students to ask Wagner to reconsider this amendment. The Keyserling papers do contain an undated document,—but it is filed along with other documents from 1934, which suggests that Frances Perkins wanted this amendment to be removed from the law and that Wagner thought that "without this amendment the law could not pass." See the document titled "Miss Perkins," undated, 1, Keyserling Papers, box 1, folder 9.

79. On the rise of the Southern Tenant Farm Union in eastern Arkansas in the early 1930s, see Michael Honey, *Southern Labor and Black Civil Rights* (Urbana: University of Illinois Press, 1993), 70.

80. Arnold T. Hill to Robert F. Wagner, April 2, 1934, Robert F. Wagner Archives, Georgetown University Archives, box 2, folder 7; Harvard Sitkoff, *A New Deal for Blacks* (New York: Oxford University Press, 2008), 127–128.

81. On the history of this clause, which finally led to the infamous *McKay* Supreme Court case, see Thomas C. Kohler and Julius G. Getman, "The Story of NLRB v. Mackay Radio & Telegraph Co.: The High Cost of Solidarity," in *Labor Law Stories*, ed. Laura J. Cooper and Catherine L. Fisk (New York: Foundation Press, 2005), 13–54.

82. Kelly Miller, "Amend the Wagner Labor Bill," undated, Wagner Archives, box 2, folder 8. The NAACP concurred, see Walter White (NAACP secretary) to Hugh S. Johnson, April 26, 1934, in Wagner Archives, box 2, folder 8. The majority rule provision remained a concern into 1935, as Congress debated the Wagner Act in its final forms; Arnold Hill to Robert Wagner, April 18, 1935, Wagner Archives, box 4, folder 38.

83. On this question, see Robert Zieger, *Jobs and Freedom: Race and Labor Since 1865* (Lexington: University Press of Kentucky, 2007).

84. Arnold T. Hill to Robert F. Wagner, April 16, 1934, "A Statement of Opinion on Senate Bill S. 2926," 3, Wagner Archives, box 2, folder 8. Dr. D. Witherspoon Dodge (chairman of the Board of Directors of the Atlanta Urban League) to Robert F. Wagner, April 20, 1934, Wagner Archives, box 2, folder 8; Maurice Moss (executive secretary of the Pittsburgh Urban League) to Robert F. Wagner, April 18, 1934, Wagner Archives, box 2, folder 8; Lloyd Garrison (treasurer of the NUL) to Robert F. Wagner, April 7, 1934, Wagner Archives, box 2, folder 8. For a general perspective on the NUL and the NNC at the time, see Thomas Sugrue, *Sweet Land of Liberty: The Forgotten Struggle for Civil Rights in the North* (New York: Random House, 2008), 33–58.

85. This may be a surprising position, but it makes sense if one remembers that the right of companies to *hire* replacement workers was not in doubt. On John Fitch's role in this debate, see Kohler and Getman, "Story of NLRB," 23.

86. *NLRB v. Hearst Pub. Inc.*, 322 U.S. 111 (1944).

87. Ibid., 111.

Chapter 3. The Sociology of Harmony

1. John R. Commons, *Myself* (Madison: University of Wisconsin Press, 1934), 28.

2. John R. Commons, *Institutional Economics: Its Place in Political Economy*, vol. 1 (1934; repr., New Brunswick, N.J.: Transaction, 1990), 1–2. George, *Progress and Poverty*; see 221–225 for his analysis of unions, where he compared unions to Hindu creditors staging a hunger strike at the door of their debtor to obtain payment—a comparison favorable to the Hindu creditor, since he enjoyed the benefit of "superstition." More generally, see Commons, *Myself*.

3. See Thorstein Veblen, "The Limitations of Marginal Utility," in *The Place of Science in Modern Civilization and Other Essays* (1919; repr., New Brunswick, N.J.: Transaction, 1990) 231–251); Emile Durkheim, *De la division du travail social* (1893; repr., Paris: PUF, 2007); Max Weber, *The Protestant Ethic and the Spirit of Capitalism* (1905; repr., London: Penguin, 2002). My reading of

the rise of economic sociology is based on Jean-Jacques Gislain and Philippe Steiner, *La sociologie économique, 1890–1920* (Paris: PUF, 1995); Jean-Jacques Gislain, "L'émergence de la problématique des institutions en économie," *Cahiers d'économie politique* 44 (2003): 19–47; Heino Heinrich Nau and Philip Steiner, "Schmoller, Durkheim, and Old European Institutionalist Economics," *Journal of Economic Issues* 36, no. 4 (December 2002): 105–124.

4. "This pressure reaches the individual through the educational media of language and social institutions. . . . Institutions rest upon ideas and beliefs, and these are epitomized in language. Language in turn, by giving names to things and relations, and by thus transmitting to each individual the accumulated race experience, gradually brings him to the consciousness of himself. This is education." John R. Commons, "Natural Selection, Social Selection," in *Selected Essays*, vol. 1, ed. Malcolm Rutherford and Warren J. Samuels (New York: Routledge, 1996), 44.

5. However, unlike Durkheim's, Commons's work was cast in the mold of evolution, and, second, he conceived of his study of political economy as a religious endeavor. In his early years he saw the social gospel as the main source of mental habits through which a "standard of living" could be secured for the masses who were forced in a position of economic subordination.

6. William D. P. Bliss, ed., *The Encyclopedia of Social Reform* (New York: Funk and Wagnalls, 1897), quoted in Howell Harris, "Industrial Democracy and Liberal Capitalism," in Harris and Lichtenstein, *Industrial Democracy in America*, 45.

7. David Montgomery, "Industrial Democracy or Democracy in Industry?," in Harris and Lichtenstein, *Industrial Democracy in America*, 2–43; Milton Derber, *The American Idea of Industrial Democracy* (Urbana: University of Illinois Press, 1970); and Harris, "Industrial Democracy and Liberal Capitalism."

8. Frank Walsh, quoted in McCartin, *Labor's Great War*, 8.

9. John R. Commons, *Labor and Administration* (New York: Macmillan, 1913), quoted in Ronald Schatz, "From Commons to Dunlop: Rethinking the Field of Industrial Relations," in Harris and Lichtenstein, *Industrial Democracy in America*, 100.

10. John R. Commons, "A Sociological View of Sovereignty" (1899), in Commons, *Selected Essays*, 70–145.

11. "Monopoly, once attained, is prone to exalt its material basis above its persuasive principles, and the interests of its hierarchy above the interests of the community." Ibid., 118.

12. John R. Commons, "A New Way of Settling Labor Disputes" (1901), in Commons, *Selected Essays*, 162–171, 171, my emphasis.

13. Mark Bevir, "Sidney Webb: Utilitarianism, Positivism, and Social Democracy," *Journal of Modern History* 74, no. 2 (June 2002): 217–252. See also the Webb's classic work, *Industrial Democracy* (London: Longman, 1893).

14. John R. Commons, "American Shoemakers" (1909), in Commons, *Selected Essays*, 209–236.

15. Ibid., 212.

16. Jett Lauck, *Political and Industrial Democracy, 1776–1928* (New York: Knopf, 1926), 7–8.

17. John R. Commons, *The Legal Foundations of Capitalism* (New York: Macmillan, 1924), 144–145, and *Institutional Economics*, 55–77.

18. Commons, *Institutional Economics*, 1.

19. Commons's disdain for recent immigrants is briefly analyzed by Maurice Isserman in "God Bless Our American Institutions," *Labor History* 17, no. 3 (1976): 316–317. On this question, see his *Immigrants and Races in America* (New York: Macmillan, 1920), chap. 6. By contrast, he did not believe that African Americans could assimilate; see his "The Negro," *Chautauquan* 38 (November 1903): 223–238, quoted by Malcolm Rutherford and Warren J. Samuels in their introduction to John R. Commons, *Selected Essays*, 6.

20. Commons, "New Way of Settling Labor Disputes," and *Myself*, 72. For a long account of the proceedings of the Joint Conference, see Arthur Suffren, *The Coal Miner's Struggle for Industrial Status* (New York: Macmillan, 1926), 11–72.

21. Lauck, *Political and Industrial Democracy*.

22. Louis Brandeis, "Testimony Before the US Commission on Industrial Relations, January 23, 1915, Senate Documents, 64th Congress, 1st Session, 1915–1916," in *Commission on Industrial Relations Report and Testimony* (Washington, D.C.: GPO, 1916), 8:7658–7676.

23. *Duplex Printing Co. v. Deering*, 254 U.S. 443 (1921), 488.

24. See the wonderful article by Pope, "Thirteenth Amendment versus the Commerce Clause."

25. Commons, *Institutional Economics*, 70–71.

26. William Leiserson, *Right and Wrong in Labor Relations* (Berkeley: University of California Press, 1938), 11.

27. See Emile Durkheim, "Représentations individuelles et representations collectives," *Revue de Métaphysique et de Morale* 6 (May 1898): 273–302.

28. William Leiserson to John Fitch, January 26, 1936, William Leiserson Papers, Wisconsin Historical Society, box 14, "Fitch" file.

29. J. Woolf, "Robert Wagner Sees a New Industrial Day," *New York Times*, November 12, 1933, 6, quoted in Mark Barenberg, "The Political Economy of the Wagner Act," *Harvard Law Review* 106, no. 7 (1993): 1379–1496, 1427. As the two following paragraphs suggest, I am largely indebted to Barenberg's meticulous research.

30. Indeed, even when, later that year, events on the shop floor suggested that industrial harmony would be harder to attain than Wagner and his aides had anticipated, the senator reaffirmed his belief that all industrial disputes could be amicably settled in the interest of both sides and according to the logic of industrial democracy as defined by institutional economics: "Out of confusion which must necessarily accompany the beginning of any new scheme of so vast a scope, have risen cross currents of distrust and antagonism between labor and industry that have no substantial basis in fact . . . all the recent conflicts can be amicably settled when the parties have been brought together to discuss their differences in an atmosphere of calmness and disinterestedness and with a clearer knowledge of their respective rights and duties. Cooperation based on mutual trust and understanding must be the keynote henceforward." Letter of Senator Wagner to the honorable Marion Smith, October 22, 1933, RG 25, National Archives, quoted in James Gross, *The Making of the National Labor Relations Board: A Study in Economics, Politics and the Law* (Albany: State University of New York Press, 1974), 33. Tellingly, Wagner proceeded to accept a presidential appointment to the National Labor Board, which was to provide mediation services to end the disputes that hampered the recovery effort. Wagner of course knew that the disputes stemmed from a widespread resistance to the idea of unionization, but he remained adamant, stating that "the chief hope that I had when accepting the President's appointment . . . was that its influence might work a change in our people's ideas about industrial disputes. See *New York Times*, November 20, 1933, 3.

31. Wagner, 79 *Congressional Record*, 4918, quoted in Barenberg, "Political Economy of the Wagner Act," 1483.

32. For Wagner on social disintegration, see 79 *Congressional Record*, 9417, "Cooperation was the only safeguard against disintegration," quoted in Barenberg, "Political Economy of the Wagner Act," 1427.

33. The reference to "hearts and minds" is noted in Barenberg, "Political Economy of the Wagner Act," 1475. This cartoon is reproduced in Alan Dawley, *Struggles for Justice* (Cambridge, Mass.: Harvard University Press, 1991), 387.

34. On this important development, see McCartin, *Labor's Great War*, 173–220.

35. "The Rights of the Man on the Job: Paul Litchfield's 29th Radio Talk to Goodyear Workers," Wagner Archives, LA 715, box 2, folder 7.

36. See Dubofsky, *State and Labor*, 107–136.

37. National Industrial Conference Board, *Individual and Collective Bargaining Under the NIRA: A Statistical Study of Present Practice* (New York: NICB, 1933), 17.

38. Gross, *Making of the National Labor Relations Board*, 24.

39. "An Attempt to Create Labor Union Dictatorship of American Industry," leaflet distributed to U.S. Steel workers, Wagner Archives, LA 715, box 2, folder 8.

40. The literature on company unionism is not extensive, mostly because there has been a tendency to dismiss them as corporate shams. However, see David Brody, *Workers in Industrial America: Essay on the Twentieth Century Struggle* (New York: Oxford University Press, 1993); David Farris, "From Exit to Voice in Shop-Floor Governance: The Case of Company Unions," *Business History Review* 69, no. 4 (Winter 1995): 494–529; Daniel Nelson, "The Company Union Movement, 1900–1937: A Reexamination," *Business History Review* 56, no. 3 (Autumn 1982): 335–527.

41. Robert Wagner, "Company Unions: A Vast Industrial Issue," *New York Times*, March 11, 1934, 21.

42. Percy S. Brown, "The Work and Aim of the Taylor Society," *Annals of the American Academy of Political and Social Science* 119 (May 1925): 134–139; Carlos E. Pabon, "The Taylor Society and Political Economy in the Interwar Period" (Ph.D. diss., University of Wisconsin, 1992).

43. Morris L. Cooke, "Who Is Boss in Your Shop?," *Annals of the American Academy of Political and Social Science* 71 (May 1917): 167–185.

44. The idea of "new unionism" and the contribution of Hillman of Hillman to the New Deal are analyzed by Fraser in *Labor Will Rule*, 259–348.

45. Robert Wagner, "Talk on Labor Relations," February 29, 1936, Wagner Archives, box 103, folder 36.

46. Mary Van Kleeck to Robert F. Wagner, March 12, 1934, 1, Wagner Archives, box 41, folder 7.

47. Ibid., 2.

48. Roger Baldwin to Robert F. Wagner, April 1, 1935, 1, 2, Wagner Archives, box 41, folder 7.

49. Robert F. Wagner to Mary Van Kleeck, May 10, 1934, Wagner Archives, box 41, folder 7. On Christopher Tomlins and the critical legal scholars who wrote against the New Deal labor relations regime in the 1980s, see my forthcoming "What Can the Critical Synthesis Teach Us Now That the Unions Have (Almost) Gone?," *Labor History*.

50. Green et al., *Labor's Charter of Rights*, 48.

51. Karl Marx, *Capital: A Critique of Political Economy* (New York: Cosimo, 2007), 451–458. The unpublished chapter 6, "The Results of the Direct Production Process," was abandoned in the course of preparation of volume 1 of *Capital*. It included a section on "Productive and Unproductive Work," which can be accessed at http://www.marxists.org/.

52. Marx, *Capital*, 451–458.

53. Commons, *Legal Foundations of Capitalism*, 155–156.

54. John R. Commons, "The Right to Work" (1899), in Commons, *Selected Essays*, 66.

55. *Allgeyer v. Louisiana*, 165 U.S. 578 (1897). On the importance of this case, see Peter H. Irons, *People's History*, 248–249.

56. Commons, *Institutional Economics*, 59–67.

57. Ibid., 64–67.

58. Ibid., 67–69. On Commons's views on Hoover's policy during the Great War, see Isserman, "God Bless Our American Institutions," 318.

59. Commons, *Institutional Economics*, 64–67.

60. Chris Nyland, "Taylorism, John R. Commons, and the Hoxie Report," *Journal of Economic Issues* 30, no. 4 (December 1996): 985–1016, on which the second half of this paragraph relies.

61. Commons, *Legal Foundations of Capitalism*, 146–147.

62. Ibid., 314–315.

63. Similarly, in France, the sociologist Maurice Halbawchs argued that the working class was characterized by the fact that it worked in relation with inanimate matter, not men. See Pierre Lantz, "Travail, Concept ou notion multifonctionnelle" (1992), quoted in Robert Castel, *Les metamorphoses de la question sociale* (Paris: Seuil, 1994), 574–576.

64. Commons, *Legal Foundations of Capitalism*, 149.

65. William Leiserson to Senator Thomas, May 9, 1939, 9, Leiserson Papers, box 28, "NLRB, 1935–41" file.

66. Quoted in Schatz, "From Commons to Dunlop," 103.

Chapter 4. Is a Foreman a Worker?

1. Ira B. Cross, "When Foremen Joined the CIO," *Personnel Journal* no. 18 (February 1940): 274–278.

2. "Excerpts from Official Report of Proceedings Before the National Labor Relations Board," Testimony of Thomas Dwyer, 430–434, *Packard v. NLRB* file, Records of the Supreme Court of the United States, RG 267, National Archives, box 4819. I have chosen to analyze the movement through the lens of the 1947 *Packard v. NLRB* Supreme Court case (330 U.S. 485) because it generated a large amount of archival documents.

3. *Matter of Packard Motor Company*, 61 NLRB 4 (decided March 1945) and 64 NLRB 204 (decided December 1945). In the first case the board agreed that foremen were "employees" within the meaning of the act, and in the second it dealt with the company's refusal to bargain with the FAA. The Supreme Court decision in *Packard* came one year later, in January 1947.

4. Cross, "When Foremen Joined the CIO," 279. Sumner Slichter did not believe that foremen should be allowed to organize; see his "The Taft-Hartley Act," *Quarterly Journal of Economics* 63, no. 1 (February 1949): 1–31; along with Don Lescohier, "The Foreman and the Union," *Personnel Journal* 15, no. 1 (August 1938): 18–25; and William Leiserson's article in *Foremen's Magazine*, "Decreased Costs and Increased Production," May 1927, 6–7.

5. Robert Scigliano, "Trade-Unionism and the Industrial Foreman," *Journal of Business* 27, no. 4 (October 1954): 293.

6. Nelson, *Managers and Workers*; Stephen Meyer, *The Five Dollar Day* (Albany: State University of New York Press, 1981); Howell Harris, *The Right to Manage* (Madison: University of Wisconsin Press, 1981).

7. Frederick Taylor, *Shop Management* (New York: Harper, 1911), 95; Sanford Jacoby, *Employing Bureaucracy: Managers, Unions, and the Transformation of Work in the Twentieth Century*, 2nd ed. (Mahwah, NJ: Lawrence Erlbaum, 2004), 30–36; Nelson, *Managers and Workers*, 34–54; Alfred Chandler, *Scale and Scope: The Dynamics of Industrial Capitalism* (Cambridge, Mass.: Harvard University Press, 1990).

8. "Excerpts from Official Report of Proceedings Before the National Labor Relations Board," testimony of James Wilkins, *Packard v. NLRB* file, 976–1032.

9. Jacoby, *Employing Bureaucracy*, 10–16. On contractors, see Montgomery, *Fall of the House of Labor*, 9–57. On Americanization efforts at Packard, see Thomas Klug, "Employer Strategies in Detroit," in *On the Line: Essays in the History of Auto Work*, ed. Nelson Lichtenstein and Stephen Meyer (Urbana: University of Illinois Press, 1989), 56–57. In other companies, however, foremen were dutiful soldiers of the struggle for Americanization, a fact that reflected the ethnic fault line separating them from the rank and file. Bethlehem Steel managers regularly conflated loyalty to the company and loyalty to the country and foremen were at the forefront of Americanization campaigns in the area of Bethlehem. Meanwhile, the company regularly organized "foremen's meetings," during which the "Americanism" of foremen was emphasized, along with their important role in securing the cooperation of "foreign-born workers." Thus, in a show of managerial unity, in May 1918 the foremen of the company signed a pledge of allegiance to America along with the superintendents, general managers, and officials of the company. See the company-dominated journal *Bethlehem Steel* 1, nos. 1–2 (May 15, 1918): 13–14, Bethlehem Area Public Library, online.

10. Montgomery, *Fall of the House of Labor*, 224–226; Nelson, *Managers and Workers*, 152–153; Chandler, *Visible Hand*; Kenneth Kolker, "The Changing Status of the Foreman," *Bulletin of the Business Historical Society* 22, no. 3 (June 1948): 84–105.

11. At Packard, there was no difference between a straw boss and an assistant foreman.

12. This paragraph is based on the testimonies of the foremen who were part of the Packard case.

13. Weirton Steel is a good example. On Ernest Weir's reliance on foremen to fight the Amal-

gamated Association of Iron and Steel Workers (AAISW) in 1934, see Gross, *Making of the National Labor Relations Board*, 172. On the persistence of traditional foremanship see also Metzgar's moving account, *Striking Steel*, 33–34.

14. Paul H. Douglas, "Plant Administration of Labor," *Journal of Political Economy* 27 (July 1919).

15. On the idea that Fordism rested on the agreement of workers, see Michael Burawoy, *Manufacturing Consent* (Chicago: University of Chicago Press, 1977); Pilon and Vatin, "Retour sur la question salariale," 93–116; McCartin, *Labor's Great War*, 75–80.

16. "Brief of Packard Motor Company," *Packard v. NLRB* file, 4. Nelson Lichtenstein, "The Man in the Middle: A Social History of Automobile Foremen," in Lichtenstein and Meyer, *On the Line*, 156. This transformation of foremanship is visible in many of the articles published in the National Association of Foremen's journal, *Foremen's Magazine*. See, e.g., "Why Is Organization Necessary in the Shop?" February 1927, 10–12.

17. See the following articles in *Foremen's Magazine*: "What Makes an Efficient Executive," June 1927; "How to Attain Leadership Over Men," June 1927; "Encouraging Thought in the Shop," June 1927, "Management and the Laws of Human Relations," October 1928; Kolker, "Changing Status of the Foreman"; Stephen P. Waring, *Taylorism Transformed: Scientific Management Theory Since 1945* (Chapel Hill: University of North Carolina Press, 1991). Notably, during the war, training was expanding to include classes on EO 8802 and the employment of women.

18. On this constitutional debate, see Leuchtenburg, *Supreme Court Reborn*.

19. "The purposes of the National Association (of Foremen) are as follows: to help in the promotion of better foremanship, by studying the needs and opportunities of industry in order to make each individual foreman a power for good in his own organization and community. To accomplish this the Association will promote: City wide foremen's clubs, Factory foremen's clubs, Educational work for workmen aspiring to be foremen, better industrial relations, stabilized employment and profit in industry. The membership includes operative foremen, job foremen, superintendents, department heads, personnel directors, educators, and all those connected with shop management." "What Is the National Association of Foremen? The Aims and Purposes of the National Association and Its Relation to Industry," *Foremen's Magazine*, August 1928, 9, 38. See also the letter from Frank H. Ireland, president of the NAF, to the members of the National Labor Relations Board, February 23, 1944, in the "Supervisory Employees" file, CMF, RG 25, National Archives, box 2; Kolker, "Changing Status of the Foreman," 101.

20. See, e.g., the following articles published in *Foremen's Magazine*: "Every Foreman a Business Manager," December 1927; "This Way Up the Ladder of Success," April 1927; John D. Rockefeller, "Character—the Foundation of Successful Business," March 1928; "Ambition—The Key to Promotion," May 1929; "The Foreman as Executive," July 1928; "The Man at the Helm," July 1928; "Can the Foreman Be a Manager?" February 1929.

21. W. J. Donkel, "The Foreman's Job Is to Make a Profit: Some Fundamental Principles That Will Assist the Foreman to Cut Costs," *Foremen's Magazine*, December 1927, 4–5, 29.

22. "Foremen Will Act in Labor Relations: New Group Call Conference Here Saturday to Pave the Way for Harmony," *New York Times*, September 28, 1938; see also Lescohier, "Foreman and the Union"; E. C. Grace, president of Bethlehem Steel Corporation, "Foremanship in Industry: A Statement by President Grace on the Foreman's Place in Employee-Management Relations," *Foremen's Magazine*, February 1928, 10.

23. James A. Smith, "Can Any Foreman Safely Rest on His Laurels?," *Foremen's Magazine*, June 1929, 13, 24. The same was the case at Ford. See Zunz, *Making America Corporate*, 136. Zunz stresses the middle-class nature of foremanship. Lichtenstein provides a different perspective in his "Man in the Middle," 158. Contrary to Zunz, Lichtenstein argues that foremen were "on the wrong side of the collar line."

24. Lichtenstein deals with these issues at greater length than I do in his "Man in the Middle." Notably, he shows that in the Detroit area, the importance of Masonry in foremen circles testified to these cultural differences; see 159.

25. "Brief for Packard Motor Company," *Packard v. NLRB* file, 15.

26. Carl Dean Snyder, *White-Collar Workers and the UAW* (Urbana: University of Illinois Press, 1973), 39–43.

27. Fritz J. Roethlisberger, "The Foreman: Master and Victim of Double Talk," *Harvard Business Review* 23 (1945): 292.

28. On the Hawthorne experiments, see Richard Gillespsie, *Manufacturing Knowledge: A History of the Hawthorne Experiments* (New York: Cambridge University Press, 1993).

29. Robert H. Keys, the president of the Foreman's Association of America, often expressed the foremen's feeling that they were not part of management: "We foremen are told in meetings and in writing that we are part of management, but there isn't one foreman in a thousand who ever knows the true costs of operating his department, for that information is withheld from him. If he tries to get the facts he gets the run around. . . . We are told that we should have knowledge of how other departments work, but when we try to learn how we are looked upon by top management." Robert H. Keys, radio broadcast, March 23, 1943, *Packard v. NLRB* file, 1698. These broadcasts were entered into the materials of the Supreme Court case as the company's exhibit no. 49-A. Oral history with Carl Brown (1974), Joe Brown Collection, UAW Archives, College of Urban, Labor and Metropolitan Affairs, Wayne State University (hereafter UAW-CULMA), 8.

30. Lichtenstein, "Man in the Middle," 162.

31. James A. Ward, *The Fall of Packard Company* (Stanford: Stanford University Press, 1995), chap. 1; "Brief for Packard Motor Company," *Packard v. NLRB* file, 1–2.

32. "New Allies in Guise of Foremen Keep Rallying to CIO Banner," *Kelsey Hayes Picket*, June 6, 1939, with notes by "JB " (most probably John Brophy) providing some explanations on the February 1938 attempt, UAW-CULMA, box 10, "Foremen and Supervisors" folder; application of United Foremen and Supervisors for a LIU Charter (application 1205), November 21, 1938, 6 pages, collection 1, CIO Archives, Catholic University of America (hereafter CUA), folder 33, box 64. Key CIO members opposing the UFS included John Brophy, the director of the National CIO Organization Department. I deal with the complex relationships between the CIO and foremen's unions in Chapter 6. Ira B. Cross, "Foremen's Union Finale," *Personnel Journal* (March 1940): 346, and "When Foremen Joined the CIO," 277. The pay cut amounted to 10 to 15 percent. On Kelsey Hayes, see Nelson Lichtenstein, *Walter Reuther: The Most Dangerous Man in Detroit* (Urbana: University of Illinois Press, 1995), 63.

33. Letter from J. R. Bell to George Stephanson granting affiliation, August 7, 1939, collection 1, CIO Archives, CUA, folder 13, box 65; "Organized Foremen Expand," *United Automobile Worker*, April 29, 1939; Cross, "When Foremen Joined the CIO," 280. I deal with this controversy at greater length in the next chapter.

34. "Excerpts from Official Report of Proceedings Before the National Labor Relations Board," Testimony of Thomas Dwyer, 437–443, Testimony of James Beyerley, 463–473, *Packard v. NLRB* file. These testimonies were recorded during the Trial Examiner's investigation. It has not been possible to determine precisely the number of Packard Foremen who joined the UFS, but it is unlikely that more than fifteen did.

35. "Agenda: Point no. 3–Report of President Thomas," UAW Executive Board Meeting Collection, UAW-CULMA, folder 12/4/39, box 2.

36. Andrew Levison, "Wartime Unionization of Foremen" (PhD diss., University of Wisconsin, 1955); Ernest Dale, "The Unionization of Foremen," AMA Research Report6, 1945, available at the Department of Labor Library (hereafter DOL), 4–34; Oral history interview with Carl Brown, former official of the FAA, November 13, 1974 (the interview was conducted by Howell Harris), UAW-CUMLA, 1–6.

37. "Excerpts from Official Report of Proceedings Before the National Labor Relations Board," Testimony of Robert H. Keys, *Packard v. NLRB* file, 72–73; Dale, "Unionization of Foremen," 8–14.

38. "Excerpts from Official Report of Proceedings Before the National Labor Relations Board," Testimony of Robert H. Keys, *Packard v. NLRB* file, 128.

39. On the technical problems attending the move to war production, see Lichtenstein, *Walter Reuther*, 161, on which this paragraph relies heavily.

40. I deal with the NLRB's work on the foremen's issue in the next chapter.

41. *Union Collieries*, 41 NLRB 174 (1942); *Maryland Drydock*, 49 NLRB 105 (1943); Charles Larrowe, "A Meteor of the Industrial Relations Horizon: Foreman's Association of America," *Labor History* 2 (1961), 259–294.

42. Levison, "Wartime Unionization of Foremen," 192–193.

43. *The Supervisor*, January 1945, 14; September 1944, 18; May 1944, 9; October 1944, 12; quoted in Levison, "Wartime Unionization of Foremen," 131.

44. Levison, "Wartime Unionization of Foremen," 178. On the debilitating effects of the no strike pledge and of bargains with the state in general, see Nelson Lichtenstein, *Labor's War at Home: The CIO in World War Two* (Philadelphia: Temple University Press, 1982); Tomlins, *State and the Unions*; and Gerald Friedman, *Reigniting the Labor Movement* (New York: Routledge, 2007).

45. "Foremen Force Shopfloor Issue," *New York Times*, May 21, 1944; Dale, "Unionization of Foremen," 13.

46. "When Foremen Organize, Here's What They Demand," *Factory Management and Maintenance* 105, no. 4 (April 1947): 64.

47. Quoted in Nelson Lichtenstein, "Great Expectations: The Promise of Industrial Jurisprudence and Its Demise," in Harris and Lichtenstein, *Industrial Democracy in America*, 113–141.

48. Quoted in Harris, *Right to Manage*, 64. Carl Brown, a foreman with Ford, painted a similar picture: "I would say it made it more difficult to maintain production schedules because prior to the recognition of the UAW, as a bargaining agent for employees, the employee was at the mercy of management." Oral history interview with Carl Brown (1974), UAW-CUMLA, 8.

49. "Excerpts from Official Report of Proceedings Before the National Labor Relations Board," Testimony of Robert Turnbull, 527, 629; Testimony of Prosper Traen, 300–301; Levison, "Wartime Unionization of Foremen," 110.

50. "Excerpts from Official Report of Proceedings Before the National Labor Relations Board," Testimony of Robert Turnbull, 617; Testimony of Prosper Traen, 319–321. "The Voice of Organized Foremen," Robert H. Key's radio address, March 16, 1944.

51. "Excerpts from Official Report of Proceedings Before the National Labor Relations Board," Testimony of Prosper Traen, 300–321. Oral history interview with Carl Brown (1974), UAW-CUMLA, 7–8.

52. "Excerpts from Official Report of Proceedings Before the National Labor Relations Board," Testimony of Prosper Traen, 291; Testimony of R. Turnbull, 544; *Report and Findings of the National War Labor Board in Certain Disputes Involving Supervisors* (Washington, D.C.: GPO, January 19, 1945), 129 (this report is available at the DOL).

53. By this I mean the lack of an objective status giving specific benefits or rights at work. I have generally refrained from using the word "status" because of its obvious historiographical connotations. See Richard Hofstadter's interpretation of Progressivism in *The Age of Reform* (New York: Knopf, 1955).

54. Letter of E. Gordon to the House Military Affairs Committee on Manpower Problems, *House Hearings Before the Committee on Military Affairs on H.R. 2239, 1742, 1728, 992*, 1st Session, April 6, 1943, 511.

55. See "Brief of Packard Motor Company," 19–20.

56. As Jennifer Klein and other historians have shown, during the 1930s an *ideology of security* took hold in American society, bringing economists, policy experts, and grassroots movements in support of policies designed to protect people from economic insecurity—the Wagner Act and the Social Security Act were pillars of this new "economic citizenship." Klein, *For All These Rights*.

57. Robert H. Keys, radio broadcast, December 16, 1943, *Packard v. NLRB* file, 1619.

58. See Klein, *For All These Rights*, 98.

59. Testimony of James Beyerley, *House Hearings Before the Committee on Military Affairs on*

H.R. 2239, 1742, 1728, 992, 1st Session, 1943, 463; Testimony of Thomas Dwyer, *House Hearings Before the Committee on Military Affairs on H.R. 2239, 1742, 1728, 992,* 1st Session, 1943, 457–458. See also the letters sent to the House Military Affairs Committee by F. A. Maas, 514–515. The record of the hearings is available at the DOL.

60. Testimony of Robert F. Turnbull, *House Hearings Before the Committee on Military Affairs on H.R. 2239, 1742, 1728, 992,* 1st session, 1943, 510.

61. This point used to be one of the most contentious debates in labor history. My paragraph reflects both labor historians' growing appreciation of the state and unions as institutions and my focus on the differences between foremen and rank-and-file workers.

62. See Zieger, *The CIO,* 168–171; Lichtenstein, *Labor's War at Home,* 75–76.

63. Levison, "Wartime Unionization of Foremen," 419.

64. *Report and Findings of the National War Labor Board,* 129. In fourteen cases the earnings of top hourly rated men exceeded those of their supervisors.

65. Ibid., 131.

66. On this question, see the excellent summary of Kennedy in *Freedom from Fear,* 746–797.

67. Letter of E. Gordon, *House Hearings Before the Committee on Military Affairs on H.R. 2239, 1742, 1728, 992,* April 6, 1943, reprinted at 512.

68. Packard Brief, *Packard v. NLRB* file, 18. Lichtenstein, *Labor's War at Home,* 117.

69. C. Wright Mills, *White Collar* (New York: Oxford University Press, 1951), 324–354. On C. Wright Mills's *White Collar,* see Nelson Lichtenstein, "Class, Collars, and the Continuing Relevance of C. Wright Mills," *Labor* 1, no. 3 (2004): 109–123; Michael Burawoy, "White Collar Revisited," *Qualitative Sociology* 30 (2007): 501–504.

70. On this question see Castel, *Les metamorphoses;* and Jean-Charles Asselain, *La France en mouvement* (Paris: Jean Bouvier, 1986).

71. Their efforts led to the creation of a new social category called *les cadres,* whose members then created unions. See Luc Boltanski, *Les cadres: Formation d'un groupe social* (Paris: Minuit, 1983). I deal at greater length with this question in the following chapter.

72. "Excerpts from Official Report of Proceedings Before the National Labor Relations Board," Testimony of Robert H. Keys, *Packard v. NLRB* file, 134–143; "History of the Movement to Organize Foremen of the Automotive Industry, General Motors Pamphlet," DOL, 3.

73. Robert H. Keys, radio broadcast, April 14, 1944, 1575; see also the letters of Bradley and Wilkins to the House Committee on Military Affairs, 512.

74. Thus E. Gordon explained that he had joined the FAA "to protect the interest of all supervision, just as labor is protected by the CIO." *House Hearings Before the Committee on Military Affairs on H.R. 2239, 1742, 1728, 992,* 1st Session, 1943, 512.

75. Theodore Bonaventura—secretary of the FAA—statement, quoted in Levison, "Wartime Unionization of Foremen," 103. Bonaventura explained that the competition between foremen was often increased by superintendents in the hope of speeding up production. Testimony of Robert F. Turnbull, *1943 House Hearings Before the Committee on Military Affairs on H.R. 2239, 1742, 1728, 992,* 507; Dale, "Unionization of Foremen," 9.

76. "Excerpts from Official Report of Proceedings Before the National Labor Relations Board," Testimony of Prosper Traen, *Packard v. NLRB* file, 383–391, 386.

77. On the American Association of Engineers, see M. P. McGirr et al., *Technologists' Stake in the Wagner Act* (Chicago: American Association of Engineers, 1944). The AAE was trying to find a middle-of-the-road approach to unionism. It had not failed to notice that the National Labor Relations Board had taken a more expansive approach to the concept of "employee" than the Department of Labor in its administration of the Fair Labor Standards Act (professional workers were excluded from the purview of the FLSA), and their main concern was to protect their professional identity. Accordingly, theirs was a cultural struggle to convince the swelling ranks of white-collar workers that professional values and collective bargaining were not incompatible. Robert H. Keys, radio broadcast, March 9, 1944, 1688. "Brief for MOU," Union Collieries Case No R-3464, informal

case files RG 25, National Archives—I deal with the miners' claim to be "employees" at greater length in the next chapter.

78. Robert Keys, radio broadcast, March 24, 1943, 1524; radio broadcast, March 31, 1943, 1564; radio broadcast, December 16, 1943: "We demand the right to bargain collectively in accordance with the procedure laid down in the Wagner Act, and we have no intention of taking a breathing spell until we get it. In making such a demand we are only asking for our constitutional rights. The rank and file of industry enjoy that right. Why should foremen be denied the same privilege?"

79. Howell Harris has studied this response in *Right to Manage*, 75–89. A good example of this cooperation was the article titled "Flash: Foremen Organize!," published in *Dodge Victory News*, March 24, 1944, reprinted in the "Brief for Packard Motor Company," *Packard v. NLRB* file, 1527.

80. "Brief for Packard Motor Company," *Packard v. NLRB* file, 3–5. See also the testimony of Clarence B. Randall, vice president of Inland Steel, *1943 House Hearings Before the Committee on Military Affairs on H.R. 2239, 1742, 1728, 992*, 88: "In industry, as in government or anywhere else, there are two classes of people; there are those who decide and those who carry out. You cannot organize human society on any other basis than there be those who decide and those who carry out. In private enterprise management is the decider. A foreman or supervisor is management." For Wagner's comment, see 74th Congress, 1st Session, 79 *Congressional Record* S. 7573 (May 15, 1935).

81. See the testimony of C. E. Wilson, *1943 House Hearings Before the Committee on Military Affairs on H.R. 2239, 1742, 1728, 992*, 62–87, as well as the testimony of Heath S. Clark (president of the Rochester and Pittsburgh Co.), 37, of Walter Gordon Merritt, 52–59, and of Edward E. Butler (executive vice president, Vinco Corporation, Detroit), 90–92. See "Businessmen Assail Unionizing Warshop Foremen: Wilson of GE and Others Use the Fall of France as Argument Against It," *New York Times*, March 31, 1943, 40.

82. "Re: Unions . . . Should Foremen Be Allowed to Organize?," *Detroit Free Press*, April 4, 1943; Kim McQuaid, *Uneasy Partners: Big Business in American Politics, 1945–1990* (Baltimore: Johns Hopkins University Press, 1994), 18–20. See also Elizabeth Fones Wolf, *Selling Free Enterprise, Selling America: The Business Assault on Labor and Liberalism, 1945–1960* (Urbana: University of Illinois Press, 1994), chap. 1; and Sanford Jacoby, *Modern Manors: Welfare Capitalism Since the New Deal* (Princeton: Princeton University Press, 1997), who argues that recalcitrant companies sought to update welfare capitalism after the 1930s.

83. This paragraph is based on Nelson Lichtenstein, *Labor's War at Home*, 118; *Walter Reuther*, 202; Harris, *Right to Manage*, 64; and George Lipsitz, *Rainbow at Midnight: Labor and Culture in the 1940s* (Urbana: University of Illinois Press, 1994), 62.

84. See Harris, *Right to Manage*, 66; Jacoby, *Employing Bureaucracy*, 171. The idea that foremen should be enlisted in the struggle derived from the belief, in the words of Ohio Bell Telephone President A. F. Carter, that "business must produce 99% of its own skill. . . . The most successful business institutions have always been those having a competent, painstaking, and above all self-perpetuating organization. Business owes itself to produce its manpower, big and little." A. F. Carter, "The Employee and the Boss," *Foremen's Magazine*, October 1929, 14.

85. In Congress, Heath S. Clark, the president Rochester and Pittsburgh Coal Company, located in Indiana, Pennsylvania, fully gave vent to those fears: "To place these men in the same labor organization with the men they boss, with the men with whom they contract, violates every principle of sound management. To permit these men to belong to the same organization, to fraternize with the men they boss, to take an oath of mutual support of one another, to logroll with each other in the negotiation of the wage contract, or in the daily operation of the mine, is fundamentally wrong, and above all it is entirely impossible and impractical. It creates an artificial community of interest which is detrimental to both sides." *House Hearings Before the Committee on Military Affairs on H.R. 2239, 1742, 1728, 992*, 1st Session, 1943, 36.

86. General Motors, *History of the Movement to Organize Foremen in the Automotive Industry*, Appendix E, 6. See also the pamphlet published by Chrysler in 1946: "Shall the Rank and File Boss the Plants?," DOL. That General Motors' C. E. Wilson should have been at the forefront of

the reaction against foremen's unionism is not surprising. At General Motors, foremen were still endowed with the authoritarian powers they needed to really control the assembly line and still had the power to hire and fire. Like Packard, since the 1920s, General Motors had followed the current of the new foremanship and taken important steps to induct foremen into the managerial hierarchy. The title "working foreman" had been abolished, and their earnings had been pegged 25 percent above those of the highest paid worker. The company also offered more than forty training programs each year. GM had also taken the lead in the public advocacy of supervisory training programs, with William Knudsen warning American managers as early as 1937, "I plead with you to go out into your factory and gather up the bottom strata. Someone else has been trying to gather it up while you were not looking." See Richard Coopey and Alan McKinlay, "Power Without Knowledge: Foucault and Fordism, c. 1900–1950," *Labor History* 51, no. 1 (2010): 117.

87. 1949 *Hearings on S. 249 Before the Senate Committee on Labor and Public Welfare*, 81st Congress, 1st Session, 2169.

88. See Atleson, *Values and Assumptions*. I am also indebted to Virginia Seitz, "The Value of *Values and Assumptions* to a Practicing Lawyer," *Buffalo Law Review* 57 (May 2009): 687–708, for my understanding of the tension between the common law and statutes.

89. *Hearings Before the Committee on Military Affairs, House of Representatives*, 78th Congress, 1943, 2.

90. Member of Congress Jennings, *Congressional Record*, February 4, 1946, 867.

91. Packard brief, *Packard v. NLRB* file, 98; Dale, "Unionization of Foremen," 29–31; testimony of C. E. Wilson, *1943 House Hearings Before the Committee on Military Affairs on H.R. 2239, 1742, 1728, 992*, 84.

92. On these debates, see Alan Brinkley, *The End of Reform* (New York: Norton, 1994); Harry B. Coen, "The Foreman as Part of Management" (paper, American Society of Mechanical Engineers, November 29–December 3, 1943), published and condensed in *Mechanical Engineering* (April 1944): 248–250, 256. See also Foner, *Story of American Freedom*, 235–237.

93. Coen, "Foreman as Part of Management," 250.

94. Packard Brief, *Packard v. NLRB* file, 81.

95. On the changing nature of the organization of capitalism, see Chandler, *Visible Hand*. In the 1960s John K. Galbraith went so far as saying that these managers represented a techno-structure that had seized power from owners and stockholders, in *The New Industrial State* (Boston: Houghton Mifflin, 1968). See, e.g., the speech delivered by Donaldson Brown, vice chairman of General Motors, before the 250th meeting of the Conference Board in New York, on March 18, 1943: "American industry has demonstrated its ability to meet the situation of the Nation's wartime production requirements. That ability has derived from the experience, skill and know-how of countless human individuals trained in the school of American industrial management. . . . The very foundations upon which management rests, and the things for which it stands, are threatened, strange to say, by those who seek to improve human relationships which industry and to improve the welfare of the individual." Inserted in the record of the *1943 House Hearings Before the Committee on Military Affairs on H.R. 2239, 1742, 1728, 992*, 229–235, quote at 229.

96. Testimony of C. E. Wilson, *1943 House Hearings Before the Committee on Military Affairs on H.R. 2239, 1742, 1728, 992*, 84.

97. *Jefferson-Standard Broadcasting Co.*, 94 NLRB 1507 (1953). The case bore upon the action of technicians accused of impugning the reputation of their company. The court found that they owed an obligation of loyalty to the company and that their dismissal was not unfair. See Atleson, *Values and Assumptions*, 84–87.

Chapter 5. The Other Side of Industrial Pluralism

1. William Leiserson to John A. Fitch, October 9, 1940, Leiserson Papers, "Speeches and Articles," box 50. In a famous letter sent to John R. Commons, Leiserson railed against the jurists:

"The lawyers seem to have the notion that the only way to arrive at the truth is by two opposing lawyers trying to keep things out of the record, and whatever gets in, that's the truth. They have no understanding of the method of inquiry that we call economic or scientific research"; quoted in James Gross, "Economics, Politics and the Law: The NLRB's Division of Economic Research," *Cornell Law Review* 55, no. 3 (1970): 321–347, 339. "Two Nice Men," *Time*, May 8, 1939, http://www.time.com/. Leiserson replaced Donald Wakefield Smith, a recess appointment, but he soon deadlocked with Edwin Smith. Only with the appointment of Harry Millis in 1940 did the board get the new majority that Roosevelt wanted. See "New Labor Chairman," *Time*, November 25, 1940, http://www.time.com/.

2. See "Two Nice Men." *Time* called Leiserson a "merry, contemplative cherub of 56." Before he became an arbitrator, Leiserson taught economics at Antioch College. After working in the needle industry, he was an arbitrator for the NRA, the petroleum field, and finally the railroad field. See Michael Eisner, *William Morris Leiserson: A Biography* (Madison: University of Wisconsin Press, 1967).

3. Notably, in 1938, the Republicans gained eight seats in the Senate and eighty-one in the House of Representatives, and the largely prolabor LaFollette Committee was replaced by the Dies Committee, or the House Un-American Activities Committee (HUAC).

4. Tomlins, *State and the Unions*. In this book, Tomlins argued that the moderate course of the NLRB was foreordained by the history of its adoption. However, he revised his position in a later article, "The New Deal, Collective Bargaining and the Triumph of Industrial Pluralism," *Industrial and Labor Relations Review* 39, no. 1 (October 1985): 19–34, in which he argues that only after the Wagner Act became law did the industrial pluralists steer it in a conservative direction. James Gross also sees the nomination as an important turning point; see James Gross, *The Reshaping of the National Labor Relations Board* (Albany: State University of New York Press, 1981), 226–259.

5. Here I am drawing on the history and sociology of expertise, which is often critical and emphasizes that the role of experts is often—in the guise of scientific disinterestedness—to maintain the established order. See Stephen Brint, *In an Age of Experts: The Changing Role in Politics and Public Life* (Princeton: Princeton University Press, 1994); and Thomas Haskell, *The Authority of Experts* (Bloomington: University of Indiana Press, 1984). On the contrary, see Romain Huret, "Les experts sociaux face à la société civile: La Campagne des pauvres et le ministère de la santé, de l'éducation et du bien-être, avril-juin 1968," *Revue d'histoire moderne et contemporaine* 51–52 (2004): 118–140; and Shelton Stromquist, "Class Wars: Frank Walsh, the Reformers, and the Crisis of Progressivism," in *Labor Histories*, ed. Eric Arnesen et al. (Urbana: University of Illinois Press, 1998), 97–124. Both emphasize the capacity of experts to go against the established order and advocate change. My own perspective here goes with Huret and Stromquist. Like Huret, however, I emphasize the lack of power of experts.

6. The foremen at this Wisconsin auto parts factory received their affiliation with the UFS-CIO in August 1939; see Chapter 4, note 33.

7. This struggle is rendered vividly in Jack Metzgar's account of the rise of the CIO in the steel industry; see Metzgar, *Striking Steel*, 31–39.

8. The role of supervisors in the antiunion struggle was one of the first questions tackled by the Division of Economic Research. See "Role of Supervisors in Spreading Employer Views," Research Memorandum 3, November 8, 1938, NLRB Archives, PCF, Former Chairmen, 1934–1970, RG 25, National Archives. For exemplary cases, see *Matter of A. S. Abell Co.*, 5 NLRB 144 (1938); *Matter of the Serrick Corporation*, 8 NLRB 621 (1938); as well as *Matter of Cooper, Wells and Co.*, 16 NLRB 27 (1939).

9. *Matter of Ford Motor Co.*, 23 NLRB 342 (1940). See also the annual reports of the board on this question.

10. The bills were submitted during the 76th Congress and were the following: S. 1000 (Walsh), H.R. 4749 (Barden), H.R. 5231 (Hartley). They are analyzed and summarized in an NLRB memo-

randum titled "Supervisory Employees," drafted by the Legal Division and dated December 17, 1946, CMF, RG 25, National Archives, box 4.

11. "Board Report to the House Committee on H.R. 4749 and 5231," 20–26, quoted in "Supervisory Employees," sec. 4. For William Leiserson's testimony in Congress on that issue, see Chapter 3, note 65.

12. See the presentation given by William Leiserson during a meeting with union leaders before the board handed down its decision in the *Union Collieries* case: "What's Evolving from Wartime Labor Relations," undated, Leiserson Papers, "Speeches and Articles," box 50; "Union Collieries, Oral Arguments at the Board," March 24, 1942, 2, NLRB Archives, RG 25, National Archives, box 3091.

13. On the elimination of the Economic Research Division see Gross, "Economics, Politics and the Law."

14. The vote was 258–129 in favor of amendments that expanded the definition of agricultural worker to include workers in food processing and protected employer free speech during elections. As for the preamble of the act, it would have been rewritten and stripped of its probargaining bias. See Dubofsky, *State and Labor*, 154–161; and Gross, *Reshaping of the National Labor Relations Board*, 85–187.

15. Led by the prominent jurist Roscoe Pound and by the American Bar Association, the controversy over the nature and accountability of the American administrative state was solved only in 1946 with the adoption of the American Procedures Act, which both specified and streamlined the procedures that should govern the development of administrative law. See Forbath, "Long Life," 189–191; Morton Horwitz, *The Transformation of American Labor Law, 1870–1960: The Crisis of Legal Orthodoxy* (New York: Oxford University Press, 1992), 214, passim; as well as Reuel Schiller, "Saint George and the Dragon: Courts and the Development of the Administrative State in the Twentieth Century," *Journal of Policy History* 17, no. 1 (2005): 110–124.

16. To the best of my knowledge, there is no full-scale account of this strike and of the role the UFS played in it. This paragraph relies on the following *United Automobile Worker Journal* articles: "CIO Smashes Chrysler," October 4, 1939; "Chrysler Gets Demands," October 11, 1939; Chrysler Workers Vote Strike," October 18, 1939; "We Accept the Challenge!" October 8, 1939; "Back to Work Move Flops," November 15, 1939. Like other union publications, the *United Automobile Worker Journal* is available at DOL. For my understanding of this strike, I have also relied on Steve Babson, *Working Detroit: The Making of a Union Town* (Detroit: Wayne State University Press, 1986), 99–102.

17. See the testimony of James Beyerley, Packard Appellate Case Files, RG 267, National Archives, box 4819, 472–473; Cross, "When Foremen Joined the CIO," 280–281; and "Chrysler Says CIO Signs Auto Foremen," *New York Times*, November 22, 1939.

18. On this question, see the previous chapter, and Lichtenstein, *Walter Reuther*, 108–109. Lichtenstein shows that General Motors avoided the decline of foremen's authority because it managed to limit the number of committeemen to 1 for every 400 workers. By contrast, at Chrysler the ratio was 1 for every 30. On the contentious nature of the strike, see "Chrysler Foremen Cause a New Crisis," *New York Times*, November 23, 1939; and "Chrysler Asks CIO to End Bid to Foremen," *New York Times*, November 24, 1939.

19. Leiserson, "What's Evolving from Wartime Labor Relations," 20. On R. J. Thomas's position, see UAW-IEB Meetings, April 4, 1939, 2, UAW Collection, Walter Reuther Library, Wayne State University, box 2; and CIO Executive Board Proceedings, April 12, 1945, during which Thomas mentioned this event.

20. John Brophy to J. R. Bell, August 20, 1940, CIO Archives, CUA, box 64, file 33.

21. In a series of cases, the board found against employers who had fired foremen for joining a labor union. Indeed, whenever all the unions involved in the representation election agreed to request it, the board accepted to include foremen and supervisors in the collective bargaining unit. In 1938, the board provided the following explanation: "Supervisory employees although eligible

for membership in competing labor organizations, are forbidden by the Act, in their capacity as the employer's agent, to interfere in the selection of employee bargaining representatives, yet there need be no conflict by reason of their dual status. It is perfectly consistent for supervisory employees to belong to labor organizations and yet be prohibited from conduct permitted to non supervisory personnel." See *Matter of Tennessee Copper Co.*, 9 NLRB 117 (1938), 119. Otherwise the best guide to these cases is the fourth annual report of the board, see National Labor Relations Board, *Fourth Annual Report For the Fiscal Year Ended June 30, 1939* (Washington DC: GPO, 1940) 93–97. In 1939, a federal court sustained the board's policy to construe foremen as *both* "employers" and "employees," noting that "a foreman, in his relation to his employer, is an employee, while in his relation to the laborers he is the representative of the employer and within section 2(2) of the Act. Nothing in the Act excepts foremen from its benefits nor from protection against discrimination nor unfair labor practices of the master." *NLRB v. Skinner and Kennedy Stationery Co.*, 113 F. (2nd) 667 (1940), 671.

22. Leiserson, "What's Evolving from Wartime Labor Relations," 20.

23. Oral history interview of David Levison with Frank Bowen, December 24, 1947, as quoted in Levison, "Wartime Unionization of Foremen," 156. Oral history with Carl Brown, November 13, 1974, p. 12, Wayne State Library.

24. The union was created in response to the layoff of a mine boss who had tried to convince the company to reorganize the working week. See Levison, "Wartime Unionization of Foremen," 328–331; and *Matter of Union Collieries Coal Company, Oakmont, Pennsylvania*, 41 NLRB 174 (1942).

25. Report of Field Examiner Henry C. Clay, December 5, 1941, 4, and Regional Director Report, November 3, 1941 1–3. Both reports can be found in *Matter of Union Collieries*, case VI-R-400, RG 25, National Archives, boxes 5449–5452. For the statement, examination, and cross examination of Frank Benny, the company's attorney, see ibid., 88–142.

26. *Matter of Godchaux Sugars Inc.*, 44 NLRB 172 (1942).

27. Leiserson, "What's Evolving from Wartime Labor Relations," 24; Harry Millis, dissenting opinion in *Maryland Drydock*, 749.

28. Leiserson, "What's Evolving from Wartime Labor Relations," 24.

29. National Labor Relations Board, *Seventh Annual Report For the Fiscal Year Ended June 30, 1942* (Washington DC: GPO, 1943) 63.

30. Harry Millis, dissenting opinion in *Maryland Drydock*, 749.

31. Ibid., 750.

32. As Eric Foner has noted, "The New Deal recast the idea of freedom by linking it to the expanding power of the National State." Foner, *Story of American Freedom*, 196. William Leiserson to John Fitch, January 28, 1936, Leiserson Papers, "Fitch" folder, box 14.

33. *Matter of Godchaux Sugars*, 877. See also *Maryland Drydock*, 746. Leiserson, "What's Evolving from Wartime Labor Relations," 23; William Leiserson to Robert Wagner, July 9, 1945, Wagner Archives, box 1, "labor."

34. Gerard Reilly, dissenting opinion in *Union Collieries*, 970–972.

35. *Matter of Union Collieries*, VI-R-400, brief for Mine Union Officials of America, 5–6, RG 25, National Archives, box 2967.

36. See note 39 in this chapter.

37. *Bills Relating to the Full Utilization of Manpower, Hearings on H.R. 2239, H.R. 1742 and H.R. 992 Before the House Military Affairs Committee*, 78th Congress, 1943, 833.

38. Joseph Slater, *Government Employee Unions, the Law and the State*, 1900–1962 (Ithaca: Cornell University Press, 2004), 158–192. See also Joseph A. McCartin, "Bringing the State's Workers In: Time to Rectify an Imbalanced US Labor Historiography," *Labor History* 47, no. 1 (2006): 73–94.

39. Again I provide here only a few examples: *Matter of Chrysler Corporation*, 1 NLRB 1964 (design engineers); *Matter of General Motors*, 36 NLRB 439 (shift engineers); *Matter of Chrysler Corporation*, 36 NLRB 593 (plant guards). The CIO's forays inside the white-collar world are told in Benjamin Stolberg, *The Story of the CIO* (New York: Viking Press, 1938), 245–267. Michael Denning provides a useful contextualization of it in his fascinating *The Cultural Front: The Laboring*

of American Culture in the Twentieth Century (New York: Verso, 1998), in which he argues that white-collar workers were essential to the building of a popular front historical bloc. See also Irving Berstein, *The Turbulent Years: A History of the American Worker, 1933–1941* (Chicago: Haymarket Books, 2010), chap. 4.

40. See Castel, *Les metamorphoses*, 519–620.

41. The invention of this new social category is analyzed in Luc Boltanski, *Les cadres*; see also Marc Descotes and Jean-Louis Robert, *Clés pour une histoire du syndicalisme cadre* (Paris: Les Editions Ouvrières, 1984), as well as Guy Groux, *Les cadres* (Paris: La Découverte, 1984) and René Mouriaux, "Le syndicalisme des ingénieurs et cadres: Histoire et historiographies," *Culture Technique* 12 (1984): 221–227.

42. Boltanski, *Les cadres*, 66–82, 155–179.

43. William T. Gossett, counsel to Ford Motor Co., as quoted in Virginia Seitz, "Legal, Legislative, and Managerial Responses to the Organization of Supervisory Employees," *American Journal of Legal History* 28 (1984): 199–243, 217.

44. *Matter of Union Collieries*, VI-R-400, brief for Union Collieries Company, 1–5, RG 25, National Archives, box 2967.

45. "Brief of Edward Burke on Behalf of the Southern Coal Producers Association," petition for a rehearing in the *Union Collieries* Case, R-3464, NLRB Archives, RG 25, National Archives, box 2967.

46. "Management, like labor, must have faithful agents—if we are to produce goods competitively and in such large quantities that people can buy them at low cost." House report 245, reprinted in *Legislative History of the National Labor Relations Act*, 307.

47. Gross, however, does note that the amount of criticism leveled at the board decreased significantly after 1940. See *Reshaping of the National Labor Relations Board*, 226–240.

48. Harry M. Millis, "A Statement Concerning the Foremen Issue," undated document (but drafted between the release of the *Union Collieries* and *Maryland* decisions) in the "Supervisory Employees" file, CMF, RG 25, box 2. For William Leiserson's own position, see "Union Collieries, Oral Arguments."

49. *Business Week*, January–March 1943, 38, as quoted in Larrowe, "Meteor on the Industrial Relations Horizon," 277. Paul Herzog, who was to be appointed to the board in 1945, later explained, "Mr. Roosevelt nominated him on the theory that he would make the board look fairly conservative, having been in the lumber business." Oral history interview with Paul Herzog, July 1975, 17, Kheel Center, Cornell University.

50. Gerald Reilly, *In the Matter of Maryland Drydock Company and Local No. 31 of the Industrial Union or Marine and Shipbuilding Workers of America*, 49 NLRB 105, 740. Reilly was quoting from Justice Cardozo's opinion in *Meinhard v. Salmon*, 249 N.Y. 458, 164 N.E. 545 (1928).

51. Mervin Bachman, "Suggested Approach to the Question Whether the Discharge of a Supervisory Employee Constitutes an Unfair Labor Practice," April 25, 1944, "Supervisory Employees" file, CMF, RG 25, box 2.

52. On Mervin Bachman, see the obituary published in the *Chicago Tribune* on August 29, 2005, by Barbara Sherlock. More is known about Farmer; see especially James Gross, *Broken Promise: The Subversion of U.S. Labor Policy* (Philadelphia: Temple University Press, 1998), 95–98.

53. Guy Farmer, "Supervisory Employees," April 14, 1944, in NLRB Archives, CMF, "Supervisory Employees" file, RG 25, National Archives, box 2. Mervin Bachman, "Suggested Approach to the Question Whether the Discharge of a Supervisory Employee Constitutes an Unfair Labor Practice," April 25, 1944, 2. As Mervin Bachman explained, "To hold at this date that Congress . . . intended to relegate to an inferior these basic guarantees and to make their availability to employees. . . . fundamental rights." A native of Chicago, Bachman (1915–2005) was a typical New Deal lawyer, graduating from Harvard Law School.

54. *Matter of Soss Manufacturing*, 56 NLRB 348, *Matter of Republic Steel*, 56 NLRB 348. The two cases were decided together. The board also noted that the right of foremen to protection was "not

an unqualified one," but was "subordinate to the organizational rights and freedom of rank and file employees and the need of an employer to maintain his neutrality"; 353–354.

55. Jesse Frieden, "Opinion on the Board's Jurisdiction over Labor Disputes Involving Supervisory Employees," March 30, 1944, NWLB Archives, RG 202, National Archives, box 585. On the NWLB, see Andrew Workman, "Creating the National War Labor Board: Franklin Roosevelt and the Politics of State Building in the Early 1940s," *Journal of Policy History* 12, no. 2 (2000): 233–264; and his dissertation, "Creating the Center" (PhD diss., University of North Carolina, 1993); and Lichtenstein, *Labor's War at Home.*

56. *Report and Findings of the National War Labor Board,* 16.

57. Ibid., 41.

58. There is no available archival material to account for this evolution (John Houston has left no personal papers). This paragraph is based on the memorandum sent by Gerard D. Reilly to John Houston and Harry Millis, December 16, 1944, available in *Matter of Packard Motor Co.,* 7-R-1884, informal file, NLRB Archives, RG 25, which is itself a response to a memorandum sent by Houston in which he announced his decision to change his position on foremen. Houston's memorandum, however, was not filed. On his gradual evolution, see the oral history interview conducted by the Kheel Center with Paul Herzog, 34–35.

59. Frank Bloom, "Memorandum Report," in *Matter of Packard Motor Co.,* 7-R-1884, informal file, NLRB Archives, RG 25. Reilly deplored Bloom's influence on Houston. See James Gross, *Reshaping of the National Labor Relations Board,* 246.

60. *Packard Motor Company,* 61 NLRB 3, 10. Millis and Houston also noted, "We cannot shut our eyes to these developments since the decision in the *Maryland Drydock* case. . . . To continue to deny such employees as a class the bargaining rights guaranteed by the Act would be to ignore the clear economic facts and invite further industrial strife—a state of affairs which the Nation can ill afford at this time which the Act was designed to mitigate." *Packard Motor Company,* 14, 21.

61. 61 NLRB 3, 25.

62. *Packard Motor Company,* 61 NLRB 204, 216. (This is the second Packard decision, in which the NLRB found against the company, which refused to bargain with the FAA after it won the election and was certified as an appropriate bargaining unit).

63. "Peace at Any Price," *Detroit Free Press,* March 28, 1945.

64. *Packard Co. v. Labor Board,* 330 U.S. 485 (1947).

65. Aaron Levenstein, *Labor Today and Tomorrow* (New York: Knopf 1946). On Walter Reuther's proposal for a kind of corporate capitalism, see Lichtenstein, *Walter Reuther;* Brinkley, *End of Reform;* Adolph Berle and Gardiner Means, *The Modern Corporation and Private Property* (1932; repr., New Brunswick, N.J.: Transaction, 1991). *Packard Co. v. Labor Board,* 494–500.

66. On this question, see Wolf, *Selling Free Enterprise;* and Kim Philips Fein, *Invisible Hands: The Making of the Conservative Movement from the New Deal to Reagan* (New York: Norton, 2009).

67. On this charter, see the CIO Executive Board meeting of April 12, 1945, in the George Meany Archives. The AFL was no part of it and bitterly criticized it. A good example of the ignorance of the foremen's issue in analyses of the antilabor bills introduced in Congress after 1946 is Philip Murray, "A Message to the Membership of the CIO and All Other Progressive Americans," September 10, 1945, 43, Legal Department, CIO archives, CUA, box 9.

68. See Gilbert Gall, *Pursuing Justice: Lee Pressman, the New Deal and the CIO* (Albany: State University of New York Press, 1999), 208. See also Irving Richter's memoir, *Labor Struggles: A Participant's View* (New York: Cambridge 1994).

69. "Statement of the Secretary of Labor Before the Senate Committee on Education and Labor on H.R. 4908," February 25, 1946, Lewis Schwellenbach Collection, RG 174, National Archives, box 4; Clark Clifford, "Points," in Clark Clifford Papers, "Case Bill, Miscellaneous" file, Truman Library, box 6. "Veto of Case Bill," http://www.presidency.ucsb.edu-ws/?pid-12414.

70. Lewis Schwellenbach to Harry Truman, June 4, 1946, 6, Lewis Schwellenbach Papers, RG 174, National Archives, box 4.

71. House Report 245, 80th Congress, 1st Session (1947), reprinted in *Legislative History of the National Labor Relations Act*, 305–308. For Truman's veto speech, see note 69.

72. Senate Report 105, 80th Congress, 1st Session (1947), reprinted in *Legislative History of the National Labor Relations Act*, 411.

73. 29 U.S.C. §152 (11).

74. Robert H. Keys to Walter Reuther, June 24, 1947, Walter Reuther Collection, Wayne State University Archives, box 96, folder 96-11.

75. For UAW leaders' statements in favor of the rights of foremen, see UAW-IEB minutes, January 22–29, 1945, 150 (adopting a motion to send to the press and the NLRB a statement urging the NLRB to protect foremen's organizing rights), and UAW-IEB minutes, October 22–30, 1943, 62 (motion adopted to support foremen in their fight).

76. UAW-IEB minutes, April 16–22, 1945, 11, 58–59. The foremen's question was broached by the IEB after an affiliation request had been issued by foremen at the Wright Plant in Paterson.

77. UAW-IEB minutes, September 10–18, 1945, UAW-IEB Collection, Wayne State Library, 64–67: "Secretary Addes explained to the committee that the Foremen's picket line was not meant for the production workers . . . and to say that because the foremen, office workers, or other groups establish a picket line the production workers shall not cross it is tantamount to having an outside organization dictate terms of policy to the UAW." The same views were expressed once again in April 1947: see UAW-IEB minutes, April 22, 1947, 163.

78. UAW-IEB minutes, April 4, 1939, 2. R. J. Thomas notably dismissed the FAA as a "company union"; see UAW-IEB minutes, March 1–10, 1943, 109; UAW-IEB minutes, October 22–30, 1943, 62. In 1943, during the hearings held in Congress on the foremen's issue, Richard Frankensteen clearly expressed his opposition to allowing foremen in the UAW: "I would not trust them to speak for the interests of the people I represent. I think they have their own problems"; *Hearings Before the Committee on Military Affairs, House of Representatives, 78th* Congress, 1943, 458. Labor leaders, however, did not speak in one voice. Unlike Frankensteen, Lee Pressman would not say whether the CIO would, later on, take foremen on; see 299–327.

79. In fact, the social definition of the American worker as a male blue-collar manual worker would remain a substantial limitation on American unions. Less than twenty-five years later, UAW leaders once again intoned a restrictive tune when they refused to support a strike of clerical workers at GM in 1971. Like foremen in the 1940s, the women who energized the strike were seen as a hindrance and a nuisance, and automobile workers readily walked through their picket lines. See Cowie, *Stayin' Alive*, 64.

80. This element in the FAA's identity is emphasized by Carl Brown in the oral history interview with Howell Harris on November 13, 1974, Wayne State University Archives of Labor and Urban Affairs.

81. UAW-IEB minutes, extraordinary session, July 1, 1947, 8. According to R. J. Thomas, "About a year ago . . . Murray called Keys to discuss with him coming in with the CIO, and at that time Keys refused." In his memoirs, Irving Richter mentions that in the wake of the Packard decision in January 1945, the CIO anticipated the affiliation of the FAA; see Irving Richter, *Labor's Struggles, 1945–1950* (New York: Cambridge University Press, 1994), 46.

82. UAW-IEB minutes, June 9–13, 1947, 8.

83. UAW-IEB minutes, extraordinary session, July 1, 1947, 1–28.

84. Ibid., 3, 8.

85. Ibid. See also Lichtenstein, *Walter Reuther*, 263–264; and Levison, "Wartime Unionization of Foremen," 302–306.

86. Levison, "Wartime Unionization of Foremen," 308–316. Then the UAW leaders once again debated the possibility of a change in the union policy, but nothing significant was done; see UAW-IEB minutes, July 9, 1947, 5–12.

87. These changes are analyzed at greater length by Seitz, on whom this development relies, in "Legal, Legislative, and Managerial Responses," 235–236.

88. Robert Korstad and Nelson Lichtenstein, "Opportunities Found and Lost," *Journal of American History* 75, no. 3 (December 1988): 786–811.

89. I thank Michael Kazin for pointing me to this useful concept.

Chapter 6. Loyalty Ascendant

1. *NLRB v. Bell Aerospace, Co.,* 416 U.S. 267 (1974), 269. "Excerpts from Official Report of Proceedings Before the National Labor Relations Board," August 28, 1970, 79, records of the Supreme Court of the United States, RG 267, National Archives, box 635 (*NLRB v. Bell Aerospace*) (hereafter *NLRB v. Bell Aerospace* Supreme Court file). This case has been discussed in a number of legal articles. See especially George Feldman, "Workplace Power and Collective Activity: The Supervisory and Managerial Exclusions in Labor Law," *Arizona Law Review* 37, no. 3 (Summer 1995): 525–562; David Rabban, "Distinguishing Excluded Managers from Covered Professionals Under the NLRA," *Columbia Law Review* 89, no. 8 (December 1989): 1776–1855; and Ben M. Germana, "Protecting Managerial Employees Under the NLRA," *Columbia Law Review* 91, no. 2 (March 1991): 405–429. My goal here is to trace the political history of this case. On the need to study the legal history of the postwar administrative state, see Reuel Schiller, "The Administrative State, Front and Center: Studying Law and Administration in Postwar America," *Law and History Review* 26, no. 2 (Summer 2008): 415–427.

2. On the development of the Sunbelt, see Bruce Schulman, *From Cotton Belt to Sunbelt: Federal Policy, Economic Development, and the Transformation of the South 1938–1980* (New York: Oxford University Press, 1991). On the rise of conservatism in that area, see Rick Perlstein, *Before the Storm: Barry Goldwater and the Unmaking of the American Consensus* (New York: Hill and Wang, 2002); Matthew Dallek, *The Right Moment: Ronald Reagan's First Victory and the Decisive Turning Point in American Politics* (New York: Free Press, 2000); and Elizabeth Tandy Shermer, *Sunbelt Capitalism* (Philadelphia: University of Pennsylvania Press, 2013).

3. Letter of Ken Bannon to Joe Ferraro, "Amalgamated Local 1286 Negotiations," June 8, 1976, UAW-TOP Collection, UAW-CULMA, box 26, file 33.

4. Carl D. Snyder, *The UAW and White Collar Unionism* (Urbana: University of Illinois Press, 1974), 41.

5. On Drucker, see Waring, *Taylorism Transformed*, 85; Nils Gilman, "The Prophet of Post-Fordism: Peter F. Drucker and the Legitimation of the Corporation," in *American Capitalism*, 109–134; Daniel Bell, *The Coming of Post-Industrial Society* (New York: Free Press, 1973). In France, the idea was advanced, albeit in a more pessimistic cast, by Alain Touraine, *La société post-industrielle, naissance d'une société* (Paris: Denoel, 1969). On the history of postindustrialist theory, see Howard Brick, *Age of Contradiction: American Thought and Culture in the 1960s* (Ithaca: Cornell University Press, 1998), 54–57, and "Optimism of the Mind: Imagining Post-industrial Society in the 1960s and 1970s," *American Quarterly* 44 (September 1992): 348–380.

6. Historians have long called for studies highlighting the paths not taken in political history. See Julian Zelizer, "Clio's Lost Tribe: Public Policy History Since 1978," *Journal of Policy History* 12, no. 3 (2000): 369–394, and Joseph A. McCartin, "A Wagner Act for Public Employees: Labor's Deferred Dream and the Rise of Conservatism," *Journal of American History* 95, no. 1 (June 2008): 123–148.

7. The following description of the work of the procurement buyers is based on the records of the investigation led by NLRB examiners in Buffalo. This type of source raises an obvious methodological question, as it was the very nature of the work done by the buyers that was at stake in the investigations. Each party to the trial thus sought to provide a depiction of the buyers' work that would justify classifying them as either "employees" or "managers." I have sought to offset this bias by using only the elements that figured in both the buyers' and the top managers' description of the buyers' work.

8. "Excerpts from Official Report of Proceedings Before the National Labor Relations Board," *NLRB v. Bell Aerospace*, Supreme Court file, 38–39, 258–260.

9. Ibid., 49–50, 80.

10. Ibid., 39–40.

11. See Hecksher, *New Unionism*, 62–71.

12. See Waring, *Taylorism Transformed*, 88–89; Marina Angel, "Professionals and Unionization," *Minnesota Law Review* 66 (1982): 383–457. See Ruth Milkman, *Farewell to the Factory* (Berkeley: University of California Press, 1997), for an analysis showing that even if workers were well paid in the 1970s, they still hated factory work for its debilitating aspects.

13. This paragraph relies heavily on Waring, *Taylorism Transformed*, 84–88. On the links between the new unionism and Taylorism, see Chapter 4.

14. "Excerpts from Official Report of Proceedings Before the National Labor Relations Board," 72–75, 107–108, 255–256. Letter from J. J. Kelly, Bell Aerospace vice-president, to John Miranda, president of Local UAW 1286, August 14, 1972, UAW-CUMLA, box 18, folder 8. Waring, *Taylorism Transformed*, 78–73; see also Hecksher, *New Unionism*, 85–113.

15. "Excerpts from Official Report of Proceedings Before the National Labor Relations Board," *NLRB v. Bell Aerospace*, Supreme Court file, 20, 36, 45–48.

16. "Reply Brief for Petitioner," 10, *NLRB v. Bell Aerospace*, Supreme Court file.

17. In *Company Men: White Collar Life and Corporate Cultures in Los Angeles, 1892–1941* (Baltimore: Johns Hopkins University Press, 2000), Clark Davis argues that the logic of security was already a matter of importance to white-collar employees before the Great Depression.

18. "Excerpts from Official Report of Proceedings Before the National Labor Relations Board," 57, 139–143. On the divided welfare system, see Klein, *For All These Rights*.

19. *Matter of Ford Motor Company*, 66 NLRB 1317 (1946), 1322.

20. 29 U.S.C. §152 (11).

21. 29 U.S.C. § 152 (12).

22. *Matter of New England Telephone*, 90 NLRB 639 (1950). The share of supervisory employees increased from 12 percent in 1948 to 16 percent in 1960 and to 19 percent in 1980; see David M. Gordon, *Fat and Mean: The Corporate Squeeze of Working Americans and the Myth of Managerial Downsizing* (New York: Free Press, 1996), 33–60, 47. None of this is to say that this struggle over definition was the only form of opposition between labor and corporate America. Strikes are an equally important element of this story, as Metzgar argues in *Striking Steel*. The idea of the "labor-management accord," once a staple of the historiography, is fully challenged in Lichtenstein, *State of the Union*, 98–140.

23. *Matter of Eastern Camera and Photo Corporation*, 140 NLRB 569 (1963).

24. *Matter of Westinghouse Electric Corp.*, 113 NLRB 337 (1955), 339: "While manufacturing engineers make recommendations on matters which are of great importance to management, that factor is usually present in the work of all professional employees, and does not in and of itself make them part of management so as to preclude their inclusion in a profession al unit."

25. Special Task Force, *Work in America*, as quoted in Waring, *Taylorism Transformed*, 132.

26. Sylvester Petro, *The Labor Policy of the Free Society* (New York: Ronald Press, 1957), and *The Kohler Strike* (Boston: Western Islands, 1961). Gross, *Broken Promise*, 98–99. On Petro, see Joseph A. McCartin and Jean-Christian Vinel, "Compulsory Unionism: Sylvester Petro and the Rise of an Anti-Union Idea," in *The Right and Labor: History, Ideology, Imagination*, ed. Nelson Lichtenstein and Elizabeth Tandy Shermer (Philadelphia: University of Pennsylvania Press, 2012), 226–251.

27. David Stebenne, *Arthur J. Goldberg: New Deal Liberal* (New York: Oxford University Press, 1996), 313. On the role of James Landis, see oral history interview with Frank McCulloch, April 28, 1967, John F. Kennedy Oral History Collection, John F. Kennedy Presidential Library, 12, and Gross, *Broken Promise*, 146, and Chapter 3 of this book. On public-sector unionism see McCartin, "Wagner Act for Public Employees."

28. On the modern presidency, see Sidney Milkis, *The President and the Parties* (New York: Oxford University Press, 1993).

29. Oral history interview with Gerald Brown (1987), 1–25, collection 5843, Kheel Center, Cornell University.

30. Oral history interview with Howard Jenkins (1988), 1–5, collection 5843, Kheel Center, Cornell University.

31. Oral history interview with Sam Zagoria (1998), 1–8, collection 5843, Kheel Center, Cornell University.

32. See Schatz, "From Commons to Dunlop," 87–112.

33. Gerald Brown, "Collective Bargaining and the NLRB in the 1970s," 9 (speech, Bowling Green State University, April 28, 1971, 1964, collection 4186, Kheel Center, Cornell University, box 5.

34. Oral history interview with Frank McCulloch (1989), collection 5843, , Kheel Center, Cornell University, 34, 136–137, my emphasis.

35. *Matter of Plochman Harrison-Cherry Lane Foods*, 140 NLRB 11. One finds an equally rosy picture of the standard of living of the community employed by Kohler company in Sylvester Petro, *Kohler Strike*, 1–4.

36. Richard S. Street, "Poverty in the Valley of Plenty: The National Farm Labor Union, DiGiorgio Farms, and the Suppression of Documentary Photography in California, 1947–1966," *Labor History* 48, no. 1 (February 2007): 25–48.

37. "The problems of collective bargaining coming before the Labor Board merely reflect the state of the technology and the current problems of the changing society in which all of us live. . . . The process of collective bargaining is bound together by the same values which hold our society together, and an institution which does not adapt to changing conditions dies or becomes useless." Brown, "Collective Bargaining and the NLRB," 7.

38. Gerald Brown, "An Administrative Agency in a Changing World" (address, Washington University, Saint Louis, Mo., January 29, 1964), collection 4186, box 5.

39. See Lichtenstein, *State of the Union*, 168. On C. Wright Mills, see Mattson, *Intellectuals in Action*, 43–96.

40. The board's new decision was upheld by the Supreme Court in 1964; see *Fibreboard Paper Products Corp. v. Labor Board*, 379 U.S. 203 (1964).

41. See Jefferson Cowie, *Capital Moves: RCA's Seventy Year Quest for Cheap Labor* (Ithaca: Cornell University Press, 1999).

42. Oral history interview with Frank McCulloch (1989). "We failed to persuade the management community that the purpose of the statute was socially valuable," McCulloch recalled. "In fact, the more I preached about that in my speeches, the more I had the feeling that they thought I was biased toward unions. I tried to tell them that I was biased toward the statute, but this didn't wash. And our numerous efforts to persuade the management community that this was a viable kind of operation—of labor management relations in a democratic community—in large part failed," 12–14, 12–13. On J. P. Stevens, see Timothy Minchin, *Don't Sleep with the Stevens: The J. P. Stevens Campaign and the Struggle to Organize the South, 1963–1980* (Gainesville: University Press of Florida, 2005).

43. *Matter of Hughes Tool*, 147 NLRB 1573. The history of this case is traced by Sophia Z. Lee, in "Hotspots in a Cold War: The NAACP's Postwar Workplace Constitutionalism, 1948–1964," *Law and History Review* 26, no. 2 (Summer 2008): 328–377. The lineage between the NLRB and the EEOC is analyzed in Hugh Graham, *Civil Rights and the Presidency* (New York: Oxford University Press, 1992), 71–72. As McCulloch explained, however, he and member Fanning believed that this was stretching the statute and that thereafter board members felt too vulnerable politically to take on both racist and antiunion practices and focused on the protection of the right to organize; see the oral history interview with Frank McCulloch (1989), 86–90. This move away from the question of racial equality reveals how entrenched the separation between labor law and individual rights had become. On this question see Reuel Schiller, "From Group Rights to Individual Liberties: Post-

War Labor Law, Liberalism, and the Waning of Union Strength," *Berkeley Journal of Employment and Labor Law* 20, no. 1 (Summer 1999): 1–73.

44. Brown, "Collective Bargaining and the NLRB," 10.

45. Oral History with Sam Zagoria (1998), 14.

46. Brown, "Administrative Agency," 14.

47. See Irving Bernstein, *Turbulent Years: The History of the American Worker, 1933–1941* (Boston: Houghton Mifflin, 1969). On the United Financial Employees Union, see "Battle of the Citadel," *Time*, April 28, 1947, http://www.time.com/. On the ESA, see *Collective Bargaining v. Collective Action* (Washington, D.C.: National Society of Professional Engineers, 1972). On teachers, see Marjorie Murphy, *Blackboard Unions: The AFT and the NEA, 1900–1980* (Ithaca: Cornell University Press, 1980). On the engineers in the electrical industry, see Geoffrey Latta, "Union Organization Among Engineers: A Current Assessment," *Industrial Labor Relations Review* 35, no. 1 (October 1981): 29–42. On public-sector unions, see Joseph A. McCartin, "Turnabout Years: Public Sector Unionism and the Fiscal Crisis," in *Rightward Bound: Making America Conservative in the 1970s*, ed. Bruce Schulman and Julian E. Zelizer (Cambridge, Mass.: Harvard University Press, 2008), 210–226; and Daniel J. Opler, *For All White Collar Workers: The Possibilities of Radicalism in New York City's Department Store Unions, 1934–1953* (Columbus: Ohio State University Press, 2007), emphasizes the negative impact of anticommunism.

48. These figures come from Benjamin Solomon and Robert E. Burns, "Unionization of White Collar Employees: Extent, Potential and Implications," *Journal of Business* 36, no. 2 (April 1963): 141–165; Conference Board, "White Collar Unionization," *Studies in Personnel Policy* 220 (1970).

49. The best illustration of this profound interest is the series "Studies in White Collar Unionism," published in the 1950s by the Industrial Relations Center at the University of Chicago, and the various conferences touching on this topic, such as the 1960 conference at the University of Pennsylvania "Industrial Relations in the 1960s—Problems and Prospects," which included several papers titled "White Collar Unionization"; Jack Barbash, "Unionizing the Professional Worker"; University of Pennsylvania, "Industrial Relations in the 1960s: Problems and Prospects" (conference proceedings, February 15, 1961), available at DOL. See also Bernard Goldstein, "Some Aspects of the Nature of Unionism Among Salaried Professionals in Industry," *American Sociological Review* 20, no. 2 (April 1955): 199–205. Along with the booklets published by the NAM, see the issues of *Studies in Personnel Policies* published by the NICB on this topic: "White Collar Unionization" (no. 101), "Unionization Among American Engineers" (no. 105), for example. The survey showing that nearly 50 percent of middle managers favored a change in the laws to compel employers to bargain with them was analyzed in Alfred T. DeMaria et al., *Manager Unions?* (New York: American Management Association, January 1973). In the 1970s, managerial fears of white-collar and managerial unionism were evident in Erwin Stanton, "White Collar Unionization: New Challenge to Management," *Personnel Journal* (February 1972): 118–139; "Would Foremen Unionize?" *Personnel Journal* (November 1970): 926–931.

50. "Summary Report and Conclusion of IUD Seminar, Collective Bargaining Problems of Professional and Technical Workers in Industry" (Industrial Union Department, 1960), DOL, 2; "Resolution on White Collar Organizing," UAW-TOP Collection, UAW-CUMLA, box 62, file 11. See also Solomon Barkin, *The Decline of the Labor Movement and What Can Be Done About It* (Santa Barbara: Center for the Study of Democratic Institutions, 1961).

51. See Paddy Riley, "Clark Kerr: From Industrial to Knowledge Economy," in Lichtenstein, *American Capitalism*, 80–82.

52. David G. Moore and Richard Renck, "The Professional Employee in Industry," *Journal of Business* 28, no. 1 (January 1955): 58–66, 66.

53. Braverman, of course, was quite critical of the industrial pluralists; Riley, "Clark Kerr," 72–87; Bernard Goldstein, "Unions and the Professional Employee," *Journal of Business* 27, no. 4 (1954): 276–284; Goldstein, "Some Aspects of the Nature of Unionism"; Robert K. Burns, "The Comparative Position of Manual and White Collar Employees," *Journal of Business* 27 (October 1954): 257.

John Dunlop et al., *Industrialism and Industrial Man* (Cambridge, Mass.: Harvard University Press, 1960), 7–8; Simon Marcson, *The Scientist in American Industry* (Princeton: Princeton University Press, 1960); Lee E. Danielson, "Management's Relations with Engineers and Scientists" (1957 proceedings, Industrial Relations Research Association); Jack Barbash, "Unionizing the Professional Worker" (University of Pennsylvania, November 18, 1960), 12–17, available at DOL.

54. Testimony of Karl M. Ruppenthal, former vice president of the ALPA, (Industrial Relations in the 1960s conference, University of Pennsylvania, November 18, 1960), 23–31, available at the DOL; Ed Modes, *The ALPA Story: A History and Study of the Background, Functions, and Organization of the Air Line Pilots Association, Intl* (Chicago: ALPA, 1954), quoted in Barbash, "Organizing the Professional Worker," 17.

55. Organization of Engineers and Scientists of America, Special Report Series, undated, quoted in Jack Barbash, "Organizing the Professional Worker," 17.

56. Ibid.

57. *Matter of North Arkansas Electric Corp.*, 168 NLRB 921 (1967).

58. Testimony of manager John Cochran, quoted in the opinion at 922.

59. James Gregory, *American Exodus* (New York: Oxford University Press, 1989). Notably, this culture was the seedbed of the giant Wal-Mart Corporation. See Nelson Lichtenstein, ed., *Wal-Mart: The Face of Twentieth Century Capitalism* (New York: Free Press, 2003).

60. *Matter of North Arkansas Electric Corp.*, 922.

61. Ibid., 924, my emphasis.

62. Ibid., 925.

63. *NLRB v. North Arkansas Electric Cooperative*, 412 F. 2nd 324 (1969), 1475.

64. National Labor Relations Board, *Thirty-Sixth Annual Report of the National Labor Relations Board* (Washington, D.C.: GPO, 1970), 40.

65. See Atleson, *Values and Assumptions*; Katherine van Wezel Stone, "The Post-War Paradigm in American Labor Law," *Yale Law Review* 90 (June 1981): 1509–80; Tomlins, *State and the Unions*. Ronald Schatz provides a good analysis of this literature in "Into the Twilight Zone: The Law and the American Industrial Relations System since the New Deal," *International Labor and Working Class History* 36 (Fall 1989): 51–60. Among the dissenters are Clark, *Like Night and Day*; and Metzgar, *Striking Steel*. See also Vinel, "What Can the Critical Synthesis Teach Us?"

66. John Dunlop, "The Social Utility of Collective Bargaining," quoted in Hecksher, *New Unionism*, 15.

67. Lichtenstein, *State of the Union*, 149. According to this theory (pluralism), the American political system ensured that no group dominated while every minority had the opportunity to make itself heard. See Robert Dahl, *Preface to Democratic Society* (Chicago: University of Chicago Press, 1956); and Robert Dahl, *Who Governs?* (New Haven: Yale University Press, 1961).

68. Howard Brick, *Daniel Bell and the Decline of Intellectual Radicalism* (Madison: University of Wisconsin Press, 1986), 164–171; Barkin, *Decline of the Labor*; Paul Jacobs, *The State of the Unions* (New York: Atheneum, 1963); Paul E. Sultan, *The Disenchanted Unionist* (New York: Harper and Row, 1963); B. J. Widick, *Labor Today* (Boston: Houghton Mifflin, 1964).

69. Arthur Ross, "Labor Organizations and the Labor Movement in Advanced Industrial Society," *Virginia Law Review* 50, no. 8 (December 1964): 1359–1385, 1362.

70. Clark Kerr et al., *Industrialism and the Industrial Man*, 292–293, quoted in Riley, "Clark Kerr," 84.

71. Michael Harrington, *The Retail Clerks* (New York: John Wiley, 1962); Ross, "Labor Organizations and the Labor Movement," 1364; Goldstein, "Some Aspects of the Nature of Unionism," 205.

72. "Your Needs Are Different," TOP leaflet, 2 pages, UAW-TOP Collection, UAW-CULMA, box 61, folder 11; "Professionalism and Union Members," draft of paper, UAW-TOP Collection, box 63, folder 49; "Emerick: Organizing Activities," box 63, folder 34.

73. Oral history interview with Frank McCulloch (1989), 16, 138.

74. Brown, "Collective Bargaining and the NLRB," 11; Oral history interview with Frank Mc-Culloch (1989), 13.

75. Jack Barbash, "AFT Philosophy and the Professional," UAW-TOP Collection, box 61, file 11.

76. Brown, "Collective Bargaining and the NLRB," 11.

77. A good synthesis of these questions is Douglas T. Miller, *On Our Own: Americans in the Sixties* (Lexington, Mass.: Heath, 1996).

78. Riley, "Clark Kerr," 79–80, 85. "I find it interesting that the ideas, practices and techniques developed in employer-employee bargaining have over-flowed to such disputes as between landlords and tenants, welfare recipients and the welfare agency, students and school administration. It may be that in the new environment, 'collective bargaining' will become so transformed as to require a new title." Brown, "Collective Bargaining and the NLRB," 9–10.

79. "A Union Target: The White Collar Worker," *Business Week*, February 7, 1948, 88–91.

80. Jack Barbash, "Unionizing the Professional Worker," 21.

81. See *NAACP v. Alabama*, 357 U.S. 449 (1958), and *Gibson v. Florida Legislative Committee*, 372 U.S. 539 (1963).

82. Peter G. Nash, "Brief for the NLRB," 7, *NLRB v. Bell Aerospace*, Supreme Court file. *ILGWU v. NLRB*, 339 F.2d 116 (1964). See also "Recognition of a Staff Union of Business Agents Under the National Labor Relations Act," *Yale Law Journal* 72, no. 5 (April 1963): 1076–1087.

83. Erwin Griswold, "Petition for Writ of Certiorari to the United States Court of Appeals for the Second Circuit," 8, 18, *NLRB v. Bell Aerospace*, Supreme Court file. Harry Blackmun was a Nixon appointee, but he penned one of the greatest opinions in the tradition of liberal legalism in *Roe v. Wade*, 410 U.S. 113 (1973).

84. Lewis F. Powell, "Memorandum to the Conference" (March 12, 1974), Papers of Thurgood Marshall, Library of Congress, box 128, "NLRB Bell Aerospace" folder.

85. *NLRB v. Bell Aerospace*, 290.

86. Louis L. Jaffe, "The Illusion of the Ideal Administration," *Harvard Law Review* 86, no. 7 (1973): 1182–1199; Theodore Lowi, *The End of Liberalism* (New York: Norton, 1969). On these issues, see the work of Reuel Schiller, "Reining in the Administrative State: WW2 and the Decline of Expert Administration," in *Total War and the Law: The American Home in Front of WW2*, ed. Daniel Ernst and Victor Jew (Westport, Conn.: Praeger, 2002), 185–206.

87. National Society of Professional Engineers, *In the Engineers' Interest: Collective Bargaining vs. Collective Action*, Report of the Task Force on Collective Bargaining (Washington, D.C.: NSPE 1973).

88. Report by Douglas Fraser, 1966, UAW-TOP Collection, box 62, file 11; Latta, "Union Organization Among Engineers," 31.

89. Lewis F. Powell, "Attack of Free Enterprise System," August 23, 1971, quoted in Michael Perelman, *The Confiscation of American Prosperity: From Right-Wing Extremism and Economic Ideology to the Next Great Depression* (New York: Palgrave Macmillan, 2005), 59.

90. None of this is to deny that Powell was a principled jurist. On the whole his career at the Court was that of a conservative moderate, which explains why the stakes in the Bork nomination were so high when he stepped down. See Henry J. Abraham, *Justices and Presidents* (New York: Oxford University Press, 1990).

91. William O'Douglas to Lewis Powell, March 12, 1974, Papers of Thurgood Marshall, Library of Congress, box 128.

92. On Douglas, see Brinkley, *End of Reform*, 63; Gary Gerstle, "The Protean Character of American Liberalism," *American Historical Review* 99, no. 4 (October 1994): 1048; Dennis J. Hutchinson, "William Orville Douglas," in *The Oxford Companion to the Supreme Court*, ed. Kermit Hall (New York: Oxford University Press, 1992), 233–235.

93. *Proceedings of the Tenth Constitutional Convention of the CIO*, November 22–26, 1948, 270, quoted in Nelson Lichtenstein, "The Eclipse of Social Democracy," in *The Rise and Fall of the New*

Deal Order, 1930–1980, ed. Stephen Fraser and Gary Gerstle (Princeton: Princeton University Press, 1989), 127.

94. *NLRB v. Bell Aerospace*, 278.

95. Here I am indebted to Gerald Friedman's insightful analysis *in Reigniting the Labor Movement*, 34–40.

96. Brick, "Postcapitalist Vision," 41; Marina Angel, "Professionals and Professionalization," *Minnesota Law Review* 66 (1982): 406–410.

97. *NLRB v. Yeshiva University*, 447 U.S. 671 (1980).

98. Ibid., 686, 699–700.

99. *Brown University*, 342 NLRB 483 (2004) reversed an older ruling, according to which teaching assistants were "employees" within the framework of the Wagner Act: *New York University*, 332 NLRB 1205 (2000).

100. "Member Brown Sworn In for New Five-Year Term," *NLRB Bulletin*, September 1966, 2, collection 4186.

101. *Packard v. NLRB*, 494–496, quoted by Powell in *NLRB v. Bell Aerospace*, 279.

102. *Machinists v. Street*, 367 U.S. 740 (1961), 776.

103. Letter from Joe Ferraro to Ken Bannon, "Amalgamated Local 1286 Negotiations," June 8, 1976, UAW-TOP Collection, box 26, folder 33.

104. Louis Jackson and Robert Lewis, *Winning NLRB Elections: Management's Strategies and Preventive Programs* (New York: Practicing Law Institute, 1972), quoted in Shawn Burton and Michael Hawkins, "*Oakwood Care*: How Textualism Saved the Supervisory Exemption," *University of Pennsylvania Journal of Labor and Employment Law* 9, no. 1 (2006): 5.

Chapter 7. The Wages of Textualism

1. This description is based on the decision handed down by the Court in *NLRB v. Kentucky River Community Care*, 532 U.S. 706 (2001), as well as the research done on this case by Marley S. Weiss. See her "Kentucky River at the Intersection of Professional and Supervisory Status: Fertile Delta or Bermuda Triangle?" in Cooper and Fisk, *Labor Law Stories*, 354–397.

2. "Hospitals are the last bulwark in our society to retain authoritarian administration," noted Theresa Wolfson on December 8, 1960, at the American Nurses Association Conference held at Cornell University, quoted in Daniel Kruger, "Bargaining and the Nursing Profession," *Monthly Labor Review* 84 (July 1961): 699–705. On the history of nursing, see Barbara Melosh, *The Physician's Hand: Work Culture and Conflict in American Nursing* (Philadelphia: Temple University Press, 1982); and David Brody, "The Job of Nursing," *Reviews in American History* 12, no. 1 (March 1984): 115–118. On public employees, see Joseph A. McCartin, "Fire the Hell Out of Them," *Labor* 2, no. 3 (2005): 67–92; as well as "Wagner Act for Public Workers."

3. See Irving Bernstein, *Turbulent Years*, chap. 4.

4. See Melosh, *Physician's Hand*, 198. Joel Seidman, "Nurses and Collective Bargaining," *Industrial and Labor Relations Review* 23 (1969): 335 shows that the ANA avoided industrial relations terminology (see 341). Kruger, in "Bargaining and the Nursing Profession," quotes an editorial in the American Nurses Association (ANA) official publication saying, "Collective bargaining is not to be confused with labor unionism. Collective Bargaining is used by many organizations other than labor unions." See 700. Joni Ketter, *A Seat at the Bargaining Table: 50 Years of Progress* (Washington, D.C.: ANA, 1996) offers ANA's own account of its history. On the notion of "security," see Chapter 4 of this book.

5. Kruger, "Bargaining and the Nursing Profession," 702; Ketter, *Seat at the Bargaining Table*, 1–9.

6. See Melosh, *Physician's Hand*, on whom this paragraph relies.

7. Max D. Kossoris, "The San Francisco Bay Area 1966 Nurses' Negotiations," *Monthly Labor Review* 90, no. 6 (1967): 8–12.

8. Robert Zieger and Gilbert Gall, *American Workers, American Unions*, 3rd ed. (Baltimore: Johns Hopkins University Press, 2002), 209–214.

9. American Nurses Association, *Summary of SNA Economic Security Activities* (1967), quoted in Seidman, "Nurses and Collective Bargaining," 343. On the Service Employees International Union (SEIU), see the testimony of Dr. Joseph Sergent, the president of the New York State Physicians Union, SEIU Local 682, *Hearings of the Subcommittee on Labor of the U.S. Congress Senate Committee on Labor and Public Welfare*, 93rd Congress, 1st Session, 58–62.

10. See John H. Fanning, "The National Labor Relations Act and the Role of the NLRB" (speech, Association of Labor Mediation Agencies, July 24, 1978), 4, on file with the Institute of Industrial Relations Library, University of California, Berkeley. According to the Wagner Act, the board's jurisdiction is coextensive with the commerce clause in the constitution, which was interpreted very broadly after the 1937 crisis. Historically, however, the board had refused to extend jurisdiction to cases involving businesses that did not have a minimal amount of dollar activity. In the case of for-profit hospitals, it was also the character of the activity that had led the board to consider that such hospitals were beyond the reach of the Wagner Act. The case in which the board changed this policy was *Butte Medical Properties*, 168 NLRB 266 (1967).

11. See "To Amend the National Labor Relations Act to Extend Its Coverage and Protection to Employees of Non Profit Hospitals and For Other Purposes," in *Hearings of the Subcommittee on Labor of the US Congress Senate Committee on Labor and Public Welfare on H.R. 11357*, August 16 and September 6, 1972, 92nd Congress, 2nd Session. The bill was passed, but there was no Senate action on the bill beyond hearings. So there were hearings again in 1973, and only on May 7, 1974, did the Senate pass S. 3203, the final version of the companion bill (see 120 *Congressional Record* 13561). The final version of the House bill was H.R. 13678 (see 120 *Congressional Record* 15660). The law was signed by President Nixon on July 26, 1974. In the meantime hearings were held on intermediary bills, H.R. 1236 and S. 794.

At the Department of Labor library I found that all the hearings (i.e., those held by the 92nd and 93rd Congresses) had been compounded into one volume, under the title "To Amend the National Labor Relations Act to Extend Its Coverage and Protection to Employees of Non Profit Hospitals and For Other Purposes," in *Hearings of the Subcommittee on Labor of the U.S. Congress Senate Committee on Labor and Public Welfare on H.R. 11357*, August 16 and September 6, 1972, 92nd Congress, 2nd Session (HD 5506 H65 A5). This is a bit confusing, since the hearings included H.R. 11357 but also the other versions of the bill, but it makes sense since the differences between them were minor. Moreover, the pagination adopted in this compilation is simple enough for the reader to find the statements that I am referring to. Hereafter, I refer to those hearings simply as *Hearings of the Subcommittee*.

12. Report of the U.S. Department of Labor sent to Harrison A. Williams, June 21, 1973, in *Hearings of the Subcommittee*, 92–95; Bureau of Labor Statistics, "Work Stoppages in Medical and Other Health Services," 1962–1971, in *Hearings of the Subcommittee*, 150.

13. Letter from the Chamber of Commerce to the Subcommittee on Labor (Committee on Labor and the Public Welfare), August 31, 1973, reprinted in *Hearings of the Subcommittee*, 593; testimony of the American Hospital Association on S. 794, July 31, 1973, *Hearings of the Subcommittee*, 131–142.

14. See the testimony of George Hardy, international president, Service Employees International Union, August 16, 1972, in *Hearings of the Subcommittee*, 63–65; Mike McDermott, Local 399, August 16, 1972, 66–69. The Wagner Act preamble was inserted into Joseph Murphy's testimony on S. 794, July 31, 1973, 48. See also the testimony of RN Bonnie Graczyk (for the American Nurses Association) on S. 794, July 31, 1973, saying that nurses were loath to strike and would not do it if there was a procedure allowing for "peaceful industrial relations," 118.

15. Senate Report 93–766 on S. 3203, 93rd Congress, 2nd Session, April 2, 1974, 3.

16. See Senator Crankston's remarks on May 2, 1974, 120 *Congressional Record* 12936–12938.

17. See the letter sent by Secretary of Labor James Hodgson to Perkins, the chairman of the

House Education and Labor Committee, on July 19, 1972, quoted by George Hardy, *Hearings of the Subcommittee*, 65. The House report also suggested that it was the decision to exempt nonprofit hospitals from the NLRA in 1947 that had led to labor conflicts in this industry; see House Report 1051, 93rd Congress, 2nd Session, 1974.

18. On this defeat of the National Public Employees Labor Relations Act, see McCartin, "Wagner Act for Public Workers."

19. On the importance of patient care, see the remarks made by Senator Cranston on May 2, 1974: "The long hours worked and the small monetary reward received by hospital workers result in a constant turnover with a consequent threat to the maintenance of an adequate standard of medical care. This was emphasized over and over again by many of the witnesses. Turnover rates for employees in several hospitals that were studied were reported by witnesses to be as high as 1,200 to 1,500 [percent] a year"; 120 *Congressional Record* 12936–12938. See also the testimony of Joseph Sergent, a physician supporting the bill "for personnel in the healthcare field union representation results in a more stable work force and better qualified people … the employment of better qualified people must logically improve the quality of the healthcare package delivered to the patient"; *Hearings of the Subcommittee,* July 31, 1973, 59; the testimony of Joseph Murphy, president of SEIU Local 47: "NLRA coverage of non profit hospital employees would enhance the quality of hospital service by improving labor relations, since workers could gain union recognition without striking." On the importance of wages see the remarks of Senator Cranston on May 2, 1974: "During the last 2½ years, hospital wage increases have lagged far behind those received by workers in other industries." 120 *Congressional Record* 12936.

20. Statement of Dr. Sergent, *Hearings of the Subcommittee,* 59. See also the individual views of Senator Dominick suggesting that the justification for the bill lay in the very need for the continuity of services: "Hospital Care is not storable … there is no stockpile from which to draw, no storage yard, or warehouse backup potential as found in many business fields"; Senate Report 93–766, 93rd Congress, 2nd Session, 39.

21. Seidman, "Nurses and Collective Bargaining," 348; Kruger, "Bargaining and the Nursing Profession," 703. The role of supervisors in organizing campaigns in mentioned in Melosh, *Physician's Hand,* 201.

22. One good example of this was the case *Sherwood Enterprises*, 175 NLRB 59 (1969). For a list of cases in the same vein, see E. A. Keller Jr., "Death by Textualism: The NLRB's 'Incidental to Patient Care' Supervisory Test for Charge Nurses," *American University Law Review* 46 (1996): 575–623, 585.

23. The Massachusetts cases were *Quincy Hospital* and *University Hospital,* 1965. See the testimony of RN Bonnie Graczyk for the ANA, on S. 794, July 31, 1973, *Hearings of the Subcommittee,* , 123. For the New York State Board decision, see the journal of the ANA, *Economic Security News,* June 23, 1967, 9, quoted in Seidman, "Nurses and Collective Bargaining," 349.

24. This executive order came in response to the request for a bargaining composed solely of supervisory nurses. EO 10988—the legal basis for unionism in public employment—required only that a unit not include employees who supervise and evaluate others in the unit. See Seidman, "Nurses and Collective Bargaining," 345.

25. Statement of Bonnie Graczyk on S. 794, July 31, 1973, *Hearings of the Subcommittee,* 115–127; statement of Charles E. Hargett on H.R. 1236, *Hearings of the Subcommittee,* 22–23; statement of Murray A. Gordon, counsel of the Committee on Interns and Residents of the New York City Municipal Hospitals, on S. 794, August 1, 1973, *Hearings of the Subcommittee,* 296–309; statement of Anthony Bottone, executive secretary of the Committee of Interns and Residents of New York City on S. 794, August 1, 1973, *Hearings of the Subcommittee,* 355–161.

26. See the testimony of RN Charles Hargett for the ANA on H.R. 1136, undated, *Hearings of the Subcommittee,* 16; as well as the testimony of Bonnie Graczyk on S. 794, July 31, 1973, *Hearings of the Subcommittee,* 122.

27. Testimony of RN Charles Hargett for the ANA on H.R. 1136, undated, *Hearings of the Subcommittee,* 17.

28. Oral interview with RN Peggy O'Maley, January 12, 2010. The charge system is described at length in the *Kentucky River* cases (see above).

29. Statement of RN Bonnie Graczyk on S. 794, July 31, 1973, *Hearings of the Subcommittee,* 121.

30. On the question of teams, see ibid., 122.

31. Testimony of Lester Asher, August 16, 1972, *Hearings of the Subcommittee,* 65. George Hardy, the president of SEIU was blunt, saying, "We are not opposed to this amendment as long a chances for the bill are not damaged." See *Hearings of the Subcommittee,* 65. For the SEIU leaders' plea of faith in the NLRB, see the testimony of Joseph Murphy, the legislative director, *Hearings of the Subcommittee,* 61–62.

32. This proposal was S. 2292. Along with imposing a restricted number of units, it would have prohibited all strikes and lockouts except in limited circumstances. It received a strong backing in the testimony of the Chamber of Commerce; see *Hearings of the Subcommittee,* 593, and the testimony of the representatives of the American Hospital Association, *Hearings of the Subcommittee,* 131–141.

33. House report on H.R. 11357, "To Amend the NLRA to Extend Its Coverage and Protection to Employees of Non Profit Hospitals and For Other Purposes," 92nd Congress, 1972, 5.

34. House Report 93–1051, 7; Senate Report 93–766, 6, my emphasis.

35. Although the Taft alternative failed, by the mid-1980s the nurses movement was thwarted by conflicting district decisions on RN units, some of which struck them down, arguing that the board should look at "disparity of interest" to create bargaining units, while others upheld them and directed the board to base its rulings on the notion of "community of interest." At stake in this legal battle was the ability of nurses to speak as a social group, mouthing common values and promoting a well-defined common interest. To solve the problem of conflicting court decision on this question, the NLRB resorted to rule making for the first time in its history. Nurses, the board noted, constitute a cohesive group of workers because their obligations are different: as a group they are on duty 24/7 and individually can all be required to work overtime. Their professional status is based not on one skill but on a "cluster of knowledge" that allows their constant interaction with patients regardless of their condition and status. Most important, the board found, nurses formed a cohesive group of "employees" for managerial and economic reasons. In a typical hospital setting, they are all supervised by one nurse, the director of nursing, but remain responsible for their acts. The board also found that nurses were overwhelmingly women suffering from a low pay scale and career ladder and were particularly affected by problems such as floating and scheduling. As their long history of collective bargaining did not reveal any degree of interaction with other professionals, the board argued, there was no reason to mandate their inclusion in broad units. See Joel D'Alba, "Legal Problems Confronting Health Care Employee Unions: An Update" (conference, Institute of Labor and Industrial Relations, University of Illinois, March 4–6, 1981), 27–39; oral interview with Alan McDonald, lawyer for the Massachusetts Nurses Association, January 13, 2011, on file with the author.

36. See *NLRB v. Yeshiva University,* 672n30.

37. Joseph J. Bean and Rene Laliberty, *Understanding Hospital Labor Relations: An Orientation for Supervisors* (Reading, Mass.: Addison-Wesley, 1976), 29.

38. See Jefferson Cowie, "'A One-Sided Class War': Rethinking Doug Fraser's 1978 Resignation from the Labor-Management Group," *Labor History* 44, no. 3 (2003): 307–314.

39. Warren H. Chaney and Thomas R. Beech, *The Union Epidemic: A Prescription for Supervisors* (Germantown, Md.: Aspen Systems, 1976).

40. Ibid., 4–5; see also 35–41. On the use of consultants in health care conflicts, see Charles T. Joyce, "Union Busters and Front-Line Supervisors: Restricting and Regulating the Use of Supervisory Employees by Management Consultants During Union Representation Election Campaigns,"

University of Pennsylvania Law Review 135 (1987): 453–493. See also the epilogue to this book. Steven Greenhouse, "Bid to Organize Nurses Faces Setback in Congress," *New York Times,* April 21, 2009, B1.

41. Herbert G. Melnick, quoted in John Logan, "Consultants, Lawyers, and the 'Union-Free' Movement in the USA Since the 1970s," *Industrial Relations Journal* 33, no. 3 (2002): 197–213.

42. See William Eskridge, "The New Textualism," *UCLA Law Review* 37 (1990): 631–692, according to whom Justice Kennedy is a textualist too; Frank H. Easterbrook, "Text, History and Structure in Statutory Interpretation," *Harvard Journal of Law & Public Policy* 17 (1994): 61–70.

43. *Beverly Enters v. NLRB,* 661 F.2d 1095 (1992).

44. For the sixth circuit decision, see ibid., 1101–1105; *Health Care & Retirement Corp. v. NLRB,* 511 U.S. 571 (1994), 580–582.

45. *Health Care & Retirement Corp. v. NLRB,* Ginsburg dissenting 591–592.

46. The classic examples are Charles Sabel and Michael Piore, *The Second Industrial Divide: Possibilities for Prosperity* (New York: Basic Books, 1986); and Thomas A. Kochan and Paul Osterman, *The Mutual Gains Enterprise* (Boston: Harvard Business School Press, 1994). For the origins of these ideas, see Waring, *Taylorism Transformed,* 155–159; and Jonathan Goldin, "Labor-Management Cooperation: Bath Iron Works's Bold New Approach," *Maine Law Review* 47 (1995): 415–500. The proposal to amend Section 8a(2) is put in historical perspective in David Brody's, *Labor Embattled, History, Power Rights* (Urbana: University of Illinois Press, 2005), 46–61. In many ways, this reform stemmed from an NLRB decision, *Electromation Inc.,* in which the board ruled that an Indiana nonunion manufacturer violated the NLRA when it set up worker action committees to address working conditions and other problems. According to 8a(2), the employer is not allowed to be a part of the organizations representing workers' interests.

47. Bryan M. Churgin, "The Managerial Exclusion Under the NLRA: Are Worker Participation Programs Next?" *Catholic University Law Review* 48 (1999): 557; and Shannon Browne, "Labor-Management Teams: A Panacea for American Businesses of the Rebirth of a Laborer's Nightmare?" *Ohio State Law Journal* 58 (1997): 243.

48. Paul Weiler, *Governing the Workplace* (Cambridge, Mass.: Harvard University Press, 1990); Hecksher, *New Unionism.*

49. The Dunlop report was clear on this: "If a more cooperative conception of the employer employee relationship is embodied in labor law so that representation does not necessarily imply the existence of an adversarial relationship, it may be necessary to reconsider whether supervisors or middle managers should be denied the right to union representation or collective bargaining." See "Fact Finding Report: Commission on the Future of Worker-Management Relations," 55. This report as well as a substantial part of the hearings conducted by the commission are available online thanks to Cornell University at http://digitalcommons.ilr.cornell.edu/dunlop/.

50. *Business Week,* April 27, 1987, 127 and May 4, 1987, 15, quoted in Mike Parker, "Industrial Relations Myth and Shopfloor Reality: The Team Concept in the Auto Industry," in Harris and Lichtenstein, *Industrial Democracy in America,* 249–274, 249.

51. See Weiler, *Governing the Workplace,* 216–217; and Lewis L. Maltby, "Statement of the American Civil Liberties Union Before the Commission on the Future of Worker-Management Relations," September 8, 1994, http://digitalcommons.ilr.cornell.edu/.

52. "Fact Finding Report," 28–30.

53. See Richard S. Meyer, "Total Quality Management and the National Labor Relations Act," *Labor Law Journal* 45 (November 1994): 718–721. For a similar view, see Burton and Hawkins, *"Oakwood Care."* Samuel Estreicher provides a rare dissenting view from the conservative side in "The Dunlop Report and the Future of Labor Reform," *Labor Lawyer* 12, no. 1 (Spring 1996): 117–135.

54. On this question, see Nelson Lichtenstein, *The Retail Revolution: How Wal-Mart Created a Brave New World of Business* (New York: Metropolitan Books, 2009). I do not mean, of course, that

companies did not proceed with the idea of job enrichment. Quite the contrary. But as the example of Toyota shows, they did not need unions for that.

55. *Business Week*, "Working . . . and Poor," May 31, 2004.

56. These points were made at length by the ANA and the AFL-CIO unions in their briefs for the *Oakwood* case. For an RN's view of collective bargaining, see also James Eggleston, "Patient Advocacy and Consumer Protection Through Union Activism," *Saint Louis Law Journal* 41 (1996–1997): 925–951, who argues that nursing unions have a unique ability to influence the quality of care that is provided by employers to their workers through health plan benefits; see 947–951.

57. The "no single lifts" provision is mentioned in Amy Albro, "Rubbing Salt in the Wound," *Northwestern Journal of Law and Social Policy* 3 (2008): 103–130, see esp. 111. U.S. Bureau of Labor Statistics, *Workplace Injuries and Illnesses in 2009* (Washington, D.C.: U.S. Bureau of Labor Statistics, 2009), table 5. Examples of contracts are available on the website of the National Nurses United. See, e.g., the Ohio Dayton Contract, available at http://www.nationalnursesunited.org/page/-/files/pdf/va/contracts/dayton-oh.pdf. For a general perspective on the taxing work of nurses, see Sara Corbett, "The Last Shift," *New York Times*, March 16, 2003, 58.

58. See "Nursing Shortage: Fact Sheet," report of the American Association of Colleges of Nursing (AACN), available at www.aacn.nche.edu/, as well as the statement of the tricouncil of nursing, available at www.aacn.nche.edu/. Peter Buerhaus et al., "The Recent Surge in Nurse Employment: Causes and Implications," *Health Affairs* 28, no. 4 (July 2009): 657–668, argue that the effects of the recession will be short-lived and project a shortage of 260,000 nurses.

59. Suzanne Gordon, *Nursing Against the Odds: How Health Care Cost Cutting, Medical Stereotypes and Medial Hubris Undermine Nurses and Patient Care* (Ithaca: Cornell University Press, 2005), 238, passim.

60. Ibid., 244–245, on which this paragraph heavily relies; and Simon Head, *The New Ruthless Economy* (New York: Oxford University Press, 2003), 23–42.

61. Douglas S. Wakefield et al., *Understanding Patient-Centered Care in the Context of Total Quality Management and Continuous Quality Improvement* (1994), quoted in Eggleston, "Patient Advocacy and Consumer Protection," 935.

62. On scripting and rounding, see Heather Boerner and Lucia Hwang, "Losing Our Voice," *National Nurse*, October 2010, 20–23.

63. Oral interview with RN Sandy Eaton, January 14, 2011, on file with the author.

64. Oral interview with RN Peggy O'Maley, January 13, 2011, on file with the author.

65. Linda Aiken et al., "Hospital Nurse Staffing and Patient Mortality, Nurse Burnout and Job Dissatisfaction," *Journal of the American Medical Association* 288, no. 16 (2002): 1987–1993.

66. See the report of the Joint Commission on Accreditation of Healthcare Organizations, *Heath Care at the Crossroads* (2002), available at http://www.jointcommission.org/assets/1/18/health_care_at_the_crossroads.pdf. In 1999, a study released by the Minnesota Nurses Association revealed that 70 percent of the nurses surveyed complained of being unable to provide basic nursing duties on a timely basis. See Gordon, *Nursing Against the Odds*, 256.

67. Agreement between the California Nurses Association and Alta Bates Medical Center, quoted in Eggleston, "Patient Advocacy and Consumer Protection," 954.

68. *Washington State Nurses Association v. NLRB*, 526 F.3d 577 (9th Cir. 2008), reviewing *Sacred Heart Medical Center*, 347 NLRB 48 (2001). See also *Mt Clemens General Hospital v. NLRB*, 328 F.3d 837 (6th Cir. 2003), reviewing *Mt Clements General Hospital*, 335 NLRB 48 (2001). On the whole the courts and the board have generally required employers to demonstrate an adverse impact to justify the prohibition of such union buttons.

69. Oral interview with Barry Adams, Boston, January 14, 2011; Barry L. Adams, "To Do the Unthinkable," in *When Chicken Soup Is Not Enough: Stories of Nurses Standing Up for Themselves, Their Patients, and Their Profession*, ed. Suzanne Gordon (Ithaca: Cornell University Press, 2010).

70. Tanya Bretherton, John Buchanan, and Suzanne Gordon, *Safety in Numbers* (Ithaca: Cornell University Press, 2008), 66–68.

71. Oral interview with Kenn Zinn, January 8, 2010, on file with the author.

72. Weiss, "Kentucky River at the Intersection of Professional and Supervisory Status," 387.

73. Ibid., 370–371.

74. See *Providence Alaska Medical Center v. NLRB, ANA and UNA* 121 F.3d 548 (9th Cir. 1997), 9887 (case 96–70595).

75. Weiss, "Kentucky River at the Intersection of Professional and Supervisory Status," 387.

76. G. Roger King, "Where Have All the Supervisors Gone? The Board's Misdiagnosis of Health Care & Retirement Corp.," *Labor Law* 13 (Fall 1997): 353–358.

77. *NLRB v. Kentucky River Community Care,* 719.

78. Burton and Hawkins, *"Oakwood Care."*

79. See *Chevron, USA, Inc. v. Natural Resources Defense Council,* 467 U.S. 837 (1984).

80. *NLRB v. Kentucky River Community Care,* 8.

81. Lester A. Heltzer, "Notice and Invitation to File Briefs," July 25, 2003, http://www.nlrb.gov/.

82. Michelle Amber, "Labor Movement Rallies Around Pending NLRB Rulings Defining Supervisors," *Daily Labor Report* (BNA), nos. 1522–5968 (July 14, 2006); EPI issue brief 225, "Supervisor in Name Only: Union Rights of Eight Million Workers at Stake in Labor Ruling," http://www.epi.org/.

83. Cited in a statement by John Sweeney and Rick Bender, "Bush's NLRB Seems Poised to Cripple American Labor," July 11, 2006, quoted in Gerald Friedman, "Labor and the Bush Administration: Down So Long, Seems Like Up to Me," *Lisa e-journal* 8, no. 1 (2010): 69–85.

84. *Matter of Oakwood Healthcare Inc.,* 348 NLRB no. 37 (2006), 5; "Employer Oakwood Healthcare Inc's Brief on Review," 1–2, http://www.nlrb.gov.

85. *Matter of Oakwood,* 348 NLRB no. 37, 689.

86. Ibid., 691, 693.

87. I am grateful to Nancy Schiffer, counsel for the AFL-CIO, for helping me with these questions. *Matter of Oakwood,* 709.

88. See Steven Greenhouse, "Board Redefines Rules for Union Exemption," *New York Times,* October 4, 2006; Paul Bigman, "Kentucky River Threatens to Swamp Labor," *Dollars & Sense,* September 2006, http://www.dollarsandsense.org/; and James Parks, "Labor Ruling May Bar Millions from Joining Unions," http://blog.aflcio.org/. Links to the Colbert report on *Kentucky River* and responses by elected officials can be found on the page devoted to the *Kentucky River* cases on the AFL-CIO website, http://www.aflcio.org/. Larry Cohen to Robert Battista, October 6, 2006, http://www.aflcio.org/.

89. This paragraph is based on oral interviews with John Hiatt (AFL-CIO), Nancy Schiffer (AFL-CIO), John Borsos (UHW), and Kenn Zinn (NNU). For agreements in which hospital managements pledge not to use the *Kentucky River* cases, see "RNs at Two California Hospitals Gain Pay Increases and Job Security Provisions," *Collective Bargaining Newsletter,* 12 COBB 43, April 12, 2007 (noting that the collective bargaining agreements for registered nurses at Stanford Hospitals & Clinics and Lucile Packard Children's Hospital in Palo Alto, California, include language prohibiting the hospital from relying upon the *Kentucky River* trilogy of cases to challenge the status of anyone currently in the bargaining unit); "NLRB Members Discuss Effects of Oakwood, Pending Cases," *Collective Bargaining Newsletter,* 12 COBB 23, February 15, 2007 (noting a similar agreement between Kaiser Permanente and the unions representing its employees). These examples are quoted in Roger King's testimony on H.R. 1644, May 8, 2007, 5.

90. From 1996 to 2006, the number of representation cases in which the "supervisory" issue was involved declined by 41 percent according to a confidential memo produced by the AFL-CIO. For a good example of a business-oriented analysis of the *Oakwood* case, see Roger King and David Birnbaum, "Kentucky River Trilogy: Recent NLRB Decisions Clarify the Meaning of 'Supervisor' Under the NLRA," *HR Advisor: Legal and Practical Guidance* 13, no. 1 (2007): 5–12.

91. Antonio Gramsci, *Selection from the Prison Notebooks* (New York: International Publishers, 1971), 276.

Epilogue

1. Statement of Sarah Fox, "Are NLRB and Court Rulings Misclassifying Skilled and Professional Employees as Supervisors?" *Joint Hearing Before the Subcommittee on Health, Employment, Labor and Pensions*, U.S. House of Representatives, May 8, 2007, 9.

2. Statement of Congressman Robert Andrews, "Are NLRB and Court Rulings Misclassifying Skilled and Professional Employees as Supervisors?" *Joint Hearing Before the Subcommittee on Health, Employment, Labor and Pensions*, 2.

3. "The Haves and the Have Nots: How American Labor Law Denies a Quarter of the Workforce Bargaining Rights," report by American Rights at Work (November 2008), 2, http://www.americanrightsatwork.org/.

4. On the decisions made early on by the Obama administration on which bills to push, see Jonathan Atler, *The Promise* (New York: Simon & Schuster, 2009), 79.

5. Cynthia Estlund, "The Ossification of Labor Law," *Columbia Law Review* 102, no. 6 (October 2002): 1530. Estlund was quoted by Sarah Fox in her testimony. For an earlier statement of this theory, see also Paul Weiler, "Promises to Keep: Securing Workers' Rights Under the NLRA," *Harvard Law Review* 96, no. 8 (June 1983): 1769–1823. Weiler argued that "contemporary American labor law resembles an elegant tombstone," 1769. See also Rick Fantasia and Kim Voss, *Des syndicats domestiqués* (Paris: Raisons d'agir, 2004).

6. "This workplace was characterized by a stable contract of hire between a single employer and employees engaged in work of a continuing nature at a fixed location, with hierarchical organization of work and promotion ladders. This model—exemplified by the manufacturing plants of the 1930s and 1940s—is increasingly anachronistic in a post-industrial and fiercely global economy.... Work is increasingly contingent"; Wilma Liebman, "Decline and Disenchantment: Reflections on the Aging of the National Labor Relations Board," *Berkeley Journal of Employment & Labor Law* 28, no. 2 (2007): 574–575.

7. Statement of Fox, 7–8.

8. Statement of Senator Dodd, "Are NLRB and Court Rulings Misclassifying Skilled and Professional Employees as Supervisors?" *Joint Hearing Before the Subcommittee on Health, Employment, Labor and Pensions*, 72.

9. Prepared statement of the American Federation of State, County and Municipal Employees (AFSCME), AFL-CIO, *Joint Hearing Before the Subcommittee on Health, Employment, Labor and Pensions*, 74.

10. Andrews actually presented the issue as the need to deal with the "Bermuda Triangle" created by the *Kentucky River* cases, which "created a category of workers who has the worst of all worlds." Statement of Andrews, *Joint Hearing Before the Subcommittee on Health, Employment, Labor and Pensions*, 2.

11. To be sure, some will argue that this would open the door to unions of executives and "real managers," which is not desirable. This is not what I am advocating here. Rather, my argument is that all people employed for wages or a salary should be free to organize if they experience the need to join a union. No doubt, many such managers and executives would eschew this possibility.

12. See Sven Beckert, "Democracy in the Age of Capital: Contesting Suffrage Rights in Gilded Age New York," in Jacobs, Novak, and Zelizer, *Democratic Experiment*, 146–169; Liette Gidlow, "Delegitimizing Democracy: Civic Slackers, the Cultural Turn, and the Possibilities of Politics," *Journal of American History* 89, no. 3 (December 2002): 922–957.

13. Heritage Foundation, "The Respect Act: Congress Should Preserve the Balance Between Management and Employees," *WebMemo*, no. 1667 (October 17, 2007), http://www.policyarchive.org/.

14. National Association of Manufacturers (NAM), "The Respect Act: Fomenting Conflict Between Employee Classes," http://www.nam.org/.

15. Letter from the National Association of Waterfront Employers to Congressman Andrews, May 18, 2007, in *Hearings of the Subcommittee*, 78.

16. Statement of Roger King and Jones Day on behalf of the U.S. Chamber of Commerce: "Oftentimes the supervisor is the difference between complying with OSHA, with the Fair Labor Standards Act, and State legislative enactments. If you don't have, as an employer, control over the workplace, compliance in those areas could be highly suspect"; 20.

17. There is, of course, no official count of the workers excluded under the NLRA definition of "employee" and "manager." In 2002, the GAO published a report counting 10.2 million first-line supervisors and higher managers who were without bargaining rights in the private sector. See General Accounting Office, "Collective Bargaining Rights: Information on the Number of Workers With or Without Bargaining Rights," GAO-02-835, 2002, 12. As the report admitted, however, this number was underestimated because it did not take into account part-time workers. Using 2005 figures, the organization American Rights at Work has counted some 13 million supervisors and managers excluded in the private sector, plus an additional 3.4 million in the public sector. See "The Haves and the Have Nots," 9. Neither of these studies takes into account the impact of the *Kentucky River* cases, which, as noted earlier, might bring an additional 8 million workers outside of the scope of the law, thus bringing the number to 24 million. My estimate of the much larger number of workers whose duties straddle the line between professional and managerial duties comes from Charles Hecksher, *New Unionism*, 68–69, 78. As Hecksher rightly noted, it is the whole group of middle managers and semiprofessionals whose rights are at risk under the legal definition of the worker.

18. Nancy Mills, organizer, quoted in Joyce, "Union Busters," 453.

19. Philip Lederer, "Management's Right to the Loyalty of Supervisors," *Labor Law Journal* 32, no. 2 (February 1981): 83–104.

20. See, e.g., Alfred T. Maria, *Managing to Stay Non-Union* (New York: Executive Enterprises, 1979); *The Supervisor's Handbook on Maintaining Non-Union Status* (New York: Executive Enterprises, 1986). See also manuals published under the aegis of the NAM to be distributed during seminars, such as "Remaining Union Free."

21. Nelson Lichtenstein, "How Labor Can Win," *In Search of Progressive America*, ed. Michael Kazin, with Franz Becker and Menno Hurrenkamp (Philadelphia: University of Pennsylvania Press, 2008), 136.

INDEX OF CASES

GENERAL INDEX

ACKNOWLEDGMENTS

I N the ten years that I have spent studying American labor and political history, I have accumulated a number of important debts. First, I would like to acknowledge the influence of Jean Kempf and Vincent Michelot, who not only supported this project in both intellectual and institutional ways, but also set an example showing me what an américaniste should be. I am also indebted to Arnaud Roujou de Boubée and the French American Commission for a one-year Fulbright Scholarship in 2001–2002 that allowed me to start the research on which this book is based.

Along the way, I benefited from the assistance of numerous librarians and archivists. This book could not have been written without the aid of staffs at the special collections at the Georgetown University Library, the Kheel Center in Ithaca, New York, the Library of Congress and the National Archives in Washington, D.C., the Truman Library in Independence, Missouri, the Walter Reuther Library at Wayne State University in Detroit, Michigan, and the Wisconsin Historical Society in Madison, Wisconsin. I have also bene-fitted from the generous help of Dominique Daniel, who provided incredible research assistance at a crucial stage in the project, and to Suzanne Gordon, who eagerly opened her home and shared her expertise and knowledge of the world of nurses.

Since 2005 I have had the good fortune to teach at the Université Paris-Diderot. My gratitude goes to Robert Mankin, the head of our research group, as well as Catherine Bernard and Jean-Marie Fournier for their gra-cious support and all the colleagues who inquired about the advancement of my project. The publication of the book also coincided with our transferring to a new, modern campus, and for me the work on the manuscript will for-ever be linked to the streets of the Marais and the joyful spirit I found there.

To the "cons gang"—Marc Olivier Baruch, Clarisse Berthezène, and Laura Lee Downs—you guys are the best. No one else mixes so well historical arguments with humor, good food, and great wine. Working with you on postwar conservatism has been a true and rare pleasure.

In addition, I am indebted to all the American and French historians who have provided me with the kind of critical but supportive comments that help a scholar stick with a project. I would like to thank particularly Sébastien Chauvin, Catherine Collomp, Daniel Ernst, Gary Gerstle, Guy Groux, Romain Huret, Robert Mason, Mark Meigs, Pap N'diaye, Johann Neem, Isabelle Richet, Alexandre Rios Bordes, Paul Schor, Maud Simonet, François Weil, and Mark Wilson. Gerald Friedman read the entire manuscript and gave this project an early boost by pushing me to publish an article in *Labor History*. I am grateful for our exchanges over the years as well as for his kind reminders that this book did not have to be my last word on the topic.

This book bears the indelible imprint of the teaching and intellectual influence of Nelson Lichtenstein, whose engaged scholarship has been a model for me ever since I met him as a graduate student at the University of Virginia. It was Nelson who first suggested that I write a paper about recent cases in which the courts had whittled down the definition of "employee," and since I decided to expand that investigation into a book reaching back into the nineteenth century, he has lent me the same energetic and upbeat support he brings to the happy few who climb mountains with him. I have argued over the implications of the difference between "worker" and "employee" for years with Joe McCartin, my sponsor for the Fulbright Scholarship in 2001–2002. Ever since, his generosity and buoyant wisdom have sustained this book in more ways than I could mention, and today I am glad to count him as a comrade and coauthor. I am also thankful for Michael Kazin's unswerving commitment to this book. As series editor, Michael not only made numerous suggestions to improve the narrative and sharpen my interpretations, but also changed my perspective on what writing history really means. If readers unacquainted with labor history can read this book, it is largely thanks to his masterly input.

At Penn I have benefitted from Bob Lockhart's expert editorship. Bob sustained the project very early on by giving me an advance contract, and then patiently waited for long-overdue chapters. Yet when he finally had the manuscript in hand, he immediately turned his attention to it and took the time to make numerous suggestions that gave the book its final shape. I am also grateful to Rachel Taube and Noreen O'Connor for their work on the production of the manuscript and to Melissa Marshall for her help with the marketing.

Then there are the greatest of debts. There are no better friends than Cyril Cammas, Becky Choi, Alexis Chommeloux, John Edwards, Bertrand Gommier, Yohan Levy, Carine Marion, Alix Martin, Matthieu and Emmanuelle Massart, Said Ouaked, and Valérie Peinot. My parents and brothers have long supported my academic endeavors, while kindly reminding me of the things that really matter beyond academic life. I could not have asked for a better family and I look forward to many more annual vacations in our hometown. I am also thankful to Michel and Eliane Ehrhardt for letting me turn a part of their home into a writing camp. Last, I have been lucky enough to share the adventure of academic life with Caroline Ehrhardt. Her love, wit, and laughter have made it a joyful one. The birth of Alice has made it perfect.